Educational Linguistics/TESOL/ICC
Graduate School of Education
University of Pennsylvania
3700 Walnut Street/Cl
Philadelphia, PA 19104

Language, Society, and Education: A Profile of Black English

The Charles A. Jones Publishing Company

International Series in Education

Adams, *Simulation Games*

Allen, Barnes, Reece, Roberson, *Teacher Self-Appraisal: A Way of Looking Over Your Own Shoulder*

Armstrong, Cornell, Kraner, Roberson, *The Development and Evaluation of Behavioral Objectives*

Braun, Edwards, *History and Theory of Early Childhood Education*

Carlton, Goodwin, *The Collective Dilemma: Negotiations in Education*

Criscuolo, *Improving Classroom Reading Instruction*

Crosswhite, Higgins, Osborne, Shumway, *Mathematics Teaching: Psychological Foundations*

Denues, *Career Perspective: Your Choice of Work*

DeStefano, *Language, Society, and Education: A Profile of Black English*

Doll, *Leadership to Improve Schools*

Drier, *K-12 Guide for Integrating Career Development into Local Curriculum*

Foster, Fitzgerald, Beal, *Career Education and Vocational Guidance*

Frymier, Hawn, *Curriculum Improvement for Better Schools*

Goodlad, Klein, Associates, *Behind the Classroom Door*

Hauenstein, *Curriculum Planning for Behavioral Development*

Higgins, *Mathematics Teaching and Learning*

Hitt, *Education as a Human Enterprise*

Leland, Smith, *Mental Retardation: Perspectives for the Future*

Lutz, *Toward Improved Urban Education*

Meyer, *A Statistical Analysis of Behavior*

National Society for the Study of Education, *Contemporary Educational Issues* (10 book series)

Nerbovig, *Unit Planning: A Model for Curriculum Development*

Overly, Kinghorn, Preston, *The Middle School: Humanizing Education for Youth*

Perry, Wildman, *The Impact of Negotiations in Public Education: The Evidence from the Schools*

Poston, *Implementing Career Education*

Pula, Goff, *Technology in Education: Challenge and Change*

Ressler, *Career Education: The New Frontier*

Rich, *Humanistic Foundations of Education*

Shane, Shane, Gibson, Munger, *Guiding Human Development: The Counselor and the Teacher in the Elementary School*

Swanson, *Evaluation in Education*

Thiagarajan, *The Programing Process: A Practical Guide*

Von Haden, King, *Innovations in Education: Their Pros and Cons*

Weber, *Early Childhood Education: Perspectives on Change*

Wernick, *Career Education in the Elementary School*

Wiles, *Changing Perspectives in Educational Research*

Wiman, *Instructional Materials*

Language, Society, and Education: A Profile of Black English

Johanna S. DeStefano

The Ohio State University

Charles A. Jones Publishing Company
Worthington, Ohio

1 2 3 4 5 6 7 8 9 10 / 77 76 75 74 73

Library of Congress Catalog Card Number: 72–93895
International Standard Book Number: 0–8396–0020–8

Printed in the United States of America

Preface

Language, Society, and Education: A Profile of Black English provides a comprehensive understanding of the urban ghetto vernacular with special emphasis on its pedagogical implications. The material represents a basic stance taken by linguists whether they approach the study of Black English, the Spanish of Chicanos and Puerto Ricans, or the American Indian languages spoken in the United States. The book also deals with the importance of teachers' attitudes toward linguistic social variety as this relates to children's learning. Thus, this book can help provide an effective assist in alleviating language barriers between teachers and their culturally different students.

Each chapter is developed to benefit educators, social scientists, and interested laymen in understanding the educational implications of Black English with particular emphasis on speakers' verbal behavior. Readable material has been selected and placed within an organization that helps the reader to see the relationships between the articles in a chapter and the scope of the entire book.

Special acknowledgment is due the pioneering work done by William Labov and his associates in New York City and by linguists at the Center for Applied Linguistics in Washington, D.C., who were among the earliest to investigate Black English and who have done some of the most significant work to date. A publication that has also been most helpful in this endeavor is the *Florida FL Reporter* edited by Alfred Aarons, which contains solid and readable articles in this area.

I would like to express my gratitude to the following people for their invaluable aid, advice, and time spent on this book: Courtney Cazden, Donald Edwards, Charles Ferguson, Kenneth and Yetta Goodman, Kenneth Johnson, William Labov, Charles Rousculp, Roger Shuy, and Walt Wolfram.

Johanna S. DeStefano

To children everywhere
        No matter what color their tongue
And to Ralph

Contents

Introduction

The selections included in this volume were chosen to provide the reader with a thorough and comprehensive view of Black English, including its speakers, and its implications for the education of black ghetto children. Pedagogical applications and implications receive major stress in the book, especially in Chapter Four through Chapter Six. The areas covered by the six chapters include selections on the linguistic model applied to Black English, on black culture and society, including its verbal behavior, descriptive studies of Black English, selections on teachers' attitudes toward Black English, on Black English and oral language in the schools, and on Black English and its implications for reading.

Chapter One is intended to give the reader preliminary information on Black English and an orientation to the viewpoint taken by the articles in this book—namely a linguistic one. But the linguistic viewpoint as developed in the chapter is not only applicable to Black English; it has also been applied to other divergent language situations in this country and around the world. It represents a basic stance taken by linguists as they approach the study of language, whether it is Black English, the Spanish of Chicanos and Puerto Ricans, or the American Indian languages spoken in the United States.

The selections on black culture and society and its verbal behavior (Chapter Two) are intended to orient the reader to the population most likely to use Black English forms in its speech. The social conditions under which Black English may be spoken are described from anthropological and sociological viewpoints. The selections on verbal behavior describe how and for what purposes Black English may be used by ghetto blacks.

The descriptive studies presented in Chapter Three are central to gaining an understanding of what Black English is seen to be, and of possible pedagogical implications (Chapters Four, Five, and Six). Included are systematic descriptions of the phonology and syntax of Black English, both at the "surface" level and at "deeper" levels which reveal the rules generating specific speech forms. Also included are descriptions of social variables which help determine the number of Black English forms which are actually realized in the speech of a black person. Thus the selections go far beyond a description of black slang, so often written about in popular literature. Some people have the impression that a language is its vocabulary. Yet

1

vocabulary changes more quickly than any other aspect of a language, and slang is especially ephemeral. What is current at the time of writing will not be current when this book is being read. So the selections deal, instead, with the systematic structure of Black English of which slang terms are a small although sometimes striking part.

Discussions of possible pedagogical implications of Black English are well represented in the literature, indicating a major educational concern in this social variety and in its import for teaching and learning. The selections in Chapter Four deal with the import of teachers' attitudes toward Black English for ghetto black children's education. The selections in Chapter Five and Chapter Six reflect an educational concern for the many ghetto black children who apparently are having language and literacy problems. However, the available literature deals largely with two problems: teaching a more "standard" English as a "second dialect" to Black English speakers, and teaching reading to this same population, both areas of lively controversy which comes clear in the articles. Evidently these problems are perceived to be among the most pressing for both teachers and students. Speech is widely thought to be a social factor of some importance in certain situations, and reading seems to be of general national concern. Unfortunately, the teaching of spelling and writing are largely unexplored areas at present so are not represented in the book.

Finally, most of the educational suggestions and applications found in Chapters Five and Six are based on the informed opinions of linguists and not so much on research findings. Research into the exact nature of Black English's role in the language and literacy questions facing black children and their teachers is badly needed.

Chapter One

A Linguistic Viewpoint
Toward Black English

Black English
Johanna DeStefano

Currently in America there are Northern urban blacks who speak a variety * of American English which is perceived to be different from surrounding groups' speech. Questions about this variety, which has been commonly labeled Black English, Negro Nonstandard English, Negro English, Negro speech, or Negro dialect, have been posed: What is it, this Black English? Who actually speaks it? Where did it come from? What significance does it have for teaching black ghetto children to read and write? The press of both current and long-standing social and educational problems lends a sense of urgency to finding at least partial answers to these questions and others. Educators are particularly feeling this press.

Linguists, as investigators of language form and use, have begun to provide information on which to base some answers; many of their initial findings and results of inquiry into Black English are reported in this volume. Since much of the investigation is in its beginning stages, the reader will note there are gaps in the knowledge needed to answer such questions as what role does Black English play in literacy learning, or even what is Black English. These gaps can only be closed by more and continued research which is urgently needed because of the importance of the questions, especially educational questions.

Taking the question "What is Black English?" some of the earliest attempts at definition were based on noting that the speech of some low socioeconomic status blacks, then in the rural South, differed from the speech of surrounding whites and higher socioeconomic blacks. These perceived differences (identified as "Negro English" or "Negro dialect") were generally not the subject of intensive or systematic study. But from the evidence, what may have existed was a degree of geographic variation throughout the South correlated with low socioeconomic status. Such speech was and is generally considered nonstandard, meaning that it deviates from the perceived standard variety † in a given area.

---

* *Variety* is used frequently in sociolinguistics to designate "a kind of language," e.g. speech treated as being different, whether it is a dialect, a sociolect, or a language such as French, in order to get away from emotional connotations which these other terms often have.

† *Standard* is variously defined, but for the purposes of this discussion it means the variety spoken by those people holding social and economic power in an area.

Then during the twentieth century black in-migration from various sections of the rural South to the urban North, the Southern black speech varieties "swamped" whatever black speech existed already in the urban areas. It is postulated that the linguistic forms in black speech from different sections of the rural South fused to help create the urban ghetto variety which is different from any found in the South, yet includes elements from them. William Labov, among other linguists, has noted the striking similarity among black speech forms found in geographically separated cities, despite different rural Southern dialectical input. There is also evidence that there was a Creole input into Black English. In other words, certain patterns occurring in Black English came from earlier Creoles which were the result of languages in contact such as colonial American English and various African languages. Finally, Black English also shares many general American English *non*standard forms such as double negatives and certain verb forms.

In much of the present linguistic literature, Black English has come to mean the speech of low socioeconomic blacks living in urban ghettos such as New York City, Detroit, Chicago, Philadelphia, Los Angeles, Oakland, and New Orleans. In Chapters Five and Six, the selections will reflect this use of Black English.

Calling Black English "Negro Dialect," Ralph Fasold and Walt Wolfram further define the parameters of this variety.

> Negro dialect, then as the term is used here, is a cohesive linguistic system which is substantially different from standard American English dialects. It is spoken by some, though not all Negroes, particularly those of the lower socioeconomic classes. Furthermore . . . almost all the features associated with Negro dialect alternate with standard English in actual speech. (1)

It is generally acknowledged that both qualitatively and quantitatively, Black English differs from other American English varieties. In other words, black ghetto speakers tend to use more nonstandard forms in their speech than other groups, but they also use some different forms as well. (This topic is discussed in greater detail in Chapter Three.)

Intra-Speaker and Inter-Speaker Variability

The alternation of Black English speech forms with more standard forms in the speech of ghetto blacks is one of the important characteristics of this variety. There is much reported intra-speaker (within speaker) variability in the forms produced among Black English speakers, probably partially dependent on the social situation the speaker perceives himself to be in. William Labov (Labov and Cohen, Chapter Three) has found, and I have also (DeStefano, Chapter Four), that the more formal the situation the Black English speaker feels he is in, the more standard English forms he will be likely to produce. Such variation is important for educators to be aware of because ghetto black children are often "sold short" on the amount of more standard forms they use.

Inter-speaker (among speakers) variability has also been reported by researchers such as Roger Shuy and Walt Wolfram. One person may produce more standard English forms in his speech than another black of approximately the same socioeconomic status who may even be a neighbor. The mechanisms responsible for such variation are poorly understood at present, but evidently age and sex are contributing factors. Again, this variation is important to educators because it implies the necessity of differing pedagogical strategies based on differing language behavior in ghetto blacks.

It is important to remember that not all blacks speak Black English, and those who are perceived to speak this ghetto specific variety do not all produce the same number of Black English forms in their speech, nor do they use an invariant number of forms in their own speech. Such variation in production is an important aspect of Black English.

Black English is often seen as a dialect very much different from other varieties of American English. In fact, some people claim it is a foreign language, a claim not accepted by most linguists and one which I reject. Black English overlaps a great deal with so-called standard varieties, and Black English speakers produce "standard" forms. Samuel Henrie reports that young black children command many more standard forms than has usually been acknowledged. He reported that:

> Two thirds of their [black five year olds] output was S[tandard] E[nglish], and there were no SE forms which the N[egro] N[onstandard] E[nglish speaking] subjects could not competently produce. (2) All three subjects produced some such complex strings as "How could I have been sleeping?" easily and with meaning. And one must bear in mind that they were chosen for the study after careful screening and preliminary testing because they were found to be among the *most frequent* producers of NNE forms from among over sixty preschool students in an urban ghetto school. Subject to further verification, we can conclude that much of the literature has presented a distorted picture of the language of the Negro ghetto child. We can speculate that this distortion is the result of a tendency to focus only on the differences and ignore the less interesting, but very important similarities between his language and that of the "advantaged" child. [See DeStefano, Chapter Four, for a discussion of his point.]

Researchers and educators who are basing decisions on reported research will do well to heed the suggestion of Labov et al. (3) that we must be responsible to the total data. "A report of a linguistic form or rule used in a speech community must include an account of the total population of utterances from which the observation is drawn, and the proportion of the expected environments in which this form did in fact occur." Far too many papers are being produced in which lists like the following are offered: (4)

Variable	Standard English	Negro Non-Standard
1.* linking verb	He IS going.	He goin'
2. verb agreement	She HAS a bicycle	She HAVE a bicycle
3. negation	He didn't go	He ain't go
4. do	No he isn't	No he don't
etc.		

One would conclude that the ghetto child could be expected to use the forms in the Negro Non-Standard column 100% of the time. But, in fact, the data in this study and in others in which the total data are reported (5) indicate that the SE forms in items 1 and 2 above are at least as typical of Negro ghetto children's speech as the NNE forms listed. And, the *SE* forms in 3 and 4 above are far more typical than are the supposed NNE forms. For example "he ain't go" occurred in these data as only 3.6% while its supposed *SE* equivalent "He didn't go" occurred 96.4% of the time.

This variability needs to be kept in mind while reading the articles in Chapter Three, and while reading about its implications for the pedagogical suggestions made in Chapters Five and Six.

Viewpoint Toward Black English

In this volume, the basic viewpoint adopted toward Black English is that of many linguists. A linguist accepts a certain set of assumptions which are relativistic in the sense that a linguist does not make judgments, for example, as to the "adequacy" or "inadequacy" of a given language in its ability to express certain concepts such as time or relativity. A given variety is assumed to be as adequate for the needs of its speakers as any other language or speech variety. Different varieties may express essentially the same concept in different ways. A linguist assumes these differences do not imply deficiencies; he assumes that one way of saying something is not intrinsically better than another way. In other words, although the surface forms of language may vary remarkably, this variation has little or nothing to do with the concept expressed by a sentence. French is thus no more logical than English, German no more inherently scientific than Italian. If a Frenchman behaves more logically than an Englishmen on a given occasion, it is assumed that at another time the Englishman may be more logical

---

* Iteration Henrie's.

in his actions. Thus two negatives as in "I ain't got nothing" do not make a positive statement, or Frenchmen have for centuries been meaning "I do have something" when they have been saying "Je n'ai rien" (I don't have nothing). The point is that different varieties have different ways of expressing negation, all of which are perfectly adequate. (See Labov's article in this chapter for a more detailed discussion of negation.)

This assumption of the adequacy of any language or variety to express concepts has been applied by linguists to the study of Black English. This variety of American English is assumed to be adequate for expressing negation, though it often uses more than one negative word in a sentence as in "It ain't no cat can't get in no coop." (6) A legitimate linguistic question is how does Black English communicate a concept as compared to a more standard English spoken by economically powerful people in the same geographical area. Thus the linguist operates on a difference rather than a deficit model when he studies Black English. Black English is considered different from other varieties of English, not inferior to them. The difference model is the one represented in the selections in this anthology.

Another assumption made by linguists is that every language variety is systematic and ordered, not irregular or haphazard. Thus, as Fasold and Wolfram note (see Chapter Three), Black English is considered systematic and not an "aberration" of a more standard form. It is a fully formed system with grammar and pronunciation rules. This assumption is implicit in the selections in this anthology and in current linguistic discussions of Black English.

The following article by William Labov states these linguistic assumptions in relationship to Black English very clearly.

References

1. Ralph W. Fasold and Walter A. Wolfram, "Some Linguistic Features of Negro Dialect," in *Teaching Standard English in the Inner City,* eds. Ralph W. Fasold and Roger W. Shuy (Washington, D.C.: Center for Applied Linguistics, 1970), p. 42 [in Chapter Three of this book].
2. Samuel N. Henrie, Jr., "A Study of Verb Phrases Used by Five-Year-Old Nonstandard Negro English Speaking Children," Mimeographed (Berkeley, Calif.: University of California, June, 1969). Reprinted by permission of Samuel Henrie, Jr.
3. William Labov et al., "A Study of the Non-Standard English of Negro and Puerto Rican Speakers in New York City," final report, Cooperative Research Project No. 3288 (Washington, D.C.: Office of Education, 1968, I and II.
4. Joan C. Baratz, "Teaching Reading in an Urban Negro School System," in *Teaching Black Children to Read,* eds. Joan C. Baratz and Roger W. Shuy (Washington, D.C.: Center for Applied Linguistics, 1969), pp. 92–116.
5. William Labov, "Contraction, Deletion and Inherent Variability of the English Copula," Mimeographed (New York: 1968).

William Labov et al., "Study of Non-Standard English"

Walter D. Loban, *Language Ability—Grade Seven, Eight and Nine* (Washington, D.C.: U.S. Department of Health, Education and Welfare, 1966).

Walter D. Loban, *Problems in Oral English: Kindergarten Through Grade Nine* (Champaign, Ill.: N.C.T.E. Research Report #5, 1966).

6. William Labov et al., "Study of Non-Standard English," p. 267.

The Logic of Nonstandard English
William Labov

In this article, William Labov presents the difference model and deficit or "verbal deprivation" model discussed in "Viewpoints Toward Black English" as well as their educational implications for ghetto black children. The following summary was written by Labov for the article.

The traditional view of nonstandard English [Black English] held by many public school teachers is that it is an illogical form of speech; that when children are taught the standard forms they are also being taught to think logically. Linguists have endeavored for many years to show that differences in language are matters of social convention established by historical processes which shift continually the social prestige of dialect variants.

Recent programs for teaching the "culturally disadvantaged," particularly those of Carl Bereiter and his associates, have revived the notion that nonstandard dialects are illogical, attributing poor educational performance to cognitive disabilities reflected in language.

The educational programs proposed are based upon sociological and linguistic misinterpretations of the data. The linguistic behavior reported by Bereiter is merely a product of a defensive posture which children adopt in an alien and threatening situation. Such behavior can be produced at will in any group of children and can be altered by changing the relevant sociolinguistic variables.

There are many important questions concerning the cognitive correlates of syntactic complexity which current research technique has not yet answered. At present, there is no basis for attributing poor educational performance to the grammatical and phonological characteristics of any nonstandard dialect of English.

In the past decade, a great deal of federally-sponsored research has been devoted to the educational problems of children in ghetto schools. In order to account for the poor performance of children in these schools, educational psychologists have attempted to discover what kind of disadvantage

From "The Logic of Nonstandard English" by William Labov. Monograph Series on Language and Linguistics, No. 22, 1969. (Washington, D.C.: Georgetown University Press, 1969). Copyright © by Georgetown University Press. Reprinted by permission of the publisher.

or defect they are suffering from. The viewpoint which has been widely accepted, and used as the basis for large-scale intervention programs, is that the children show a cultural deficit as a result of an impoverished environment in their early years. Considerable attention has been given to language. In this area, the deficit theory appears as the concept of "verbal deprivation": Negro children from the ghetto area receive little verbal stimulation, are said to hear very little well-formed language, and as a result are impoverished in their means of verbal expression: they cannot speak complete sentences, do not know the names of common objects, cannot form concepts or convey logical thoughts.

Unfortunately, these notions are based upon the work of educational psychologists who know very little about language and even less about Negro children. The concept of verbal deprivation has no basis in social reality: in fact, Negro children in the urban ghettos receive a great deal of verbal stimulation, here more well-formed sentences than middle-class children, and participate fully in a highly verbal culture; they have the same basic vocabulary, possess the same capacity for conceptual learning, and use the same logic as anyone else who learns to speak and understand English.

The notion of "verbal deprivation" is a part of the modern mythology of educational psychology, typical of the unfounded notions which tend to expand rapidly in our educational system. In past decades linguists have been as guilty as others in promoting such intellectual fashions at the expense of both teachers and children. But the myth of verbal deprivation is particularly dangerous, because it diverts attention from real defects of our educational system to imaginary defects of the child; and as we shall see, it leads its sponsors inevitably to the hypothesis of the genetic inferiority of Negro children which it was originally designed to avoid.

The most useful service which linguists can perform today is to clear away the illusion of "verbal deprivation" and provide a more adequate notion of the relations between standard and nonstandard dialects. In the writings of many prominent educational psychologists, we find a very poor understanding of the nature of language. Children are treated as if they have no language of their own in the preschool programs put forward by Carl Bereiter and Siegfried Engelmann. (1) The linguistic behavior of ghetto children in test situations is the principal evidence for their genetic inferiority in the view of Arthur Jensen. (2) In this paper, I will examine critically both of these approaches to the language and intelligence of the populations labelled "verbally" and "culturally deprived." I will attempt to explain how the myth of verbal deprivation has arisen, bringing to bear the methodological findings of sociolinguistic work, and some substantive facts about language which are known to all linguists. I will be particularly concerned with the relation between concept formation on the one hand, and dialect differences on the other, since it is in this area that the most dangerous misunderstandings are to be found.

1. Verbality

The general setting in which the deficit theory has arisen consists of a number of facts which are known to all of us: that Negro children in the central urban ghettos do badly on all school subjects, including arithmetic and reading. In reading, they average more than two years behind the national norm. Furthermore, this lag is cumulative, so that they do worse comparatively in the fifth grade than in the first grade. Reports in the literature show that this bad performance is correlated most closely with socioeconomic status. Segregated ethnic groups, however, seem to do worse than others: in particular, Indians, Mexican-Americans, and Negro children. Our own work in New York City confirms the fact that most Negro children read very poorly; however, our studies in the speech community show that the situation is even worse than has been reported. If one separates the isolated and peripheral individuals from the members of the central peer groups, the peer group members show even worse reading records, and to all intents and purposes are not learning to read at all during the time they spend in school. (3)

In speaking of children in the urban ghetto areas, the term "lower-class" is frequently used as opposed to "middle-class." In the several sociolinguistic studies we have carried out, and in many parallel studies, it is useful to distinguish a "lower-class" group from "working-class." Lower-class families are typically female-based or "matrifocal," with no father present to provide steady economic support, whereas for the working-class there is typically an intact nuclear family with the father holding a semiskilled or unskilled job. The educational problems of ghetto areas run across this important class distinction; there is no evidence, for example, that the father's presence or absence is closely correlated with educational achievement. The peer groups we have studied in South Central Harlem, representing the basic vernacular culture, include members from both family types. The attack against "cultural deprivation" in the ghetto is overtly directed at family structures typical of lower-class families, but the educational failure we have been discussing is characteristic of both working-class and lower-class children.

In the balance of this paper, I will therefore refer to children from urban ghetto areas, rather than "lower-class" children; the population we are concerned with are those who participate fully in the vernacular culture of the street and who have been alienated from the school system. We are obviously dealing with the effects of the caste system of American society —essentially a "color marking" system. Everyone recognizes this. The question is, by what mechanism does the color bar prevent children from learning to read? One answer is the notion of "cultural deprivation" put forward by Martin Deutsch and others: the Negro children are said to lack the favorable factors in their home environment which enable middle-class children to do well in school. (4) These factors involve the development of various cognitive skills through verbal interaction with adults, including the ability to reason abstractly, speak fluently, and focus upon long-range goals. In their publications, these psychologists also recognize broader social factors. However, the deficit theory does not focus upon the interaction of the Negro child with white society so much as on his failure to interact with his mother at home. In the literature we find very little direct observation of verbal interaction in the Negro home; most typically, the investigators ask the child if he has dinner with his parents, and if he engages in dinner-table conversation with them. He is also asked whether his family takes him on trips to museums and other cultural activities. This slender thread of evidence is used to explain and interpret the large body of tests carried out in the laboratory and in the school.

The most extreme view which proceeds from this orientation—and one that is now being widely accepted—is that lower-class Negro children have no language at all. The notion is first drawn from Basil Bernstein's writings that "much of lower-class language consists of a kind of incidental 'emotional' accompaniment to action here and now." (5) Bernstein's views are filtered through a strong bias against all forms of working-class behavior, so that middle-class language is seen as superior in every respect—as "more abstract, and necessarily somewhat more flexible, detailed and subtle." One can proceed through a range of such views until one comes to the practical program of Carl Bereiter, Siegfried Engelmann and their associates. (6) Bereiter's program for an academically oriented preschool is based upon their premise that Negro children must have a language with which they can learn, and their empirical finding that these children come to school without such a language. In his work with four-year-old Negro children from Urbana, Bereiter reports that their communication was by gestures, 'single words,' and 'a series of badly-connected words or phrases,' such as *They mine* and *Me got juice.* He reports that Negro children could not ask questions, that "without exaggerating . . . these four-year-olds could make no statements of any kind." Furthermore, when these children were asked

"Where is the book?" they did not know enough to look at the table where the book was lying in order to answer. Thus Bereiter concludes that the children's speech forms are nothing more than a series of emotional cries, and he decides to treat them "as if the children had no language at all." He identifies their speech with his interpretation of Bernstein's restricted code: "the language of culturally deprived children . . . is not merely an underdeveloped version of standard English, but is a basically non-logical mode of expressive behavior." (7) The basic program of his preschool is to teach them a new language devised by Engelmann, which consists of a limited series of questions and answers such as *Where is the squirrel? The squirrel is in the tree.* The children will not be punished if they use their vernacular speech on the playground, but they will not be allowed to use it in the schoolroom. If they should answer the question *Where is the squirrel?* with the illogical vernacular form *In the tree* they will be reprehended by various means and made to say, *The squirrel is in the tree.*

Linguists and psycholinguists who have worked with Negro children are apt to dismiss this view of their language as utter nonsense. Yet there is no reason to reject Bereiter's observations as spurious—they were certainly not made up—on the contrary, they give us a very clear view of the behavior of student and teacher which can be duplicated in any classroom. In our own work outside of the adult-dominated environments of school and home, (8) we do not observe Negro children behaving like this, but on many occasions we have been asked to help analyze the results of research into verbal deprivation in such test situations.

Here, for example, is a complete interview with a Negro boy, one of hundreds carried out in a New York City school. The boy enters a room where there is a large, friendly white interviewer, who puts on the table in front of him a block or a fire engine, and says "Tell me everything you can about this." (The interviewer's further remarks are in parentheses.)

[12 seconds of silence]
(What would you say it looks like?)
    [8 seconds of silence]
A space ship.
(Hmmmm.)
    [13 seconds of silence]
Like a je-et.
    [12 seconds of silence]
Like a plane.
    [20 seconds of silence]
(What color is it?)
Orange. [2 seconds]. An' whi-ite. [2 seconds]. An' green.
    [6 seconds of silence]

(An' what could you use it for?)
  [8 seconds of silence]
A je-et.
  [6 seconds of silence]
(If you had two of them, what would you do with them?)
  [6 seconds of silence]
Give one to some-body.
(Hmmm. Who do you think would like to have it?)
  [10 seconds of silence]
Cla-rence.
(Mm. Where do you think we could get another one of these?)
At the store.
(Oh ka-ay!)

We have here the same kind of defensive, monosyllabic behavior which is reported in Bereiter's work. What is the situation that produces it? The child is in an asymmetrical situation where anything he says can literally be held against him. He has learned a number of devices to *avoid* saying anything in this situation, and he works very hard to achieve this end. One may observe the intonation patterns of which Negro children often use

$$\begin{array}{l} ^{3}\text{'o'}\; ^{2}\text{know} \\ \hline ^{1}\text{a} \\ \hline ^{2}\text{a space}\; ^{2}\text{shi}\; \text{ip}^{3} \end{array}$$

when they are asked a question to which the answer is obvious. The answer may be read as "Will this satisfy you?"

If one takes this interview as a measure of the verbal capacity of the child, it must be as his capacity to defend himself in a hostile and threatening situation. But unfortunately, thousands of such interviews are used as evidence of the child's total verbal capacity, or more simply his "verbality;" it is argued that his lack of verbality *explains* his poor performance in school. Operation Head Start and other intervention programs have largely been based upon the "deficit theory"—the notions that such interviews give us a measure of the child's verbal capacity and that the verbal stimulation which he has been missing can be supplied in a preschool environment.

The verbal behavior which is shown by the child in the test situation quoted above is not the result of the ineptness of the interviewer. It is rather the result of regular sociolinguistic factors operating upon adult and child in this asymmetrical situation. In our work in urban ghetto areas, we have often encountered such behavior. Ordinarily we worked with boys 10–17 years old; and whenever we extended our approach downward to 8 or 9 year olds, we began to see the need for different techniques to explore the verbal capacity of the child. At one point we began a series of interviews with younger brothers of the "Thunderbirds" in 1390 5th Avenue. Clarence Robins returned after an interview with 8-year-old Leon L., who showed the following minimal response to topics which arouse intense interest in other interviews with older boys.

CR: What if you saw somebody kickin' somebody else on the ground,
        or was using a stick, what would you do if you saw that?
Leon: Mmmm.
CR: If it was supposed to be a fair fight—
Leon: I don' know.
CR: You don' know? Would you do anything . . . huh? I can't hear you.
Leon: No.
CR: Did you ever see somebody got beat up real bad?
Leon: . . . Nope ? ? ?
CR: Well--uh--did you ever get into a fight with a guy?
Leon: Nope.
CR: That was bigger than you?
Leon: Nope.
CR: You never been in a fight?
Leon: Nope.
CR: Nobody ever pick on you?
Leon: Nope.
CR: Nobody ever hit you?
Leon: Nope.
CR: How come?
Leon: Ah 'on' know.
CR: Didn't you ever hit somebody?
Leon: Nope.
CR: [incredulous] You never hit nobody?
Leon: Mhm.
CR: Aww, ba -a-a-be, you ain't gonna tell me that.

It may be that Leon is here defending himself against accusations of wrong-doing, since Clarence knows that Leon has been in fights, that he has been taking pencils away from little boys, etc. But if we turn to a more neutral subject, we find the same pattern:

CR: You watch—you like to watch television? . . . Hey, Leon . . . you
        like to watch television? [Leon nods] What's your favorite program?
Leon: Uhhmmmm . . . I look at cartoons.
CR: Well, what's your favorite one? What's your favorite program?
Leon: Superman . . .
CR: Yeah? Did you see Superman--ah--yesterday, or day before yester-
        day: when's the last time you saw Superman?
Leon: Sa-aturday . . .

CR: You rem--you saw it Saturday? What was the story all about? You remember the story?
Leon: M-m.
CR: You don't remember the story of what--that you saw of Superman?
Leon: Nope.
CR: You don't remember what happened, huh?
Leon: Hm-m.
CR: I see--ah--what other stories do you like to watch on T.V.?
Leon: Mmmm ? ? ? ? . . . umm . . . [glottalization]
CR: Hmm? [4 seconds]
Leon: Hh?
CR: What's th'other stories that you like to watch?
Leon: ^{2}Mi - ighty ^{2}Mouse^2 . . .
CR: And what else?
Leon: Ummmm . . . ahm . . .

This nonverbal behavior occurs in a relatively *favorable* context for adult-child interaction; since the adult is a Negro man raised in Harlem, who knows this particular neighborhood and these boys very well. He is a skilled interviewer who has obtained a very high level of verbal response with techniques developed for a different age level, and he has an extraordinary advantage over most teachers or experimenters in these respects. But even his skills and personality are ineffective in breaking down the social constraints that prevail here.

When we reviewed the record of this interview with Leon, we decided to use it as a test of our own knowledge of the sociolinguistic factors which control speech. We made the following changes in the social situation: in the next interview with Leon, Clarence

1) brought along a supply of potato chips, changing the "interview" into something more in the nature of a party;

2) brought along Leon's best friend, 8-year-old Gregory;

3) reduced the height imbalance (when Clarence got down on the floor of Leon's room, he dropped from 6 ft. 2 in. to 3 ft. 6 in.);

4) introduced taboo words and taboo topics, and proved to Leon's surprise that one can say anything into our microphone without any fear of retaliation.

The result of these changes is a striking difference in the volume and style of speech.

CR: Is there anybody who says *your momma drink pee?*
{Leon: [rapidly and breathlessly] Yee-ah!
{Greg: Yup!
Leon: And your father eat doo-doo for breakfas'!
CR: Ohhh! ! [laughs]

Leon:	And they say *your father--your father eat doo-doo for dinner!*
Greg:	When they sound on me, I say *C.B.M.*
CR:	What that mean?
⎰ Leon:	Congo booger-snatch! [laughs]
⎱ Greg:	Congo booger-snatcher! [laughs]
Greg:	And sometimes I'll curse with *B.B.*
CR:	What that?
Greg:	Black boy! [Leon—crunching on potato chips] Oh that's a *M.B.B.*
CR:	M.B.B. What's that?
Greg:	'Merican Black Boy!
CR:	Ohh . . .
Greg:	Anyway, 'Mericans is same like white people, right?
Leon:	And they talk about Allah.
CR:	Oh yeah?
Greg:	Yeah.
CR:	What they say about Allah?
⎰ Leon:	Allah--Allah is God.
⎱ Greg:	Allah--
CR:	And what else?
Leon:	I don' know the res'.
Greg:	Allah i--Allah is God, Allah is the only God, Allah-
Leon:	Allah is the *son* of God.
Greg:	But can he make magic?
Leon:	Nope.
Greg:	I know who can make magic.
CR:	Who can?
Leon:	The God, the *real* one.
CR:	Who can make magic?
Greg:	The son of po'--[CR: Hm?] I'm sayin' the po'k chop God! He only a po'k chop God! [Leon chuckles].

The "nonverbal" Leon is now competing actively for the floor; Gregory and Leon talk to each other as much as they do to the interviewer.

One can make a more direct comparison of the two interviews by examining the section on fighting. Leon persists in denying that he fights, but he can no longer use monosyllabic answers, and Gregory cuts through his façade in a way that Clarence Robins alone was unable to do.

CR:	Now, you said you had this fight, now, but I wanted you to tell me about the fight that you had.
Leon:	I ain't had no fight.
⎰ Greg:	Yes you did! He said Barry,
⎱ CR:	You said you had one! you had a fight with Butchie,
⎰ Greg:	An he say Garland . . . an' Michael.
⎱ CR:	an' Barry . . .
⎰ Leon:	I di'n'; you said that, Gregory!
⎱ Greg:	You did.
⎰ Leon:	You know you said that!
⎱ Greg:	You said Garland, remember that?

{ Greg:	You said Garland!	Yes you did!	
{ CR:			You said Garland, that's right.

Greg: He said Mich--an' I say Michael.

{ CR: Did you have a fight with Garland?
{ Leon: Uh-uh.

CR: You had one, and he beat you up, too!

Greg: Yes he did!

Leon: No, I di--I never had a fight with Butch! . . .

The same pattern can be seen on other local topics, where the interviewer brings neighborhood gossip to bear on Leon and Gregory acts as a witness.

CR: . . . Hey Gregory! I heard that around here . . . and I'm 'on' tell you who said it, too . . .

Leon: Who?

{ CR: about you . . .
{ Leon: Who?
{ Greg: I'd say it!

CR: They said that--they say that the only person you play with is David Gilbert.

{ Leon: Yee-ah! yee-ah! yee-ah! . . .
{ Greg: That's who you play with!

{ Leon: I 'on' play with him no more!
{ Greg: Yes you do!

Leon: I 'on' play with him no more!

Greg: But remember, about me and Robbie?

Leon: So that's not--

Greg: and you went to Petey and Gilbert's house, 'member? *Ah haaah!* !

Leon: So that's--so--but I would--I had came back out, an' I ain't go to his house no more . . .

The observer must now draw a very different conclusion about the verbal capacity of Leon. The monosyllabic speaker who had nothing to say about anything and cannot remember what he did yesterday has disappeared. Instead, we have two boys who have so much to say they keep interrupting each other, who seem to have no difficulty in using the English language to express themselves. And we in turn obtain the volume of speech and the rich array of grammatical devices which we need for analyzing the structure of nonstandard Negro English (NNE): negative concord *(I 'on' play with him no more)*, the pluperfect *(had came back out)*, negative perfect *(I ain't had)*, the negative preterite *(I ain't go)*, and so on.

One can now transfer this demonstration of the sociolinguistic control of speech to other test situations—including I.Q. and reading tests in school. It should be immediately apparent that none of the standard tests will come anywhere near measuring Leon's verbal capacity. On these tests he will show up as very much the monosyllabic, inept, ignorant, bumbling child of our first interview. The teacher has far less ability than Clarence Robins to elicit speech from this child; Clarence knows the community, the things that Leon has been doing, and the things that Leon would like to talk about. But the power relationships in a one-to-one confrontation between adult and child are too asymmetrical. This does not mean that some Negro children will not talk a great deal when alone with an adult, or that an adult cannot get close to any child. It means that the social situation is the most powerful determinant of verbal behavior and that an adult must enter into the right social relation with a child if he wants to find out what a child can do: this is just what many teachers cannot do.

The view of the Negro speech community which we obtain from our work in the ghetto areas is precisely the opposite from that reported by Deutsch, Engelmann and Bereiter. We see a child bathed in verbal stimulation from morning to night. We see many speech events which depend upon the competitive exhibition of verbal skills: sounding, singing, toasts, rifting, louding—a whole range of activities in which the individual gains status through his use of language. We see the younger child trying to acquire these skills from older children—hanging around on the outskirts of the older peer groups, and imitating this behavior to the best of his ability. We see no connection between verbal skill at the speech events characteristic of the street culture and success in the schoolroom.

2. Verbosity

There are undoubtedly many verbal skills which children from ghetto areas must learn in order to do well in the school situation, and some of these are indeed characteristic of middle-class verbal behavior. Precision in spelling, practice in handling abstract symbols, the ability to state explicitly the meaning of words, and a richer knowledge of the Latinate vocabulary, may all be useful acquisitions. But is it true that *all* of the middle-class verbal habits are functional and desirable in the school situation? Before we impose middle-class verbal style upon children from other cultural groups, we should find out how much of this is useful for the main work of analyzing and generalizing, and how much is merely stylistic—or even dysfunctional. In high school and college middle-class children spontaneously complicate their syntax to the point that instructors despair of getting them to make their language simpler and clearer. In every learned journal one can find examples of jargon and empty elaboration—and complaints about it. Is the "elaborated code" of Bernstein really so "flexible, detailed and subtle" as some psychologists believe? (9) Isn't it also turgid, redundant, and empty? Is it not simply an elaborated *style,* rather than a superior code or system? (10)

Our work in the speech community makes it painfully obvious that in many ways working-class speakers are more effective narrators, reasoners and debaters than many middle-class speakers who temporize, qualify, and lose their argument in a mass of irrelevant detail. Many academic writers try to rid themselves of that part of middle-class style that is empty pretension, and keep that part that is needed for precision. But the average middle-class speaker that we encounter makes no such effort; he is enmeshed in verbiage, the victim of sociolinguistic factors beyond his control.

I will not attempt to support this argument here with systematic quantitative evidence, although it is possible to develop measures which show how far middle-class speakers can wander from the point. I would like to contrast two speakers dealing with roughly the same topic—matters of belief. The first is Larry H., a 15-year-old core member of the Jets, being interviewed by John Lewis. Larry is one of the loudest and roughest members of the Jets, one who gives the least recognition to the conventional rules of politeness. For most readers of this paper, first contact with Larry would produce some fairly negative reactions on both sides: it is probable that you would not *like* him any more than his teachers do. Larry causes trouble in and out of school; he was put back from the eleventh grade to the ninth, and has been threatened with further action by the school authorities.

JL: What happens to you after you die? Do you know?
Larry: Yeah, I know.
JL: What?
Larry: After they put you in the ground, your body turns into--ah--bones, an' shit.
JL: What happens to your spirit?
Larry: Your spirit--soon as you die, your spirit leaves you.
JL: And where does the spirit go?
Larry: Well, it all depends . . .
JL: On what?
Larry: You know, like some people say if you're good an' shit, your spirit goin' t'heaven . . . 'n' if you bad, your spirit goin' to hell. Well, bullshit! Your spirit goin' to hell anyway, good or bad.
JL: Why?
Larry: Why? I'll tell you why. 'Cause, you see, doesn' nobody really know that it's a God, y'know, 'cause I mean I have seen black gods, pink gods, white gods, all color gods, and don't nobody know it's really a God. An' when they be sayin' if you good, you goin' t'heaven, tha's bullshit, 'cause you ain't goin' to no heaven, 'cause it ain't no heaven for you to go to.

Larry is a paradigmatic speaker of nonstandard Negro English (NNE) as opposed to standard English (SE). His grammar shows a high concentration of such characteristic NNE forms as negative inversion (*don't nobody know*. . .), negative concord (*you ain't goin' to no heaven*. . .), invariant *be* (*when they be sayin'*. . .), dummy *it* for SE *there* (*it ain't no heaven*. . .), optional copula deletion (*if you're good*. . . *if you bad*. . .), and full forms of auxiliaries (*I have seen*. . .). The only SE influence in this passage is the one case of *doesn't* instead of the invariant *don't* of NNE. Larry also provides a paradigmatic example of the rhetorical style of NNE: he can sum up a complex argument in a few words, and the full force of his opinions comes through without qualification or reservation. He is eminently quotable, and his interviews give us many concise statements of the NNE point of view. One can almost say that Larry *speaks* the NNE culture. (11)

It is the logical form of this passage which is of particular interest here. Larry presents a complex set of interdependent propositions which can be explicated by setting out the SE equivalents in linear order. The basic argument is to deny the twin propositions

    (A) If you are good,   (B) then your spirit will go to heaven.
    (-A) If you are bad,   (C) then your spirit will go to hell.

Larry denies (B), and asserts that *if (A) or (-A), then (C)*. His argument may be outlined as follows:

1) Everyone has a different idea of what God is like.

2) Therefore nobody really knows that God exists.

3) If there is a heaven, it was made by God.

4) If God doesn't exist, he couldn't have made heaven.

5) Therefore heaven does not exist.

6) You can't go somewhere that doesn't exist.

(-B) Therefore you can't go to heaven.

(C) Therefore you are going to hell.

The argument is presented in the order: (C), because 2) because 1), therefore 2), therefore (-B) because 5) and 6). Part of the argument is implicit: the connection 2) therefore (-B) leaves unstated the connecting links 3) and 4), and in this interval Larry strengthens the propositions from the form 2) *Nobody knows if there is*. . . to 5) *There is no*. . . Otherwise, the case is presented explicitly as well as economically. The complex argument is summed up in Larry's last sentence, which shows formally the dependence of (-B) or 5) and 6):

    An' when they be sayin' if you good, you goin' t'heaven,
    [The proposition, if A, then B]

Tha's bullshit,
[is absurd]
'cause you ain't goin' to no heaven
[because -B]
'cause it ain't no heaven for you to go to.
[because 5) and 6)].

This hypothetical argument is not carried on at a high level of seriousness. It is a game played with ideas as counters, in which opponents use a wide variety of verbal devices to win. There is no personal commitment to any of these propositions, and no reluctance to strengthen one's argument by bending the rules of logic as in the 2–5) sequence. But if the opponent invokes the rules of logic, they hold. In John Lewis' interviews, he often makes this move, and the force of his argument is always acknowledged and countered within the rules of logic. In this case, he pointed out the fallacy that the argument 2–3–4–5–6) leads to (-C) as well as (-B), so it cannot be used to support Larry's assertion (C):

JL: Well, if there's no heaven, how could there be a hell?
Larry: I mean--ye-eah. Well, let me tell you, it ain't no hell, 'cause this is hell right here, y'know!
JL: This is hell?
Larry: Yeah, this is hell right here!

Larry's answer is quick, ingenious and decisive. The application of the 3–4–5) argument to hell is denied, since hell is here, and therefore conclusion (C) stands. These are not ready-made or preconceived opinions, but new propositions devised to win the logical argument in the game being played. The reader will note the speed and precision of Larry's mental operations. He does not wander, or insert meaningless verbiage. The only repetition is 2), placed before and after 1) in his original statement. It is often said that the nonstandard vernacular is not suited for dealing with abstract or hypothetical questions, but in fact speakers from the NNE community take great delight in exercising their wit and logic on the most improbable and problematical matters. Despite the fact that Larry H. does not believe in God, and has just denied all knowledge of him, John Lewis advances the following hypothetical question:

JL: . . . But, just say that there is a God, what color is he? White or black?
Larry: Well, if it is a God . . . I wouldn' know what color, I couldn' say, --couldn' nobody say what color he is or really *would* be.
JL: But now, jus' suppose there was a God—
Larry: Unless'n they say . . .

JL: No, I was jus' sayin' jus' suppose there is a God, would he be white or black?

Larry: . . . He'd be white, man.

JL: Why?

Larry: Why? I'll tell you why. 'Cause the average whitey out here got everything, you dig? And the nigger ain't got shit, y'know? Y'understan'? So--um--for--in order for *that* to happen, you know it ain't no black God that's doin' that bullshit.

No one can hear Larry's answer to this question without being convinced that they are in the presence of a skilled speaker with great "verbal presence of mind," who can use the English language expertly for many purposes. Larry's answer to John Lewis is again a complex argument. The formulation is not SE, but it is clear and effective even for those not familiar with the vernacular. The nearest SE equivalent might be: "So you know that God isn't black, because if he was, he wouldn't have arranged things like that."

The reader will have noted that this analysis is being carried out in standard English, and the inevitable challenge is: why not write in NNE, then, or in your own nonstandard dialect? The fundamental reason is, of course, one of firmly fixed social conventions. All communities agree that SE is the "proper" medium for formal writing and public communication. Furthermore, it seems likely that SE has an advantage over NNE in explicit analysis of surface forms, which is what we are doing here. We will return to this opposition between explicitness and logical statement in sections 3 and 4. First, however, it will be helpful to examine SE in its primary natural setting, as the medium for informal spoken communication of middle-class speakers.

Let us now turn to the second speaker, an upper-middle-class, college educated Negro man being interviewed by Clarence Robins in our survey of adults in Central Harlem.

CR: Do you know of anything that someone can do, to have someone who has passed on visit him in a dream?

Chas. M.: Well, I even heard my parents say that there is such a thing as something in dreams some things like that, and sometimes dreams do come true. I have personally never had a dream come true. I've never dreamt that somebody was dying and they actually died, (Mhm) or that I was going to have ten dollars the next day and somehow I got ten dollars in my pocket. (Mhm). I don't particularly believe in that, I don't think it's true. I do feel, though, that there is such a thing as --ah--witchcraft. I do feel that in certain cultures there is such a thing as witchcraft, or some sort of *science* of witchcraft; I don't think that it's just a matter of believing hard enough that there is such a thing as witchcraft. I do believe that there is such a thing that a person can put himself in a state of *mind* (Mhm), or that--er--something could

be given them to intoxicate them in a certain--to a certain frame
of mind--that--that could actually be considered witchcraft.

Charles M. is obviously a "good speaker" who strikes the listener as well-educated, intelligent and sincere. He is a likeable and attractive person—the kind of person that middle-class listeners rate very high on a scale of "job suitability" and equally high as a potential friend. His language is more moderate and tempered than Larry's; he makes every effort to qualify his opinions, and seems anxious to avoid any misstatements or over-statements. From these qualities emerge the primary characteristic of this passage—its *verbosity.* Words multiply, some modifying and qualifying, others repeating or padding the main argument. The first half of this extract is a response to the initial question on dreams, basically:

1) Some people say that dreams sometimes come true.

2) I have never had a dream come true.

3) Therefore I don't believe 1).

Some characteristic filler phrases appear here: *such a thing as, some things like that, particularly.* Two examples of dreams given after 2) are after-thoughts that might have been given after 1). Proposition 3) is stated twice for no obvious reason. Nevertheless, this much of Charles M.'s response is well-directed to the point of the question. He then volunteers a statement of his beliefs about witchcraft which shows the difficulty of middle-class speakers who (a) want to express a belief in something but (b) want to show themselves as judicious, rational and free from superstitions. The basic proposition can be stated simply in five words:

But I believe in witchcraft.

However, the idea is enlarged to exactly 100 words, and it is difficult to see what else is being said. In the following quotations, padding which can be removed without change in meaning is shown in brackets.

1) "I (do) feel, though, that there is (such a thing as) witchcraft." *Feel* seems to be a euphemism for 'believe'.

2) "(I do feel that) in certain cultures (there is such a thing as witchcraft.)" This repetition seems designed only to introduce the word *culture,* which lets us know that the speaker knows about anthropology. Does *certain cultures* mean "not in ours" or "not in all"?

3) "(or some sort of *science* of witchcraft.)" This addition seems to have no clear meaning at all. What is a "science" of witchcraft as opposed to just plain witchcraft? The main function is to introduce the word "science," though it seems to have no connection to what follows.

4) "I don't think that it's just (a matter of) believing hard enough that

(there is such a thing as) witchcraft." The speaker argues that witchcraft is not merely a belief; there is more to it.

5) "I (do) believe that (there is such a thing that) a person can put himself in a state of *mind . . .* that (could actually be considered) witchcraft." Is witchcraft as a state of mind different from the state of belief denied in 4)?

6) "or that something could be given them to intoxicate them (to a certain frame of mind) . . ." The third learned word, *intoxicate,* is introduced by this addition. The vacuity of this passage becomes more evident if we remove repetitions, fashionable words and stylistic decorations:

> But I believe in witchcraft.
> I don't think witchcraft is just a belief.
> A person can put himself or be put in a state of mind that is witchcraft.

Without the extra verbiage and the O.K. words like *science, culture,* and *intoxicate,* Charles M. appears as something less than a first-rate thinker. The initial impression of him as a good speaker is simply our long-conditioned reaction to middle-class verbosity: we know that people who use these stylistic devices are educated people, and we are inclined to credit them with saying something intelligent. Our reactions are accurate in one sense: Charles M. is more educated than Larry. But is he more rational, more logical, or more intelligent? Is he any better at thinking out a problem to its solution? Does he deal more easily with abstractions? There is no reason to think so. Charles M. succeeds in letting us know that he is educated, but in the end we do not know what he is trying to say, and neither does he.

In the previous section I have attempted to explain the origin of the myth that lower-class Negro children are nonverbal. The examples just given may help to account for the corresponding myth that middle-class language is in itself better suited for dealing with abstract, logically complex and hypothetical questions. These examples are intended to have a certain negative force. They are not controlled experiments: on the contrary, this and the preceding section are designed to convince the reader that the controlled experiments that have been offered in evidence are misleading. The only thing that is "controlled" is the superficial form of the stimulus: all children are asked "What do you think of capital punishment?" or "Tell me everything you can about this." But the speaker's interpretation of these requests, and the action he believes is appropriate in response is completely uncontrolled. One can view these test stimuli as requests for information, commands for action, as threats of punishment, or as meaningless sequences of words. They are probably intended as something altogether different: as requests for display; but in any case the experimenter is normally unaware of the problem of interpretation. The methods of educational psychologists like Deutsch, Jensen and Bereiter follow the pattern designed for animal experiments where motivation is controlled by such simple methods as withholding food until a certain weight reduction is reached. With human subjects, it is absurd to believe that an identical "stimulus" is obtained by asking everyone the "same question." Since the crucial intervening variables of interpretation and motivation are uncontrolled, most of the literature on verbal deprivation tells us nothing about the capacities of children. They are only the trappings of science: an approach which substitutes the formal procedures of the scientific method for the activity itself. With our present limited grasp of these problems, the best we can do to understand the verbal capacities of children is to study them within the cultural context in which they were developed.

It is not only the NNE vernacular which should be studied in this way, but also the language of middle-class children. The explicitness and precision which we hope to gain from copying middle-class forms are often the product of the test situation, and limited to it. For example, it was stated in the first part of this paper that working-class children hear more well-formed sentences than middle-class children. This statement may seem extraordinary in the light of the current belief of many linguists that most people do not speak in well-formed sentences, and that their actual speech production or "performance" is ungrammatical. But those who have worked with any body of natural speech know that this is not the case. Our own studies of the "Grammaticality of Every-day Speech" show that the great majority of utterances in all contexts are complete sentences, and most of the rest can be reduced to grammatical form by a small set of "editing rules." (12) The proportions of grammatical sentences vary with class backgrounds and styles. The highest percentage of well-formed sentences are found in casual speech, and working-class speakers use more well-formed sentences than middle-class speakers. The widespread myth that most speech is ungrammatical is no doubt based upon tapes made at learned conferences, where we obtain the maximum number of irreducibly ungrammatical sequences.

It is true that technical and scientific books are written in a style which is markedly "middle-class." But unfortunately, we often fail to achieve the explicitness and precision which we look for in such writing; and the speech of many middle-class people departs maximally from this target. All too often, "standard English" is represented by a style that is simultaneously over-particular and vague. The accumulating flow of words buries rather than strikes the target. It is this verbosity which is most easily taught and most easily learned, so that words take the place of thought, and nothing can be found behind them.

When Bernstein describes his "elaborated code" in general terms, it emerges as a subtle and sophisticated mode of planning utterances, achieving structural variety, taking the other person's knowledge into account, and so on. But when it comes to describing the actual difference between middle-class and working-class speakers, we are presented with a proliferation of "I think," of the passive, of modals and auxiliaries, of the first person pronoun, of uncommon words; these are the bench marks of hemming and hawing, backing and filling, that are used by Charles M., devices which often obscure whatever positive contribution education can make to our use of language. When we have discovered how much middle-class style is a matter of fashion and how much actually helps us express our ideas clearly, we will have done ourselves a great service; we will then be in a position to say what standard grammatical rules must be taught to nonstandard speakers in the early grades.

3. Grammaticality

Let us now examine Bereiter's own data on the verbal behavior of the children he dealt with. The expressions *They mine* and *Me got juice* are cited as examples of a language which lacks the means for expressing logical relations—in this case characterized as "a series of badly connected words." (13) In the case of *They mine,* it is apparent that Bereiter confuses the notions of logic and explicitness. We know that there are many languages of the world which do not have a present copula, and which conjoin subject and predicate complement without a verb. Russian, Hungarian, and Arabic may be foreign; but they are not by that same token illogical. In the case of nonstandard Negro English we are not dealing with even this superficial grammatical difference, but rather with a low-level rule which carries contraction one step farther to delete single consonants representing the verbs *is, have,* or *will.* (14) We have yet to find any children who do not sometimes use the full forms of *is* and *will,* even though they may frequently delete it. Our recent studies with Negro children four to seven years old indicate that they use the full form of the copula *is* more often than preadolescents 10 to 12 years old, or the adolescents 14 to 17 years old. (15)

Furthermore, the deletion of the *is* or *are* in nonstandard Negro English is not the result of erratic or illogical behavior: it follows the same regular rules as standard English contraction. Wherever standard English can contract, Negro children use either the contracted form or (more commonly) the deleted zero form. Thus *They mine* corresponds to standard *They're mine,* not to the full form *They are mine.* On the other hand, no such deletion is possible in positions where standard English cannot contract: just as one cannot say *That's what they're* in standard English, *That's what they* is equally impossible in the vernacular we are considering. The internal constraints upon both of these rules show that we are dealing with a phonological process like contraction, sensitive to such phonetic conditions as whether or not the next word begins with a vowel or a consonant. The appropriate use of the deletion rule, like the contraction rule, requires a deep and intimate knowledge of English grammar and phonology. Such knowledge is not available for conscious inspection by native speakers: the rules we have recently worked out for standard contraction (16) have never appeared in any grammar, and are certainly not a part of the conscious knowledge of any standard English speakers. Nevertheless, the adult or child who uses these rules must have formed at some level of psychological organization clear concepts of "tense marker," "verb phrase," "rule ordering," "sentence embedding," "pronoun," and many other grammatical categories which are essential parts of any logical system.

Bereiter's reaction to the sentence *Me got juice* is even more puzzling. If Bereiter believes that *Me got juice* is not a logical expression, it can only be that he interprets the use of the objective pronoun *me* as representing a difference in logical relationship to the verb: that the child is in fact saying that *the juice got him* rather than *he got the juice!* If on the other hand the child means "I got juice," then this sentence form shows only that he has not learned the formal rules for the use of the subjective form *I* and oblique form *me.* We have in fact encountered many children who do not have these formal rules in order at the ages of four, five, six, or even eight. It is extremely difficult to construct a minimal pair to show that the difference between *he* and *him,* or *she* and *her,* carries cognitive meaning. In almost every case, it is the context which tells us who is the agent and who is acted upon. We must then ask: what differences in cognitive, structural orientation are signalled by the fact that the child has not learned this formal rule? In the tests carried out by Jane Torrey it is evident that the children concerned do understand the difference in meaning between *she* and *her* when another person uses the forms; all that remains is that the children themselves do not use the two forms. Our knowledge of the cognitive correlates of grammatical differences is certainly in its infancy; for this is one of very many questions which we simply cannot answer. At the moment we do not know how to construct any kind of experiment which would lead to an answer; we do not even know what type of cognitive correlate we would be looking for.

Bereiter shows even more profound ignorance of the rules of discourse and of syntax when he rejects *In the tree* as an illogical, or badly-formed answer to *Where is the squirrel?* Such elliptical answers are of course used by everyone; they show the appropriate deletion of subject and main verb, leaving the locative which is questioned by *wh + there*. In reply *In the tree* demonstrates that the listener has been attentive to and apprehended the syntax of the speaker. Whatever formal structure we wish to write for expressions such as *Yes* or *Home* or *In the tree,* it is obvious that they cannot be interpreted without knowing the structure of the question which preceded them, and that they presuppose an understanding of the syntax of the question. Thus if you ask me "Where is the squirrel?" it is necessary for me to understand the process of *wh*-attachment, *wh*-attraction to the front of the sentence, and flip-flop of auxiliary and subject to produce this sentence from an underlying form which would otherwise have produced *The squirrel is there.* If the child had answered *The tree,* or *Squirrel the tree,* or *The in tree,* we would then assume that he did not understand the syntax of the full form, *The squirrel is in the tree.* Given the data that Bereiter presents, we cannot conclude that the child has no grammar, but only that the investigator does not understand the rules of grammar. It does not necessarily do any harm to use the full form *The squirrel is in the tree,* if one wants to make fully explicit the rules of grammar which the child has internalized. Much of logical analysis consists of making explicit just that kind of internalized rule. But it is hard to believe that any good can come from a program which begins with so many misconceptions about the input data. Bereiter and Engelmann believe that in teaching the child to say *The squirrel is in the tree* or *This is a box* and *This is not a box* they are teaching him an entirely new language, whereas in fact they are only teaching him to produce slightly different forms of the language he already has.

4. Logic

For many generations, American school teachers have devoted themselves to correcting a small number of nonstandard English rules to their standard equivalents, under the impression that they were teaching logic. This view has been reinforced and given theoretical justification by the claim that nonstandard Negro English lacks the means for the expression of logical thought.

Let us consider for a moment the possibility that Negro children do not operate with the same logic that middle-class adults display. This would inevitably mean that sentences of a certain grammatical form would have different truth values for the two types of speakers. One of the most obvious places to look for such a difference is in the handling of the negative; and here we encounter one of the nonstandard items which has been stigmatized as illogical by school teachers: the double negative, or as we term it, negative concord. A child who says *He don't know nothing* is often said to be making an illogical statement without knowing it. According to the teacher, the child wants to say *He knows nothing* but puts in an extra negative without realizing it, and so conveys the opposite meaning 'he does not know nothing' which reduces to "he knows something." I need not emphasize that this is an absurd interpretation: if a nonstandard speaker wishes to say that "he does *not* know *nothing,*" he does so by simply placing contrastive stress on both negatives as I have done here (He *don't* know *nothing*) indicating that they are derived from two underlying negatives in the deep structure. But note that the middle-class speaker does exactly the same thing when he wants to signal the existence of two underlying negatives: "He doesn't know *nothing.*" In the standard form *He doesn't know anything,* the indefinite *anything* contains the same superficial reference *nothing* does. In the corresponding positive sentences, the indefinite *something* is used. The dialect difference, like most of the differences between the standard and nonstandard forms, is one of surface form, and has nothing to do with the underlying logic of the sentence.

The Anglo-Saxon authors of the Peterborough Chronicle were surely not illogical when they wrote *For ne waeren nan martyrs swa pined alse he waeron,* literally "For never weren't no martyrs so tortured as these were." The "logical" forms of current standard English are simply the accepted conventions of our present-day formal style.

We can summarize the ways in which the two dialects differ in the following table:

Table 1

	SE	NNE
Positive	He knows something.	He know something.
Negative	He doesn't know anything.	He don't know nothing.
Double negative	He <u>doesn't</u> know <u>nothing</u>.	He <u>don't</u> know <u>nothing</u>.

This array makes it plain that the only difference between the two dialects is in superficial form. When a single negative is found in the deep structure, SE converts *something* to the indefinite *anything,* NNE converts it to *nothing.* When speakers want to signal the presence of two negatives, they do it in the same way. No one would have any difficulty constructing the same table of truth values for both dialects.

English is a rare language in its insistence that the negative particle be incorporated in the first indefinite only. Russian, Spanish, French and Hungarian show the same negative concord as nonstandard English, and they are surely not illogical in this. What is termed "logical" in standard English is of course the conventions which are habitual. The distribution of negative concord in English dialects can be summarized in this way:

1) In all dialects of English, the negative is attracted to a lone indefinite before the verb: *Nobody knows anything,* not *Anybody doesn't know anything.*

2) In some nonstandard white dialects, the negative also combines optionally with all other indefinites: *Nobody knows nothing, He never took none of them.*

3) In other white nonstandard dialects, the negative may also appear in preverbal position in the same clause: *Nobody doesn't know nothing.*

4) In nonstandard Negro English, negative concord is obligatory to all indefinites within the clause, and it may even be added to preverbal position in following clauses: *Nobody didn't know he didn't* meaning "Nobody knew he did."

Thus all dialects of English share a categorical rule which attracts the negative to an indefinite subject, and they merely differ in the extent to which the negative particle is also distributed to other indefinites in preverbal position. It would have been impossible for us to arrive at this analysis if we did not know that Negro speakers are using the same underlying logic as everyone else.

Negative concord is more firmly established in nonstandard Negro English than in other nonstandard dialects. The white nonstandard speaker shows variation in this rule, saying one time *Nobody ever goes there* and the next *Nobody never goes there;* core speakers of the NNE vernacular consistently use the latter form. In the repetition tests which we conducted with adolescent Negro boys, standard forms were regularly repeated back instantly with negative concord. Here, for example, are three trials by two 13-year-old members of the "Thunderbirds."

Model:	Nobody ever sat at any of those desks, anyhow.
Boot-1:	Nobody never sa--No [whitey] never sat at any o' tho' dess, anyhow.
-2:	Nobody never sat at any o' tho' dess, anyhow.
-3:	Nobody [es'] ever sat at no desses, anyhow.
David-1:	Nobody ever sat in-in-in-in- none o'--say it again?
-2:	Nobody never sat in none o' tho' desses anyhow.
-3:	Nobody--aww! Nobody never ex--Dawg!

It can certainly be said that Boot and David fail the test; they have not repeated the sentence back "correctly"—that is, word for word. But have they failed because they could not grasp the meaning of the sentence? The situation is in fact just the opposite: they failed because they perceived only the meaning and not the superficial form. Boot and David are typical of many speakers who do not perceive the surface details of the utterance so much as the underlying semantic structure, which they unhesitatingly translate into the vernacular form. Thus they have an asymmetrical system:

Perception:	Standard	Nonstandard
Production:	Nonstandard	

This tendency to process the semantic components directly can be seen even more dramatically in responses to sentences with embedded questions:

Model: I asked Alvin if he knows how to play basketball.
Boot: I ax Alvin do he know how to play basketball.
Money: I ax Alvin if--do he know how to play basketball.
Model: I asked Alvin whether he knows how to play basketball.
Larry F.-1: I axt Alvin does he know how to play basketball.
      -2: I axt Alvin does he know how to play basketball.

Here the difference between the words used in the model sentence and in the repetition is striking. Again, there is a failure to pass the test. But it is also true that these boys understand the standard sentence, and translate it with extraordinary speed into the NNE form—which is here the regular Southern colloquial form. This form retains the inverted order to signal the underlying meaning of the question, instead of the complementizer *if* or *whether* which standard English uses for this purpose. Thus Boot, Money, and Larry perceive the deep structure of the model sentence:

Figure 1

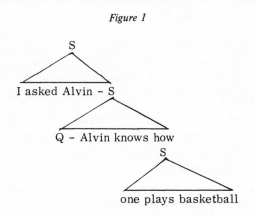

The complementizers *if* or *whether* are not required to express this underlying meaning; they are merely two of the formal options which one dialect selects to signal the embedded question. The colloquial Southern form utilizes a different device—preserving the order of the direct question. To say that this dialect lacks the means for logical expression is to confuse logic with surface detail.

To pass the repetition test, Boot and the others have to learn to listen to surface detail. They do not need a new logic; they need practice in paying attention to the explicit form of an utterance rather than its meaning. Careful attention to surface features is a temporary skill needed for language learning—and neglected thereafter by competent speakers. Nothing more than this is involved in the language training in the Bereiter and Engelmann program, or in most methods of "teaching English." There is of course nothing wrong with learning to be explicit—as we have seen, that is one of the main advantages of standard English at its best—but it is important that we recognize what is actually taking place, and what teachers are in fact trying to do.

I doubt if we can teach people to be logical, though we can teach them to recognize the logic that they use. Piaget has shown us that in middle-class children logic develops much more slowly than grammar, and that we cannot expect four-year-olds to have mastered the conservation of quantity, let alone syllogistic reasoning. Whatever problems working-class children may have in handling logical operations are not to be blamed on the structure of their language. There is nothing in the vernacular which will interfere with the development of logical thought, for the logic of standard English cannot be distinguished from the logic of any other dialect of English by any test that we can find.

5. What's wrong with being wrong?

If there is a failure of logic involved here, it is surely in the approach of the verbal deprivation theorists, rather than in the mental abilities of the children concerned. We can isolate six distinct steps in the reasoning which has led to programs such as those of Deutsch, Bereiter and Engelmann:

1) The lower-class child's verbal response to a formal and threatening situation is used to demonstrate his lack of verbal capacity, or verbal deficit.

2) This verbal deficit is declared to be a major cause of the lower-class child's poor performance in school.

3) Since middle-class children do better in school, middle-class speech habits are seen to be necessary for learning.

4) Class and ethnic differences in grammatical form are equated with differences in the capacity for logical analysis.

5) Teaching the child to mimic certain formal speech patterns used by middle-class teachers is seen as teaching him to think logically.

6) Children who learn these formal speech patterns are then said to be thinking logically and it is predicted that they will do much better in reading and arithmetic in the years to follow.

In sections 1–4 of this paper, I have tried to show that these propositions are wrong, concentrating on 1), 4), and 5). Proposition 3) is the primary logical fallacy which illicitly identifies a form of speech as the *cause* of middle-class achievement in school. Proposition 6) is the one which is most easily shown to be wrong in fact, as we will note below.

However, it is not too naive to ask, "What is wrong with being wrong?" There is no competing educational theory which is being dismantled by this program; and there does not seem to be any great harm in having children repeat *This is not a box* for twenty minutes a day. We have already conceded that NNE children need help in analyzing language into its surface components, and in being more explicit. But there are serious and damaging consequences of the verbal deprivation theory which may be considered under two headings: 1) the theoretical bias, and 2) the consequences of failure.

1) It is widely recognized that the teacher's attitude towards the child is an important factor in his success or failure. The work of Robert Rosenthal on "self-fulfilling prophecies" shows that the progress of children in the early grades can be dramatically affected by a single random labelling of certain children as "intellectual bloomers." (17) When the everyday language of Negro children is stigmatized as "not a language at all" and "not possessing the means for logical thought," the effect of such a labelling is repeated many times during each day of the school year. Every time that a child uses a form of NNE without the copula or with negative concord, he will be labelling himself for the teacher's benefit as "illogical," as a "nonconceptual thinker." Bereiter and Engelmann, Deutsch and Jensen are giving teachers a ready-made, theoretical basis for the prejudice they already feel against the lower-class Negro child and his language. When they hear him say *I don't want none* or *They mine,* they will be hearing through the bias provided by the verbal deprivation theory: not an English dialect different from theirs, but the primitive mentality of the savage mind.

But what if the teacher succeeds in training the child to use the new language consistently? The verbal deprivation theory holds that this will lead to a whole chain of successes in school, and that the child will be drawn away from the vernacular culture into the middle-class world. Undoubtedly this will happen with a few isolated individuals, just as it happens in every school system today, for a few children. But we are concerned not with the few but the many, and for the majority of Negro children the distance between them and the school is bound to widen under this approach.

Proponents of the deficit theory have a strange view of social organization outside of the classroom: they see the attraction of the peer group as a "substitute" for success and gratification normally provided by the school. For example, Whiteman and Deutsch introduce their account of the deprivation hypothesis with an eye-witness account of a child who accidentally dropped his school notebook into a puddle of water and walked away without picking it up.

> A policeman who had been standing nearby walked over to the puddle and stared at the notebook with some degree of disbelief. (18)

The child's alienation from school is explained as the result of his coming to school without the "verbal, conceptual, attentional and learning skills requisite to school success." The authors see the child as "suffering from feelings of inferiority because he is failing; . . . he withdraws or becomes hostile, finding gratification elsewhere, such as in his peer group."

To view the peer group as a mere substitute for school shows an extraordinary lack of knowledge of adolescent culture. In our studies in South Central Harlem we have seen the reverse situation: the children who are rejected by the peer group are quite likely to succeed in school. In middle-class suburban areas, many children do fail in school because of their personal deficiencies; in ghetto areas, it is the healthy, vigorous popular child with normal intelligence who cannot read and fails all along the line. It is not necessary to document here the influence of the peer group upon the behavior of youth in our society; but we may note that somewhere between the time that children first learn to talk and puberty, their language is restructured to fit the rules used by their peer group. From a linguistic viewpoint, the peer group is certainly a more powerful influence than the family. Less directly, the pressures of peer group activity are also felt within the school. Many children, particularly those who are not doing well in school, show a sudden sharp down turn in the fourth and fifth grades, and children in the ghetto schools are no exception. It is at the same age, at nine or ten years old, that the influence of the vernacular peer group becomes predominant. Instead of dealing with isolated individuals, the school is then dealing with children who are integrated into groups of their own, with rewards and value systems which oppose those of the school. Those who know the sociolinguistic situation cannot doubt that reaction against the Bereiter-Engelmann approach in later years will be even more violent on the part of the students involved, and that the rejection of the school system will be even more categorical.

The essential fallacy of the verbal deprivation theory lies in tracing the educational failure of the child to his personal deficiencies. At present, these deficiencies are said to be caused by his home environment. It is traditional to explain a child's failure in school by his inadequacy; but when failure reaches such massive proportions, it seems to us necessary to look at the social and cultural obstacles to learning, and the inability of the school to adjust to the social situation. Operation Head Start is designed to repair the child, rather than the school; to the extent that it is based upon this inverted logic, it is bound to fail.

2) The second area in which the verbal deprivation theory is doing serious harm to our educational system is in the consequences of this failure, and the reaction to it. If Operation Head Start fails, the interpretations which we receive will be from the same educational psychologists who designed this program. The fault will be found not in the data, the theory, nor in the methods used, but rather in the children who have failed to respond to the opportunities offered to them. When Negro children fail to show the significant advance which the deprivation theory predicts, it will be further proof of the profound gulf which separates their mental processes from those of civilized, middle-class mankind.

A sense of the "failure" of Operation Head Start is already in the air. Some prominent figures in the program are reacting to this situation by saying that intervention did not take place early enough. Bettye M. Caldwell notes that:

> . . . the research literature of the last decade dealing with social-class differences has made abundantly clear that all parents are not qualified to provide even the basic essentials of physical and psychological care to their children. (19)

The deficit theory now begins to focus on the "long-standing patterns of parental deficit" which fill the literature. "There is, perhaps unfortunately," writes Caldwell, "no literacy test for motherhood." Failing such eugenic measures, she has proposed "educationally oriented day care for culturally deprived children between six months and three years of age." The children are returned home each evening to "maintain primary emotional relationships with their own families," but during the day they are removed to "hopefully prevent the deceleration in rate of development which seems to occur in many deprived children around the age of two to three years." (20)

There are others who feel that even the best of the intervention programs, such as those of Bereiter and Engelmann, will not help the Negro child no matter when they are applied—that we are faced once again with the "inevitable hypothesis" of the genetic inferiority of the Negro people. Many readers of this paper are undoubtedly familiar with the paper of Arthur Jensen in the *Harvard Educational Review* (21) which received early and widespread publicity. Jensen begins with the following quotation from the United States Commission on Civil Rights as evidence of the failure of compensatory education.

> The fact remains, however, that none of the programs appear to have raised significantly the achievement of participating pupils, as a group, within the period evaluated by the Commission.

Jensen believes that the verbal deprivation theorists with whom he had been associated—Deutsch, Whiteman, Katz, Bereiter—have been given every opportunity to prove their case—and have failed. This opinion is part of the argument which leads him to the overall conclusion that "the preponderance of the evidence is . . . less consistent with a strictly environmental hypothesis than with the genetic hypothesis," that racism, or the belief in the genetic inferiority of Negroes, is a correct view in the light of the present evidence.

Jensen argues that the middle-class white population is differentiated from the working-class white and Negro population in the ability for "cognitive or conceptual learning," which Jensen calls Level II intelligence as against mere "associative learning" or Level I intelligence:

> certain neural structures must also be available for Level II abilities to develop, and these are conceived of as being different from the neural structures underlying Level I. The genetic factors involved in each of these types of ability are presumed to have become differentially distributed in the population as a function of social class, since Level II has been most important for scholastic performance under the traditional methods of instruction.

Thus Jensen found that one group of middle-class children were helped by their concept-forming ability to recall twenty familiar objects that could be classified into four categories: animals, furniture, clothing, or foods. Lower-class Negro children did just as well as middle-class children with a miscellaneous set, but showed no improvement with objects that could be so categorized.

The research of the educational psychologists cited here is presented in formal and objective style, and is widely received as impartial scientific evidence. Jensen's paper has already been reported by Joseph Alsop and William F. Buckley Jr. as "massive, apparently authoritative . . ." (N.Y. Post 3/20/69) It is not my intention to examine these materials in detail;

but it is important to realize that we are dealing with special pleading by those who have a strong personal commitment. Jensen is concerned with class differences in cognitive style and verbal learning. His earlier papers incorporated the cultural deprivation theory which he now rejects as a basic explanation. He classifies the Negro children who fail in school as "slow-learners" and "mentally-retarded," and urged that we find out how much their retardation is due to environmental factors and how much is due to "more basic biological factors." (22) His conviction that the problem must be located in the child leads him to accept and reprint some truly extraordinary data. To support the genetic hypothesis he cites the following table of Heber for the racial distribution of mental retardation.

Table 2
Estimated Prevalence of Children with IQ's Below 75.

SES	White	Negro
1	0.5	3.1
2	0.8	14.5
3	2.1	22.8
4	3.1	37.8
5	7.8	42.9

This report, that almost half of lower-class Negro children are mentally retarded, could be accepted only by someone who has no knowledge of the children or the community. If he had wished to, Jensen could easily have checked this against the records of any school in any urban ghetto area. Taking IQ tests at their face value, there is no correspondence between these figures and the communities we know. For example, among 75 boys we worked with in Central Harlem who would fall into Heber's SES 4 or 5, there were only three with IQs below 75: one spoke very little English, one could barely see, and the third was emotionally disturbed. When the second was retested, he scored 91, and the third retested at 87. (23) There are of course hundreds of realistic reports available to Jensen: he simply selected one which would strengthen his case for the genetic inferiority of Negro children, and deliberately deleted the information that this was a study of an area selected in advance because of its high incidence of mental retardation.

In so doing, Jensen was following a standing tradition among the psychologists who developed the deficit hypothesis. The core of Martin Deutsch's environmental explanation of low school performance is the Deprivation Index—a numerical scale based on six dichotomized variables. One variable is "The educational aspirational level of the parent for the child." Most people would agree that a parent who did not care if a child finished high school would be a disadvantageous factor in the child's educational career. In dichotomizing this variable Deutsch was faced with the embarrassing fact that the educational aspiration of Negro parents is in fact very high—higher than for the white population, as he shows in other papers. In order to make the Deprivation Index work, he therefore set the cutting point for the deprived group as "college or less." (24) Thus if a Negro child's father says that he wants his son to go all the way through college, the child will fall into the "deprived" class on this variable. In order to receive the two points given to the "less deprived" on the index, it would be necessary for the child's parent to insist on graduate school or medical school! This decision is never discussed by the author: it simply stands as a *fait accompli* in the tables. This is the type of data manipulation carried on by those who are strongly committed to a particular hypothesis; the selection and presentation of the data are heavily determined by the desire of the writers to make things come out right.

No one can doubt that the inadequacy of Operation Head Start and of the verbal deprivation hypothesis has now become a crucial issue in our society. The controversy which is beginning over Jensen's article will undoubtedly take as given that programs such as Bereiter and Engelmann's have tested and measured the verbal capacity of the ghetto child. The cultural sociolinguistic obstacles to this intervention program are not considered; and the argument proceeds upon the data provided by the large, friendly interviewers that we have seen at work in the extracts given above.

6. The Linguistic View

Linguists are in an excellent position to demonstrate the fallacies of the verbal deprivation theory. All linguists agree that nonstandard dialects are highly structured systems; they do not see these dialects as accumulations of errors caused by the failure of their speakers to master standard English. When linguists hear Negro children saying *He crazy* or *Her my friend* they do not hear a "primitive language." Nor do they believe that the speech of working-class people is merely a form of emotional expression, incapable of expressing logical thought.

All linguists who work with nonstandard Negro English recognize that it is a separate system, closely related to standard English, but set apart from the surrounding white dialects by a number of persistent and systematic differences. Differences in analysis by various linguists in recent years are the inevitable products of differing theoretical approaches and perspectives as we explore these dialect patterns by different routes—differences which are rapidly diminishing as we exchange our findings. For example, Stewart differs with me on how deeply the invariant *be* of *She be always messin' around* is integrated into the semantics of the copula system with *am, are,* etc. The position and meaning of *have . . . -ed* in NNE is very unclear, and there are a variety of positions on this point. But the grammatical features involved are not the fundamental predicators of the logical system. They are optional ways of contrasting, foregrounding, emphasizing, or deleting elements of the underlying sentence. There are a few semantic features of NNE grammar which may be unique to this system. But the semantic features we are talking about here are items such as "habitual," "general," "intensive." These linguistic markers are essentially *points of view*—different ways of looking at the same events, and they do not determine the truth values of propositions upon which all speakers of English agree.

The great majority of the differences between NNE and SE do not even represent such subtle semantic features as these, but rather extensions and restrictions of certain formal rules, and different choices of redundant elements. For example, SE uses two signals to express the progressive: *be* and *-ing,* while NNE often drops the former. SE signals the third person in the present by the subject noun phrase and by a third singular *-s;* NNE uses redundant negative elements in negative concord, uses possessives like *mines,* uses *or either* where SE uses a simple *or,* and so on.

When linguists say that NNE is a "system," we mean that it differs from other dialects in regular and rule-governed ways, so that it has equivalent ways of expressing the same logical content. When we say that it is a "separate" sub-system, we mean that there are compensating sets of rules which combine in different ways to preserve the distinctions found in other dialects. Thus as noted above NNE does not use the *if* or *whether* complementizer in embedded questions, but the meaning is preserved by the formal device of reversing the order of subject and auxiliary.

Linguists therefore speak with a single voice in condemning Bereiter's view that the vernacular can be disregarded. I have exchanged views on this matter with all of the participants in the Round Table [Georgetown University Round Table on Language and Linguistics], and their response shows complete agreement in rejecting the verbal deprivation theory and its misapprehension of the nature of language. The other papers in this series will testify to the strength of the linguistic view in this area. It was William Steward who first pointed out that Negro English should be studied as a coherent system; and in this all of us follow his lead. Dialectologists like Raven McDavid, Albert Marckwardt, and Roger Shuy have been working for years against the notion that vernacular dialects are inferior and illogical means of communication; and their views are well represented here. As the overwhelming testimony of this conference shows, linguists agree that teachers must know as much as possible about nonstandard Negro English as a communicative system.

The exact nature and relative importance of the structural differences between NNE and SE are not in question here. It is agreed that the teacher must approach the teaching of the standard through a knowledge of the child's own system. The methods used in "teaching English as a foreign language" are invoked, not to declare that NNE is a foreign language, but to underline the importance of studying the native dialect as a coherent system for communication. This is, in fact, the method that should be applied in any English class.

Linguists are also in an excellent position to assess Jensen's claim that the middle-class white population is superior to the working-class and Negro populations in the distribution of "Level II" or "conceptual" intelligence. The notion that large numbers of children have no capacity for conceptual thinking would inevitably mean that they speak a primitive language, for even the simplest linguistic rules we discussed above involve conceptual operations more complex than those used in the experiment cited by Jensen. Let us consider what is involved in the use of the general English rule that incorporates the negative with the first indefinite. To learn and use this rule, one must first identify the class of indefinites involved: *any, one, ever,* which are formally quite diverse. How is this done? These indefinites share a number of common properties which can be expressed as the concepts "indefinite," "hypothetical," and "nonpartitive." One might argue that these indefinites are learned as a simple list by "association" learning. But this is only one of the many syntactic rules involving indefinites—rules known to every speaker of English, which could not be learned except by an understanding of their common, abstract properties. For example, everyone "knows" unconsciously that *anyone* cannot be used with preterite verbs or progressives. One does not say, *Anyone went to the party* or *Anyone is going to the party.* The rule which operates here is sensitive to the property (+hypothetical) of the indefinites. Whenever the proposition is not inconsistent with this feature, *anyone* can be used. Everyone "knows" therefore that one can say *Anyone who was anyone went to the party,* or *If anyone went to the party . . .* or *Before anyone went to the party . . .* There is another property of *anyone* which is grasped unconsciously by all native speakers of English: it is (+distributive). Thus if we need one more man for a game of bridge or basketball, and there is a crowd outside, we ask, *Do any of you want to play?* not *Do some of you want to play?* In both cases, we are considering a plurality, but with *any* we consider them one at a time, or distributively.

What are we then to make of Jensen's contention that Level I thinkers cannot make use of the concept "animal" to group together a miscellaneous set of toy animals? It is one thing to say that someone is not in the habit of using a certain skill. But to say that his failure to use it is genetically determined implies dramatic consequences for other forms of behavior, which are not found in experience; the knowledge of what people must do in order to learn language makes Jensen's theories seem more and more distant from the realities of human behavior. Like Bereiter and Engelmann, Jensen is handicapped by his ignorance of the most basic facts about human language and the people who speak it.

There is no reason to believe that any nonstandard vernacular is in itself an obstacle to learning. The chief problem is ignorance of language on the part of all concerned. Our job as linguists is to remedy this ignorance: Bereiter and Engelmann want to reinforce it and justify it. Teachers are now being told to ignore the language of Negro children as unworthy of attention and useless for learning. They are being taught to hear every natural utterance of the child as evidence of his mental inferiority. As linguists we are unanimous in condemning this view as bad observation, bad theory, and bad practice.

That educational psychology should be strongly influenced by a theory so false to the facts of language is unfortunate; but that children should be the victims of this ignorance is intolerable. It may seem that the fallacies of the verbal deprivation theory are so obvious that they are hardly worth exposing; I have tried to show that it is an important job for us to undertake. If linguists can contribute some of their available knowledge and energy towards this end, we will have done a great deal to justify the support that society has given to basic research in our field.

References

1. Carl Bereiter and Siegfried Engelmann, *Teaching Disadvantaged Children in Preschool* (Englewood Cliffs, N.J.: Prentice-Hall, 1966).
2. Arthur Jensen, "How Much Can We Boost IQ and Scholastic Achievement?" *Harvard Educational Review,* 39, No. 1 (1969).
3. See William Labov and Clarence Robins, "A Note on the Relation of Reading Failure to Peer-Group Status in Urban Ghettos," *Teachers College Record,* 70, No. 5, (1969) [in Chapter Six of this book].
4. Martin Deutsch and Associates, *The Disadvantaged Child* (New York: Basic Books, 1967).

   Martin Deutsch, Irwin Katz, and Arthur R. Jensen, eds., *Social Class, Race, and Psychological Development* (New York: Holt, 1968).

5. Arthur Jensen, "Social Class and Verbal Learning," in *Social Class, Race, and Psychological Development,* p. 118.
6. Carl Bereiter et al., "An Academically Oriented Pre-School for Culturally Deprived Children, "in *Pre-School Education Today,* ed. Fred M. Hechinger (New York: Doubleday, 1966), pp. 105–37.
   Bereiter and Engelmann, *Teaching Disadvantaged Children in Preschool.*
7. Bereiter et al., "Academically Oriented Pre-School," p. 113.
8. The research cited here was carried out in South Central Harlem and other ghetto areas in 1965–1968 to describe structural and functional differences between nonstandard Negro English and standard English of the classroom. It was supported by the Office of Education as Cooperative Research Projects 3091 and 3288. Detailed reports are given in Labov, Cohen, and Robins (1965), Labov (1965), and Labov, Cohen, Robins, and Lewis (1968).
9. Jensen, "Social Class and Verbal Learning," p. 119.
10. The term *code* is central in Bernstein's description of the differences between working-class and middle-class styles of speech. The restrictions and elaborations of speech observed are labelled as "codes" to indicate the principles governing selection from the range of possible English sentences. No rules or detailed description of the operation of such codes are provided as yet, so that this central concept remains to be specified.
11. William Labov, Paul Cohen, Clarence Robins, and John Lewis, "A Study of the Non-Standard English of Negro and Puerto Rican Speakers in New York City," final report, Cooperative Research Project No. 3288 (Washington, D.C.: Office of Education, 1968), II, pp. 38, 71–3, 291–2.
12. The editing rules are presented in Labov, "On the Grammaticality of Every-day Speech," paper given at the annual meeting of the Linguistic Society of America, New York City (December 1966).
13. Bereiter et al., "Academically Oriented Pre-School," 113 ff.
14. Labov, Cohen, Robins, and Lewis. "A Study of the Non-Standard English of Negro and Puerto Rican Speakers in New York City," sect. 3.4.
15. From work on the grammars and comprehension of Negro children four to eight years old being carried out by Professor Jane Torrey of Connecticut College in extension of the research cited above in Labov, Cohen, Robins, and Lewis (1968).
16. Labov, Cohen, Robins, and Lewis, "Study of Non-Standard English," sect. 3.4.
17. Robert Rosenthal and Lenore Jacobson, "Self-Fulfilling Prophecies in the Classroom: Teachers' Expectations as Unintended Determinants of Pupils' Intellectual Competence," in *Social Class, Race, and Psychological Development.*
18. Martin Whiteman and Martin Deutsch, "Social Disadvantage as Related to Intellective and Language Development," in *Social Class, Race, and Psychological Development,* pp. 86–7.
19. Bettye M. Caldwell, "What is the Optimal Learning Environment for the Young Child?" *American Journal of Orthopsychiatry,* XXXVII, No. 1 (1967), p. 16.
20. Caldwell, "Optimal Learning Environment," p. 17.
21. Jensen, "How Much Can We Boost IQ?" p. 138.
22. Jensen, "Social Class and Verbal Learning," p. 167.
23. Heber's studies of 88 Negro mothers in Milwaukee are cited frequently throughout Jensen (1969). The estimates in this table are not given in relation to a particular Milwaukee sample, but for the general population. Heber's study was specifically designed to cover an area of Milwaukee which was known to contain a large concentration of retarded children, Negro and white, and he has stated that his findings were "grossly misinterpreted" by Jensen. (*Milwaukee Sentinel,* June 11, 1969).
24. Whiteman and Deutsch, "Social Disadvantage as Related to Intellective and Language Development," p. 100.

Chapter Two
Black Society and Black Talk

What is the population like which contains speakers of Black English? Do Black English speakers use their variety of American English in different ways from the "mainstream" culture of middle-class America? The preliminary answers to these questions indicate that Black English speakers often participate in a culture which differs in important ways from middle-class "mainstream" society. And part of their black culture includes using Black English in ways different from middle class uses of so-called standard English. Thus the selections in this chapter assume a multi-cultural view of the United States. Black culture is one of the many cultures in America and is seen not as an inferior "perversion" of middle-class society. Hannerz' viewpoint is of particular significance in that he brings an anthropological approach to the study of ghetto society, one which reflects an awareness of cultural differences rarely found in other disciplines. Note the objectivity of his description.

The need for educators to know about the culture of the Black English speaker is crucial to the realization of Black English speaking children's educational chances. One has only to read the dropout figures from large city school systems such as New York City, Chicago, or Philadelphia to sense the urgency of this need.

Black talk (culture specific verbal behavior) and black nonverbal behavior accompanying that talk are also often judged ethnocentrically against middle-class cultural standards. Yet this system of "speaking behavior" which Abrahams describes in this chapter is an integral part of black urban ghetto society. And a black who performs well in using Black English is given a great deal of status. Yet certain language forms used especially by boys in ghetto culture often strike teachers negatively as they are unaware of the cultural motivation behind their use. So the teacher may be punitive about black talk which is highly functional in the child's culture.

The four selections in this chapter were chosen specifically to provide the reader with insights into black life of which black talk is an integral part. The two selections of Ulf Hannerz and St. Claire Drake describe the population among whom Black English speakers are usually found. Black society sketched by Hannerz and Drake is, for the majority of blacks in America, a society of poverty and racial isolation. Both authors describe the powerlessness of ghetto blacks in the face of "mainstream" society, and the "victimization" they experience in America. In the urban North, where Black English is most studied, ghettoization is an outstanding characteristic of black life. All these forces contribute to shaping black society and the black ghetto child's behavior. It is crucial for educators to know about the child's culture because it provides important cues as to why he often behaves in ways different from middle-class children. His society makes different demands on him than does middle-class society on the more affluent child, and his behavior is conditioned by those demands.

His verbal behavior, or black talk, with its concomitant nonverbal behavior may also be different from a teacher's expectations about how children should use language. The article by Roger Abrahams gives insight into how black communication patterns, verbal and nonverbal, function in the ghetto as an expressive system of great power and adaptability. It is important for educators to understand those patterns if they are to understand the black ghetto child they are responsible for educating. William Labov's selection is quite specific as to the negative consequences of not understanding a black child's verbal behavior and of judging it ethnocentrically. It affords a great deal of insight into the necessity for knowing the black child and his culture.

The Setting
Ulf Hannerz

In this selection from *Soulside, Inquiries into Ghetto Culture and Community*, Ulf Hannerz graphically describes some of the most salient characteristics of black ghetto existence. One of the most important is that the Winston Street neighborhood is a more or less self-contained community in its own right. It has a social organization in which the street's dwellers participate in different ways and to greater or lesser degree. It is definitely not a mere collection of poor blacks who happen to be physically present in the same area. The residents generally have in common being black, holding unskilled or semi-skilled jobs if employed at all, making relatively low incomes, and having a limited formal education. Their children's educational chances are characterized as not much better because of the *de facto* segregation of the inner city schools. However, there are blacks living in Winston Street who do have more money, could afford to move to better housing, but may stay for reasons of racial solidarity. According to Hannerz, this racial dimension is extremely important in the lives of Winston Street dwellers. Winston Street is also very definitely a part of the larger Washington, D.C. ghetto; Hannerz places it into the large setting. Finally, Hannerz describes the political powerlessness of the urban black which basically keeps him in a slum such as Winston Street whether he wants to be there or not.

Winston Street

At one end of Winston Street is a yellow wall with a number of graffiti—a list of boys, *Jimmy, Norman, Eddie, Marvin, Robert,* and a list of girls next to it, *Barbie, Debbie, Sarah, Peaches, Janice.* There is a secretive *Leroy loves somebody,* and a couple of four-letter words scrawled by an uncertain hand. A little to the side, the message is that *Your mother drink wild irish rose,* with the reply *So do your cat.* Wild Irish rose is the drink of the winos, "wineheads" or "juiceheads" in ghetto parlance.

Winston Street, Washington, D.C., is a narrow, one-way ghetto street, one block long and lined by brick row houses, two or three stories high and

From *Soulside, Inquiries into Ghetto Culture and Community* by Ulf Hannerz. (New York: Columbia University Press, 1969). © 1969 by Columbia University Press. Reprinted by permission of the publisher.

in varying states of repair. In the windows of some of them are flower pots, bright curtains, or even venetian blinds. Others have broken blinds, dirty plastic sheets, or nothing at all. Sometimes a house is condemned as unfit to live in, and its doors and windows are covered with boards. It is largely a residential street, and since it is not really a thoroughfare, its pedestrian and auto traffic is largely confined to the street's own residents and their visitors. At the corners of Winston Street and the surrounding streets are small business establishments: groceries, liquor stores, carry-out food shops, variety stores, laundromats, shoeshine shops, barber shops, beauty salons: all very modest in appearance. These are the establishments which cater to the day-to-day needs, and supply the few luxuries, of ghetto living. The consumption of liquor is considerable. The carry-outs find most of their customers among the many single men who cannot prepare food in their rented rooms, as well as among the children and adolescents who spend much of whatever money they can get on extra food and goodies. Variety stores sell candy, school equipment, cheap toys, and a variety of other inexpensive odds and ends. The carry-outs, the barber shops, and the shoe-shine shops serve not only their manifest function but are also the hangouts, the centers of sociability, of teenagers and adult men. To serve as locales of leisure, they add some more items to their furnishings: newspapers, vending machines for cigarettes and soft drinks, a pinball machine, a juke box, a public telephone. No one establishment would have them all, some would have none of this, but many have some of it. So this becomes the place of small talk, perhaps sweet talk with the girl behind the carry-out counter.

Much of this leisurely interaction takes place on the street itself, however, where people stand at the corner or sit on the high staircases in front of houses. During the cold months there are few people out, although there are usually some men at the corners. But in March and April when the early spring sun shines through from the south end of Winston Street, there will already be people sitting on the front steps and children playing in the street, and through the hot and humid summer months the street scene is a lively one until late at night. Many men and some women stand or sit around talking, children throw balls, hula-hoop, ride bikes, push each other in carts, or skip rope. Sometimes the fire hydrant at the end of the street is switched on, and the children shower in the water spray and bathe in the gutter. People go back and forth to the laundromat or to Mr. Rubin's grocery store at the corner, doing the shopping for the day or just picking up a soda or an onion. A young man in sunglasses comes up the street carrying a transistor radio and listening to the soul music of station WOL. Two teenage girls, walking elbow to elbow, exchange news about boys.

"And then I told him, 'Child, I couldn't care less if you come or not'!" The old man who goes from door to door on his mission for the Jehovah's Witnesses walks by, eyes fixed on the ground and with a brown briefcase in his hand. Since the people on the staircases know most of the passersby, they greet them and sometimes stop them for a chat. Some, of course, avoid greeting each other, for there is animosity between them. And there are also the people who have not lived very long on the block and who are thus not very well known. On the other hand, some of the long-time watchers of the Winston Street scene actually reside somewhere else, on some neighboring street, just coming down regularly to the street to spend their free time there. And of course, in the same way some of the people of Winston Street have their regular hangouts on other streets.

The street has its regular events. In the evening, the word is spread about what is the winning number in the numbers game, one of the ghetto's illegal but nonetheless central institutions. Now and than a fortunate player may collect some money from a nearby agent, but most of the time there is no luck. "758? I was two off again. I had 742." During the warmer months of the year, the ice cream vendor's car also comes around in the evening, drawing the children's attention with its jingling bell.

The adult streetcorner men want other refreshments. Just talking, playing a game of cards, or shooting dice, they usually get around to pooling their money for something to drink, and one of them goes to the liquor store—or to a bootlegger, if it is Sunday, or too late on a weekday evening—to get some gin, of the kind which is $1.10 a half-pint at the cheapest store, or wine, of the kind that is 35 cents a half-pint (a higher price from the bootlegger). When he comes back, they try to share their drink somewhere out of the public view, as it is illegal to drink in public places. They go into a house or into the back alley, where they may not be seen, although of course it is no more lawful to drink there. The alley has a few trees, a rose bush, overflowing garbage cans, and lots of trash on the ground, including empty and broken bottles. Here and there is a clothesline. Some children play there, dogs guard the back yards, and there are heavy-weight rats running around. Some of the men also go there to "take a leak" if there is no toilet within reach.

There are slums which are more like villages and others which are more like jungles. At times one would look down Winston Street, see only the neighborliness and tranquility, and place this neighborhood close to the village end of the spectrum. But the people who live there know that it also has some attributes of the urban jungle. Some people and places mean trouble, and there is danger in the dark and the unknown. There is the mentally disturbed woman who shouts at the men loafing below her window: "Get away from down there or I'll pour lye over you all." There is the young man who is shunned by the girls and the younger women because of his reputation:

> That boy Chuck is crazy about sex. He goes to a bar and picks up a girl and brings her home and then he locks her up and screws her, and when he has to go out to work he locks her up and won't leave food or cigarettes or anything for her, and then he comes home and goes right on screwing her again. And that nice old mother of his don't say a word, I guess she don't dare, so she just acts as if she knows nothing about it. I've seen girls come out of there, and he keeps them in there for weeks locked up, and they look pretty near dead when they get out. Everybody is afraid of him and the girls around here won't go near him.

There is also Winston Street's own major trouble spot, the corner where the rougher streetcorner men hang out. Fights are rather common there, and the men occasionally show up with fresh knife wounds. True, most of the fights are within the group, and most of the people who have lived in the neighborhood for some time know the men well and are reasonably friendly with them; even so they warn newcomers and visitors about this corner. Yet, it is not so bad there, Winston Street people feel, as on the neighboring street where tough teenage boys hang out and are a menace to everybody who passes by. And the nearby playground is also worse. Some young men go there only to play basketball and table tennis, of course, but there is also a rougher clique which is held responsible for the fact that some people who have passed by have been "yoked"—robbed. Thus the playground is a place to stay away from, particularly after dark, according to neighborhood concensus. And if some young man whom one should happen to know begins to be seen with this clique, one points out the dangers of such company. As one young man was given a jail sentence for his participation in a holdup, an older acquaintance of his commented:

> It had to happen sooner or later, you know. He used to work as some kind of an instructor for the kids up there on the playground, and then when he lost that job he should have stayed away from there from then on, but no, he kept on hanging out there with those no-good fellows, gorillas, that's what they are, all of them. So he got mixed up in this holdup in this liquor store, and they ain't going to let him out for a while. I guess he thinks about what we all told him now.

Potential trouble spots such as those just described can, of course, be reasonably well avoided. But sometimes it is quite difficult. The people who could cause trouble may have their recurrent gatherings on the front stair-case of a house which for some reason is well placed for the purpose while they are not necessarily on terms of personal friendship with the occupants of the house—or at least not with all the occupants. Sometimes the friends of one household occupy the whole front stairs leading to several apartments, thus making entry difficult. At times their conversation gets loud and boisterous, disturbing the people inside the house, and it may erupt into a fight. The empty bottles, paper bags, cigarette packets and other things which assemble during the gatherings are often left behind littering the sidewalk, the gutter, or the little patch of grass—or bare earth—which is in front of some buildings. Some residents who want to avoid trouble do not give any expression of their resentment to the people on the staircase, only occasionally voicing it in private to others—"They should have more sense." If they are on better terms with the loiterers, and in particular if the latter are not "gorillas" but more peaceful streetcorner men, they may occasionally reprimand them for the intrusion into other people's rights, or make a gesture of mild annoyance now and then.

Thus the people of the ghetto maintain a working knowledge of the potential for trouble in their environment. This knowledge undergoes constant revision, of course; and the concern with danger may also fluctuate, although it seems generally to be rather strong. At Winston Street people seem to be a little extra worried during the weeks before Christmas, when it is widely held that robberies and holdups increase in number—"People are desperate for money then, you know, to have something extra." (Besides, the victims may also carry more money, and it gets dark rather early.) One man who had been robbed of his pay envelope a few days before the holiday and woke up to find himself in a police car on the way to the hospital said the following:

> I'm just gonna go over and get myself some wine and something to eat, you know, so I got something in the frigidaire for the next few days, 'cause I'm not going to go out if I don't have to the next few days, and I won't let my old lady go out either.

Some periods generally defined as troubled times are of a more idiosyncratic nature. For a while during early 1967, people in the Winston Street neighborhood felt that the general mood was "kind of tense." A number of factors seemed to contribute. Some long-standing conflicts between families who had been in the neighborhood for many years reached a stage where one observer said, "Bricks could start flying any time now." The reason for the intensification never became particularly clear; some quarrels apparently made the tension more acute. Second, there were some unexpected and undesired pregnancies among teenage girls, and as one neighbor put it, "Their fathers may never have been very good fathers, but that only

makes them more upset about this thing, so they need a scape-goat."
Furthermore, a group of tough teenage boys from another part of the
Washington ghetto started hanging out in the neighborhood and were
responsible for two assaults within a few days. A couple of adult men with
a reputation for violence also came back after a period of absence, and this
was seen as an ominous sign. Another factor, not directly involving interpersonal violence in the neighborhood but yet contributing to the general
gloom, was the state of the national politics of black-white relations. In the
preceding summer black power had made its debut, and there was much
talk of a "white backlash." The Vietnam war overshadowed the war on
poverty, and cutbacks in funds for the latter were predicted. A more conservative congress was elected. These facts were described and commented
on extensively in the newspapers, and there was also frequent mention of
them on the radio. Ghetto dwellers read, heard, and commented to each
other about this, and the expressed view was that it was going badly for
black people. During this period which lasted about a month and then
gradually expired, some of the people who generally contribute most to the
village atmosphere of Winston Street life—by standing about, going around
visiting, and being generally present in public places—felt that it was wiser
to spend more time in the haven of their homes.

It can certainly be helpful for the people of the ghetto to map the trouble
potential of their environment in these ways. When it comes to going about
their daily life, however, they must necessarily compromise between safety
and freedom of movement, for trouble remains very unpredictable, and to
try to avoid every possible danger would be intolerably constraining. So the
only possible general rule is that "you better be on the alert when you're
walking on those streets." This is particularly important at night when it
is easy for an attacker to hide in the dark and when the streets are empty.
If a group of men have been drinking together and someone has a long way
to go home, he may agree with the host to stay overnight rather than try
to make his way home intoxicated, an easy prey for yoking. But certainly
one cannot always be so cautious, and some day one may have to face the
consequences. This is what one middle-aged man said when encountered
at a street corner near Winston Street after he has been absent for some
time:

> No, I sure ain't seen you for a long time, not since I was yoked—yes, just
> across the street from here. Remember last time I saw you, over at the
> Robinson's house? Yeah, I was worried about you going home that night
> —remember how I told you to watch out? And then I was yoked, and I left
> just after you! If I lost anything? I damn near lost my life! And I was in
> hospital for six weeks, and all my teeth was knocked out, and I got to pay

the dentist five hundred bucks. Yeah, I got a pretty good idea who they was, I've seen them outside that bar up the street—actually, don't look now, but that's one of them going into the liquor store behind me right now. I ain't going to no court, probably wouldn't do any good, and I got to think of my family. I got a wife and daughter, you know, and I don't want them to get into trouble. If I was alone it might have been another thing. Well, anyway, that's why you don't see me around so much any more, 'cause I don't want to go out of the house too much.

But despite the dangers people in the Winston Street neighborhood still face, many of those who have been acquainted with the street for the last few decades say that in some ways it has calmed down. One man who has been there on and off for seventeen years said that "this used to be the baddest damn street I've seen in my life." There was a time, it is claimed, when a stranger could be happy if he managed to get from one end of the street to the other alive, and he certainly would not have a whole lot of money left. There were signs which the natives used between one another to show if the person going down the side-walk was fair game. In those days, Winston Street also had a great number of bootleggers, some of whom made their own whiskey, and people came from all over town to buy from them. The bootleggers then spent a great deal of their money gambling with each other. That way, one man said, "it all stayed in the family." Sonny, a former jazz saxophonist who lives off the street but spends most of his day on it, says that when he arrived in Washington from Florida some thirty years ago, his mother placed Winston Street off limits for him. But there was always some way of sneaking up there to watch the action.

These were also the times of organized gang conflicts among adolescents. The men who are now in their thirties have memories of this warfare at its height, but now such gangs, with names, offices, and all their *West Side Story* paraphernalia, are few in Washington.

The recollections of Winston Street in the past are most likely exaggerated. Probably they should be seen as interesting pieces of jungle imagery rather than as good historical evidence. Yet there is a notable unanimity among various informants, and there can hardly be a doubt that the street had a reputation as a stronghold of shady activities. Since then, some of the people who engaged in them moved to other parts of the ghetto without changing their way of life much. Among the hustlers at the corner of Seventh and T Streets there are some who can describe in detail the social organization of illegal activities at Winston Street in the old days. Others have moved on up and out, to more respectable jobs and better dwellings in other parts of the city. Then there are those who remain on the street but have undergone a similar change there. One man who used to make whiskey in his Winston Street home is now a janitor in an apartment house.

His sons, growing up in the old days, have taken different paths. One is an office clerk, another is an apartment house receptionist, two are on-and-off construction workers one of whom still occasionally makes a handsome profit from gambling while the other is an alcoholic. A few people have remained in business while a couple of newcomers have taken over where someone left off, but they manage their affairs discreetly. Of course, since their activities are illegal, they may sometimes go out of business at least temporarily. Occasionally a bootlegger gets raided. One raid which caused many hearty laughs in the neighborhood was described by one young man:

> You know up the corner of Piedmont Street where there are bootleggers in three houses in a row? Somebody had tipped off the man about one of them, so they came with a search warrant with this person's name on it. But they got the wrong house number, you see, they went to his next-door neighbor, and when he saw that they had a search warrant he didn't look closer at it 'cause he just thought his whole thing was over. So they went in and found all those half-pints, and only when they were on their way out did they find out they got the wrong guy. But then of course the fellow next door had seen there was a raid going on, so he had got all his stuff into the car and drove off. And of course they didn't know that they could have gone to any one of these three places and caught someone.

Today's bootleggers in the area do not make their own liquor but buy it at a discount and sell it at higher prices—something like 25 per cent higher than regular store prices—when the legitimate liquor stores are closed.

But of course, the large majority of people, whether remaining from the past or more recent arrivals on the street, hold ordinary jobs or are unemployed, and their contact with illegal activities may be non-existent or confined to their positions as customers and, now and then, victims.

What kind of people are those who live at Winston Street now? Like other people in the black ghettos of Northern cities, they are part of what is in a way an immigrant community. Certainly, their ancestry has been American longer than that of many groups which have been assimilated more quickly into mainstream American society. But black people do have a "back home" of their own. The trails from the rural South to the big cities are well established. Washington, D.C., has not been the goal of most migrants from the Deepest South—Alabama, Mississippi—who have usually gone more directly north. The majority of the black migrants have come from the states of the Southeastern seaboard, and this is mirrored in the Winston Street population. Among the adults there, about a fourth were born in South Carolina, and a similar proportion in North Carolina. Smaller numbers came from Virginia and Maryland, the neighboring states. A few came from other states, and about a third were born in the District of

Columbia. But many of those who are from outside the District came there while they were young, brought by their parents, and most of the children and younger people are native Washingtonians. Yet now and then a new family arrives from the South and moves into the neighborhood, and among those who are less recent arrivals many maintain contacts "down country" by visiting relatives there during holidays or sending the children to spend a part of their summer vacation with cousins.

However, the second generation of Northern city dwellers, and even more the following generations, often have only a more general idea of the South and know less about their specific ties to kinsmen and towns. There remains a more general sense of the South as the origin of the ghetto dwellers or their ancestors, and as a place where life was worse than it is in the city—here the news media seem to contribute as much to knowledge as the ghetto oral tradition, although they can complement and support each other in their effects. As ghetto dwellers see governor Wallace on TV a few unappreciative comments are exchanged between them, and when the cottonfield scene comes on in the Sidney Poitier movie, *In the Heat of the Night,* the audience in the U Street movie house howls and murmurs. The King David Carry-Out at the corner of Winston Street and many others like it proclaim that its specialty is "Southern Home Cooking," and streetcorner groceries advertise chitterlings, greens and other Southern foods on their window posters.

In their economic situations, a certain diversity emerges among the Winston Street people. As a ghetto street, it has a majority of low-income people, but there are some who stay on although they achieve a higher income. Their reasons for remaining may vary. The additional cost and the extra difficulties which still appear for black people trying to find a home outside the ghetto keep many from ever trying to move out. "Sure, the suburbs are nice, you know. But I don't particularly want to go where nobody wants me although I know they are wrong and I'm right." Others are reasonably satisfied with the ghetto and know that they would leave most of their friends behind if they moved. A few have vested interests in the ghetto which are best served by remaining there. Businesses, legal or illegal, provide one reason for staying even when it would be possible to move out. Especially among some younger people, a motive occasionally offered for remaining in the ghetto is racial solidarity. Leaving less fortunate "brothers" behind is "copping out." The ghetto can be defined in both racial and economic terms, but there is a conscious emphasis on the racial dimension.

Despite all this, some of those who have reached an economic threshold do indeed trickle out of the ghetto. If they have some kind of attachment to their old neighborhood they may come to visit friends occasionally, but on the whole the ghetto remains in many ways a community to itself without extensive ties of personal friendship with people in other parts of the city.

But most people have no choice of whether to stay in the ghetto or not. Although they may have jobs, they cannot afford to live anywhere else. It is difficult to establish exactly what proportion of the people in the Winston Street neighborhood are employed. Clearly, at any given point in time, a majority of the adult males hold jobs. They are in a strong majority among those who are functioning husbands and fathers in childrearing households. The problem in arriving at more exact figures stems primarily from two sources; there is a variable employment situation over time, and the number of men who should be seen as inhabitants of the neighborhood can only be decided with difficulty, and then in a rather arbitrary manner. Many men drift in and out of jobs, with or without prolonged periods of unemployment between. Some are in occupations which have periods of unemployment, such as the many construction workers in the neighborhood who are laid off during the winter. As for the instability in the neighborhood population of adult men, it is particularly the rather regularly unemployed men who are sometimes in the neighborhood, sometimes out of it; now they live there, next they sleep somewhere else but spend their free time at Winston Street, later again they are completely out of the picture only to turn up again a few months later, resuming their old place.

Most of the employed men are in unskilled or at best semiskilled occupations: general laborers, construction workers, garbage men, janitors, messengers, gas station attendants, truck drivers, etc. There is a bartender, a cook, a baker and a railroad trackman. But there are also a few white-collar workers; clerks in low-level government service or other offices, the receptionist in a downtown apartment building mentioned before, a drugstore clerk. One man operates his own business, a furniture refinishing shop. Obviously, most of the men make their living outside the ghetto.

Among the adult women who are not aged, those who have employment and those who do not are about equal in number. In those childrearing households where no adult male is present in the husband-father role, somewhat more women hold jobs outside the home than in the two-parent families where the male is usually employed. Women are usually in service occupations; a great many are domestic workers for white families, often in the suburbs. There are also hotel maids, laundresses, waitresses in cafeterias and at luncheon counters. A few are secretaries and clerks in minor positions.

Most inhabitants of the neighborhood, then, are in low-income occupations, and this is of course to some extent (that is, apart from discrimination in the labor market and some other factors) due to their limited formal education. One younger man in the neighborhood holds a degree from a Negro college and now works for the city's recreation department, but he takes little part in neighborhood interaction. The overwhelming majority of the inhabitants of the neighborhood have only a high school education, and most of them a rather poor one. Many dropped out of school before graduating, and whether they went to school in the South or in Washington, they usually went to segregated schools of low standard. Some of the adults have less than five years of schooling and are functionally illiterate. Of course, the Washington, D.C., public school system is officially integrated, but residential *de facto* segregation has resulted in overwhelmingly segregated schools. Thus the generation now growing up in the ghetto continues to be poorly prepared for social mobility—although it may be argued that segregation in schools need not in itself cause poor education, it is generally agreed that ghetto schools are in fact ill-equipped for their purpose.

How much do the Winston Street people earn on their jobs? The majority is definitely at a low-income level. The greater number of the households earn between $2,000 and $5,000 with about an equal number below and above $3,000. Some make even less (usually one-person households or elderly people), some make more. A few households state their income as more than $10,000 per year, but some qualifications and additional information need then be given. Some would earn that much if employment were steady. This is not always true, either because of shifts in the labor market or because of personal matters; one skilled worker with a potentially high income earns substantially less because he is a chronic alcoholic, working only irregularly. Secondly, in most cases when a household income reaches higher figures, it is the consequence only of many household members holding jobs. In the three cases on Winston Street where incomes above $10,000 are earned at legitimate jobs, three members have steady employment—a car inspector, a domestic worker, and a hotel maid; a skilled construction worker, a hotel maid, and a recreation specialist (the young college graduate mentioned above); and a truck driver, a laundress, and a typist. Of course, there are also households of lower income where more than one member are employed and contribute to the household economy, and a few individuals increase their incomes by holding two jobs.

For many of the households at the lowest income levels, earnings from employment are only a part or none at all of the income. A number of Winston Street households derive some of or their entire means of living from public welfare payments, particularly from the programs concerned with aid to families with dependent children (AFDC) and old-age assistance. Among the men, some who were disabled in recent wars draw veterans' pensions, and others qualify for unemployment compensation.

The Ghetto

The Winston Street neighborhood is not a world to itself. As a neighborhood, it has its own web of social relations, but it is also a part of larger entities. As far as trouble is concerned, it is in "number seventeen," an all-ghetto police precinct. The small children of the neighborhood start at the nearby Elijah M. Poole Elementary School, but as they get older they go to junior high schools and high schools further away, where they come into contact with children from much wider areas of the ghetto. And the adults also have their interests spread out over the ghetto. They may have lived somewhere else in it before, and they have friends and kinsmen scattered over it with whom they get together more or less frequently. They also make use of a number of ghetto locales which are outside their own neighborhood. The setting for their life in the community is thus wider than just the few blocks closest to home.

The ghetto has many streets like Winston Street, with the same kinds of row houses, occasionally a larger apartment house, and many of the small businesses—the groceries, the barber shops, the liquor stores. There is a rather high turnover among these, as many of them are rather unsuccessful operations, and there are often vacant premises. Some of these become the homes of storefront churches which advertise their services and Sunday school programs in the erstwhile shop windows, most of which are white painted or covered by self-adhesive plastic imitations of stained glass. The diversity of their names—*The Full Speed Gospel Church of God in Christ, The Peaceway Temple, The Miracle Temple of Truth, The Christian Home Penecostal* (sic) *Holiness Church of God of the Americans, The Maranatha Gospel Hall, The Solid Rock Church of God in Christ, The Way Back to Pentecost Church, The Full Gospel Tabernacle Church of the Living God* and a multitude of other combinations—is one pointer to their independence of old, large and well-established churches. These storefront churches, "Spiritual," "Holiness," or "Sanctified," have small congregations of perhaps a couple of dozen members and are led by preachers who may be male or female but are more often male. The tiny congregations usually have little or no connection with any other church. On a Sunday one may hear through the open door a preacher's staccato sermon, shout-singing and tambourines, or a slow and peaceful hymn, in the weak and cracking voices of older women. On the staircase of the house next door sit a few men who could have been their one-time husbands. A fragrance of pork chops hangs in the air as a message about someone's Sunday dinner, and one of the men may jokingly suggest that they track it down to the source.

The ghetto also has its main arteries. Some of them are the thoroughfares of the people of the suburbs and outer city who get a glimpse of the ghetto on their way to and from the downtown business area and its office buildings. There are also commercial establishments which cater as much to a white as to a black public, or more—gas stations, car dealers, repair shops, warehouses, small industries, and the like—spilling out into the ghetto from the downtown area. In a motley arrangement with the homes of ghetto dwellers, with their variety of shapes, sizes, colors, and states of upkeep, and 'empty lots covered with litter, these establishments give the ghetto a very cluttered look. It also appears rather spacious. Most buildings are not very tall, and the street plan of the nation's capital, with the streets and wide avenues lined by trees, also encompasses the ghetto. During the summer when the trees are green, the ghetto may even look idyllic; but from fall to spring, when cold winds shake the trees and envelop the loafers who huddle together in their aging worn-out overcoats, the view is a bleak one.

The ghetto main streets, however, are not only thoroughfares but also lifelines of the ghetto community. Seventh Street, Fourteenth Street, and U Street in Northwest Washington, and H Street in the Northeast section, cater to the ghetto public in many ways. There are the large chain supermarkets competing with the small streetcorner groceries; there are bars and restaurants, pool halls and a few movie theaters showing the same movies as the downtown theaters, usually only slightly later and at lower prices; record stores and big churches; clothing and furniture stores, for both new and used merchandise; employment agencies, drug stores, occult advisors, and funeral homes. Interspersed among them are more of the same kinds of small businesses as cluster at the street corners in the Winston Street neighborhood. But the barber shops and carry-outs which are routine hangouts for rather stable groups in the neighborhood take on much more urban anonymity on the main streets. There may be fleeting sociability among customers as well as between them and the staff, but there is more reason to "watch out" as one cannot be quite sure what kind of person one is dealing with. One middle-aged white-collar worker, also involved in numbers running and with rather moderate political opinions commented on the increasingly militant mood among some ghetto dwellers:

> You know, nowadays if I see somebody in the barber shop I don't know I keep my mouth shut if somebody starts talking about politics. You never can tell if there's a Muslim or one of those black power people in there and they might jump you if you say something they don't like. I keep my mouth shut.

The larger establishments on the ghetto main streets are seldom owned by black people, although some to the ghetto dwellers may find employment in them. However, some of the smaller or medium-sized businesses are black owned and operated. They are the ones which have "soul brother" written on their windows when the Washington ghetto erupts into violence, as it did after Martin Luther King's death in April, 1968. Thus they hope to establish themselves as a part of the ghetto moral community, an effort which has more often than not been successful.

The intersections of the main streets are among the landmarks of the ghetto. Where U Street crosses Fourteenth Street, and where it meets Florida Avenue near the corner of Seventh Street, there are always people on the move, as well as people not on the move but just looking. These corners are where beggars, prostitutes, and dope pushers do some of their best business. One block south of the corner of Seventh and Florida is Seventh and T, already mentioned as a home of hustlers—pimps, gamblers, narcotics pushers and others—as well as plain "gorillas," men who, if the situation is propitious, are quick to use their fists and to jump on a passer-by who might have money. These, at least, are the terms in which ghetto dwellers speak of Seventh and T. If any one place in the ghetto sums up the imagery of an urban jungle, it is this corner, with its many bars and pool rooms. This, perhaps, is also the opinion of the preacher who sometimes takes a place on the sidewalk there, speaking out against all this sin in a stentorian voice to which the passers-by and loafers seem to pay scant attention.

But of course most people passing by Seventh and T go unharmed and unnoticed, including the audience at the Howard Theatre. The Howard has been a major entertainment spot in the ghetto for many decades, and a lot of black stage personalities who have since turned to large white audiences have played the Howard at earlier points in their career. Nowadays, the Howard usually alternates between rock-and-roll shows, with jazz and an occasional comedian thrown in now and then, and third-rate movies. The stage shows draw audiences ranging from small children to adults in their early middle age. The Sunday matinees have very youthful audiences crying out when their favorites come on, singing along and dancing in the rows and aisles; the evening shows, and particularly the Saturday midnight shows, draw more mature crowds. The emcees, usually disc jockeys from local black radio stations, adjust to these differences and spice their remarks more heavily as the afternoon yields to evening and night. This is one place where the ghetto public meets its stars alive—singers such as James Brown, Joe Tex, Wilson Pickett, soul groups like the Marvellettes, the Impressions, the Flamingoes, and comedians like Moms Mabley and Clay Tyson. Some young white people from nearby colleges occasionally drop in, but on the whole, the Howard is a ghetto institution *par preference.*

It is a rather small theater, however, and some big stars would rather play a one-nighter for a large audience than stay a week at the Howard. So when some of the big names turn up in Washington, they are billed at the top of a show held at some place with a larger capacity. The Coliseum, also used for a variety of sports events, has been a frequently used setting for this kind of shows, but after a minor riot at a Temptations show, its management has been more reluctant to book such events. Weeknight boxing and the roller-skating rink are also there as great attractions. The latter, however is not the only one of its kind in the ghetto.

A few bowling alleys and a great number of pool halls are among the other foci of leisure life in the ghetto. The pool halls have an imagery of wickedness attached to them; they are all-male institutions where the air is heavy with smoke and where small-time hustlers in flashy outfits mingle with laborers on their way home from work. They are also places where one may lose a good deal of money. This is Sonny, the former saxophonist, reminiscing again about a couple of his friends:

> Bee Jay shoots a pretty good game of pool, but he loses his cool. You know, one or two shots go wrong and he goes to pieces. I remember once he was playing Henry, and you know Henry is a very cool player and so he is very good although he is close to seventy years old. So Bee Jay was playing him, and Henry won something like thirty dollars, and Bee Jay was sure he'd win everything back in the end, so he went and got his hundred and twenty-five dollar suit and took it to the pawn shop, and then they went on playing. But Bee Jay was all excited, so Henry got that money too.

The bowling alleys, on the other hand, have men as well as women among their patrons (although the men are more numerous), and generally you do not play for money there. The women are usually in their twenties or possibly late teens, the men have a somewhat wider age range from the late teens to the middle forties. Presumably, the women stop bowling when they become tied down by their families, while the men cease to go when they feel too old. During the week business at the bowling alley is rather slow, but it picks up during the weekend, particularly on Saturday nights when the teams compete in leagues. The teams may be of one sex or both; since leagues are sex-integrated the games can be too, even when the teams are sex-segregated. Thus the bowling alley is a possible arena for making new contacts with the opposite sex. Girls do not stop bowling as soon as the adumbrations of family life occur; many unmarried pregnant girls continue to hold their place on the team, and later they may appear at the alley with a child with whom they play between their turns and who is passed over to someone else when their turn comes to bowl.

Except for the lanes, the alley usually frequented by people from Winston Street also houses pinball machines, soft drink vending machines, and a snack bar, with the ordinary hamburgers and hot dogs as well as some Southern specialties. The snack bar also serves beer; the players sometimes bring in stronger beverages in secret.

The persons present on a Saturday night are not only the regular members of the teams but also friends who come to see the games or people who just drop in to look around, have a snack, and perhaps work the pinball machines. Since some team member may fail to show up, there is always a chance that one of these extra persons will be asked to play instead. Occasionally members of the staff at the alley are asked to fill a vacant position for the night.

Bars are also locales for leisure. However, there is more drinking going on away from bars than in them, and most visits to them also have other purposes than just drinking. The middle-aged men who drink in the back alley and in their rooms during the week go to the beer garden on Friday night, because that is when they want a good time. They go from one table to another, exchanging greetings, pleasantries, reminiscences, and occasionally hot arguments with friends and acquaintances. Although the poster on the wall expressly forbids dancing, some men take a few steps to the music of the jukebox, alone or with one of the few middle-aged women, usually of more or less explicit prostitute status, who also frequent these establishments. Sometimes a fight develops; now and then someone is too drunk to stand up. In both cases, the management and the other patrons make efforts to get the delinquents to either shut up or get out.

The younger public usually prefers bars or "clubs" with some form of entertainment, usually live music or go-go girls. They are often at least somewhat more elegant than the beer gardens of the older men. More women come into them, and one important reason for visiting them is meeting persons of the opposite sex. Put more bluntly, they are often pick-up places. Since these bars are accepted as such by generally shared definition, any party made up of members from one sex only which enters the place leaves itself open to approaches from others. Although men usually take the first step, this is not always the case. A number of the women in these places are prostitutes or semi-prostitutes, both among visitors and waitresses, and it is sometimes open to question who picks up whom.

Freddy, Fats, and Big Jimmy were standing at the corner of Piedmont Street, trying to collect money for a half-pint of gin and talking about the waitresses in the beer garden down the street. Fats said he was talking "real sweet" to one of them, the yellow-skinned girl with the high hairdo, trying to convince her to take him home with her that night when she handed him an envelope full of nudie pictures of herself out of her handbag. "Ain't that a bitch," said Freddy, and they all chuckled.

Other bars have become established in the public knowledge as hangouts for more specialized clienteles: gamblers, "gorillas," homosexuals. Those ghetto dwellers who do not belong to such categories will usually avoid such places. There grows up an identification between people and the places where they hang out, and nobody would want to get an unearned stigma attached to himself. Besides, it is again a question of the mapping of trouble. If one spends time around a setting of trouble, one may run an immediate risk of violence, and in the long run there is the possible influence of bad company. Mr. Robinson, a 62-year old janitor, walks past a bar with a clientele of "young hoodlums"—as people in the area describe them—who are not only inside but who also stand around in front of the bar; he sees his 19 year-old nephew among them. Afterwards, he comments to his own son:

> You know who I saw outside the Crystal Bar? Frank. That boy sure ain't got no sense. You know how worried his mother is he'll get into trouble, and there he is with all them gorillas outside the Crystal. I bet you he'll get himself into a mess one of these days.

Washington, D.C.

The people of the Washington ghetto obviously find some of the satisfactions of life in their own black community. It is also the source of some of their troubles. But the ghetto is also a part of the Washington whole; we have already seen how its inhabitants are integrated into the economy of the wider community. In politics, too, the ghetto is a dependency.

The black ghetto in Washington, D.C., has grown much over the last decades. In the late nineteen-fifties, black people became a majority of the city's population. It was the first large American city where this occurred, but it is only one of many urban centers in the nation where large low-income black populations stay in the inner city while there is an exodus of white people to the suburbs. Thus much of what are now parts of Washington's black ghetto were white or at least more mixed until the forties and fifties. (Winston Street, however, has always been a home of poor black people.)

The ghettoization trend has continued in Washington. In the late sixties, about two thirds of the population of the District of Columbia are black people. But the situation is naturally a different one in the metropolitan area as a whole, including the suburbs in Virginia and Maryland, and this makes black dominance in Washington largely a chimera. In this larger area, the whites are about three quarters of the total population. About eighty percent of them live in the suburbs, while only some fifteen percent of the black people are suburbanites. The whites who reside within the boundaries of the District of Columbia are to a disproportionate extent unmarried or at least childless. The childrearing white families have gone to the suburbs.

The development of numerical dominance of black people within the District of Columbia has not made a great difference in their status, and their situation is largely the same as that of black people in a number of other large American cities. Their employers, their landlords, their rulers are ultimately white outsiders. Even though most of them are poor, the black people of the District of Columbia should be able to have more political power by virtue of their being in majority; but the District, as the nation's capital, does not have home rule. It has only been allowed to participate in presidential elections since the 1964 election. Executive power for the District of Columbia is vested in a local government appointed by the President of the United States. Legislation for the District is handled by two standing congressional committees, one of the Senate and one of the House of Representatives, and bills concerning the District must be passed by them before they are sent to Congress for general debate and vote. The committees have often been dominated by conservatives from rural areas, and these have frequently had little understanding of the problems peculiar to cities. Thus there is a chronic conflict between the government and much of the District's population, and many of the ghetto dwellers who are most politically aware feel that they live under a colonial type of government. Although the loss of a form of self-government occurred already in 1874 and was caused primarily by economic mismanagement, the role of race relations in the continuation of federal rule into the present is not easily denied. To a great many white Americans with representatives in Congress, the view of black people governing the nation's capital is apparently distasteful. A change to home rule may come sooner or later, and the issue has certainly been in the focus of interest of political and civil rights groups in the District during recent years. Yet it has so far been impossible to get Congress to approve of such a change.

Without general participation in elections, political activity in the ghetto is rather limited. Although most ghetto dwellers are certainly in favor of increasing their citizens' rights, their active articulation of such demands has so far been largely missing. Local political organizations and civil rights groups—and branches of national ones—have been relatively small. The new black power groups have apparently not yet extended their organizations significantly beyond the cadre, although their influence is certainly growing. The leaders of the older organizations, and most of their active members, belong to the sizeable black middle class, which usually lives out of the low-income ghetto in either integrated areas or black areas of a higher standing. Their interest in ghetto problems may arise from civic concern, from involvement with the ghetto through business or as professional employees of government or civil rights organizations, or from church work (as usual, there are many black ministers in the leadership), and not necessarily from a grass roots ghetto origin. Thus many of them are a kind of caretakers, defining and articulating the problems of the ghetto. But their everyday channels of communication to large segments of the people of the ghetto are not always very wide. Thus the ghetto dwellers are in one way a "people without politics," in that their personal voices are rarely heard in the political community to which they are assigned. The widest setting of the ghetto dweller, the polity and economy of Washington, D.C., and the United States, is one where there is little black power and much white.

The Social and Economic Status of the Negro in the United States

St. Clair Drake

In this article which is a classic on the status of the American Negro, St. Clair Drake, a noted black scholar, deals with the development and description of black ghettos and "life styles" within those ghettos. Using a wealth of detail to carefully document his contentions, Drake traces how the black subculture in America, more fully described by Hannerz in "Setting," was generated by the "victimization" of the blacks which prevents them from becoming part of the middle class. Thereby black "life styles" are kept different from white.

Drake proposes that a caste-class system has been imposed on the black, creating the "victimization" which he discusses in detail. The caste system developed in the South, while the class system evolved in the urban North where there were large groups of immigrants who became socioeconomically mobile. Both systems oppressed the black who has been kept in the lower caste and in the lower class. For example, the average ghetto black suffers from a lower average income than a white worker, from lessened job opportunities, from poorer health and fewer medical services, and from poor schools on which less money is expended than on suburban schools.

The black, according to Drake, also suffers from an identification problem at the psychological level. Drake maintains the black often has trouble answering "Who am I?" because the white physical and social image is the prevalent one in America. So blacks have been psychologically, as well as socially and economically, "victimized." They have been kept "powerless" in black-white relations and have been made to feel that powerlessness, much to their detriment.

And now, Drake points out in this article, even though blacks are "winning through" a bit more in some areas such as job opportunities, new victimizations are creeping in to replace some of the old. Drake cites the integration of middle class blacks as robbing the lower class black masses of leadership. He calls it "skimming off the cream" to further victimize the majority of black Americans. Although some of the specific statistics have changed since the article was written, Drake's major points about victimization remain valid and offer valuable insights for the teacher into black life.

From "The Social and Economic Status of the Negro in the United States" by St. Clair Drake. Reprinted by permission from *Daedalus,* Journal of the American Academy of Arts and Sciences, Boston, Massachusetts, Vol. 94, No. 4, 1965.

Caste, Class, and "Victimization"

During the 1930's W. Lloyd Warner and Allison Davis developed and popularized a conceptual scheme for analyzing race relations in the Southern region of the United States which viewed Negro-white relations as organized by a color-caste system that shaped economic and political relations as well as family and kinship structures, and which was reinforced by the legal system. Within each of the two castes (superordinate white and subordinate Negro), social classes existed, status being based upon possession of money, education, and family background as reflected in distinctive styles of behavior. "Exploitation" in the Marxist sense was present within this caste-class system, but also much more; for an entire socio-cultural system, not just the economic order, functioned to distribute power and prestige unevenly between whites and Negroes and to punish any individuals who questioned the system by word or behavior.

Students of the situation in the North rarely conceptualized race relations in terms of caste, but tended rather to view specific communities as areas in which *ethnic* groups were involved in continuous competition and conflict, resulting in a hierarchy persisting through time, with now one, and again another, ethnic group at the bottom as previous newcomers moved "up." Each ethnic group developed a social class structure within it, but as individuals acquired better jobs, more education, and some sophistication, they and their families often detached themselves from immigrant colonies (usually located in slum areas) and sometimes from all ethnic institutions as well. They tended to become a part of the middle class. The negroes who migrated North in large numbers during World War I were the latest arrivals in this fluid and highly competitive situation, but their high visibility became a crucial factor limiting their upward mobility. Upwardly mobile Negroes could not "disappear" into the middle class of the larger society as did European ethnics.

Thus, on the eve of World War II, students of race relations in the United States generally described the status of Negroes as one in which they played subordinate roles in a caste system in the South and an ethnic-class system in the North. The actions of persons toward those of another race were explained not in terms of some vaguely defined emotions connected with "prejudice," but rather in terms of the behavior they felt was expected of them by others in various positions within the social structure, and as attempts to protect and maximize whatever power and prestige accrued to them at their locus in the system. . . .

. . . Of the racial and ethnic groups in America only Negroes have been subjected to caste-deprivations; and the ethnic-class system has operated to their disadvantage as compared with European immigrants. In other words, Negroes in America have been subject to "victimization" in the sense that a system of social relations operates in such a way as to deprive them of a chance to share in the more desirable material and non-material products of a society which is dependent, in part, upon their labor and loyalty. They are "victimized," also, because they do not have the same degree of access which others have to the attributes needed for rising in the general class system—money, education, "contacts," and "know-how."

The concept of "victimization" implies too, that some people are used as means to other people's ends—without their consent—and that the social system is so structured that it can be deliberately manipulated to the disadvantage of some groups by the clever, the vicious, and the cynical, as well as by the powerful. The callous and indifferent unconsciously and unintentionally reinforce the system by their inaction or inertia. The "victims," their autonomy curtailed and their self-esteem weakened by the operation of the caste-class system, are confronted with "identity problems." Their social condition is essentially one of "powerlessness."

Individual "victims" may or may not accept the rationalizations given for the denial to them of power and prestige. They may or may not be aware of and concerned about their position in the system, but, when they do become concerned, victimization takes on important social psychological dimensions. Individuals then suffer feelings of "relative deprivation" which give rise to reactions ranging from despair, apathy, and withdrawal to convert and overt aggression. An effective analysis of the position of the Negro in these terms (although the word "victimization" is never used) may be found in Thomas F. Pettigrew's *A Profile of the Negro American.* (1)

Concepts developed by Max Weber are useful for assessing the degree of victimization existing within the American caste-class system. (2) Individuals and groups can be compared by examining what he refers to as "life chances," that is, the extent to which people have access to economic and political power. *Direct victimization* might be defined as the operation of sanctions which deny access to power, which limit the franchise, sustain job discrimination, permit unequal pay for similar work, or provide inferior training or no training at all. *Indirect victimization* is revealed in the consequences which flow from a social structure which decreases *"life chances,"* such as high morbidity and mortality rates, low longevity rates, a high incidence of psychopathology, or the persistence of personality traits and attitudes which impose disadvantages in competition or excite derogatory and invidious comparisons with other groups. Max Weber also compared individuals and groups in terms of differences in *"life styles,"* those ways of behaving which vary in the amount of esteem, honor, and prestige attached to them. Differences in "life chances" may make it impossible to acquire the money or education (or may limit the contacts) necessary for adopting and maintaining prestigious life styles. The key to understanding many aspects of race relations may be found in the fact that, in American society, the protection of their familiar and cherished life styles is a dominating concern of the white middle classes, who, because many Negroes have life styles differing from their own, have tried to segregate them into all-Negro neighborhoods, voluntary associations, and churches.

The "Ghettoization" of Negro Life

Pressure upon Negroes to live within all-Negro neighborhoods has resulted in those massive concentrations of Negro population in Northern metropolitan areas which bitter critics call "concentration camps" or "plantations" and which some social scientists refer to as "Black Ghettos." (3) Small town replicas exist everywhere throughout the nation, for the roots of residential segregation lie deep in American history. In older Southern towns slave quarters were transformed into Negro residential areas after Emanicipation—a few blocks here, a whole neighborhood there, often adjacent to white homes. In newer Southern towns and cities a less secure upwardly mobile white population usually demanded a greater degree of segregation from ex-slaves and their descendants. Prior to World War I, the residential patterns did not vary greatly between North and South, but the great northward migration of Negroes between 1914 and 1920 expanded the small Negro neighborhoods into massive Black Belts. Middle-class white neighbors used "restrictive-covenants" as their main device for slowing down and "containing" the expansion of Negro neighborhoods. Thus, with continued in-migration and restricted access to housing in "white neighborhoods," the overcrowded Black Ghetto emerged with its substandard structures, poor public services, and high crime and juvenile delinquency rates.

Scholars know from careful research, and increasingly wider circles are becoming aware of the fact, that Negroes do not depress property values, but that middle-class white attitudes toward Negroes do. As long as Negroes, as a group, are a symbol of lower social status, proximity to them will be considered undesirable and such social attitudes will be reflected in the market place. The problem is complicated by the fact that a very high proportion of Negro Americans actually does have lower-class attributes and behavior patterns. The upward mobility of white Americans, as well as their comfort and personal safety, is facilitated by spatial segregation.

(Older cities in the South have been an exception.) The white middle class could protect its values by acting solely in terms of class, letting middle-class Negro families scatter into white neighborhoods irrespective of race. Instead, the white middle class in American cities protects its own neighborhoods from behavior patterns it disapproves of and from chronic social disorganization by "ghettoizing" the Negro. Real-estate operators, black and white, have exploited the fears of the white middle class from the beginning of the northern migration by "block busting," that is, by buying property for less than its normal market value and reselling it at a higher price to Negroes barred from the open market or by charging them higher rentals. Eventually the profit-potential in residential segregation was maximized by the institutions which controlled mortgage money and refused to finance property for Negro residence outside of the Black Belts except under conditions approved by them.

In 1948, the Supreme Court declared racial restrictive covenants unenforceable in the courts, but this action tended to accelerate rather than reverse the process of ghettoization, for many whites proceeded to sell to Negroes at inflated prices and then moved to the suburbs, or they retained their properties, moved away, and raised the rents. The Court's decision was based partly upon a reevaluation of the concept of civil rights and partly upon a recognition of the fact that serious economic injustice was a by-product of residential segregation, a situation summed up by Thomas Pettigrew:

> While some housing gains occurred in the 1950's the quality of Negro housing remains vastly inferior relative to that of whites. For example, in Chicago in 1960, Negroes paid as much for housing as whites, despite their lower incomes. . . . This situation exists because of essentially two separate housing markets; and the residential segregation that creates these dual markets has increased steadily over past decades until it has reached universally high levels in cities throughout the United States, despite significant advances in the socio-economic status of Negroes. . . . (4)

The trend has not yet been reversed despite F.H.A. administrative regulations and Supreme Court decisions.

The spatial isolation of Negroes from whites created Negro "communities." Within these Negro neighborhoods, church and school became the basic integrative institutions, and Negro entrepreneurs developed a variety of service enterprises—barbershops and beauty parlors, funeral homes and restaurants, pool parlors, taverns, and hotels—all selling to what came to be called "The Negro Market." Successful banking and insurance businesses also grew up within some Negro communities. A Negro "subculture" gradually emerged, national in scope, with distinctive variations upon the general American culture in the fields of literature, art, music, and dance, as well as in religious ritual and church polity.

The spatial isolation of Negroes from whites in "Black Belts" also increased consciousness of their separate subordinate position, for no whites were available to them as neighbors, schoolmates, or friends, but were present only in such roles as school teachers, policemen, and social workers, flat janitors and real-estate agents, merchants and bill collectors, skilled laborers involved in maintenance, and even a few white dentists and doctors with offices in the Black Belt. Such a situation inevitably generated anti-white sentiments (often with anti-Semitic overtones), and the pent-up feelings have occasionally erupted in anti-white riots. Normally, however, this intense racial consciousness finds expression in non-violent forms of social protest and is utilized by Negro leaders to sanction and reinforce Negro institutions and their own personal welfare. It has also lent powerful support to the segments of municipal political machines existing within Negro neighborhoods. As long as ghettos remain, race consciousness will be strong.

Residential segregation created the demographic and ecological basis for "balance of power" politics, since the possibility of a Negro bloc vote had to be recognized by both political parties. Northern Black Belt voters are not only occasionally the decisive factor in municipal elections, but have also sent a half-dozen Negroes to Congress. Indeed, it is ironic that one of the most effective weapons against segregation and discrimination in the South has been the political power generated in Negro precincts and wards of Northern Black Ghettos, thus reinforcing the direct action tactics of the civil rights movement. In the South, too, with the passage of the Civil Rights Act of 1964 and subsequent legislation, the political strength of newly enfranchised voters lies in their spatial concentration. There is some evidence that fear of this strength may operate as a factor in Northern cities to support "open occupancy," desegregation being considered preferable to Negro dominance.

While the development of machine politics has brought some gains to Negro communities, it has also resulted in various forms of indirect victimization. Local Negro leaders often co-operate with the city-wide machine in the protection of "the rackets"—policy, dope, and prostitution—and sacrifice group welfare to personal gain for self and party. They have not hesitated, in some places, even to drag their heels in the fight for residential desegregation rather than risk wiping out the base of their power. Being saddled with a "bought leadership" is one of the greatest burdens Black Ghettos have had to bear. Economic victimization is widespread, too. In the "affluent society" of the sixties, consumption-oriented and given to the "hard sell," Negroes like other Americans are under social pressure to spend beyond their means. Given the lack of sophistication of many recent migrants and the very low median income of those with less than a high-school education, it is not surprising that loan sharks and dubious credit merchants (of all races) make the Black Ghetto a prime target. Negroes pay a high price for "protection" of the white middle-class way of life, since those who aspire to leave the ghetto are trapped, and those who are content to stay develop a limited and restricted view of the world in which they live.

Folkways and Classways Within the Black Ghetto

Black Ghettos in America are, on the whole, "run down" in appearance and overcrowded, and their inhabitants bear the physical and psychological scars of those whose "life chances" are not equal to those of other Americans. Like the European immigrants before them, they inherited the worst housing in the city. Within the past decade, the white "flight to the suburbs" has released relatively new and well-kept property on the margins of some of the old Black Belts. Here, "gilded ghettos" have grown up, indistinguishable from any other middle-class neighborhoods except by the color of the residents' skin. The power mower in the yard, the steak grill on the rear lawn, a well stocked library and equally well stocked bar in the rumpus room—these mark the homes of well-to-do Negroes living in the more desirable portions of the Black Belt. Many of them would flee to suburbia, too, if housing were available to Negroes there.

But the character of the Black Ghetto is not set by the newer "gilded," not-yet run down portions of it, but by the older sections where unemployment rates are high and the masses of people work with their hands—where the median level of education is just above graduation from grade school and many of the people are likely to be recent migrants from rural areas.

The "ghettoization" of the Negro has resulted in the emergence of a ghetto subculture with a distinctive ethos, most pronounced, perhaps, in Harlem, but recognizable in all Negro neighborhoods. For the average Negro who walks the streets of any American Black Ghetto, the smell of barbecued ribs, fried shrimps, and chicken emanating from numerous restaurants gives olfactory reinforcement to a feeling of "at-homeness." The beat of "gut music" spilling into the street from ubiquitous tavern juke boxes and the sound of tambourines and rich harmony behind the crude folk art on the windows of store-front churches give auditory confirmation to the universal belief that "We Negroes have 'soul.' " The bedlam of an occasional brawl, the shouted obscenities of street corner "foul mouths," and the whine of police sirens break the monotony of waiting for the number that never "falls," the horses that neither win, place, nor show, and the "good job" that never materializes. The insouciant swagger of teen-age drop-outs (the "cats") masks the hurt of their aimless existence and contrasts sharply with the ragged clothing and dejected demeanor of "skid-row" types who have long since stopped trying to keep up appearances and who escape it all by becoming "winoes." The spontaneous vigor of the children who crowd streets and playgrounds (with Cassius Clay, Ernie Banks, the Harlem Globe Trotters, and black stars of stage, screen, and television as their role models) and the cheerful rushing about of adults, free from the occupational pressures of the "white world" in which they work, create an atmosphere of warmth and superficial intimacy which obscures the unpleasant facts of life in the overcrowded rooms behind the doors, the lack of adequate maintenance standards, and the too prevalent vermin and rats.

This is a world whose urban "folkways" the upwardly mobile Negro middle class deplores as a "drag" on the "The Race," which the upper classes wince at as an embarrassment, and which race leaders point to as proof that Negroes have been victimized. But for the masses of the ghetto dwellers this is a warm and familiar milieu, preferable to the sanitary coldness of middle-class neighborhoods and a counterpart of the communities of the foreign-born, each of which has its own distinctive subcultural flavor. The arguments in the barbershop, the gossip in the beauty parlors, the "jiving" of bar girls and waitresses, the click of poolroom balls, the stomping of feet in the dance halls, the shouting in the churches are all *theirs* —and the white men who run the pawnshops, supermarkets, drug stores, and grocery stores, the policemen on horseback, the teachers in blackboard jungles—all these are aliens, conceptualized collectively as "The Man," intruders on the Black Man's "turf." When an occasional riot breaks out, "The Man" and his property become targets of aggression upon which pent-up frustrations are vented. When someone during the Harlem riots of 1964 begged the street crowds to go home, the cry came back, "Baby, we *are* home!"

But the inhabitants of the Black Ghetto are not a homogeneous mass. Although, in Marxian terms, nearly all of them are "proletarians," with nothing to sell but their labor, variations in "life style" differentiate them into social classes based more upon differences in education and basic values (crystallized, in part, around occupational differences) than in meaningful differences in income. The American caste-class system has served, over the years, to concentrate the Negro population in the low-income sector of the economy. In 1961, six out of every ten Negro families had an income of less than $4000.00 per year. This situation among whites was just the reverse: six out of every ten white families had *over* $4000.00 a year at their disposal. (In the South, eight out of ten Negro families were below the $4000.00 level.) This is the income gap. Discrimination in employment creates a job ceiling, most Negroes being in blue-collar jobs.

With 60 percent of America's Negro families earning less than $4000.00 a year, social strata emerge between the upper and lower boundaries of "no earned income" and $4000.00. Some families live a "middle-class style of life," placing heavy emphasis upon decorous public behavior and general respectability, insisting that their children "get an education" and "make something out of themselves." They prize family stability, and an unwed mother is something much more serious than "just a girl who had an accident"; pre-marital and extra-martial sexual relations, if indulged in at all, must be discreet. Social life is organized around churches and a welter of voluntary associations of all types, and, for women, "the cult of clothes" is so important that fashion shows are a popular fund raising activity even in churches. For both men and women, owning a home and going into business are highly desired goals, the former often being a realistic one, the latter a mere fantasy.

Within the same income range, and not always at the lower margin of it, other families live a "lower-class life-style" being part of the "organized" lower class, while at the lowest income levels an "unorganized" lower class exists whose members tend always to become *dis*organized—functioning in an anomic situation where gambling, excessive drinking, the use of narcotics, and sexual promiscuity are prevalent forms of behavior, and violent interpersonal relations reflect an ethos of suspicion and resentment which suffuses this deviant subculture. It is within this milieu that criminal and semi-criminal activites burgeon.

The "organized" lower class is oriented primarily around churches whose preachers, often semi-literate, exhort them to "be in the 'world' but not of it." Conventional middle-class morality and Pauline Puritanism are preached, although a general attitude of "the spirit is willing but the flesh is weak" prevails except among a minority fully committed to the Pentecostal sects. They boast, "We *live* the life"—a way of life that has been portrayed with great insight by James Baldwin in *Go Tell it on the Mountain* and *The Fire Next Time*.

Young people with talent find wide scope for expressing it in choirs, quartets, and sextets which travel from church to church (often bearing colorful names like The Four Heavenly Trumpets or the Six Singing Stars of Zion) and sometimes traveling from city to city. Such groups channel their aggressions in widely advertised "Battles of Song" and develop their talent in church pageants such as "Heaven Bound" or "Queen Esther" and fund-raising events where winners are crowned King and Queen. These activities provide fun as well as a testing ground for talent. Some lucky young church people eventually find their fortune in the secular world as did singers Sam Cooke and Nat King Cole, while others remain in the church world as nationally known gospel singers or famous evangelists.

Adults as well as young people find satisfaction and prestige in serving as ushers and deacons, "mothers," and deaconesses, Sunday-school teachers and choir leaders. National conventions of Negro denominations and national societies of ushers and gospel singers not only develop a continent-wide nexus of associations within the organized lower class, but also throw the more ambitious and capable individuals into meaningful contact with middle-class church members who operate as role models for the less talented persons who seek to move upward. That prestige and sometimes money come so easily in these circles may be a factor militating against a pattern of delaying gratifications and seeking mobility into professional and semi-professional pursuits through higher education.

Lower-class families and institutions are constantly on the move, for in recent years the Negro lower class has suffered from projects to redevelop the inner city. By historic accident, the decision to check the expansion of physical deterioration in metropolitan areas came at a time when Negroes were the main inhabitants of sub-standard housing. (If urban redevelopment had been necessary sixty years ago immigrants, not Negroes, would have suffered.) In protest against large-scale demolition of areas where they live, Negroes have coined a slogan, "Slum clearance is Negro clearance." They resent the price in terms of the inconvenience thrust upon them in order to redevelop American cities, and the evidence shows that, in some cities, there is no net gain in improved housing after relocation.

At the opposite pole from the Negro lower class in both life styles and life chances is the small Negro upper class whose solid core is a group in the professions, along with well-to-do businessmen who have had some higher education, but including, also, a scattering of individuals who have had college training but do not have a job commensurate with their education. These men and their spouses and children form a cohesive upper-class stratum in most Negro communities. Within this group are individuals who maintain some type of contact—though seldom any social relations—with members of the local white power élite; but whether or not they participate in occupational associations with their white peers depends upon the region of the country in which they live. (It is from this group that Negro "Exhibit A's" are recruited when white liberals are carrying on campaigns to "increase interracial understanding.") They must always think of themselves as symbols of racial advancement as well as individuals, and they often provide the basic leadership at local levels for organizations such as the N.A.A.C.P. and the Urban League. They must lend sympathetic support to the more militant civil rights organizations, too, by financial contributions, if not action.

The life styles of the Negro upper class are similar to those of the white upper *middle* class, but it is only in rare instances that Negroes have been incorporated into the clique and associational life of this group or have intermarried into it. (Their participation in activities of the white upper class occurs more often than with those whites who have similar life styles because of Negro upper-class participation as members of various civic boards and interracial associations to which wealthy white people contribute.) Living "well" with highly developed skills, having enough money to travel, Negroes at this social level do not experience victimization in the same fashion as do the members of the lower class. Their victimization flows primarily from the fact that the social system keeps them "half in and half out," preventing the free and easy contact with their occupational peers which they need; and it often keeps them from making the kind of significant intellectual and social contributions to the national welfare that they might make if they were white. (They are also forced to experience various types of nervous strain and dissipation of energy over petty annoyances and deprivations which only the sensitive and the cultivated feel. Most barbershops, for instance, are not yet desegregated, and taxi drivers, even in the North, sometimes refuse Negro passengers.)

The Negro upper class has created a social world of its own in which a universe of discourse and uniformity of behavior and outlook are maintained by the interaction on national and local levels of members of Negro Greek-letter fraternities and sororities, college and alumni associations, professional associations, and civic and social clubs. It is probable that if all caste barriers were dropped, a large proportion of the Negro upper class would welcome complete social integration, and that these all-Negro institutions would be left in the hands of the Negro middle class, as the most capable and sophisticated Negroes moved into the orbit of the general society. Their sense of pride and dignity does not even allow them to imagine such a fate, and they pursue their social activities and play their roles as "race leaders" with little feeling of inferiority or deprivation, but always with a tragic sense of the irony of it all.

The Negro middle class covers a very wide income range, and whatever cohesion it has comes from the network of churches and social clubs to which many of its members devote a great deal of time and money. What sociologists call the Negro middle class is merely a collection of people who have similar life styles and aspirations, whose basic goals are "living well," being "respectable," and not being crude. Middle-class Negroes, by and large, are not concerned about mobility into the Negro upper class or integration with whites. They want their "rights" and "good jobs," as well as enough money to get those goods and services which make life comfortable. They want to expand continuously their level of consumption. But they also desire "decent" schools for their children, and here the degree of victimization experienced by Negroes is most clear and the ambivalence toward policies of change most sharp. Ghetto schools are, on the whole, inferior.

Awareness of the poor quality of education grew as the protest movement against *de facto* school segregation in the North gathered momentum. But while the fight was going on, doubt about the desirability of forcing the issue was always present within some sections of the broad Negro middle class. Those in opposition asked, "Are we not saying that our teachers can't teach our own children as well as whites can, or that our children can't learn unless they're around whites? Aren't we insulting ourselves?" Those who want to stress Negro history and achievement and to use the schools to build race pride also express doubts about the value of mixed schools. In fact, the desirabilitiy of race consciousness and racial solidarity seems to be taken for granted in this stratum, and sometimes there is an expression of contempt for the behavior of whites of their own and lower income levels. In the present period one even occasionally hears a remark such as "Who'd want to be integrated with *those* awful white people?"

A sober analysis of the civil rights movement would suggest . . . , that the striking fact about all levels of the Negro community is the absence of "false consciousness," and the presence of a keen awareness of the extent of their victimization, as well as knowledge of the forces which maintain it. Not lack of knowledge but a sense of powerlessness is the key to the Negro reaction to the caste-class system.

Few Negroes believe that Black Ghettos will disappear within the next two decades despite much talk about "open occupancy" and "freedom of residence." There is an increasing tendency among Negroes to discuss what the quality of life could be within Negro communities as they grow larger and larger. At one extreme this interest slides over into Black Nationalist reactions such as the statement by a Chicago Negro leader who said, "Let all of the white people flee to the suburbs. We'll show them that the Black Man can run the second largest city in America better than the white man. Let them go. If any of them want to come back and integrate with *us* we'll accept them."

It is probable that the Black Belts of America will increase in size rather than decrease during the next decade, for no city seems likely to commit itself to "open occupancy." And even if a race-free market were to appear, Negroes would remain segregated unless drastic changes took place in the job ceiling and income gap. Controlled integration will probably continue, with a few upper- and upper-middle-class Negroes trickling into the suburbs and into carefully regulated mixed neighborhoods and mixed buildings within the city limits. (5) The basic problem of the next decade will be how to change Black Ghettos into relatively stable and attractive "colored communities." Here the social implications of low incomes become decisive.

Social Implications of the Job Ceiling and the Income Gap

Nowhere is direct victimization of Negroes more apparent than with respect to the job ceiling and the income gap; but indirect victimization which is a consequence of direct victimization is often less obvious. For instance, it has been mentioned that family incomes for Negroes are lower than for whites; but family income figures are inadequate tools for careful sociological analysis unless we know which, and how many, members of a family labor to earn a given income. In 1960, half of the white families were being supported by a husband only, while just a few more than a third of the Negro families could depend solely upon the earnings of one male breadwinner. In six out of ten nonwhite families where both a husband and wife were present, two or more persons worked; yet less than half of the white families had both husband and wife working. But even in those families which commanded an income of over $7,000.00 a year, twice as many nonwhite wives had to help earn it as white. (6) One not unimportant consequence is that a smaller proportion of Negro than white wives at this income level can play roles of unpaid volunteers in civic and social work, a fact which should be remembered by those who criticize Negroes in these income brackets for not doing more to "elevate their own people."

One of the most important effects of the income gap and the job ceiling has been the shaping of social class systems within Negro communities which differ markedly in their profiles from those of the surrounding white society. Negro class structure is "pyramidal," with a large lower class, a somewhat smaller middle class, and a tiny upper class (made up of people whose income and occupations would make them only middle class in the white society). White class profiles tend to be "diamond shaped," with small lower and upper classes and a large middle class. Unpromising "life chances" are reflected in inferior "life styles," and Black Ghettos are on the whole "rougher" and exhibit a higher degree of social disorganization than do white communities.

The job ceiling and the income gap do not create classways—for these reflect educational levels and cultural values, as well as the economic situation—but job ceiling and income gap do set the limits for realization of class values. It is a fact of American life (whether one approves of it or not) that as long as Negroes are predominantly lower-class they will, as a group, have low esteem. Yet, Negroes are victimized in the sense that the job ceiling and the income gap make it more difficult for them than for whites to maintain middle-class standards equivalent to those obtaining among whites. A given life style demands a minimum level of income, but it is evident that Negroes are victimized in the sense that their effort as reflected in the acquisition of an education does not bring equal rewards in terms of purchasing power, for they have less to spend than their white counterparts at any given educational level. Nonwhite family heads in 1960 had a smaller median income than whites for every educational level. (7) [Over a decade later, this tendency has still not changed.]

In a sense, getting an education "pays off" for Negroes as for all other Americans; but while some individuals "get ahead" of other Negroes, education has not yet raised their earning power to the level of whites with equivalent training. In fact, the average income for a nonwhite family with a male head who had finished high school was less than that of a white male head who had finished only the eighth grade. Since any aspects of the caste-class system which make it more difficult for Negroes than for whites to achieve middle-class norms of family behavior retard the process of eventual "integration," the income differential and the necessity for more members of the family to work operate in this negative fashion. Even more serious in determining deviations from general middle-class family norms is the manner in which both income distribution and the occupational structure function to reinforce the number of families without fathers and to lower the prestige of Negro males *vis-à-vis* their mates, prospective mates, and children. Thus a pattern of male insecurity which originated under slavery persists into the present. In fact, the struggle of Negro men, viewed as a group, to attain economic parity with Negro women has, up to the present, been a losing fight. Norval Glenn, in an exhaustive study of this problem, (8) has concluded that "Among full-time workers, non-white females were, in 1959, less disadvantaged relative to whites than were non-white males." Women were obtaining employment at a relatively faster rate than men and sustained a more rapid proportionate increase in income between 1939 and 1959. According to Glenn, there was an actual reversal in the income growth pattern of Negro males and females during a twenty-year period, and he notes that if their respective rates remain the same it will take twice as long for Negro males to catch up with white males as for Negro women to catch up with white women (93 years to achieve occupational equality and 219 to achieve equality of income). This is a case of *relative* deprivation, of course, but is significant nevertheless. An impressive body of evidence indicates that rather serious personality distortions result from the female dominance so prevalent in the Negro subculture, since the general norms of the larger society stress the opposite pattern as more desirable.

The interplay between caste evaluations and economic and ecological factors has tended not only to concentrate a low-income Negro population within ghettos, but has also concentrated a significant proportion of them in vast public housing projects—sometimes "high rise." In the 1930's public housing projects were often exciting experiments in interracial living, but there has been a tendency in many cities for them to become ghettos within ghettos. Within housing projects as well as out, a small hard core of mothers without husbands and a larger group of youth without jobs are developing a pattern which social psychologist Frederick Strodtbeck has called "the poverty-dependency syndrome." Here and there an integrated program of professional family services has proved its usefulness, but, in general, family case-work becomes a mere "holding operation."

Only the future will tell whether a large-scale "Poverty Program" coordinated through federally sponsored agencies will break the interlocking vicious circles which now victimize urban Negro populations. The dominant pattern in the American economic system has never been one of racial segregation. In fact, the racial division of labor has always involved considerable close personal contact, while demanding that Negroes play subordinate occupational roles carrying the lesser rewards in terms of economic power and social prestige. Doctrines of racial inferiority originated as dogmas to defend the use of African slave labor and were later used by white workers to defend their own privileged position against Negro competition. Trade union restrictionism reinforces employer preference in maintaining a job ceiling. Often, even when an employer decided it was profitable to use Negro labor, white workers used intimidation or violence against both white employer and black employee.

Access to new roles in the economic structure has occurred during periods of a great shortage of labor, as in the North during both world wars. Negroes entered at the bottom of the hierarchy, but were "last hired and first fired." Yet the job ceiling *was* raised, and, beginning with the organization of industrial unions in the 1930's and reaching a climax in the civil rights movement of the 1960's, ideological factors have reinforced economic interest in breaking the job ceiling. Now, for the first time in American history the full weight of top leadership in labor, industry, and government has been thrown in the direction of "fair employment practices," and public opinion is tolerating an all-out drive against job discrimination (partly because the economy is still expanding). [Now that this expansion seems to be largely curtailed, it remains to be seen if public opinion will *still* be in favor of job equality.] Yet so drastic are the effects of the past victimization of the Negro that any decisive alteration in the caste-class structure without more drastic measures seems remote. Thomas Pettigrew, after an analysis of recent changes, concludes:

> At the creeping 1950–1960 rate of change, non-whites in the United States would not attain equal proportional representation among clerical workers until 1992, among skilled workers until 2005, among professionals until 2017, among sales workers until 2114, and among business managers and proprietors until 2730! (9)

"In Sickness and in Death"

The consequences of being at the bottom in a caste-class system are revealed clearly in comparative studies of morbidity, mortality, and longevity, the latter being a particularly sensitive index to the physical well-being of groups. Comparing Negroes and whites with respect to longevity, Thomas Pettigrew notes that:

> At the turn of this century, the average non-white American at birth had a life expectancy between 32 and 35 years, 16 years less than that of the average white American. By 1960, this life expectancy had risen from 61 to 66 years. . . . But while the percentage gain in life expectancy for Negroes over these sixty odd years has been twice that of whites, there is still a discrepancy of six to eight years. . . . (10)

In other words, Negroes were "catching up," but, as a Department of Labor study pointed out in 1962, they ". . . had arrived by 1959 at about the longevity average attained by whites in 1940." (11) They were twenty years behind in the race toward equality of longevity.

Differences in longevity reflect differences in morbidity rates. Among the communicable diseases, for instance, the Negro tuberculosis rate is three times greater than that of whites, and the rates for pneumonia and influenza are also higher. The incidence of venereal disease is substantially higher among Negroes, although the Public Health Service figure of a syphilis rate ten times larger than that for whites has been questioned in Dr. Ann Pettigrew's study. (12) Twice as many Negro children per thousand as white children suffer from measles, meningitis, diphtheria, and scarlet fever.

Given such differences between Negroes and whites in the incidence of specific diseases, it is not surprising to find that the *death* rate from childhood diseases is six times higher among Negroes than whites and that the tuberculosis death rate is four times higher in all age-groups. (13)

The analysis of mortality rates provides one tool for studying the effects of the caste-class system which victimizes the Negro population. A United States government report for the year 1963 noted that "The age pattern of mortality . . . as in previous years, is similar for each of the color-sex groups—high rates in infancy, lower rates until the minimum is reached during grade-school age, then rising rates for the older age-groups." (14) Although the *pattern* was the same, there were racial differentials in the actual rates; for instance, "The relative increases in the 1963 death rates over the prior years were slightly greater for non-white persons than for white. . . ."

Two causes of death on the list for nonwhite males are probably directly related to the caste situation. The death rate for hypertensive heart disease is over twice that for whites and ranks fifth as a cause of death, compared to ninth for whites. Thomas Pettigrew, commenting on all types of hypertension, notes that some students feel that it is related to "psychosocial influences" and that, with regard to the high rates for Negroes, ". . . the problem of repressing hostility against whites . . . may be an important factor." (15) A homicide death rate nine times higher than that for whites, and appearing among the ten leading causes of death for nonwhite males, reflects the overt terror in the Black Belt, the explosions of in-caste aggression, and the anomic lower-class situation, as well as the distinctive ethos of the Negro subculture where crimes of passion among the lower-class are not condemned to the extent that they are in some other segments of American society.

It was once both fashionable and scientifically respectable to explain these differences [in mortality] in terms of differential racial susceptibility to various diseases, but as Thomas Pettigrew points out:

> The many improvements in his situation since 1900 rendered a dramatic increment in the Negro's health, providing solid evidence that corrosive poverty and inadequate medical care were the reasons for his short life span in the past . . . this difference [between Negro and white rates] can be traced to the diseases which are treatable, preventable and unnecessary. (16)

This is now the generally accepted view among serious students of the problem, and "corrosive poverty" and "inadequate medical care" are aspects of the victimization to which Negroes have been subjected. Further improvement in the health status of Negroes depends upon the eradication of poverty and all its accompanying side effects as well as upon access to adequate medical care.

Much of the "corrosive poverty" has been associated with life in the cotton fields, the logging camps, the mines, and the small-town slums of a poverty-striken South. Conditions were bad for most people, and the caste-system made them worse for the Negro. Dr. Ann Pettigrew has presented convincing evidence that the massive shift of Negro population into Northern and Western cities during the past two decades has resulted in some health gains for the Negro, and these gains have been due largely to greater access to medical advice and medical care. (17) But, the differentials are still large, even in the North, especially for tuberculosis, pneumonia, and venereal diseases. "Ghettoization," with its associated overcrowding, has been one important factor in keeping these rates high; but for these, as well as for other ailments, hospital discrimination is a primary factor limiting access to adequate medical care.

Hospital discrimination is only one facet of a complex process involving both direct and indirect victimization which leads to a lower level of physical and mental well-being among Negroes and which is reflected in morbidity and mortality rates. Health hazards for most of the Negro population begin even before birth, and they affect both mother and child. These hazards are greatest in the rural South, but they exist in urban situations as well, both Northern and Southern. Premature births occurred 50 per cent more frequently among Negroes than among whites during 1958–1959 and maternal mortality rates among Negroes were four times higher. (18) A higher proportion of Negro mothers failed to receive prenatal care, and a higher proportion died in childbirth. The most authoritative testimony on the disadvantaged position of the Negro expectant mother has been supplied by an eminent obstetrician, Dr. Phillip F. Williams, who has called attention to the fact that "one survey of maternal mortality is cited which found errors in judgment and technique as well as neglect on the part of the physician, as much as fifty per cent more frequently in the case of Negro than white mothers." He pointed out, too, that Negro women who were pregnant and those who had babies were victims of a set of interlocking conditions which included a lack of concern by husbands and putative fathers, a relatively high exposure to gonorrhea and syphilis, and, in the South ". . . a scarcity of physicians that has resulted in an inferior grade of attendance at birth (the untrained midwife). . . ." (19) In both North and South, hospital facilities are still inadequate and all of these factors combine to create a situation ". . . more or less adversely affecting the chances of survival of the Negro mother at childbirth." They affect the chances of the baby's surviving, too. Studies made soon after World War II revealed that, for Negroes as compared with whites, fewer Negro babies were delivered in hospitals and therefore more of them died at birth or during the first year after (and more died before they could be born, too).

Immunization of children was less common among Negroes and childhood diseases more prevalent and more often fatal. (20) Negro children, on the average, received fewer of the benefits of deliberately planned feeding, and fewer parents, in proportion, ate according to the more advanced nutritional standards.

Insofar as the job ceiling, the income gap, and ghettoization preserve and reinforce lower-class behavior patterns among Negroes to a greater extent than in the general society, the general health status of the Negro will be affected. For instance, a less adequate nutritional level than is found among whites is one factor often cited in accounting for the poorer average health status of Negroes. It is conceivable that Negroes could improve their nutritional status immediately by altering their present patterns of food consumption, but this is likely to occur less as a result of education and propaganda than as a by-product of changes in the caste-class situation. Except in wartime or during depressions, food habits are among the most difficult to change, unless change is related to mobility strivings. Maximizing the opportunity for Negroes to achieve the values and norms of the general American middle class is likely to do more to change the eating habits of the Negro population than all of the written or spoken exhortations of home economists or the most seductive of television commercials. A shift in social class supplies the motivation to change, and such a shift is dependent upon an increase in the number and proportion of Negroes entering white collar occupations.

Maintaining a style of living consonant with any occupational roles demands a minimum level of income. Success in improving the health status of the Negro population may ultimately depend upon an indirect rather than frontal assault. One student of the problem gives us a clue to the strategy when he observes that ". . . the much lower income level of the American Negro, to the extent that it is a measure of standard of living, explains, in part at least, the differences in health status and longevity between whites and non-whites in the United States." (21) Carefully controlled studies "point up the intimate relationship between physical illness and economic . . ." (22) to use Dr. Ann Pettigrew's expression. Economic factors not only partially explain, or serve as indices of, the causes of divergent morbidity and mortality rates, but they also give us the clues to a strategy for change, namely, working toward a continuously rising standard of living. Whether hope or pessimism is warranted depends upon the possibility of drastically changing the economic status of the Negro over the next decade, of eliminating economic "victimization."

Closing the income gap is crucial, or alternatively, the provision of a subsidy for medical services. Large masses of Negroes will never become members of the white-collar class, but better job opportunities in commerce and industry will place many of them in a position to benefit from privately sponsored health and insurance plans. These will be of maximum benefit, however, only if hospital discrimination is eliminated. Also, the wider extension of adequate medical care to all citizens through the use of public funds, and the more effective use of social workers and educators, will automatically benefit those Negroes who are not upwardly mobile.

Chronic illness, as well as frequent periods of sickness, not only results in loss of man-hours of production, but also increases stress and strain in interpersonal relations and deprives individuals of the maximum amount of pleasure to be derived from a sense of physical well-being and from recreation and pleasurable interaction with other human beings. Insofar as the general health level of Negroes is lower than that of whites they suffer more from these deprivations. Tendencies to escape from pain and its consequences by habitual use of alcohol and drugs, or the anodyne of excessive preoccupation with the supernatural world, may be related to the general health situation within the Negro lower class. These less tangible and immeasurable disabilities are as real as the financial burdens imposed by sickness.

The Identification Problem

Some of the most damaging forms of indirect victimization manifest themselves at the psychological level. The Black Ghetto and the job ceiling are the key variables in accounting for differences in morbidity and mortality rates, and for the persistence of subcultural behavior patterns which deviate from middle-class norms. At the subjective level they also determine the crucial points of social reference for the individual Negro when answering the questions "Who am I today?" and "What will I be tomorrow?" The Black Ghetto forces him to identify as a Negro first, an American second, and it gives him geographical "roots." The job ceiling is an ever present reminder that there are forces at work which make him a second-class American. But the Black Ghetto and the job ceiling are only two components of a caste-class system now undergoing revolutionary transformation —an institutional complex which includes the courts, schools, churches, voluntary associations, media of mass communication, and a network of family units. Like all other persons, the individual Negro receives his orientation to this social nexus first from his family and later from his peer group. Exposure to schools and the mass media continues the process of socialization and personality formation while membership in voluntary associations provides a tie to the class system and constitutes an aid to upward mobility.

The white middle class is the reference group for those who are mobile; yet the entire system operates to emphasize identity with "The Race," since defensive solidarity must be maintained against the white world. Inner conflicts are inevitable; and conventional, as well as idiosyncratic, adjustments to this situation have been thoroughly studied. Ann Pettigrew suggests that ". . . the perception of relative deprivation, the discrepancy between high aspirations and actual attainments . . . is a critical psychological determinant of mental disorder. And certainly racial discrimination acts to bar the very achievements which the society encourages individuals to attempt." (23) A disparity in psychosis rates reflects this discrepancy, but for most Negroes the reaction to oppression is less severe. Neither insanity nor suicide is a *typical* Negro reaction.

Both Negroes and whites are "victims" of one persisting legacy of the slave trade—the derogation of "negroidness." The idea that a dark skin indicates intellectual inferiority is rapidly passing, but at the esthetic level derogatory appraisal of thick lips, kinky hair, and very dark skin is still prevalent. That many Negroes reject their own body image is evident from advertisements for skin lighteners in the major Negro publications, and Negro children in experimental situations begin to reject brown dolls for white ones before the age of five. The ever present knowledge that one's negroid physiognomy is evaluated as "ugly" lowers self-esteem and, therefore, weakens self-confidence. The rise of new African states has given a psychological "lift" to those American Negroes who still look more African than *metis,* but extreme Negro physical traits are still a source of inner disquiet—especially for women. (There is no equivalent in America of the African cult of *negritude* whose poets idealize the black woman.) [On the other hand, some of these negative attitudes may be changing in the black community. We often hear "Black is beautiful." Among certain black groups, the hair is left natural and not processed. So Drake's comment may need to be updated for the 1970's.] These negative esthetic appraisals are a part of a larger stereotype-complex which equates Africa with primitiveness and savagery and considers Negro ancestry a "taint." A frontal assault on a world-wide scale is necessary to undo this propaganda of the slave era which still exists as a form of cultural lag which has lost even the excuse of the functional utility it once had in rationalizing an integral part of the Western economic system—Negro slavery.

Negroes in America, as a numerical minority, always have a feeling of being "on the outside looking in," of not being "in the main stream." Yet, the mere fact of being only one in ten does not automatically generate this feeling; the "victimization" flows, rather, from the values of the majority who refuse to accept every individual upon his own merit, but insist upon ascription of status on the basis of membership in a racial group. (Bahia, Brazil, presents an interesting case where the opposite is true, where individual achievement can almost completely over-ride racial origin.) (24) This sense of alienation is reinforced by traditional or deliberate omission of Negroes from the decision-making process. That they are absent from the boards of major corporations is not surprising; but it is surprising that they are virtually absent from the boards of foundations and professional associations. Only in the realm of public administration and the world of sports and entertainment are Negroes present in sufficient numbers to be "visible," and to serve as role models for Negro youth.

These omissions are particularly crucial in a society where numerous illustrated publications function as the image-makers. A Negro child seldom sees a person like himself in an advertisement or in illustrations accompanying fiction. The children in the textbooks are all white. The image of the powerful, the desirable, the admirable is set very early as "white." There is an increasing awareness of the seriousness of this problem, and by 1964 the television industry was making a half-hearted attempt to use a few Negroes in commercials, and one or two Northern cities were experimenting with "integrated textbooks." But still, Negro newspapers and magazines alone cater to this hunger to see the Negro image in print. These publications also give prominence to whatever interracial participation is taking place, but they cannot eliminate the feeling of resentment over exclusion from the collective representations of the larger society. [Although the Negro is still not represented in proportion to his percentage of the population, nevertheless there are more blacks seen in the media and in textbooks now than at the time this article was written.]

Leaders in the civil rights movement frequently refer to the process of desegregation and integration as having the goal of "bringing Negroes into the main stream." This sense of isolation from "the main stream" was given poetic expression by the late Dr. W. E. B. Du Bois in the 1890's when he spoke of living behind, or within, "The Veil." This isolation not only generates distorted perceptions of the total society and occasionally bizarre definitions of situations, but it also results in cognitive crippling. The communication flow needed to provide data for rational decision making is often impeded. Incomplete information is available for "playing the game" the way it is played in various segments of the larger society, and in a highly mobile society it is all-important to know "who is who" and "what is what." There is some evidence, for instance, to indicate that lower-middle-class and lower-class Negro parents often have high aspirations for their children but have no clear idea how to realize them. Negro students in segregated colleges and high schools are also often woefully ignorant of opportunities and techniques for succeeding. (25)

One cannot be mobile without learning the professional codes and the folkways of other social strata. It was this which the Supreme Court had in mind when it ruled some years ago that a separate law school for Negroes cut the student off from those contacts which were necessary to make a person a first-class lawyer and therefore could not meet the criterion of equality. It is this contact which most Negro physicians are denied. Also, in a society where the social ritual is so much a part of the business world, Negroes are generally not in a position to secure the cues and tips needed for competition on a basis of complete equality. If they cannot meet their peers at professional meetings and in the informal gatherings of persons who pursue similar occupations and professions, they, of necessity, will see only "through a glass darkly." Very clever and ambitious individuals (and persistent ones) sometimes rip aside "The Veil," but such persons are rare within any ethnic group. Most individuals remain victims of the communication blockage, and special efforts will be necessary to open the channels of communication. Participation across race lines with persons in similar occupations is the first step toward structural integration.

In social system which forces Negroes to think of themselves *first* as Negroes and only second as Americans, a problem of "double identification" is posed for those who are partially integrated. Guilt feelings sometimes arise over the charge hurled by others that they are "running away from the Race." Negroes who represent the country abroad are exposed to the criticism of Africans and Asians as being "the tool of the white man." Personnel officers, political leaders, and work-supervisors are always open to the charge that they are "Uncle Toms," have "sold out," or have "forgotten the Race." This problem will be intensified if the process of integration at upper levels of power and prestige is not accompanied by the complete disappearance of racial barriers to upward mobility, or if the masses of Negroes are doomed to be America's permanent lower class. In the meanwhile, the rise of Malcolm X and the appeal of the Black Muslims and various local Black Nationalist groups suggest that the lower classes and lower middle classes can work their way out of the problem of double identification by rejecting "white" values and by proudly proclaiming their psychological independence. Such a solution is not available to the more sophisticated Negroes, but the possibility is not to be excluded that, since America insists upon limited integration rather than complete acceptance, increased identification of educated Negroes with some aspects of the Negro subculture and with the cultural renaissance taking place in Africa may become the norm. (26)

The Condition of Powerlessness

The problem of "identification" is crucial, but Charles Silberman in *Crisis in Black and White* (27) puts his finger upon the most critical aspect of Negro-white relations in the United States when he stresses the psychological effect of being "powerless." Negroes realize that, as a minority in "the white man's country," they do not set the rules of the game. Unlike Negroes in Africa and the West Indies they do not fight for national independence, but rather for "desegregation" and "integration," and they can attain these goals only if the white majority sanctions them as legitimate and desirable. "Integration," in the final analysis, also means that the Negro community must increasingly become more middle-class in values and behavior if it is to win respect and approval. Negroes do not determine the ends for which they struggle, nor the means. The most they can expect is an increasingly greater share in the *joint* determination of their future. The problem of maintaining dignity and some autonomy in such a situation is, for sensitive personalities, a continuous one, even within the civil rights movement, for white friends, even in liberal-left circles, often strive to bend Negroes to their will and not to ask their advice as co-workers.

In the past, this sense of "powerlessness" to determine their own destiny or to change their position in the caste-class system has been one important factor in accentuating in-group aggression among lower class Negroes, in the diversion of energy and financial resources into the over-elaboration of the church-voluntary association complex, and in the development of those styles of life which E. Franklin Frazier portrayed so unsympathetically in *Black Bourgeoisie.* Black Belt crime, juvenile delinquency, and cynical exploitation have also been interpreted by some sociologists as one reaction to a state of "powerlessness." Within the lower class and lower middle class, hostility and resentment become "socialized" for a few in the form of Black Nationalism and take organized form in movements such as the Black Muslims. Among the rootless masses, the anger flowing from frustration bursts forth periodically in verbal abuse and violent assault, in arson and looting, in attacks upon policemen and property—thus the tragedy of Harlem, Rochester, and Philadelphia in 1964 and of Los Angeles and Chicago in 1965 [and of many other cities since then]. The feeling of having made the conquest of power, of being in control of their own fate, if only for a moment, is symbolized in a widely circulated photograph of jubilant Negroes giving the V-for-Victory sign on top of a shattered police car in Los Angeles. But these Black Belt explosions underscore a basic fact—that no revolution can follow the storming of the Bastille by Negroes in America. . . .

Conventional politics has been the most realistic approach to gaining at least the semblance of power. Recent demographic trends, including the flight of whites to the suburbs, have placed some Negro communities in a strategic position to play "balance of power" politics more effectively, and the civil rights movement may result in increased political power for Negroes in the South. Yet, all Negro leaders know the limits of their ability to wield decisive political influence. (And in the world of "big business" their influence is even less.) Silberman has suggested the importance—cathartic and practical—of grass-roots movements, with "middle-level" leadership, fighting for limited goals where results can be achieved, and Thomas Pettigrew has stressed the psychologically liberating effect of participation in the civil rights movement. (28) The feed-back in terms of an increased incentive to secure more education or to get better jobs can be sustained only if society actually provides the rewards in terms of expanded occupational mobility. Then sense of being powerless can disappear, however, only if the social system eventually changes to the extent that Negroes will not need to organize *as Negroes* to defend their interests and if color ceases to be a factor in membership in the "power structure." Riots will cease only when Americans allow Black Ghettos to dissolve.

The Myth of "Separate but Equal"

Negroes have been "victimized" throughout the three hundred fifty years of their presence on the North American continent. The types of social systems which have organized their relations with whites have been varied —over two hundred years of slavery and indenture, ten years of post-Civil War Reconstruction in the South, and eighty years of experimentation with a theory of "separate but equal" ostensibly designed to replace caste relations with those of class. The "separate but equal" doctrine has now been repudiated by the federal government and a broad section of public opinion as unjust and inimical to the national welfare. The period of desegregation has begun. Yet, the legacy of the past remains. As a transition to some new, and still undefined system of race relations takes place, it is relevant to examine the extent to which victimization persists, probing for its more subtle and covert manifestations. An estimate, too, should be made of whether or not what Merton has called "the unintended consequences of purposive social action" carry a potential for new forms of victimization.

By 1900 the doctrine had become firmly established that it was desirable for Negroes and whites to be members of two functionally related segments of a bi-racial society in which families, intimate friendship groups, and voluntary associations (including churches) would be separate, although members of both races were participating in a common economic system and political order. Both Negro and white leaders emphasized the point that "social equality" was not a Negro aspiration, and Booker T. Washington's famous Atlanta Compromise address delivered in 1895 made this point very explicit with his symbolism of the five fingers, separate and distinct, but joined together at the palm.

The theory of "separate but equal" visualized a future in which Negroes would gradually acquire wealth and education on such a scale as to develop a social-class system within the Negro community paralleling that of the white community. Then, as the sociologist Robert Park once phrased it, Negroes and whites would "look over and across" at each other, not "up and down." Defenders of "bi-racialism" believed that although institutional life—including schools and neighborhoods—should remain separate, Negroes should be allowed to compete freely for jobs and should gradually acquire the full voting rights which they had lost in the South after 1875. It was considered unwise, however, to make a frontal assault upon segregation in public places since the key to the ultimate dissolution or transformation of the caste system lay in the acquisition of education and economic well-being—not in protest. The "correct" behavior of an enlarged Negro middle class would eventually win acceptance by the white middle class. The doctrine of "separate but equal" was given legal sanction in a number of Supreme Court decisions, the most famous being that of *Plessy vs. Ferguson,* and it became the operating ideology among Southern white liberals between the two world wars.

During the first decade after World War II the doctrine of "separate but equal" was abandoned as a guide to the formulation of public policy insofar as the armed forces, public transportation, public accommodations, and public schools were concerned. Experience between the two world wars had demonstrated that, while it might be theoretically possible to achieve equality within the framework of a segregated school system in the South, it seemed impossible in actual practice. In the field of public transportation, no matter how many shiny new coaches replaced the old rickety "Jim Crow" coaches, Negroes did not consider them "equal," and they never ceased to be resentful that there were two American armies instead of one. The cost of duplicating facilities to make public accommodations and schools truly equal would have been exorbitant even if Negroes welcomed the idea. Thus, a demand for change was in the air when the historic 1954 decision requiring school desegregation was taken, and the Court cut through to a fundamental question which had often been evaded: whether or not it was possible to maintain any kind of *forced* segregation in an open society without pejorative implications. Did not the very insistence upon separation imply inferiority? The caste-class system organizing race relations was recognized for what it really was—a system which, irrespective of the intent of individuals, resulted in the victimization of Negroes. Makers of national policy have now embarked upon a thoroughgoing program of desegregation coupled with an assault upon all institutionalized forms of racial discrimination. But the white public has not accepted the concept of "total integration."

Some Paradoxes of Progress

The abandonment of the doctrine of "separate but equal" has forced consideration of many provocative questions, such as: "Can the victimization resulting from unequal treatment of Negroes in the past be eliminated without preferential treatment for present-day victims?" There are those who contend that justice demands more than equality, that it requires a "revolutionary break-through" in the form of preferential hiring, distinctive programs of education, and special scholarship schemes. The existence of entrenched patterns of residential segregation also raises the question of the desirability and probability of the persistence of Negro neighborhoods and institutions. If *forced* separation eventually disappeared would separateness cease to be an index of victimization? Would it then lose its pejorative implications? Would the right to choose, if it ever came, mean that some Negroes will choose *not* to be "integrated" except in the economic and policital order?

New types of victimization are emerging which are not only indirect but are also unintended consequences of actions designed to eliminate victimization. For instance, in several Northern cities an earnest effort is being made to facilitate and speed up the process of residential desegregation at the middle-class level. Negroes whose incomes and life styles approximate those of the white middle class are accepted into neighborhoods and apartment buildings in limited numbers in order not to excite fear and panic among white residents. The goal, as one Chicago neighborhood association states it, is "an integrated neighborhood with high community standards," to reverse the process of ghettoization. However, without a commitment to "open occupancy" at the city level, attainment of this goal demands a neighborhood-by-neighborhood approach, which calls for studying "tipping points" and setting up "benign quotas" in order to maintain a "racial balance." It may also involve a program which forces all lower-class residents to leave irrespective of their color, while integrating a small number of middle-class Negroes into neighborhoods or specific apartment buildings.

One effective technique has been clearance of slums followed by rebuilding at a high enough rent level to keep the proportion of Negroes automatically very low. This process is frequently called "controlled integration." Actions such as these often result in the concentration of many lower-class Negroes into almost completely segregated public housing projects. What is gained for some in terms of better physical surroundings is lost in increased "ghettoization." Other displaced persons increase the degree of overcrowding in already overcrowded neighborhoods or filter into middle-class Negro neighborhoods and disorganize them.

Serious problems also arise within the middle class at the psychological level. Insofar as Negro families have to cooperate actively in setting and maintaining quotas on the number of Negroes who enter, and in eliminating lower-class Negroes from the neighborhood, they become vulnerable to attack by other Negroes. Some sensitive individuals suffer from a feeling of guilt over manipulating the situation to maintain exclusiveness; others feel a loss of dignity in carrying on continuous discussion about race with white people. They dislike dealing with themselves as "a problem." A few people simply withdraw from such "integrated" situations into the comfort of the middle-class "gilded ghetto." This situation is only a special case of a more general problem confronting some Negroes in this Era of Integration—how to reconcile being a "loyal Negro" or a "Race Man" with new middle-class interracial relations or new occupational roles.

Rapid and fairly complete "integration" of middle-class Negroes into neighborhoods, churches, educational, and voluntary associations could have a profound effect upon Negro institutional life, "skimming off the cream" of the Negro élites to the disadvantage of the larger Negro community. This would result in a kind of victimization of the Negro masses which would be permanent unless the conditions of life for the lower classes were drastically changed.

Unfortunately there are few signs of hope that the Negro masses will profit from current economic changes, for at the very moment when the civil rights movement has been most successful, and when access to training is being made more widely available to Negroes, forces are at work which could render these gains meaningless. Whitney Young, Jr., of the National Urban League, emphasizing economic problems facing Negroes, stated upon one occasion: "Unless we identify these problems and take steps to meet them, we will find the masses of Negroes five years from today with a mouthful of rights, living in hovels with empty stomachs." (29) [Now that it is more than five years later, it is unfortunate to note that Young's prophesy was apparently right. Overall gains for blacks are not that striking.] About 12 per cent of the nonwhite labor force were unemployed in 1960, twice the rate for white workers. In some urban areas it was between

15 and 20 per cent. It was higher for Negro men than for women. Unemployment rates are particularly high for Negro youth. In 1961, nonwhite boys and girls between fourteen and nineteen had the highest unemployment rate of any age-color group in the nation, while the unemployment rate for Negro high-school graduates between the ages of sixteen and twenty-one was twice that for white youth and higher than the rate for whites who had *not* attended high school. One out of five Negro high-school graduates were unable to find jobs. If high-school graduates face such a situation, the plight of the untrained Negro is likely to be even worse. It was estimated in 1964 that automation was wiping out about 40,000 unskilled jobs a week, the sector of industry where Negro workers are concentrated. This trend is likely to continue for some time. (30)

If Negroes are not to become a permanent *lumpen-proletariat* within American society as a result of social forces already at work and increased automation, deliberate planning by governmental and private agencies will be necessary. Continued emphasis upon "merit hiring" will benefit a few individuals, but, in the final analysis, structural transformations will have to take place. (31) There are those who feel that only a radical shift in American values and simultaneous adjustments of economy and society will wipe out, forever, the victimization of the Negro. If such a situation does occur it is not likely to be the result of any cataclysmic proletarian upheaval, but rather through drift and piece-meal pragmatic decisions. One straw in the wind has been raised to test the temper of the time. Gunnar Myrdal and twenty-nine other scholars, writers, and political scientists have released a statement on "The Cybernation Revolution, the Weaponry Revolution, and the Human Rights Revolution." In discussing the need for adjustment to the effects of largescale automation, they made a revolutionary suggestion:

> We urge, therefore, that society, through its appropriate legal and governmental institutions, undertake an unqualified commitment to provide every individual and every family with an adequate income as a matter of right. . . .

Should this ever happen, Negroes would, of course, profit even more than whites, but demands for radical reforms of this type have not arisen from within the Civil Rights Movement whose leaders generally accept a middle-class work ethic which is incompatible with such a solution. (32)

References

1. Thomas F. Pettigrew, *A Profile of the Negro American* (New York: Litton Educational Publishing Inc., 1964). Reprinted by permission of Van Nostrand Reinhold Company.

2. For a discussion of these concepts see Hans Gerth and C. Wright Mills, *From Max Weber: Essays in Sociology* (New York: Oxford University Press, 1946), chapter on "Caste, Class and Party."
3. St. Clair Drake and Horace R. Cayton, in *Black Metropolis* (New York: Harper & Row Publishers, 1962), use the term "Black Ghetto" to refer to the involuntary and exploitative aspect of the all-Negro community and "Bronzeville" to symbolize the more pleasant aspects of the segregated community. Robert C. Weaver, another Negro scholar, called his first book *The Negro Ghetto* (New York: Harcourt, Brace & World, 1948). The term is widely used by contemporary Negro leaders with pejorative implications.
4. Pettigrew, *Profile of the Negro American*, p. 190. His wife, Dr. Ann Pettigrew, M.D., collaborated with him on the chapter dealing with health.
5. A successful experiment in "controlled integration" has been described by Julia Abrahamson in *A Neighborhood Finds Itself* (New York: Harper & Row Publishers, 1959).
6. Jacob Schiffman, "Marital and Family Characteristics of Workers, March, 1962," in *Monthly Labor Review*, U.S. Department of Labor, Bureau of Labor Statistics, Special Labor Force Report No. 26 (January 1963).
7. *Ibid.*
8. Norval D. Glenn, "Some Changes in the Relative Status of American Nonwhites: 1940–1960," *Phylon*, 24, No. 2 (Summer 1963).
9. Pettigrew, *Profile of Negro American*, p. 188.
10. *Ibid.*, p. 99; see also Marcus S. Goldstein, "Longevity and Health Status of Whites and Non-Whites in the United States," *Journal of the National Medical Association*, 46, No. 2 (March 1954), p. 83. Among other factors, the author emphasizes the relationship between nutrition and racial mortality differentials.
11. Marion Haynes, "A Century of Change: Negroes in the U.S. Economy, 1860–1960," *Monthly Labor Review*, U. S. Department of Labor, Bureau of Labor Statistics (December 1962).
12. Pettigrew (*Profile of Negro American*, p. 87) comments that some research indicates that ". . . these group differences are inflated through disproportionate underreporting of whites. . . ."
13. The rates cited are from Pettigrew, *Profile of Negro American*, Chap. 4, "Negro American Health."
14. *Monthly Vital Statistics Report*, National Center for Health Statistics, U.S. Department of Health, Education and Welfare, Public Health Service, 13 (November 2, 1964), p. 8.
15. Pettigrew, *Profile of Negro American*, p. 96.
16. *Ibid.*, p. 99.
17. *Ibid.*, pp. 82–94, "Communicable Diseases," and pp. 97–98, "Economics and Physical Health."
18. Note Pettigrew, *Profile of Negro American*, p. 97, which cites "lack of prenatal care, poor family health education, inadequate diet and inexpert delivery" as factors.
19. Philip F. Williams, "Material Welfare and the Negro," *Journal of American Medical Association*, 132, No. 11 (November 16, 1946), pp. 611–14.
20. M. Gover and J. B. Yaukey, "Physical Impairments of Members of Low-Income Farm Families," *Public Health Reports*, 61, No. 4 (January 25, 1946), and Marion E. Altenderfer and Beatrice Crowther, "Relationship Between Infant Mortality and Socio-economic Factors in Urban Areas," *Public Health Reports*, 64, No. 11 (March 18, 1949), pp. 331–9.
21. Marcus S. Goldstein, "Longevity and Health Status," p. 93.
22. Dr. Ann Pettigrew cites a study carried out in Chicago, using 1950 data, in which, when Negroes and whites of the same economic level were compared, mortality rates were about the same although the rates for Negroes as a group when compared with those for whites as a group were higher. Other studies using the same body of data indicate sharp differences in mortality rates as between laborers and skilled workers among Negroes, a situation similar to that found among whites (Pettigrew, *Profile of Negro American*, p. 98).
23. *Ibid.*, p. 80.

24. The extent to which the pattern in Bahia, Brazil, differs from that in the United States is analyzed by Donald Pierson in *Negroes in Brazil* (Chicago: University of Chicago Press, 1942).

25. Wilson Record, "Counseling and Communication," *Journal of Negro Education,* 30, No. 4 (Fall 1961).

26. Note Harold Isaacs, *The New World of Negro Americans* (New York: Day, 1963), and St. Clair Drake, "To Hide My Face? An Essay on Pan Africanism and Negritude," in *Soon One Morning,* ed. Herbert Hill (New York: Alfred A. Knopf & Co, 1963).

27. Charles Silberman, *Crisis in Black and White* (New York: Random House, 1964).

28. Pettigrew, *Profile of Negro American,* pp. 161–168, "The New Role of the Equal Citizen."

29. Quoted by James Reston in a column, "The Ironies of History and the American Negro," *The New York Times,* May 15, 1964.

30. Pettigrew, *Profile of Negro American,* p. 169.

31. *Ibid.,* "Some Needed Societal Reforms," pp. 168–176.

32. Dr. Drake acknowledges with gratitude the assistance of Miss Odessa D. Thompson.

The Advantages of Black English
Roger D. Abrahams

Roger Abrahams points out to teachers in this article that not only is Black English a series of linguistic forms (see Chapter Three for this type of description) but that it is also an "entire system of speaking behavior" which contains non-verbal cues as well. He describes distinct differences between this black system and the system used by so-called standard English speakers, differences which can and do cause breakdowns in communication between the groups, including teachers and black students.

One of the major differences Abrahams describes is that of "performance." In black culture, speakers use their language to create a performance while in "mainstream" culture (see Hannerz) a distinction is made between performance (non-casual) and other interactions which are more casual in nature. He notes how in Black English performances the audience interacts much more with the speaker than it does in what Abrahams calls the "standard English" mode. He then shows how much deeper this distinction goes by describing standard English performance as a "thing," a distinct entity, while Black English performance is seen as a procss involving both speaker and audience in an on-going experience. One is more or less static; the other dynamic. And the Black English speaker (performer) who is good at performance has a great deal of status in the speech community. He is not a peripheral figure as are most verbal performers in mainstream society. Abrahams also describes briefly male-female differences in using Black English, men's talk often containing more stigmatized forms than women's talk.

Finally, the author suggests that teachers need to understand that the black expressive system he has described has endured despite white pressure to give it up because it is adaptable to black cultural needs and also is a solidarity device to express togetherness. The black child needs his Black English in order to be a part of his culture.

. . . The only way that the teacher can utilize Black English is first of all to *listen* to it; he must learn to recognize not only its basic linguistic features but also such elements as who is speaking to whom, for what purpose and to what effect, realizing that behavior observed in one situation with one age-group will change radically when the circumstances are al-

From *Dimension: Languages 70,* "The Advantages of Black English" by Roger D. Abrahams. Reprinted with permission of the Southern Conference On Language Teaching, 1970.

tered. It is such features which must be explored as a system if we are to understand the functional operations of Black English.

Every language, from the social point of view, is made up of a number of varieties, each designating and symbolizing membership in one segment of the speaking community. These varieties are codes, like baby or child talk, man or woman talk, which contain cuing features recognizable to members of the speaking community, and used by them to designate some grouping within their society. A variety may exist on a purely formal level, or on a casual level; it may be used in a wide range of communications situations. Each speaking system is made up of a number of these varieties, each of which is describable in terms of its own discrete performance traits. These discrete features are not hard to discover, as they are commonly conscious to both the primary users of the variety and to most other members of the community as well. One can easily elicit the basic features, for instance, of baby talk in middle-American English, as any informant could describe with little hesitation the major markers of this subsystem. Black English is like all other languages, when viewed from this perspective: the sum of its varieties.

Unfortunately, even those sociolinguists who have done the most precise reporting of Black English have not considered these different codes in their descriptions. Because such code-distinctions were not made, we are provided little idea from which variety or varieties these distinctly BE features have been derived. But this is not to fault these observers, only to point out the limitations of their perspective. What is needed is a framework in which the larger patterns of communicative interactions may be analysed, a framework which will not only bear on *linguistic* differences between Black English and standard English but also on the differences in the entire *system of speaking behavior.*

There are crucial differences between Black English and standard English * in regard to the rules, boundaries, and expectations carried into communicative encounters, and the means by which disruptions of these expectations are taken care of. Though there are differences on the linguistic level, there are numerous other devices of communication which differ in less immediately perceivable but equally far-reaching ways. The difference between eye-contact behaviors, for instance, has often been commented upon lately because failure to recognize the discrepancy has led many teachers to misunderstand and stereotype black students. The unwillingness of blacks to look a teacher in the eye has commonly been read as either a sign of inattention, or hostility, or embarrassment, or worse; but if the

---

* Black English and Standard English will be referred to as BE and SE in this article.

teacher had observed the behavior of black children at home he would have noted that such eye-aversion signals proper deference to older people. What is perhaps more important is that if a student, especially a teenager, *does* look the teacher in the eye, this might be better read as a sign of an impending, more overt display of hostility. There are, of course, numerous other inter-cultural failures of this sort, committed because of a lack of familiarity with such differences in BE behaviors—a lack arising from an unwillingness to acknowledge the existence of a different communications-decorum system, or simply from an assumption that the blacks operate in terms of no system at all.

There are many other failures of communications which stem from a misreading of some facet of BE. Gerald Suttles points out an example of this in interactions between Italians and Negroes in a Chicago slum neighborhood, centering on the use of "jive talk," one of the varieties of BE recognized by both blacks and whites as characteristically Afro-American:

> . . . The Italians seldom use any of this vocabulary even to the point of understanding it. In the case of "jive," however, the Italians do not regard language differences so much as an attempt to talk behind someone's back, "show off" one's knowledge of urban ways or display one's emancipation from the homely virtues of family, ethnic group, and neighbors. To the Italians, the use of "jive" often indicates a person who has scuttled the surest signs of human feeling and concern for the bonds that secure personal relations within the neighborhood. To the Negroes, . . . a familiarity with this youthful jargon is only a sign of a willingness to expand the magic circle of trust beyond that of family, ethnic group, and territorial compatriots. (1)

The point here is that speech differences exist in dimensions other than pronunciation or sentence structure, evidence of more deep-seated cultural disparities. Learning to understand one another goes far beyond the development of a mutually comprehensible universe of discourse, for there is a clash of values (linguistic and otherwise) as well as of style.

Another example of a failure of communication arising from such cultural differences recently came to my attention. In a classroom of black students one day recently, there was a good deal of uproar of the usual sort. The white teacher, seeking to bring the situation to a halt, saw one of the students opening his mouth and making communicative sounds, what she interpreted (and probably rightly) to be words. She thereupon called out his name and told him "to stop talking." His reply was "I wasn't talking." An extensive altercation then occurred because the student clung to his story. This episode, observed and reported to me by a black teacher-trainer raised in a lower class community, was interpreted by her as a failure in intercultural communication. The teacher was justified within her own frame of reference to refer to the boy's activities as "talking." But they obviously meant different things in their use of the word. What she meant was that he was speaking discrete words; what he seems to have meant was that to merit that accusation he would have had to have been commanding the attention of the others in the class, and that he therefore could not be accused of "talking," of being the instigator of the speaking event. He was saying, at least in part, that he was simply responding in an appropriate way to one of his peers who *was* "talking," he was answering "talk" with "sounds" (functionally analogous to the "amen-saying" of black sermonizing.)

BE is not then just a linguistic system; it is the expressive system of Black Culture. This system includes not only linguistic features, but also the numerous paralinguistic traits which are recognizably characteristic of black speech (elongation of words or raising pitch level for emphasis, use of a wide range of vocal effects from falsetto to false bass to growl, unexpected slowing or speeding of delivery, emphasizing unexpected syllables or words, and so on).

There are at least two sociolinguistic levels on which BE and SE differ in vital ways. On the sociocultural level, the disparity is felt in the different configuration of varieties within BE and in who uses what code with whom and for what purposes; this is the level on which one would investigate the range of varieties and the correlations between these varieties and the social segmentation within the speaking community. (In the case of BE, it would also, of necessity, include the ways in which features of BE are used to define the community of blacks vis-a-vis the white community.) The second important level is that of perspective or world view. BE and SE differences turn on the disparity between how the two groups organize their environments, especially with regard to what expectations are carried into a communicative encounter. (2)

In the black expressive system, life is constantly viewed as a performance and speech acts are judged accordingly. Where the SE universe of discourse makes a strong distinction between non-casual performances and casual interactions (such as conversations), this is a distinction simply not made in BE. Rather, *all* expressive behavior is judged as a performance—that is, in terms of its ability to affect onlookers, drawing them into some type of sympathetic participation. This point cannot be overemphasized. Performances, as in all societies, are judged first by the standards of appropriateness, and then as to whether the audience has been stimulated into participation. This is true of white audiences as well, but the style of participation for blacks differs enormously. BE performances call for more overt demonstrations of sympathetic involvement, through movement and sounds (Recall the student who was not "talking" but merely responding with sounds). Thus, there are differences both in terms of how the performer acts and how the audience reacts. For instance, an SE speaker will expect conversations to appear spontaneous even though this convention is not consciously carried into the encounter. (We come to know the rules only through the breaking of them, in situations of embarrassment or in social gaffes.) BE casual encounters, on the other hand, gravitate toward conscious stylization and the speaker therefore expects to be judged in terms of how well he invests his performance energies and uses his conversational devices. He knows that among other things his variety of BE will be judged by its appropriateness and that he will be judged in terms of his command of that variety. This is not just true of jive-talkers; the very women within the black community who most scorn that code, (regarding it as rude and rightly sensing it an attack on them) constantly remark on each other's control over the variety appropriate to their family-centered life-style.

The distinctions between different modes of performance, like song, dance, and speech, which are strongly felt in the SE system are not nearly so central in BE. Rather, there is a much stronger concern with modalities or qualities—like "cool," "hard," "heavy"—and with performance styles and strategies—like "jiving," "signifying," "marking" (mocking). Of importance here is that these focal terms characterize any mode of performance; jiving, for instance, is not just a verbal style but also a kinesthetic one—there is jiving dance, a jive-walk and so on. This reflects a performance environment in which song commonly elicits dance, and a speech may become a song. Mode distinctions simply are not important, while the total involvement of the participants is.

Perhaps the most important discrepancy between SE and BE is the distinctions made in SE but not in BE between performer and audience, speaker and hearer, and so on. In SE interactions attentive silence is expected on the part of the hearer, whether in conversation or virtuoso performance. Response is expected only when there is a cue given by the speaker or performer. There is consequently great psychic distance created between performer and audience in SE stylized interactions, a distance which is capitalized upon by the performer in the development of his virtuoso art. Any feedback in such a situation, unless it is under strong controls, is reacted to by the performer as a threat and will generally modify the effect of the participative interaction. This sense of removal has become progressively institutionalized with the greater reliance on media of record which permit total control of noise by the performer—in books, recordings, TV, and the movies.

The psychic distance of the SE performance system is regarded as coldness by BE users, for they expect a high degree of complementary audience participation in answer to their efforts. This is how they judge their effectiveness, and how they are judged by the audience. The black performer has the task of getting the audience "into it," setting up rhythms that will elicit the vital response of the audience. In fact, he attempts in some way to establish a dialog relationship with them, and his best performances will arise when dialog turns into playful competition. Further, performance contests produce the most active response on the part of both participants and audience and result in the best exhibition of their abilities. It is, of course, this BE performance pattern which elicits the charge of overemotionalism by Euro-Americans.

This set of differences in performance patterns and expectations reveals an even deeper difference of world views. Performance to an SE audience (and to Westerners in general) is regarded as a *thing*, to be judged in terms of integrity, verisimilitude, and control over media. A work of art is developed upon, most commonly, in regard to how it will end. It is successful if it has a sense of wholeness to it, especially if it enlists our interest (quieting us), builds upon this, bringing it to a climax, and providing us with a sense of relief or catharsis when the climax comes. Black performance, on the other hand, is not a thing but an aspect of a process, and that process is coterminous with life itself. Therefore, performance goes on all of the time, not just in performances but in principle. The performer activates this ideal of performance, being the channel through which vitality achieves formal expression. His task is not to make a thing but to bring about an experience in which not only his creative energies but the vitality of others may find expression. Therefore his specific performances need have no sense of wholeness; they are part of what Leroi Jones has called the ongoing "Art of Be-ing." Energy exists; it is up to the performer to activate it and then for the group to demonstrate it together, the performer acting as leader. (For examples of this, you need only go to a lower class black religious observance or to a James Brown concert. Or more dramatically because of our usual expectations, go to a movie in an Afro-American neighborhood.) In the system of BE performances, the subject-object split is anathema, as is the SE focus on the work of art and the effect of catharsis. The need for catharsis engenders the pattern of tension and relief; that is, through enactment of troubling matters and their resolution in the safe environment of a play world the problem is taken care of. Black performances rather than insisting on this controlled play world, focus on performance as epitomizing life, intensifying it, and thus revealing the underlying orders and energies of cultural existence.

To this point, the discussion of the social dimensions of Black English has emphasized the performance pattern and the way in which the community expects this pattern to be carried out in eliciting participation and a total verbal and kinesthetic response. In an environment of this sort, because it is the performance which brings the group together, celebrating life and the community of experience, performance is constantly expected and valued, and the performer is given a very high degree of status. The performer is not just a person who places himself in the center of the performance operation, capitalizing upon these expectations; he must demonstrate his control over the expressive devices appropriate to the occasion. This means, among other things, that the adept performer will be one who is highly conscious of the alternative varieties of language and who will therefore be able to manipulate these differences to demonstrate his control.

This focus on the performer as epitomizing the highest capacities of the group by channeling vitality into participation is, then, another feature of black culture which departs considerably from that of middle America. One of the by-products of our object-and usefulness-orientation has been a relegation of the performance to the periphery of our main cultural processes. The art objects or set-pieces which are the performer's stock-in-trade are valued, to be sure, but they are not regarded in the same way that a useful piece of machinery is. The performer is given license to perform so long as he doesn't intrude too deeply into our everyday lives. He lives on the periphery of our existence, unless we happen to function in an artists' society.

This difference of focus is reflected not only in performance patterns but in the devices available, by convention, to the performers. The configuration of techniques characteristic of black performances contributes to a focus on the performer and his acts, whether in contest or not. Perhaps most important of the devices is the large number of intensifying techniques which call attention to the performer's role in setting things in motion: metaphors, slang terms, highly kinesthetic verbs, nouns descriptive of stylish items, and the already described paralinguistic features of elongation, variable stress patterns, and so on. Furthermore, since the performer as hero is identified with the experiences common to the group, he is free to use the first person singular pronouns, a technique which I have in the past referred to as the "intrusive 'I'." (3) He calls upon terms which are ambiguous in their denotative meanings, which can mean one thing or its opposite, and therefore the performer's usage must be closely attended to for meaning to be established. ("Funky" and "heavy" are examples.) Finally, and perhaps most important, the black performer has learned to take high affect words and attitudes which are negative in the SE world and to convert them into positive features. He has done this with words like "bad," "tough" and "cold," and with the entire white set of negative stereotype traits of blacks, which are embodied in their narratives as positive attributes. (4)

The aspects which I have emphasized are most observable in adolescent and young adult talk, and are mostly associated with men. This brings us to the basic problem in designating the defining features of BE, for there are a number of segments of the lower class black community each of which is identified with a specific variety of BE. Some of these seem more black only because they contain more dramatically different and/or stigmatizing features than the other varieties.

This is true, for instance, of recent immigrants from rural Southern communities, for their speech is old-fashioned and therefore from the men's perspective not "hip," and from the women's not as "sweet" as they would have it (by which they often mean too distant from conversational SE.) Similarly, the peer-grouping which is so important in the socialization of blacks is reflected in the rejection of "kid talk" (except among kids), once again judging in "jive" terms. Jive, in another frame of reference, is associated with carefree, friendship-oriented male society and is therefore contrasted by women with their more genteel "sweet" manner of speaking. Woman talk is associated by them with their code of "respectability" and with the values of the home. Their approved variety is closer to certain aspects of SE—one reason why the women have found greater linguistic acceptance and social mobility. Man talk, on the other hand, is deeply involved in the proclamation of masculine, style-centered self-image or "reputation." (5) It is much more troubling to whites because of its defiant strength and its maximizing of the differences between it and the "sweet" talk of women. Here the similarities between woman talk and SE are also crucial, for a dramatic rejection by men of the standards of the former is read by whites (especially teachers) as a rejection of the latter.

Black English includes all of these varieties, city and country, man and woman, and many more. Each of them is maintained as long as the group persists which the variety symbolically represents. Some groups, like kids and country people, often shed their stigmatized variety and take on other varieties. Others see stigmatization as simply a part of their social well-being, for they see the stigmatizing group as the enemy. They therefore maintain their speaking behavior as a way of contesting with these others; this is especially so in the opposition between the jive talk of the young and the variety spoken by their parents and other elders, and in the opposition between men and women which arises after adolescence. This is also increasingly true of the talk of black militants in confrontations with whites; there we have witnessed black speakers of what most would regard as SE utilizing some of the most stigmatized features of BE to achieve their contentious effects vis-a-vis whites, as well as solidarity with their ghetto brothers.

Having made this brief survey of devices, patterns, varieties and uses of Black English, we are now in a better position to ask the biggest question confronting the language arts teacher—Why has it persisted in spite of the obvious pressures from the white community for the black community to lose it? Clearly the answer lies in two directions: BE has maintained itself because of its *adaptability* in a situation in which flexibility means ability to contend and endure; and more specifically, the use of BE provides an on-going and vital *cohesive* device, recognizable as characteristically and uniquely black. Through BE performances the group may act together, grooving together to the same rhythms. This is, as I understand it, what is usually meant by "soul." These performances embody the process-oriented, creatively competitive world view, in an act of Be-ing.

But if this black esthetic were the only basis for retaining BE, that speaking system would at least have gravitated away from the most stigmatizing of the BE traits. A number of other social forces enter here. The variety a black child first learns to speak is filled with the most conservative and stigmatizing of BE linguistic traits because they learn to speak from those immediately older then themselves. (This is more true of the boys than the girls.) This is the only code that most of them will bring into the first-grade classroom. To be sure, other varieties are added in the course of black socialization, but these codes may also contain stigmatizing features, especially if the child is male. Because of the subsequent oppositions between youths and adults, and between men and women, a number of these other stigmatized traits have been maintained and have proliferated. They are strongly identified by the young and by men with a stylish and positive image of themselves. The cultural necessity in the ghetto to maintain the friendship-based peer grouping in which these varieties operate is stronger than those influences from mainstream America which would change the most disparate of black cultural patterns, including certain varieties and features of Black English. But BE is one of the adaptive patterns so crucial to the ability to endure; we would be asking a great deal to expect lower class blacks to give up this adaptable expressive system that has served them so well for so long.

References

1. Gerald D. Suttles, *The Social Order of the Slums: Ethnicity and Territory in the Inner City* (Chicago: University of Chicago Press, 1968).

2. For a fuller sociolinguistic description of Black English, see these works, especially "Rapping and Capping."

Roger D. Abrahams, *Deep Down in the Jungle* . . . (Hatboro, Pa.: Folklore Associates, 1964).

Abrahams, "Public Drama and Common Values in Two Caribbean Communities," *Trans-Action,* July/August (1968), pp. 62–71.

Abrahams, *Positively Black* (Englewood Cliffs, N.J., 1970).

Abrahams, "Rapping and Capping: Black Speech as Art" in *Black Americans,* ed. John Szwed (New York: Basic Books, 1970).

3. Abrahams, *Deep Down in the Jungle.* . . .
4. Abrahams, *Positively Black.*
5. Peter J. Wilson, "Reputation and Respectability: Suggestions for Caribbean Ethnology," *Man,* 4 (1969), pp. 70–84.

Additional References

James E. Alatis, *Report of the Twentieth Annual Round Table Meeting on Linguistics and Language Studies* (Washington, D.C., 1970).

J. L. Dillard, "Non-Standard Negro Dialects—Convergence or Divergence," *The Flordia FL Reporter,* 6:2 (1968).

Ralph Fasold, "Distinctive Linguistic Characteristics of Black English" in Alatis, pp. 233–38.

Ulf Hannerz, *Soulside,* (New York: Columbia University Press, 1969) [in Chapter Two of this book].

William Labov, "The Logic of Non-Standard English," in Alatis, pp. 1–44 [in Chapter One of this book].

Claudia Mitchell-Kernan, *Language Behavior in a Black Urban Community,* Working Paper No. 23 (Berkeley, Calif., 1969).

Roger W. Shuy, "Sociolinguistic Research at the Center for Applied Linguistics" preprint ms., 1969.

William A. Stewart, "Sociolinguistic Factors in the History of American Negro Dialects," *The Flordia FL Reporter,* 5:2 (1967).

Stewart, "Continuity and Change in American Negro Dialects," *The Flordia FL Reporter,* 6:1 (1968).

Stewart, "Historical and Structural Bases for the Recognition of Negro Dialect," in Alatis, pp. 239–47.

Walter A. Wolfram, "Linguistic Correlates of Social Differences in Negro Communities," in Alatis, 1970, pp. 249–57.

Modes of Mitigation and Politeness
William A. Labov

In this selection from *A Study of Nonstandard English,* William Labov notes that Black English speaking children participate in a culture which has different verbal strategies for disagreeing with authority. He suggests that these children may not have learned the middle-class strategies of polite disagreement in the school situation. Using the case of Junior, an adolescent who was generally a failure in school but a verbal leader in his own group, Labov indicates how the boy came into verbal conflict with his teachers over his refusal to act on their commands.

Labov analyzes the structure of commands, showing how certain things such as ability to carry out the command are presupposed before the command is given. Each of these presuppositions plays a part in polite, mitigated middle-class responses to commands by teachers. Junior, a black ghetto child, did not use any of the mitigated forms expected by middle-class teachers, and so, according to Labov, could conceivably have become a school failure because of his inability to handle middle-class verbal forms. In other words, his teachers reacted so forcefully to his verbal behavior, they came to see him as incorrigible and a trouble maker.

Obviously the cultural conflict demonstrated by the different forms of verbal behavior has important implications for teachers who need to be aware that black ghetto children may not control certain middle-class forms of mitigation and politeness. Rather they are responding from their own culture and are not necessarily "impolite" and "bad."

We are only beginning to describe the rules for the use of language, but in this area we can observe many differences between nonstandard and standard speakers. The nonstandard speaker is undoubtedly handicapped in many ways by his lack of control over mitigating forms which are more highly developed in middle class and school language. These forms are used to avoid conflict between individuals who meet in some kind of face-to-face encounter. The child may not know the mitigating ways of disagreeing with the teacher which make such disagreement acceptable in the school situation. It is not uncommon for Negro children to simply accuse the teacher of lying where middle class white children might say, "There's another way

---

From *A Study of Nonstandard English* by William Labov. ERIC. 1969. Reprinted by permission of William Labov.

of looking at it." Faced with the statement "You a lie!" most teachers find
it necessary to react forcefully. After one or two such confrontations, most
students learn to say nothing. But some students continue to object without
learning the means of doing so without conflict. In the school records of
boys we have studied, we find many cases where they have been repri-
manded, even demoted, for their failure to use mitigating forms of politeness. For one fourteen-year-old named Junior, who can be described as a
verbal leader of his subgroup, we find such entries as the following:

Nov. 63 Frequently comes to school without a tie. . . . He frequently calls
out answer. When told not to call out he made an expression of
disgust. He then refused to accept the rexographed sheet the
teacher gave to the class.

Nov. 63 When asked to re-write a composition he adamantly refused. He
said, "I will not." He doesn't practice any self control.

Dec. 63 Was fighting with another boy in class today . . .

Sept. 66 *F* in Citizenship.

May 67 Mother has been in touch with school regarding son's truancy.

This record can be interpreted in several ways. Junior may be unable to
compete with the smart kids and finds a way out in being "bad." Or it may
be that he does not care at all about school and is simply expressing his
defiance for the system. It is just as hard for us to interpret the school record
by itself as it is for the teacher to deal with the student in this formal
situation without any knowledge of the vernacular culture.

When we listen to Junior speaking outside of school, we can see that he
has a natural command of language and has no difficulty in expressing his
ideas. The following quotations are taken from a session with Junior, a black
fieldworker, and Ronald, one of Junior's best friends. First of all, it is
apparent that Junior does have strong feelings of resentment against the
school and white society.

Junior: Like I'ma tell you the truth. They jus' want everythin' taken
away from us. . . . Who do we work for? Whities! Who do we
go to school for? Whities! Who's our teachers? Whities! . .

Inter-
viewer: If the whitey's not different from you, how come he has everything?

Ronald: They don't have everything.

Junior: Yes they do!

It is important to note here that Junior and Ronald are members of the
Jets, a group which is quite indifferent and even hostile to black nationalism

and the Muslim religion. Junior has not been taught to be militant; the resentment expressed here is a product of Junior's own thinking—the result of his own experience. Despite his antagonism towards the dominant white society, he has retained a strong sense of realism in his evaluation of it. An argument with Ronald as to whether high school diplomas are necessary:

Ronald: And I'm 'onna tell you; I'm 'onna say *why* what they say you have to have a high school diploma. Some whitey's probably ain't got a high school diploma, and he still go out to work. My father ain't got a high school diploma.

Junior: Your father ain't no whitey, is he?

Ronald: No, but he has no high school deploma, but he go out there and work, right?

Junior: O.K.!. . . . But . . . I'ma tell you, you're wrong in a *way*—cause ev'ry whitey—ev'ry whitey, if they out o' school, they went through *high* school. If they didn't go to college they went through *high* school. If the whities didn't go through high school, how come they got everything? . . . . 'Cause they had the *knowledge.*

It seems clear that Junior is a much better speaker than Ronald. In complex arguments of this sort, Ronald's syntax gets him into problems like the double *but* clauses or the unsolved labyrinth of his first sentence quoted above. Junior has no such difficulty expressing his ideas. Furthermore, he has the ability to put one argument on top of another which is characteristic of those who win verbal contests.

Junior: If you—if you was in a high school—right? Why do people graduate?

Ronald: 'Cause they try hard to grad—'cause they *want* to graduate.

Junior: 'Cause they *learn*. . . 'cause they *learn*. If they didn't learn, and they just stood around, they wouldn't have everything. 'Cause you got to *work* to get to high school, you got to *work* to get from elementary to junior high . . .

In this dialogue, Junior seems to express very well the values of middle class society. He shows a full cognitive awareness of the importance of education. It comes as something of a shock then to learn that at the time of this interview he was in the eighth grade and his reading score was 4.6—more than three years behind grade. And the disciplinary record cited above indicates that he is very unlikely to be graduating from high school himself. Note that the *they* of *they learn* seems at first reading to refer to a very general *people* who graduate; it seems to be an inclusive rather than an exclusive *they*. But when Junior says "*they* wouldn't have everything . . ." it is clear that he is not including himself among the people who graduate.

Is there any internal evidence within this record as to why Junior is not learning to read—why he is not taking advantage of the school system to get what he so plainly wants? It is obviously not a question of his verbal intelligence. A reading of disciplinary events shows serious sources of conflict between him and his teachers which are preventing him from using his intelligence for the acquisition of knowledge. Each of these reported incidents was the occasion for an interruption in his school work, a violent confrontation with authority. The teachers report that he "calls out answers" and "doesn't practice any self control." The kinds of skills which Junior is lacking appear to be those verbal routines of mitigation which would make it possible for him to object and refuse without a major confrontation. Of course the record reflects the teachers' subjective impressions rather than what actually happened, but we can see enough to reconstruct the kinds of events involved and to isolate the problems for further study. Note that Junior's disciplinary record begins in the fifth grade, when he was eleven. The exchange between him and the teacher must have been something like this:

Teacher:	Junior, this is very sloppy work.
Junior:	No it isn't!
Teacher:	Now you take that composition and write it over again!
Junior:	I will not!

The sentence "I will not" was striking enough to be quoted in the teacher's report. It is an elliptical response, short for "I will not write that composition over again," but it is certainly not illogical. We hear a good deal about the faults of nonstandard language, but its strong points certainly include brevity and clarity. The problem with "I will not" is that it is altogether too clear: it lacks the verbal indirection which could have been used to make the objection and perhaps win the argument. Instead, the direct refusal without mitigation led to the end of the verbal exchange ("You go right down to the office . . .").

To show what Junior did not do, it is necessary to analyze the rules for commands, and for refusing commands, which prevail for standard English and the middle class society in which that language is embedded. Commands and refusals are actions; declarations, interrogatives, imperatives are linguistic categories—things that are said, rather than things that are done. The rules we need will show how things are done with words and how one interprets these utterances as actions: in other words, relating what is done to what is said and what is said to what is done. This area of linguistics can be called "discourse analysis"; but it is not well known or developed. . . .

We have, however, begun work in this field relative to requests and commands, so that it is possible to indicate what Junior might have done besides answering "I will not." Commands or requests for action are essentially instructions from a person A to a person B to carry out some action X at a time T.

$$A \rightarrow B: X!/T$$

This is the explicit form of such a command. But there are a number of unstated preconditions which must hold if the receiver B is to hear the command as valid (or a "serious" command). It is necessary that he believe that the originator A believes four things: that, at time T,

a) X should be done.

b) B has the obligation to do X.

c) B has the ability to do X.

d) A has the right to request that B do X.

These four preconditions are not only part of the process of judging and reacting to a command. They are also used for indirect ways of making the command or request. Either a statement or a question about any of these four preconditions can stand for and be heard as the command itself. Thus the teacher could have said:

a) This has to be done over. *or*
   Shouldn't this be done over?

b) You'll have to do this over. *or*
   Don't you have to do neater work than this?

c) You can do better than this. *or*
   Don't you think you can do neater work than this?

d) It's my job to get you to do better than this. *or*
   Can I ask you to do this over?

Some of these forms are heard as forceful requests, but many are heard as mitigated and very polite forms, even more than "Would you please . . .?" Furthermore, not only are these preconditions used in making requests, but they are also utilized for mitigated forms of refusal. Denials of any of these preconditions, or questions about them, will serve the same purpose as "I will not" as far as the activity of refusing is concerned. Thus Junior could have said:

a) I don't think it's sloppy enough to do over. *or*
   It's not that sloppy, is it?

b) I'm not supposed to be doing penmanship today. *or*
   If it's right it doesn't have to be pretty, does it?

c) I sprained my wrist and I can't write good. *or*
   That's the best I've done so far, isn't it?
d) You have no right to tell me that. *or*
   Are you telling me to do everything twice?

Except for the last two forms, which concern the teacher's rights and are therefore extremely challenging, these kinds of refusals leave the door open for further negotiation. They are heard as partial refusals, in the sense that it is clear Junior will not rewrite the composition unless the teacher repeats the command. But most importantly, they are *deniable* refusals. If someone is accused of refusing a command by such forms, he is entitled to say, "I didn't refuse, I was only . . ." Furthermore, if the teacher wants to retreat, he too can say that Junior did not refuse, avoiding the loss of face involved in accepting a refusal. There are thus many adult ways of doing business in this situation. But the form "I will not" stands in contrast to all of these and signals an unwillingness to use the mitigated forms; it thus represents a direct challenge to the authority of the teacher. Perhaps Junior was angry and wanted to precipitate a crisis: the question is, did this eleven-year-old have the skills to avoid that crisis if he wanted to? . . .

Chapter Three
Descriptions of Black English

If an educator is to intelligently plan pedagogical strategies for teaching urban ghetto black children to read, write, spell, and learn to maximize their verbal potential, he needs to have information on the language system Black English speaking children bring to school with them. Obviously, need for information about any child's language is imperative, whether the child speaks Spanish, one of the American Indian languages, or an American rural dialect. For example, undoubtedly many a well meaning teacher has said to a black child who read "I been home" for "I have been home," "Rodney, that was a mistake. You missed a word. Go back and read it again." What she did not understand was that "I been" is the Black English semantic equivalent of "I have been," so the child has obviously understood the content of the sentence enough to rephrase it in his own variety's forms. (In Chapters Five and Six these pedagogical implications will be more fully presented.) In this case, the teacher has made the mistake, not the child. And the mistake grew from her ignorance of the language variety the child used.

The system of Black English is at least partially revealed in the three descriptive articles in this chapter. I say partially, because Black English, like any other variety, is highly complex and is not yet fully described. Each article stresses the systematic nature of black ghetto speech; Ralph Fasold and Walt Wolfram's article and William Labov and Paul Cohen's article both organize their information according to the sets of rules they see governing Black English. These rules are descriptive, so are very different from the prescriptive rules found in school grammar texts which *tell* one what is acceptable or not acceptable to say. The rules in this chapter do not tell but instead describe the formal system of Black English. Although Fasold and Wolfram's set of rules differs in some ways from Labov and Cohen's, both articles are concerned with explaining the system of Black English.

However, description of the Black English speech forms and the rules organizing them does not take into account the variation in the number of these forms used by different black speakers or used by the same speaker on different occasions. Description of another sort is considered necessary, a description which accounts for some of the possible reasons as to why ghetto blacks differ as to how many Black English forms they produce in speech. From the preliminary investigations which have been made, social factors are seen as playing an important role in accounting for that variation. Walt Wolfram (1), who conducted Black English research in Detroit, found that social factors such as socio-economic status, sex, and age affected the production of Black English forms. For example, black ghetto women often used fewer Black English forms than ghetto men. Adults normally used fewer Black English forms than teen-agers and children.

According to Labov and Cohen, differences in style from casual to careful speech helped account for the variation they found within the same speaker. For example, a single black speaker may use fewer double negatives in his speech in a formal social situation such as talking with a white stranger than when he is talking to his friends over a card game. This type of variation is what I would call *register switching* rather than *style switching*. But whatever the term, the situation seems to be that when social situations change, people change the way they talk. (This concept is more fully developed by me in Chapter Four.) If a situation is perceived as being more formal, the speech is adjusted accordingly toward using more "standard" forms which are considered more formal by many ghetto blacks. The opinion is sometimes expressed that the actual difference between Black English and other varieties is the relatively higher number of times certain nonstandard forms are used in black speech, plus some phonological and intonational differences. In other words, the forms themselves are not considered specific to Black English or Black English *per se*.

William Stewart also correlates this variation in the number of Black English forms used in speech with social variables. He found informal social structures in the ghetto environment which he felt exercised some control over the production of Black English forms.

A description of the forms which are considered to be Black English is too simplistic, then, without an attendent description of the possible factors, social and linguistic, which help account for the variation in the number of forms actually used in the speech of ghetto blacks. This variation seems inherent in Black English.

Both the forms associated with Black English and variations in their production are crucial knowledge for educators as pedagogical strategies cannot be intelligently planned without such knowledge. For example, if a child uses a Black English form sometimes and its more standard equivalent sometimes, he knows both. The teacher then does not need a strategy to teach the so-called standard equivalent although this is often done because the variation in the child's speech is ignored. [See DeStefano, Chapter Four, for a discussion of this problem.]

Reference

1. Walter A. Wolfram, *A Sociolinguistic Description of Detroit Negro Speech* (Washington, D.C.: Center for Applied Linguistics, 1969).

Some Linguistic Features of Negro Dialect
Ralph W. Fasold and Walt Wolfram

Linguists have become interested in the systematic description of Black English as it is spoken today in urban ghettos. One of the most comprehensive of these descriptions is in the article done by Ralph Fasold and Walt Wolfram, based on data gathered from a survey of the current literature on Black English. They make the traditional linguistic division between phonology (sound) and syntax (grammar), but in both sections present phonological and syntactic rules which have been proposed to account for the system of actual Black English forms they describe. Since speech in any language variety is seen as rule-governed verbal behavior although the rules may vary from variety to variety, the actual speech forms are presented more revealingly when linked to a system of rules. Having a system of rules based on the actual usage of Black English speakers is seen to give the organization necessary for a systematic description of this social variety.

There are essentially three sources of information on the features of Negro dialect. (1) First, there are detailed technical linguistic analyses which are difficult for non-specialists to read. Another source of information is in the form of lists which usually sacrifice adequacy in favor of simplicity. A third source of information is articles about the history of Negro dialect in which certain features are emphasized, but in which no comprehensive analysis is attempted. Our purpose here is to present the information currently available on the linguistic features of Negro dialect in non-technical language, but in sufficient detail to be useful, if not to teachers themselves, at least to those who would like to write teaching materials but do not feel secure in their knowledge of the features involved. The details of the analysis being presented are based on careful research and while no extensive references to this research are made in the course of the presentation, all the source material can be found in the references at the end of this article.

Before discussing the features themselves, it is necessary to clarify several

From "Some Linguistic Features of Negro Dialect" by Ralph W. Fasold and Walt Wolfram, in *Teaching Standard English in the Inner City,* edited by Ralph W. Fasold and Roger W. Shuy. (Washington, D.C.: Center for Applied Linguistics, 1970). © 1970 by Center for Applied Linguistics. Reprinted by permission of the publisher.

facts about Negro dialect. First, it should be understood that not all Negroes speak Negro dialect. There are many Negroes whose speech is indistinguishable from others of the same region and social class, and there are many whose speech can be identified as Negro only by a few slight differences in pronunciation and vocal quality. Second, Negro dialect shares many features with other kinds of English. Its distinctiveness, however, lies in the fact that it has a number of pronunciation and grammatical features which are not shared by other dialects. It is important to realize that Negro dialect is a fully formed linguistic system in its own right, with its own grammar and pronunciation rules; it cannot simply be dismissed as an unworthy approximation of standard English. In fact, there are some grammatical distinctions which can be made more easily in Negro dialect than in standard English. Negro dialect, then, as the term is used here, is a cohesive linguistic system which is substantially different from standard American English dialects. It is spoken by some, though not all Negroes, particularly those of the lower socioeconomic classes. Furthermore, as will be brought out in the discussion, almost all the features associated with Negro dialect alternate with standard English forms in actual speech. To avoid forming a distorted picture of how speech is actually used in the lower socioeconomic black community, this variation or alternation should be kept in mind when reading the descriptions which follow. . . .

Pronunciation

It is important to keep separate the two kinds of differences between standard English and Negro dialect. Some of these features, like the pronunciation of *then* as *den,* are the result of differences in the pronunciation systems of two kinds of American English. Other differences, like the use of "double" or multiple negatives, are grammatical in nature. Sometimes it is not obvious which kind of feature is involved. For example, we will see that the rule which causes speakers of Negro dialect to say *He go* where standard English speakers say *He goes* is a grammatical rule. On the other hand, the rule by which speakers of Negro dialect say *He walk* where standard dialect speakers say *He walked* is a pronunciation rule. Some of the reasons for this conclusion and for the importance of the distinction between the two types of rules will be given in the description to follow.

Word-final Consonant Clusters

1. *General.* Standard English words ending in a consonant cluster or blend often have the final member of the cluster absent in Negro dialect.

(2) As we shall see, the reduction of some clusters which are formed by the addition of the *-s* suffix can be attributed to a grammatical difference between standard English and Negro dialect (see pp. 132, 141–143). Other types of cluster "reductions," however, do not result from grammatical differences, but are the product of pronunciation differences in final consonant clusters. In Negro dialect, words such as *test, desk, hand,* and *build* are pronounced as *tes', des', han',* and *buil'* respectively. Because of this, we find that pairs of words such as *build* and *bill, coal* and *cold,* and *west* and *Wes* have identical pronunciations in Negro dialect.

It is important to distinguish two basic types of clusters which are affected by this sort of reduction. First of all, clusters in which both members of the cluster belong to the same "base word" (3) can be reduced, as in *tes', des', han',* and *buil'.* But reduction also affects final *t* or *d* which results when the suffix *-ed* is added to the "base word." In all varieties of English, the *-ed* suffix has several different phonetic forms, depending on how the base word ends. If it ends in *d* or *t,* the *-ed* suffix is pronounced something like *id* (e.g. *wantid, countid*); otherwise it is pronounced as *t* or *d.* When the word ends in a voiced sound, it is pronounced as *d,* so that words with *-ed* like *rubbed* or *rained* are actually pronounced as *rubd* and *raind* respectively. Consonants like *b, n,* and *g* are pronounced with vocal cords vibrating, that is, they are voiced. If the base word ends in a voiceless consonant, the cluster ends in *t,* so that *messed* and *looked* are actually pronounced as *mest* and *lookt,* respectively. Consonants such as *s, k,* and *f* are pronounced without the vibration of the vocal cords, that is, they are voiceless. In Negro dialect, when the addition of the *-ed* suffix results in either a voiced or voiceless cluster, the cluster may be reduced by removing the final member of the cluster. This affects *-ed* when it functions as a past tense marker (e.g. *Yesterday he move' away*), a participle (e.g. *The boy was mess' up*) or an adjective (e.g. *He had a scratch' arm*), although its association with the past tense is the most frequent. The list of clusters affected by this process and the examples of the two types of consonant cluster reduction are given in the following table: Type I represents clusters which do not involve *-ed* and Type II represents clusters which result from the addition of the *-ed* suffix.

Note that in the table, such clusters as [mp] (e.g. *jump, ramp*), [nt] (e.g. *count, rent*), [lt] (e.g. *colt, belt*), [ŋk] (e.g. *crank, rank*), and [lp] (e.g. *gulp, help*) are not included. The reason is that the reduction rule operates only when both members of the cluster are either voiced or voiceless. Words like *mind, cold,* or *rained* (pronounced *raind*) end in two voiced sounds, *n* and *d.* On the other hand, words like *jump, count, belt, crank,* and *help* end in one voiced and one voiceless sound; *m, n, l* and [ŋ] sound are voiced, while *t, k* and *p* are voiceless. Since final consonant clusters can be reduced only when both consonants are voiced or when both consonants are voiceless, these words ending in one of each kind of consonant never have reduced clusters.

Table 3.

Consonant Clusters in Which the Final Member of the Cluster May Be Absent

Phonetic Cluster	Examples*	
	Type I	Type II
[st]	test, post, list	missed, messed, dressed
[sp]	wasp, clasp, grasp	
[sk]	desk, risk, mask	
[št]		finished, latched, cashed
[zd]		raised, composed, amazed
[žd]		judged, charged, forged
[ft]	left, craft, cleft	laughed, stuffed, roughed
[vd]		loved, lived, moved
[nd]	mind, find, mound	rained, fanned, canned
[md]		named, foamed, rammed
[ld]	cold, wild, old	called, smelled, killed
[pt]	apt, adept, inept	mapped, stopped, clapped
[kt]	act, contact, expect	looked, cooked, cracked

*Where there are no examples under Type I or II, the cluster does not occur under that category.

In some ways, the absence of the final member of the consonant cluster in Negro dialect is like a process which can also be observed in standard English; in other ways, however, it is quite different. In standard English, the final member of the cluster may be absent if the following word begins with a consonant, so that *bes' kind, col' cuts,* and *wes' side* are common and acceptable in spoken standard English. (4) In standard English, however, this reduction can take place only when the following word begins with a consonant. While *col' cuts,* does not violate the pronunciation rules of standard English, *col' egg* does. In Negro dialect, this reduction not only takes place when the following word begins with a consonant, but it may also take place when it is followed by a vowel or a pause of some type. Thus *wes' en', bes' apple,* or *col' egg* are all acceptable according to Negro dialect rules of pronunciation. Items such as *Yesterday he was mess' up* occur because of this pronunciation rule and not because past tense is absent in Negro dialect. In standard English it is not at all unusual to hear a sentence such as *Yesterday I burn' my hand,* since the potential cluster in *burned* is followed by a word beginning with a consonant. But a sentence such as *It was burn' up,* acceptable in Negro dialect, would not be acceptable in standard English since the potential cluster is followed by a word beginning with a vowel.

2. *Plural formation.*   Related to the reduction of final consonant clusters in Negro dialect is a particular pattern of pluralization involving the *-s* and *-es* plural forms. In all varieties of English, there are several different phonetic forms for the plural suffix. If the word ends in an *s*-like sound (i.e. a sibilant such as *s, sh, z, zh*), the plural suffix is formed by adding *-es;* phonetically, this is pronounced something like *-iz*. Thus *bus, bush,* and *buzz* are pluralized as *buses, bushes,* and *buzzes* respectively. If the word does not end in an *s*-like sound, then *-s* is added; phonetically this is *z* after voiced sounds and *s* after voiceless sounds. Thus, the plural of *pot, coat, bud,* and *pan* is *pots, coats, buds* (phonetically *budz*) and *pans* (phonetically *panz*) respectively. In Negro dialect, words ending in *s* plus *p, t* or *k* add the *-es* plural instead of the *-s* plural. (5) Thus, words like *desk, ghost, wasp,* and *test* are pluralized as *desses, ghoses, wasses,* and *tesses.* Because the *p, t,* and *k* are so often removed by the rule discussed above, these plurals are formed as if *desk, test,* and *wasp* ended in *s,* instead of *sk, st,* or *sp.* It is essential to understand that this is a regular pluralization pattern due to the status of final consonant clusters in Negro dialect.

Attempting to learn standard English pluralization patterns, speakers will sometimes pluralize words like *desk* and *test* as *deskes* and *testes* respectively. These forms result from the failure to eliminate Negro dialect pluralization after realizing that words like *test* and *desk* are to be pronounced with a cluster. Technically, this is known as "hypercorrection."

3. *The status of word-final clusters.*   Because consonant clusters occur so infrequently at the end of words in Negro dialect, one might ask whether these word-final clusters can be considered an integral part of the Negro dialect system. That is, are speakers of Negro dialect at all familiar with what words may and what words may not end in clusters? This question is crucial for teaching, since clusters must be taught as completely new items

if Negro dialect speakers are completely unfamiliar with them. On the other hand, if clusters are a part of the dialect and simply different from standard English because they can undergo reduction in certain contexts where reduction is not possible in standard English (e.g. when the following word begins with a vowel), the teaching problem is of a different nature. What must be taught in the latter case, is the contexts in which cluster reduction is not possible in standard English but is possible in Negro dialect, while the lists of standard English words ending in clusters must be taught as completely new items if clusters are not an integral part of the dialect.

This question can be answered most clearly by observing what happens when suffixes beginning with a vowel are added to a base word ending in a cluster in standard English. This includes *-ing* as in *testing* or *scolding*, *-er* as in *tester* or *scolder* and *-est* as in *coldest* or *oldest*. If a consonant cluster is presented in such constructions (e.g. *testing, tester*), we may assume that the speaker is fully acquainted with the cluster, but that it can be reduced in places where it is not possible in standard English. For the vast majority of Negro dialect speakers in the North, this is exactly how the rule concerning consonant clusters operates. These speakers may reduce the cluster in the context of *tes' program* or *tes' idea,* but retain the cluster in *tester.* There is, however, also a group of Negro dialect speakers, most typically Southern children, who not only show the absence of the final member of the cluster in *tes' program* or *tes' idea,* but in *teser* as well. For these speakers, the teaching of standard English must start with the list of standard English words which end in consonant clusters.

We may summarize our observations about the word-final consonant clusters in Table 4, which represents how standard English and the two varieties of Negro dialect function with respect to final consonant clusters. The three contexts mentioned above are: 1) the following word begins with a consonant, 2) the following word does not begin with a consonant, and 3) a suffix beginning with a vowel follows.

Table 4.

Consonant Cluster Reduction

	(1) ___#C	(2) ___#	(3) ___-V
Standard English	tes' program	test idea	testing
Negro dialect 1	tes' program	tes' idea	testing
Negro dialect 2	tes' program	tes' idea	tes'ing

On the basis of this table, we can draw some general conclusions about the social significance of consonant cluster reduction. We see, for example, that Negro dialect is very much like standard English when the following word begins with a consonant; a reduction of the cluster therefore has little social significance in this context. When not followed by a consonant, however, it is socially stigmatized. Absence of the cluster is most stigmatized when a suffix beginning with a vowel is added.

The th-Sounds

1. *General.* In standard English, the letters *th* actually represent two different types of sound. First, they represent the voiced sound in words such as *the, they,* and *that* (i.e. a voiced interdental fricative). Second, they represent the voiceless sound as in words like *thought, thin,* and *think* (a voiceless interdental fricative). In Negro dialect, the regular pronunciation rules for the sounds represented by *th* are quite different. The particular sounds which *th* represents are mainly dependent on the context in which *th* occurs. That is, the sounds for *th* are dependent on where *th* might occur in a word and/or what sounds occur next to it.

2. *Word-initial.* At the beginning of a word, the *th* in *the* is frequently pronounced as a *d* in Negro dialect, so that words such as *the, they,* and *that* are pronounced as *de, dey,* and *dat* respectively. It has been pointed out that a limited amount of *d* for *th* is also characteristic of standard English in the most casual or informal speech style. In Negro dialect, however, it is much more frequent so that the pronunciation *de* for *the* is the regular pronunciation. It is important to note here that the pronunciation of *d* for *th* in Negro dialect is not simply an error in pronunciation, but the result of a regular and patterned rule.

In the case of *th* in words such as *thought, think* or *thin* (the voiceless interdental fricative), *th* is sometimes pronounced as *t,* so that *thought, think* or *thin* are pronounced as *tought, tink* and *tin* respectively. However, most Negro dialect speakers who pronounce *thought* as *tought* will also sometimes pronounce it as *thought.* That is, both the *th* and *t* pronunciations for *thought* are appropriate for Negro dialect. If *th* is followed by *r* as in *throat* or *three* still another pronunciation is possible. These words may be pronounced with an *f,* so that *three* and *throat* can be pronounced as *free* and *froat* respectively. This means that items such as *three* and *free* may be pronounced the same in Negro dialect.

3. *Within a word.* In the middle of the word, there are several different pronunciations for *th* in Negro dialect. For the voiceless sound as in *nothing, author,* or *ether,* most frequently it is pronounced as *f.* Thus, *nothing,*

author, and *ether* are pronounced as *nuf'n, ahfuh,* and *eefuh* respectively. For the voiced sound, as in *brother, rather* or *bathing, th* is pronounced as *v* in some varieties of Negro dialect, so that these words are pronounced as *bruvah, ravah,* and *bavin',* respectively.

In addition to *f* and *v* for *th* in the middle of a word, several other pronunciations may occur. When *th* is followed by a nasal sound such as *m* or *n, th* may be pronounced as *t.* Thus *'ritmetic* for *arithmetic, nut'n* for *nothing* or *montly* for *monthly,* are patterns frequently used in Negro dialect. There are also several items in which no consonant at all is found. For example, *mother* may be pronounced as *muh* (with a lengthened vowel) and *brother* may be pronounced as *bruh.* This pattern, however, is relatively infrequent and only takes place when the vowel sounds preceding and following *th* are similar.

4. *Word-final.* At the end of a word, *f* is the predominant pronunciation of *th* in words such as *Ruth, tooth,* and *south,* which are pronounced as *Ruf, toof,* and *souf,* respectively. Whereas most speakers fluctuate between the pronunciation of *f* and *th* in the middle of the word, some speakers exclusively use *f* and *v* at the ends of these words. In addition to *f* and *v* at the ends of these words, several other sounds may be represented by *th,* dependent upon the sounds which precede it. (6) When the preceding sound is the nasal sound *n, t* may occur so that *tenth* and *month* are pronounced as *tent'* and *mont',* respectively. The stop *t* or *d* may also be used with the preposition *with,* so that it is pronounced as *wit* or *wid.* Next to the nasal *n,* it is also possible to have no consonant at all present. This means that *month* and *tenth* may be pronounced as *mon'* and *ten'.*

r and *l*

1. *After vowels.* The pronunciation rule for *r* and *l* in Negro dialect operates in a way quite similar to white speech in certain parts of the South. At the beginning of a word, *r* and *l* are always pronounced, as in *run, lip, rub,* or *lamp.* In other positions, however, *r* and *l* are sometimes reduced to a vowel-like quality pronounced something like *uh.* The most important context to recognize in discussing the so-called "loss' of *r* and *l* is when they follow a vowel (technically called "post-vocalic"). In such items as *steal, sister, nickel,* or *bear,* only a "phonetic vestige" of *r* or *l* is pronounced, so that we hear *steauh, sistuh, nickuh,* and *beauh* respectively. Preceding a consonant in a word (e.g. *wart, tart*) some speakers do not have any phonetic vestige of *r* or *l;* this means that *help* and *hep* and *taught* and *torte* may be pronounced identically by these speakers. In some areas of the South, Negro dialect may also reveal no vestige of *r* following the vowels

o or *u.* For these speakers, *door* and *doe, four* and *foe,* and *sure* and *show* may be pronounced alike. Although it has been suggested that *l* may also be completely absent at the end of a word following *o* or *u,* there seems to be some small phonetic vestige so that *toll* and *toe* or *mole* and *mow* do not sound exactly alike in Negro dialect.

In some "r-less" American English dialects the word which follows *r* or *l* is important in determining whether or not *r* and *l* loss may take place. For example, in the *r*-less dialect of New England, *r* is consistently absent when the following word begins with a consonant, as in *brothuh Mike* or *fouh people;* when followed by a word that begins with a vowel, the *r* is consistently present, as in *brother Ed* or *four apples.* In Negro dialect, however, it may be absent in both types of contexts, although it is more frequently absent when followed by a word beginning with a consonant (e.g. *fouh people*) than when followed by one beginning with a vowel (e.g. *fouh apples*).

2. *Between vowels.*   Not only may *r* or *l* be absent when followed by another word beginning with a vowel, but *r* absence is occasionally observed between two vowels within a word. Thus, it is possible to get *Ca'ol, sto'y* or *ma'y* for *Carol, story* and *marry* respectively.

3. *Effect on vocubulary and grammar.*   The consistent absence of *r* at the end of a word has led to several "mergers" of vocabulary items. That is, because of the similarity of two words after a particular pronunciation rule has taken place, one word has assumed the function of what was originally two words. For example, when the phonetic vestige which re-places the *r* is removed, there is only a small difference which separates *they* from *their* or *you* from *your.* The forms *they* and *you* can be used as possessive as in *It is they book* or *It is your book* in Negro dialect as a result of this merging process (cf. Undifferentiated pronouns, p. 142).

Like *r,* the loss of *l* may have important implications for grammatical functions. The most crucial of these deals with the loss of *l* on a contracted form of the future modal *will.* We may get a sentence such as *Tomorrow I bring the thing* for *Tomorrow I'll bring the thing,* where *will* becomes *'ll* and then is lost completely. This pronunciation process accounts for use of *be* in Negro dialect as an indicator of future time, as in *He be here in a few minutes.* The pronunciation rule for the loss of the contracted form of *l* takes place most frequently when the following word begins with *b, m* or *w* (i.e. labial sounds).

4. *After initial consonants.*   Before leaving our description of the rules for *r* and *l* in Negro dialect, we must note that in certain words, *r* may be absent when it follows a consonant. Two main types of contexts can be cited to account for this phenomenon. First, *r* may be absent when the following

vowel is either *o* or *u*, so that we get *th'ow* for *throw*, and *th'ough* for *through*. Second, *r* may be absent in unstressed syllables, so that *protéct* and *proféssor* are pronounced as *p'otéct* and *p'oféssuh*, respectively.

5. *Social stigma.* On the whole, *r* and *l* absence has not been as socially stigmatized as many other grammatical and pronunciation rules of Negro dialect. This is probably due to the fact that certain types of *r* absence are generally recognized as legitimate regional characteristics of some dialects of standard English. Because of the relatively slight stigmatization, the rule for *r* and *l* absence is often found in the speech of middle class Negroes living in regions characterized by the presence of *r* and *l*.

Final b, d, and g

1. *Devoicing.* At the end of a syllable, the voiced stops *b, d,* and *g* (and, to a lesser extent, all voiced consonants except nasals *r, l, w* and *y*) are often pronounced as the corresponding voiceless stops, *p, t,* and *k,* respectively. This means that words such as *pig, bud,* and *cab* end in *k, t,* and *p,* respectively. Before concluding that *pig* and *pick, bud* and *butt,* and *cab* and *cap* sound identical in Negro dialect, it is essential to note that they are still distinguished by the length of the vowel. English vowels are held slightly longer when the following sound is voiced (i.e. the vowel in *bud* is held slightly longer than the vowel in *butt*). In the case of Negro dialect, the vowel is lengthened before sounds such as *d* in *bud,* even though the *d* is actually pronounced *t.* As a result, *bud* does not sound the same as *butt* because the *u* is "stretched out" a little in *bud* but not in *butt.*

In some varieties of standard English, "devoicing" can take place in an unstressed syllable, so that we can get *salat* for *salad, hundret* for *hundred,* or *acit* for *acid.* Negro dialect not only has the rule for devoicing in unstressed syllables, but stressed syllables as well, so that we hear *mut* for *mud, goot* for *good* and *loat* for *load.*

The *-ed* suffix, when attached to verb bases ending in a vowel, is represented by *d* in all varieties of English. The devoicing rule applies to this *d* of *mud, good,* and *load.* For this reason, *played* is sometimes pronounced *playt* in Negro dialect.

2. *Deletion of d.* In addition to the devoicing rule, there are some speakers who may have the complete absence of the stop *d,* although this is not nearly as frequent as devoicing. This results in pronunciations such as *goo' man* and *ba' soldier.* The rule for the absence of *d* occurs more frequently when *d* is followed by a consonant than when followed by a vowel (e.g. *goo' soldier* is more frequent than *goo' egg*); *d* absence is most common before *s* or *z.* For this reason, the addition of an *-s* suffix

often results in pronunciations such as *kiz* for *kids,* and *boahz* for *boards.*
    d-absence is also possible when *d* represents the *-ed* suffix with verbal
bases ending in vowels. It is possible to observe sentences like *Yesterday
he play it* and *He had play it the day before.* However, since this rule is much
less frequently applied than the rule eliminating the second member of a
consonant cluster, there are many more cases of sentences like *Yesterday
he miss it* than *Yesterday he play it.*

Nasalization

There are several different aspects of the nasals *m, n,* and *ng* (phonetically
[ŋ]) which must be discussed with reference to Negro dialect. Some of these
are quite characteristic of all nonstandard English dialects, others are characteristic of southern standard as well as nonstandard dialects, and still
others are unique to Negro dialect.
    1. *The -ing suffix.* The use of the *-in* suffix for *-ing* (e.g. *singin', buyin',
swimin'*) is a feature which is characteristic of all socially stigmatized
varieties of English. Because of the spelling of [ŋ] as *ng* this is sometimes
referred to as a "dropping of the *g.* "Although *in* in such words as *singin',
comin'* and *doin'* occurs in all socially stigmatized varieties of American
English, its frequency is somewhat greater in Negro dialect than in other
nonstandard dialects. In fact, there may be some speakers who do not use
the *-ing* form at all. This form is one of the most stereotyped phonological
features of nonstandard speech in the American language.
    2. *Nasalized vowels.* Another feature which is found in Negro dialect
is the use of a nasalized vowel instead of the nasal consonant. Generally,
this only takes place at the end of a syllable. In words like *man, bun,* or
bum the final consonant is sometimes not pronounced, but a nasalization
of the preceding vowel is found similar to the type of nasalization of vowels
that is found in a language such as French. This means that words such
as *rum, run,* and *rung* might all sound alike in Negro dialect (that is, they
may all be produced as [rə̃] phonetically where [˜] stands for nasalization).
As many other features in Negro dialect, this feature does not occur
categorically. That is, there is always fluctuation between the use of the
nasalized vowel and the nasal consonant.
    3. *The influence of nasals on i and e.* Finally, we should mention the
influence that nasal consonants have on the vowels *i* and *e.* Before a nasal
consonant, *i* and *e* do not contrast, making words such as *pin* and *pen* or
tin and *ten* sound identical. This pronunciation rule of Negro dialect is quite
like some standard varieties of Southern speech, and only has social significance in a Northern context.

Vowel Glides

In some parts of the South, the vowel glides represented as *ay* (e.g. *slide, time*) and *oy* (e.g. *boy, toy*) are generally pronounced without the glide. Thus, *slide* and *time* may be pronounced as *sahd* and *tahm* and *boy* and *toy* as *boah* and *toah*. This feature of some Southern standard as well as nonstandard dialects has been adopted as an integral part of Negro dialect. The absence of the glide is much more frequent when it is followed by a voiced sound or a pause than it is when followed by a voiceless sound. This means that the absence of a glide is much more likely in words such as *slide, time*, or *toy* than it is in *kite, bright*, or *flight*. Many speakers never have a glide when followed by voicing but always have one when followed by a voiceless sound (e.g. they always have *tahm* for *time* but never have *kaht* for *kite*). Because the rule for vowel glides is found among middle class speakers in the South, its social significance is limited to Northern areas, where it is associated with class and race. Even in Northern areas, however, its stigmatization is minimal.

Indefinite Articles a and an

In standard English, when the following word begins with a vowel, the indefinite article *an* is used as in *an apple* or *an egg;* when it is followed by a word beginning with a consonant, *a* occurs as in *a boy* or *a dog*. In Negro dialect, as in some varieties of white Southern speech, the article *a* is used regardless of how the following word begins. With a selected group of words (of more than one syllable) which may begin with a vowel similar to *a* (phonetically [ə]), the article may also be completely absent (or, at least, "merge" with the vowel); this results in sentences such as *He had eraser* or *He had erector set*. Less frequently, and mostly among younger children, this article may be absent in other types of constructions (e.g. *I have pencil*), but this type of absence seems to be a grammatical rather than a pronunciation feature.

Stress

Stress or accent in Negro dialect operates quite like the stress patterns of standard English with several exceptions. One exception can be found when standard English words of more than one syllable have their stress on the second syllable rather than the first. In Negro dialect, some of these words may be stressed on the first rather than the second syllable. This only affects a small subset of words such as *políce, hotél*, or *Julý*, which in Negro dialect are pronounced as *pólice, hótel* and *Júly*.

Another difference which can be traced to stress is the absence of the first syllable of a word when the first syllable is unstressed. For example, we find *'rithmetic, 'member, 'cept* or *'bout,* respectively. Because this pattern results in the absence of certain types of prefixes, some speakers may occasionally "overuse" the prefix *re-*. This overuse of *re-* may result in formations such as *revorce* or *remorial* for *divorce* and *memorial,* according to William A. Stewart.

Other Pronunciation Features

In addition to the systematic patterns which have been mentioned above, there are several features which are quite restricted. One such feature is the pronunciation of *ask* as *ax,* so that it sounds like *axe.* This feature, which is quite prominent in some speakers of Negro dialect, can be related to an Old English pronunciation which has been preserved in Negro dialect as well as white Appalachian speech.

Another rule which is quite limited is the absence of *s* in a word which ends in *x* (phonetically [ks]). This pattern results in the pronunciation of *box* as *bok* and *six* as *sik* (homophonous with *sick*). For the most part, this feature is limited to a few items ending in *x* and is more frequently found in Southern speakers of Negro dialect than it is in Northern speakers.

Finally, we may mention rules for the *str* clusters in such words as *string* and *street,* which may be pronounced as *skring* and *skreet,* respectively. At the end of a word, *st* may also be changed to *sk,* so that *wrist* and *twist* are occasionally pronounced as *wrisk* and *twisk* when speakers are trying to approximate a standard English norm.

There are, of course, other restricted types of differences between the pronunciation rules of Negro dialect and standard English which might be mentioned. Other examples, however, are either so limited in terms of the numbers of items affected or so unobtrusive in terms of their social significance, that it is sufficient for the teacher to have a firm understanding of the pronunciation features which we have described above. Indeed, the teacher who fully understands and respects the pronunciation rules of Negro dialect discussed here will have taken a necessary step in the effective teaching of standard English.

Grammar

Other features of Negro dialect are due to the fact that some of the rules of Negro dialect grammar are different from grammatical rules in standard English. These rules deal with the verb system, with negation, with noun suffixes, with question formation, and with pronouns. Some of the features in the following section, however, are technically pronunciation features, but are described as grammatical features because they are usually perceived as such.

Verbs

Many of the most significant features of Negro dialect are to be found in its verb system. The differences in the verb structure of Negro dialect as compared to standard American English are mainly found in the tense systems of the two dialects and in their treatment of the verb *to be*.

Past Forms

1. *The -ed suffix.*   As we have seen already, the *-ed* suffix which marks past tense and past participial forms, as well as derived adjectives, is sometimes not pronounced in Negro dialect because of pronunciation rules (pp. 139 and 149). When *-ed* is added to a verb base ending in a consonant, as in *missed,* it can be removed by application of the consonant cluster reduction rule. When *-ed* is added to a verbal base which ends in a vowel, it can be removed by the rule for deletion of syllable-final *d.* As we have already pointed out, the *d*-deletion rule applies much less often than the consonant cluster reduction rule, so that *-ed* is much more frequently absent from bases ending in a consonant which is not *t* or *d* than from bases ending in a vowel.

When *-ed* is added to a base ending in *t* or *d,* it is pronounced something like *id,* (7) as we have mentioned before. In this form, it is rarely absent in Negro dialect. However, this *id* form can be reduced to *d* alone in Negro dialect and also in standard English by some fairly complex, but very regular rules. In casual speech, the words *want* and *start* are the most frequently occurring verbs which are eligible for these rules. If they apply, the *i*-sound of *id* can be eliminated. The verb then ends in *dd* or *td* which is simplified to *d.* These operations result in sentences like *He stard crying* (from *He started crying*) and *He wanda go* (from *He wanted to go*). Such sentences are common in all varieties of American English and are not considered nonstandard. In the case of *stard,* Negro dialect (but not standard English) has a rule for the elimination of the remaining *d,* especially when the verb occurs before a gerund, as in *He sta crying* (the *r* of *start* is absent for reasons we have already discussed). The verb *started* is virtually the only verb to undergo this process. (8)

These rules are pronunciation rules. This means that the missing *-ed* suffix does not reflect a grammatical difference between Negro dialect and standard English. The suffix is a part of the grammar of both kinds of

English. Any attempt to teach the *-ed* suffix as a grammatical entity, then, will be superfluous.

Another important implication is that children who speak Negro dialect should not be required to learn the careful pronunciation of *-ed* where speakers of standard English usually do not pronounce it. When *-ed* is phonetically *t* or *d* and is the second member of a consonant cluster, and when the next word begins with a consonant, as in *Yesterday I burned my hand,* Negro dialect speakers should be allowed to pronounce *burned* as *burn',* the way standard English speakers do.

2. *Irregular verbs.* Verbs which form their past tenses in an irregular way distinguish present and past forms in the overwhelming majority of cases in Negro dialect. The occurrence of sentences like *Yesterday he give it to me* are rare. However, some verbs which have irregular past forms in standard English have the same form for past and present tenses in Negro dialect. There are also such verbs in standard English (*They hit him yesterday; They hit him every day*). A few verbs, notably *say,* behave like *hit* for some speakers of Negro dialect, giving, for example, *He say it every day; He say it yesterday.* In the case of *say,* the situation is complicated by the fact that some speakers who actually use *said* will be heard by speakers of standard English as having said *say* because the *d* of *said* has been removed by the word-final *d*-elimination rule.

Perfective Constructions

1. *General.* The perfective constructions in Negro dialect discussed below are first illustrated in Table 5.

Table 5.

The Perfective Constructions in Negro Dialect and Standard English

	Negro Dialect	Standard English
Present Perfect	I have walked I('ve) walked	I have walked I've walked
Past Perfect	I had walked	I had walked I'd walked
Completive	I done walked	
Remote Time	I been walked	

2. *Omission of forms of have.* In standard American English, the present tense forms of auxiliary *have* can be contracted to *'ve* and *'s,* giving sentences like *I've been here for hours* and *He's gone home already.* In Negro dialect, the contracted forms *'ve* and *'s* can be removed, giving *I been here for hours* and *He gone home already.* Rules for removing the remnants of contraction account for at least three of the most noticed features of Negro dialect, as we shall see. The frequent operation of this rule, together with the relatively infrequent use of the present perfective tense can lead to the conclusion that *have* + past participle is not part of Negro dialect. It is true that the present perfect tense is quite infrequent. But the past perfect construction with *had* is, if anything, even more common in Negro dialect narratives than in narratives by speakers of standard American English. Sentences like *He had found the money* appear strikingly often in story-telling. Negro dialect speakers do not select the present perfect as often as do speakers of standard English, but they select the past perfect more often than standard English speakers. As with the *-ed* suffix, pronunciation rules have removed forms which are present grammatically.

3. *The past participle.* While it is quite clear that the tenses formed grammatically with *have* and *had* are part of Negro dialect, it is less clear whether or not there are past participles in its grammar. In standard English, most past participles are formed with the *-ed* suffix and so are identical with the past tense form. But there are a number of semi-regular and irregular verbs for which the past participle and past tense are formally distinguished (e.g. *came* versus *has come; ate* versus *has eaten,* etc.). In Negro dialect, however, it seems that there may not be any irregular verbs for which the past tense and past participle are distinct. Sometimes the standard English past participle form is generalized to serve both functions (*He taken it; He have taken it*), but more commonly the simple past form is used in both kinds of constructions (e.g. *He came; He have came*). For a few verbs, some Negro dialect speakers generalize one form while others generalize the other (e.g. *He done it; He have done it; He did it; He have did it*). It is possible, then, that the Negro dialect equivalents of the present and past perfect tenses are not formed with forms of *have* plus the past participle, but rather with a form of *have* plus a general past form.

4. *The completive aspect with done.* Where standard American English has only two aspectual contrasts of the perfective type, Negro dialect has four. With standard English, Negro dialect has perfective tense (or aspect) constructions with *have* and *had.* In addition, Negro dialect has a complement construction and a remote time construction. The completive aspect is formed from the verb *done* plus a past form of the verb. Because of the uncertain status of the past participle in the grammar of the dialect, it is

difficult to determine whether this form is the past participle or not. This construction occurs in sentences like *I have tried hard all I know how* and *I done forgot what you call it.*

5. *The remote time construction with been.*   A similar construction with *been* indicates that the speaker conceives of the action as having taken place in the distant past. The remote aspect is used in *I been had it there for about three or four years* and *You won't get your dues that you been paid.* Often, the *been* construction is used with emphatic stress to doubly emphasize the total completion of an action, although it is not always used in this way. Unlike the *done* construction, the *been* construction is used only in Negro dialect. Both constructions are rather rare, at least in Northern cities.

The Third Person Singular Present Tense Marker

1. *General.*   In standard American English, the suffix *-s* (or *-es*) is used to identify the present tense of a verb if the subject of that verb is in the third person singular. The paradigm is:

Singular	*Plural*
I walk	we walk
you walk	you walk
he walks; the man walks	they walk; the men walk

In a sense, the use of the *-s* suffix to mark present tense with third person singular subjects is an irregularity, since no suffix is used to mark present tense with other persons. The paradigm in Negro dialect is more regular:

Singular	*Plural*
I walk	we walk
you walk	you walk
he walk; the man walk	they walk; the men walk

It is important to realize that the *-s* suffix is not carelessly "left off" by speakers of Negro dialect. This suffix is simply not part of the grammar of the dialect.

2. *Auxiliary don't.*   The verb *do* is used as an auxiliary in negative and other kinds of sentences. In Negro dialect, the *-s* suffix is absent from the auxiliary *don't* in the present tense when the subject is in the third person singular, just as it is from other third person singular present tense verbs. The equivalent of the standard English sentence *He doesn't go,* then, is *He don't go.* Some other nonstandard dialects of English lack the *-s* suffix only with auxiliary *don't.* Speakers of such dialects rarely or never use sentences like *He walk,* but frequently use such sentences as *He don't walk.* The use

of *don't* for *doesn't* in Negro dialect does not apply only to auxiliary *don't*, but is part of a general pattern involving all present tense verbs with subjects in the third person singular. (9)

3. *Have and do.*   The verb *have* in standard English is unique in that the combination of *have* and the *-s* suffix results in *has* rather than *haves*. Similarly, when the *-s* suffix is added to *do*, the vowel quality changes and the result is *does*, not *dos*. Since the *-s* suffix does not exist in the verb system of Negro dialect, the verbs remain *have* and *do* with third person singular subjects in the present tense. For this reason, we observe sentences like *He have a bike, He always do silly things*, and *I don't know if he like you, but I think he do.*

4. *Hypercorrect forms.*   The absence of the *-s* suffix in Negro dialect causes a real language learning problem when Negro dialect speakers come in contact with standard English. They observe that speakers of standard English have a suffix *-s* on some present tense verbs. But the grammatical rules restricting its use to sentences with third person singular subjects is just like a rule in the grammar of a foreign language. Like a foreign language learner, Negro dialect speakers begin to use the feature, but do not restrict it according to the rules of the new dialect. The result is that the *-s* subject is sporadically used with present tense verbs with subjects other than third person singular. This accounts for sentences like *I walks, you walks, the children walks*, etc., as well as the appropriate standard English *He walks*. Occasionally, the suffix is also added to non-finite forms, giving sentences like *They want to goes*. No Negro dialect speakers, however, add the *-s* suffix to all present tense verbs with non-third person singular subjects.

The use of sentences like *I walks* has a quite different status from the use of sentences like *He walk*. A speaker of Negro dialect uses *walk* instead of *walks* with a subject like *he* because this is the correct form according to the grammatical rules of his dialect. He uses *walks* with subjects like *I*, not because this grammar calls for this form but because of a partial learning of the grammar rules of a different dialect.

Future

1. *Gonna.*   A very frequent future indicator in Negro dialect, as in other dialects of English, is the use of *gonna*. The rule for deleting *is* and *are* (see pp. 135–136) operates very frequently when *gonna* follows, giving sentences like *He gonna go* and *You gonna get in trouble*. So rarely is a form of *be* used with *gonna* that it may seem that *gonna* is not related to standard English *be going to*, but is an auxiliary in its own right. However, the behavior of *gonna* as compared with true auxiliaries like *can* shows that

this is not the case. In questions and in abbreviated sentences, *can* and *gonna* function quite differently (*Can he go?* but never *Gonna he go?; He can sing, I know he can* but *He gonna vote for you, I know he is,* not *I know he gonna*). As Labov and his associates have pointed out, the phonetic form of *gonna* can be reduced in a number of ways in Negro dialect which are different from its reductions in standard English. When the subject of the sentence is *I* in standard dialects of American English, *gonna* can be reduced to *ngna* (*I'ngna go*). In Negro dialect, there are three reductions not possible in standard English, *mana* (*I'mana go*), *mon* (*I'mon go*) and *ma* (*I'ma go*).When the subject is something other than *I*, Negro dialect may give the reduced form *gon* (*He gon go*). (10)

2. *Will.* The use of *will* to indicate future time reference is also part of both Negro dialect and standard English. As in the case of *has* and *have, will* can be contracted (to *'ll*). This contracted form, like *'ve* and *'s,* can be eliminated, as we have seen, especially if the next word begins with a labial consonant, as in *He miss you tomorrow.* This makes it appear that the future is sometimes indicated by the use of the main verb alone.

Invariant Be

1. *General.* When the verb *to be* is used as a main verb in standard English, it appears as one of the five variant inflected forms *is, are, am, was* or *were,* depending on the verb tense and the person and number of the subject. In Negro dialect, the form *be* can be used as a main verb, regardless of the subject of the sentence as in *I be here this afternoon* and *Sometime he be busy.* This use of invariant *be* in Negro dialect has two explanations; deleted *will* or *would* and distributive *be.*

2. *Will be or would be.* Since *be* begins with a labial consonant, the *'ll* contraction of *will* is often absent before *be.* This is fairly common in Negro dialect, but also happens occasionally in standard English, giving sentences like *He be here pretty soon.* The contracted form of *would* is *'d,* which can merge with the *b* of *be* or be removed by the final *d* elimination rule. This process is another source for invariant *be* and is quite common in standard English as well. A sentence like *If you gave him a present he be happy* is possible both in standard dialects and in Negro dialect.

It may seem that an intolerable number of ambiguous sentences would result from the removal of the remnants of contraction. But the context usually makes the intended meaning clear. The same sort of thing happens in standard English, not only in the occasional removal of *'ll* and *'d,* but in the contraction of *'d* of both *had* and *would.* The sentence *He'd come home* is ambiguous by itself. But in contexts like *He'd come home before I got there* or *He'd come home if he could,* the meaning is clear.

3. *Distributive or non-tense be.* The other source for invariant *be* is very different. This type of invariant *be* occurs because *to be* is possible in Negro dialect without tense specification with a meaning something like "object or event distributed intermittently in time." This use of *be,* as in *Sometime he be there and sometime he don't,* occurs only in Negro dialect and is usually misunderstood by standard English speakers. It is common for standard English speakers to take non-tense *be* as a deviant form of *am, is,* or *are,* when in fact it contrasts with these forms. To say *I'm good* is to assert a permanent quality of oneself. To say *I be good* means that the speaker is good only intermittently. Unlike the cases of invariant *be* which are derived from *will be* or *would be,* non-tense *be* usage is highly stigmatized socially. Because there are three sources for invariant *be* in Negro dialect, any positive statement containing invariant *be* is potentially three-ways ambiguous. In the sentence *If somebody hit him, Darryl be mad,* if the use of *be* is taken as coming from *would be,* it is a hypothesis about how Darryl might act if he were hit. If *will be* is understood, it is a prediction as to how Darryl will react. If distributive *be* is the interpretation, it is a statement of Darryl's reaction to a certain kind of intermittent event. The sentence is only ambiguous because it is a positive statement. In negative sentences, contraction of *will* and *would* is not possible. The three interpretations above would each be denied in a different way. The hypothesis would be denied by *Darryl wouldn't be mad,* the predication by *Darryl won't be mad,* and the statement by *Darryl don't be mad.*

Absence of Forms of To Be

1. *General.* When the *is* or *are* forms of *to be* are expected in standard English, Negro dialect may have no form at all. When the subject is *I,* and the expected standard English form is *am,* however, *am* or its contraction *'m* is almost always present. For most varieties of Negro dialect, the absence of forms of *to be* represents the elimination of the contracted forms *'s* and *'re* of *is* and *are,* much as the contractions of *have, has, will* and *would* are removed. Just as in these cases and in the case of the *-ed* suffix, the *to be* forms are grammatically present and are known to the speaker, but have been removed by a pronunciation rule. It is not necessary to teach the present tense forms of *to be* to speakers of Negro dialect, but they will need to learn to contract these forms without also deleting the remnants of contraction.

2. *Is.*   As we have seen, the absence of *is* is common before *gonna.* Some Southern dialects of English besides Negro dialect show the absence of *is* in this context. In Negro dialect, unlike other English dialects, *is* can be absent wherever it can be contracted in standard English. We observe sentences like *He a man, He running to school, That dude bad,* as well as *He gonna go.* When the subject of a sentence is *it, that,* or *what,* [and] the next word is *is,* an *s*-sound is usually heard. This is not the *'s* from the contraction of *is,* however. The *s* in such sentences is the result of the following process. First, *is* is contracted to *'s.* Then, the *t* of *it, that* and *what* is transformed into *s* under the influence of the *'s* from *is.* This leaves *is's, thas's,* and *whas's.* But these forms are never heard because the *'s* from *is* is then eliminated as it almost always must be when it follows a sibilant. This leaves the pronunciation *iss, thas* and *whas* for these three words. Apparently something similar happens in the case of *let's* (pronounced *les*) even though the *'s* comes from *us* rather than *is.*

3. *Are.*   The form *are* is present less often than the form *is* in the speech of Negro dialect speakers. *Are* is also absent in white Southern dialects of English which do not allow the absence of *is,* including some which are socially standard. The English contraction rule provides for the removal of all but the final consonant of certain auxiliaries (*are* to *'re, will* to *'ll, have* to *'ve,* etc.). In dialects which lack *r* after most stressed vowels, *are* has no final consonant (i.e. it is pronounced *ah*). Regular pronunciation rules of English reduce this *ah* to *uh.* Applying the contraction rule to this pronunciation eliminates the word *are* entirely, without utilizing the Negro dialect rule for removing the consonant. Because of this there are speakers who have *are* absence but do not have *is* absence.

4. *Agreement with forms of to be.*   Some speakers show no person-number agreement with full forms of *to be* are used. The past tense form is *was* regardless of the subject, giving sentences like *They was there, You was there,* etc. When the full forms of the present tense form is used, *is* is used by these speakers for all persons, e.g. *The boys is there, You is there,* etc. However, some Southern speakers of Negro dialect occasionally use *are* or even *am* as the general form of the present tense of *to be* (*There she are, You am a teacher,* etc.).

Negation

The Use of Ain't

Due to a series of phonetic changes in the history of English, the negative forms of *is, are, am,* and auxiliary *have* and *has* became *ain't.* Although *ain't* is used by educated speakers in casual conversation in some parts of the country, the use of *ain't* in this way is one of the clearest and universal markers of nonstandard speech of all kinds. In some varieties of Negro dialect, *ain't* also corresponds to standard English *didn't*. This probably developed from rather recent phonetic changes. In Negro dialect, negative forms of auxiliary *do* can lose the initial *d* in casual speech. This gives, for example, *I 'on't know* for standard English *I don't know*. In the case of *didn't*, the second *d* can merge with the following *n*. The result of these two developments is the pronunciation *int* for *didn't*. This form is so similar in pronunciation and function to the already existing *ain't* that the two forms merged. For speakers of Negro dialect who have this use of *ain't*, there are sentences like *He ain't do it* as well as *He ain't done it* (or *He ain't did it*) and *He ain't there*. The unfamilarity of this usage to speakers of standard English often leads to misunderstanding between speakers of the two dialects. A Negro dialect speaker may say *He ain't touch me* which should be translated as *He didn't touch me* in standard English but be understood as having meant *He hasn't touched me* (with the *-ed* suffix supplied by the hearer). *Ain't* is often used with multiple negation, leading to sentences like *He ain't nobody, He ain't did nothing* and *He ain't go nowhere*.

Multiple Negation

1. *General.* "Double negatives" or, more accurately, multiple negation is another very common feature of nonstandard dialects. A frequent misconception about multiple negation is that it leads to misunderstanding because "two negatives make a positive." For example, it is often said of a sentence like *He doesn't know nothing* that the intention of the speaker is reversed because if he doesn't know *nothing*, he must know *something*. But in actual usage, sentences with multiple negatives are always understood as the speaker intends them, by other speakers of nonstandard English and usually by speakers of the standard dialects as well. The reason is that there is basically only one negative in *He doesn't know nothing* which is expressed in more than one place in the sentence. Standard English allows negatives to be expressed only once; nonstandard dialects have no such restriction. Yet there are strict grammar rules in nonstandard dialects of English which govern precisely at which places in a sentence a negative can be expressed.

2. *Three negative placement rules in standard English.* To understand these facts, it is necessary to introduce a new concept of grammar rule. We will conceive of all sentences as starting out at an abstract level with an

abstract structure which is not actually pronounced. What grammar rules do is to take this unpronounceable abstract structure and convert it, step by step, into an ordinary sentence which can actually be spoken. These rules are partly the same for all dialects of English, but partly different. These differences account for the fact that the same basic structure can be expressed in different ways in different dialects.

As an example, we will see what happens when the abstract structure of the sentence *Nobody knows anything* is operated on by the rules of standard English. At the abstract level, we can think of the structure of *Nobody knows anything* as: NOT+ANY-BODY+DOE-S+KNOW+ANY-THING. The element NOT is to be understood as denying the truth value of the rest of the sentence. All dialects of English have a rule which requires that this NOT be placed into any noun phrase containing the indefinite element ANY, if that noun phrase comes before the main verb. Because of this rule, the first rule of negative placement, there are no dialects of English which have such sentences as *Anybody doesn't know anything* or *Anybody knows nothing.* We can symbolize the fact that NOT has been incorporated into ANY by changing the first plus sign to a dash. This means that the element NOT is now part of the same word as ANYBODY. The result is: NOT-ANY-BODY+DOE-S+KNOW+ANY-THING. Since standard English allows the basic negative element NOT to be expressed only once, this is the only negative placement rule which can be applied to this sentence. Later on, there will be a rule to convert cases of NOT-ANY into *no.* There is another rule which removes DO in sentences like this one and attaches the -S to main verbs like KNOW. The final result is *Nobody knows anything.*

In the sentence *He doesn't know anything,* there is no ANY in the noun phrase which comes before the verb. The abstract structure would be NOT +HE+DOE-S+KNOW+ANY-THING. Because there is no ANY before the verb, the first negative placement rule does not operate. NOT must be placed by the second negative placement rule in this sentence. This rule stipulates that the element NOT will be attached to the main verb phrase, if the first rule is not applicable. The effect on our abstract structure is: HE +DOE-S+NOT+KNOW+ANY-THING. There is a later rule which contracts *does not,* giving *doesn't.*

In formal styles of standard English speech, it is possible to use sentences such as *He knows nothing.* This sentence results from the third negative placement rule, which may be applied, but is not required. This rule allows a negative to be removed from the main verb phrase and be attached to the first ANY which follows the verb phrase. This rule operates on the result of the second negative placement rule. As we know, the structure which results from the application of this rule is HE+DOE-S+NOT+ KNOW+ANY-THING. If the third negative placement rule is selected, the structure of HE+DOE-S+NOT+KNOW+ANY-THING is converted to HE+DOE-S+KNOW+NOT-ANY-THING. After the rules for removing DO and converting NOT-ANY to NO have been applied, HE+DOE-S +KNOW+NOT-ANY-THING becomes *He knows nothing.*

3. *The three negative placement rules in nonstandard English.* In standard English, the three negative placement rules operate under the general restriction that the negative element NOT can be expressed in the final version of any sentence only once. If the first rule applied, the second and third rules do not. If the conditions for the use of the first rule are not met, the second rule applies. In some styles of speech, it is possible to use the third rule, but if it is used, NOT is removed from the position given it by the second rule. In nonstandard dialects, the second and third rules are copying rules, not placement rules in the strictest sense. These rules make a copy of the original NOT somewhere else in the sentence, but leave the first NOT in its original position. Let us examine the abstract structure NOT+ANY-BODY+DOE-S+KNOW+IT, which would be expressed in standard dialects as *Nobody knows it.* The first negative placement rule, as we have seen, operates in all dialects of English. In any variety of English, the result of the first rule is NOT-ANY-BODY+DOE-S+KNOW+IT. In standard English, the second and third rules are not allowed to operate if the first rule has been applied. In some kinds of nonstandard English, including Negro dialect, the second negative placement rule is allowed to apply to NOT-ANY-BODY+DOE-S+KNOW+IT as a copying rule. That is, it makes a copy of NOT in the main verb phrase of the sentence, but leaves the original NOT where it is. The result is: NOT-ANY-BODY+ DOE-S+NOT+KNOW+IT. When the rules which convert NOT-ANY to *no* and contract *not* have been applied, the sentence comes out as *Nobody doesn't know it.* (11) At this point it is essential to keep in mind that *Nobody doesn't know it* comes from exactly the same abstract structure as the standard English *Nobody knows it* and means the same thing. The *n't* of *doesn't* is a mere copy of the *no* of *nobody.* Unlike most kinds of multiple negation, sentences to which both the first and second rules have been applied are likely to be misunderstood by speakers of standard English. Standard English speakers would not expect *Nobody doesn't know it* to have a negative meaning.

The third negative placement rule operates differently in nonstandard dialects from the way in which it operates in standard dialects. Like the nonstandard use of the second rule above, the third rule in nonstandard English acts as a copying rule. Consider the following structures:

NOT+ANY-BODY+DOE-S+KNOW+ANY-THING+ABOUT+ANY-
THING (the basis for standard English *Nobody knows anything about
anything*), and NOT+HE+DOE-S+KNOW+ANY-THING+ABOUT+
ANY-THING (the basis for standard English *He doesn't know anything
about anything* or *He knows nothing about anything*). The first negative
placement rule converts NOT+ANY-BODY+DOE-S+KNOW+ANY-
THING+ABOUT+ANY-THING   to   NOT-ANY-BODY+DOE-S+
KNOW+ANY-THING+ABOUT+ANY-THING, incorporating NOT
into ANY-BODY. In standard English, the second and third placement
rules can never apply if the first rule applies. We have seen that the second
negative placement rule can apply in some nonstandard dialects as a copying rule, even if the first rule has already operated. In most nonstandard
dialects, whether or not the second rule is allowed to operate as a copying
rule, the third rule is allowed to operate as such. In this form, the third
rule stipulates that NOT may be copied with every ANY in the sentence,
but also must be left in its original position. When this rule applies in these
nonstandard dialects, it converts NOT-ANY-BODY+DOE-S+KNOW+
ANY-THING   to   NOT-ANY-BODY+DOE-S+KNOW+NOT-ANY-
THING+ABOUT+NOT-ANY-THING. After the rule about NOT-ANY
and the rule about DOES have operated, the result is: *Nobody knows nothing about nothing.* Again it is imperative to keep in mind that the sentences
*Nobody knows anything about anything, Nobody knows nothing about noth-
ing* and *Nobody doesn't know nothing about nothing* are all equivalent in
meaning. The multiple negative expressions are simply different ways of
copying the one basic sentence-negating NOT.

If we take the structure, NOT+HE+DOE-S+KNOW+ANY-THING+
ABOUT+ANY-THING, we notice that the first rule does not apply, since
the first noun phrase does not contain ANY. If the first rule does not apply,
all dialects of English require that the second rule apply, which places the
NOT in the main verb phrase. The result is HE+DOE-S+NOT+KNOW
+ANY-THING+ABOUT+ANY-THING. The third negative placement
rule can apply, but does not necessarily have to, in standard English. If it
does apply, it removes the NOT from the verb phrase and attaches it to
the first ANY. The ultimate result is *He knows nothing about anything.* In
nonstandard dialects, there are two differences. First, the rule is a copying
rule, so the original NOT remains in the main verb phrase. Furthermore,
the NOT is copied with every ANY in the sentence, so that the resulting
structure is HE+DOE-S+NOT+KNOW+NOT-ANY-THING+ABOUT
+NOT-ANY-THING, and the ultimate sentence is *He doesn't know nothing about nothing.*

For some speakers of Negro dialect, the third rule must apply to every
sentence with ANY after the main verb phrase. For these speakers, there

are no such sentences as *Nobody knows anything about anything* and *He doesn't know anything about anything;* the grammar of this variety requires *Nobody knows nothing about nothing* and *He doesn't know nothing about nothing.* Another way of putting it is that the word *any* can never appear in the spoken form of a negative sentence.

4. *Multiple negation in two clauses.* The nonstandard applications of the second and third negative placement rules above only apply within a single clause. There is another type of multiple negation, which is possible for some Negro dialect speakers, in which negation may be marked in two different clauses. These speakers use sentences like *Nobody didn't know it didn't rain* meaning *Nobody knew it rained.* But such sentences are extremely rare.

5. *Multiple negation with negative adverbs.* Negation can be expressed with negative adverbs, as well as in verb phrases and by incorporation into ANY. Multiple negation can be expressed by a negative adverb and also by one of these other methods in the same sentence. The result is the utterance of sentences like *He doesn't hardly come to see us anymore,* or more commonly, *He doesn't come to see us any more, hardly.* Standard English speakers who never use other kinds of multiple negation sometimes use sentences like the above. In Negro dialect, the marking of negation in the verb phrase or with ANY in sentences which contain *hardly* is the rule rather than the exception. Negro dialect, along with other nonstandard English dialects, also allows negation to be multiply expressed when the same sentence contains the adverbs *never* and *neither.*

6. *Negativized auxiliary pre-position.* If a sentence has an indefinite noun phrase containing a negative marker *(nobody, nothing, no dog)* before the verb, the negativized form of the verbal auxiliary *(can't, wasn't, didn't)* may be placed at the beginning of the sentence. The result is sentences like *Can't nobody do it, Wasn't nothing wrong,* and *Didn't no dog bite him.* Although these sentences appear to be questions in their written form, the intonation of the spoken form in Negro dialect makes it clear that they are statements. If the noun phrase before the verb does not contain a negativized indefinite, pre-position of the auxiliary is not possible, so that a sentence like *Don't the man do it* will not occur as a statement.

-*s* Suffixes

Possessive

1. *With common nouns.* Where the *'s* possessive appears in standard English, Negro dialect indicates possessive by the order of the words. The phrase *The boy hat* corresponds to *The boy's hat* in the standard dialect.

In Northern urban Negro dialect, apparently no one uses the zero form of the possessive exclusively; it alternates with the 's form. In Southern varieties of Negro dialect it seems possible to find speakers who do not use 's for possessive at all. There is some reason to believe that the presence of the 's possessive suffix is more common at the end of a clause (i.e. in absolute position, as in *The hat is the boy('s)* than in the attributive possessive *(The boy('s) hat)*. It has been claimed that the 's in this situation is regularly present. However the absence of the 's suffix in the absolute possessive suffix has been observed with some frequency in the speech of Northern urban Negro dialect speakers and has been found to be extremely common in Southern Negro dialect data. Pedagogically, it would seem wise to deal with both kinds, but to emphasize the attributive construction.

2. *With personal names.*   Because the position of the 's possessive is somewhat unstable in the grammar of Negro dialect, some speakers use the 's suffix inappropriately with personal names when attempting to speak standard English. In standard English, of course, the rule is that the 's suffix is attached to the surname when the possessor is identified by his full name *(Jack Johnson's car)*. Occasionally, a Negro dialect speaker will attach the 's suffix to both names *(Jack's Johnson's car)* or to the first name *(Jack's Johnson car)*. This feature is not part of the grammar of Negro dialect but is a hypercorrection in attempting to use standard English (cf. the hypercorrections in connection with the 's third person singular present tense marker on p. 133).

3. *Mines.*   Some speakers of Negro dialect use the form *mines* for *mine* in the absolute possessive construction (never in the attributive construction) giving sentences like *This mines.* This is a regularization in Negro dialect of the absolute possessive form of the first person pronoun to conform to the other pronoun forms which end in *s (his, hers, its, yours, ours, theirs)*.

4. *Undifferentiated pronouns.*   Some speakers of Negro dialect use the standard English nominative or accusative forms of personal pronouns for possession in attributive constructions *(he book, him book, we book,* etc.). This feature, which is probably to be ascribed to the lingering influence of the grammar of Caribbean Creole languages in Negro dialect, is extremely rare in the North but apparently somewhat more common in the speech of young children in the South.

Plural

1. *Absence of the plural suffix.*   The -s (or -es) suffixes which mark most plurals in standard English are occasionally absent in the speech of Negro

dialect speakers. This results in sentences like *He took five book* and *The other teacher, they'll yell at you.* The absence of the plural suffix in Northern urban Negro dialect occurs considerably less often than the absence of the possessive suffix and far less than the absence of the third person singular present tense marker. (12) There is no question that most Northern speakers of Negro dialect have the use of the plural suffix as part of their grammar. Much of the absence of the plural suffix is due to a difference in the classification of certain nouns in Negro dialect from standard English. A few nouns do not take the plural suffix at all in standard English *(one sheep, two sheep).* Words which are so classified in Negro dialect, but which take the regular *-s* plural in standard English include *cent, year,* and *movie.* It is possible that the absence of the plural suffix in words like *cent* and *year* is because the grammar of Negro dialect allows the optional absence of the plural marker with nouns of measure. Such a rule is also part of the grammar of a number of white regional dialects. For some speakers of Southern Negro dialect, particularly young children, the plural suffix is almost always absent and may well not be part of the grammar of their dialect at all. The occasional claim that the plural suffix may only be absent when the plural noun is preceded by a quantifier (*two, several,* etc.), and not otherwise, is invalid. There are a great many examples of plural nouns not preceded by a quantifier which lack the plural suffix.

2. *Regular plurals with irregular nouns.*   Some nouns in standard English form plurals by a vowel change *(one foot, two feet),* or with no suffix at all *(one deer, two deer).* For many Negro dialect speakers, these nouns take the regular *-s* suffix *(two foots, two deers).* This is another example of a classification difference between the two kinds of English.

3. *Double plurals.*   Where standard English forms plurals irregularly, Negro dialect may add the *–s* suffix to the irregular plural *(peoples, childrens).* A possible historical reason relates to an earlier stage of Negro dialect in which the plural category was not part of the grammar. (13) In learning standard English, speakers of the dialect tended to add the *-s* suffix to words which were already pluralized in an irregular way. These doubly pluralized words became fossilized and are preserved to the present. Words most frequently affected are *childrens, peoples,* and *mens.*

Questions

Inversion

The form which questions take in standard English depends on whether the question is direct or indirect. If the question is direct, word-order inversion takes place, but if the question is indirect, the basic word order is retained. Inversion affects the questioned element, if any, and the verbal auxiliary or copula, transferring them to the beginning of the sentence. The statement *He went somewhere* can be content-questioned or yes-no-questioned. To form the content question, *somewhere* is replaced by *where,* the auxiliary *did* is added and both are moved to the head of the sentence, giving *Where did he go.* The yes-no question simply requires the insertion of the auxiliary *did* and its transfer to the head of the sentence, giving *Did he go somewhere.* The indirect question involves the transfer of the questioned element to the head of the clause only. In the case of yes-no questions, *if* or *whether* is used in the construction. Examples of the two types of indirect questions corresponding to *He went somewhere* would be *I want to know where he went* and *I want to know if (whether) he went somewhere.* In Negro dialect spoken in the North, the inverted form of the question is used for both direct and indirect questions and the words *if* and *whether* are not used to form indirect yes-no questions. The direct questions for *He went somewhere* are the same as the standard English examples given above. But the two indirect questions would be *I want to know where did he go* and *I want to know did he go somewhere.* The Negro dialect grammar rules for question formation are more regular than the standard English rules, since they apply in the same way to both kinds of questions. (14) Some speakers, on the other hand, have the uninverted form for direct questions, at least in content questions. These speakers use questions like *What that is?* and *Where the white cat is?*.

A historical process something like the following may explain this state of affairs. The uninverted construction is probably the older one. As Negro dialect began to approximate standard American English more closely, its speakers noticed that the standard dialect had inverted direct questions. Since there was no distinction in Negro dialect between direct and indirect questions, inversion may have been generalized to both types.

The Absence of Preposed Auxiliaries

In inverted direct questions, the auxiliary or copula form of the main verb phrase is moved to the front of the sentence, as we have seen. In this position, some of these elements are especially vulnerable to deletion. This gives questions like *He coming with us?* (deletion of *is*), *Where you been?* (deletion of *have*), and *You understand?* (deletion of *do*). Although this is frequently cited as a feature of nonstandard dialects, deletion of these auxiliaries in direct questions is very common in spoken standard English.

Therefore, attempting to eliminate this kind of auxiliary deletion from the speech of inner-city Negro children would be a low-priority task.

Pronouns

A number of usages involving personal, demonstrative and relative pronouns are sometimes cited as examples of nonstandard dialect usage. We will discuss only two of them here.

Pronominal Apposition

A well-known, but little understood feature of nonstandard English dialects including Negro dialect, is pronominal apposition. Pronominal apposition is the construction in which a pronoun is used in apposition to the noun subject of the sentence. Usually the nominative form of the pronoun is used, as in *My brother, he bigger than you* or *That teacher, she yell at the kids all the time.* Occasionally, the objective or possessive pronoun is used in apposition as well, as in *That girl name Wanda, I never did like her* or *Mr. Smith, I got one F in his class one time.* It was discovered in a study of Detroit speech that pronominal apposition was used by all speakers whether they were speakers of standard English or not. It seems likely that the length of the modifying material which intervenes between the noun and the pronoun has an effect on acceptability; the more intervening material, the more acceptable the pronoun in apposition. For example, pronominal apposition in a sentence like *That man that I met on the train to Chicago last week, he turned out to be a Congressman* is more acceptable than in a sentence such as *My mother, she's here now.* (15) But the exact restrictions on the acceptable usage of pronominal apposition have yet to be discovered. Negro dialect speakers who use the stigmatized kinds of pronominal apposition do not use it in every sentence. It has been suggested that the use of pronominal apposition is related to the entry and re-entry of participants in a narrative, but this hypothesis has not been thoroughly investigated.

Existential It

Where standard English uses *there* in an existential or expletive function, Negro dialect has *it.* This results in sentences like *It's a boy in my room name Robert* and *Is it a Main Street in this town?* where standard English would have *There's a boy . . .* and *Is there a Main Street . . .* This difference in the choice of one word in a single construction, affects the understanding of a considerable number of sentences in ordinary speech. For example, a television advertisement for a brand of powdered soup contained the line *Is it soup yet?* This was intended to mean something like *Has it become soup yet?* and was no doubt so understood by the standard English speaking audience, except possibly in parts of the South. But speakers of Negro dialect might well understand the same sentence as something like *Is there any soup yet?*

Conclusion

It should be clear from our approach to the features discussed here that we are not using the terms "grammar rule" and "pronunciation rule" in the traditional sense. As in the physical sciences, in which laws are discovered by observing natural phenomena and are not imposed on nature by scientists, so grammar rules and pronunciation rules are discovered by observing actual usage rather than taken as given and imposed on people's speech. For this reason, we can speak meaningfully of the grammar and pronunciation rules of a nonstandard dialect. For this reason also, some of the rules cited for standard American English will appear startling. In both cases, the rules are discovered from careful observation of usage. It is proper to refer to "rules" because in no speech (except possibly in the speech of the mentally ill or brain-damaged) are words randomly put together. Negro dialect and other nonstandard linguistic systems operate under rules just as do socially favored dialects. But the rules are different. . . .

References

1. We will assume throughout this article that the question of whether or not there is such a thing as "Negro dialect" distinct from white nonstandard dialects has been answered in the affirmative. Discussion of this issue is to be found in any of the articles by William A. Stewart listed in the bibliography. The use here of the term "Negro dialect" is equivalent to our use of "Black English" elsewhere and approximately equivalent to the use of "Negro Non-Standard English" by others. Unfortunately, there is no consensus about an adequate label for this variety of English, so that we have adopted the more traditional term.
2. "Consonant blends" is sometimes used by educators where we have used consonant clusters, but the meaning is the same.
3. "Base word" refers to the part of the word to which inflections may be added. For example, in the words *drowned* and *drowns, drown* is considered the base part of the word.
4. The rules which govern standard English as it is actually spoken are often quite different from the prescriptive norms that are set up in school grammar textbooks.
5. In standard English, these sequences are often pronounced by lengthening the *s* instead of pronouncing the full sequence (e.g. *tess* for *tests* or *dess* for *desks*).

6. In some parts of the South *t* or *d* occurs at the end of the word in Negro dialect, regardless of what precedes *th.* Thus we may get *toot* or *Rut'* for *tooth* and *Ruth.*
7. There are, however, two exceptions. Some verbs, like *berate,* end in *t* or *d* followed by "silent *e.*" When *-ed* (actually only *d*) is added to these verbs, the pronunciation is still *id.* In the second case, English has a set of verbs ("strong verbs") like *hit* and *cost,* which never take the *-ed* suffix. All "strong verbs" end in *t* or *d.*
8. This seems to be a different rule from the *d*-elimination rule discussed in the pronunciation section of this article.
9. Teachers are sometimes doubly surprised when they hear sentences like *He don't suppose to bring his books to class.* Not only is the *-s* suffix absent from auxiliary *don't,* but the presence of *don't* instead of a form of *to be* is strikingly different from standard English. In Negro dialect, the word is not the participle *supposed,* but is a verb *suppose* which functions grammatically like the verb *intend.* Thus we get *He don't suppose to bring . . .* parallel with *He don't intend to bring . . .*
10. It is difficult to indicate the pronunciations intended by the spellings *mon* and *gon.* The *on* in each case is to be taken as a nasalized *o*-like vowel (giving [mɔ̃] and [gɔ̃]).
11. In Negro dialect, of course, the third person singular *-s* suffix would ordinarily not be present and this sentence would be *Nobody don't know it.* For simplicity in comparing standard and nonstandard sentences, we will ignore this fact.
12. This was true of studies in New York, Detroit, and Washington, D.C.
13. This statement is not to be taken as implying that Negro dialect at this or any other stage is a cognitively deficient system. Many languages in which there is an abundance of philosophical and literary works, like Chinese, also lack plural as a grammatical category.
14. There seems to be some evidence that this regularization is coming into standard English, since sentences like the last two are sometimes heard in the standard dialects.
15. Fasold once tested the sentence *That man that I met on the train to Chicago last week, he turned out to be a Congressman* for acceptability with a class of university graduate students and none found it ungrammatical.

Additional References

Non-Technical Descriptions

Joan C. Baratz. "Teaching Reading in an Urban Negro School System," *Teaching Black Children to Read,* eds. Joan C. Baratz and Roger W. Shuy, 91–116 (Washington, D.C.: Center for Applied Linguistics, 1969). Presents arguments, backed by experimental evidence, that Negro dialect is a different, but not deficient, kind of English from standard English and suggests implications for reading education.

William A. Stewart. "Sociolinguistic Factors in the History of American Negro Dialects," *The Florida FL Reporter* 5:2 (1967) 11, 22, 24, 26.

Stewart, 1968. "Continuity and Change in American Negro Dialects," *The Florida FL Reporter* 6:1 (1968) 3–4, 14–16, 18. These two articles outline the historical development of Negro dialect and give examples of modern survivals from a putative early slave Creole language.

Stewart, 1969. "On the Use of Negro Dialect in the Teaching of Reading," in *Teaching Black Children to Read,* eds. Joan C. Baratz and Roger W. Shuy, 156–219 (Washington, D.C.: Center for Applied Linguistics, 1969) [In Chapter Six of this book]. Proposes that Negro dialect texts be used in reading education and outlines the language interference problems which make this necessary.

Walter A. Wolfram and Ralph W. Fasold. "Toward Reading Materials for Speakers of Black English: Three Linguistically Appropriate Passages," in *Teaching Black Children to Read,* eds. Joan C. Baratz and Roger W. Shuy, 138–55 (Washington, D.C.: Center for Applied Linguistics, 1969). A discussion of the use of Negro dialect reading materials including three sample passages with annotations to the grammatical features they contain.

Technical Descriptions

Ralph W. Fasold. "Tense and the Form *Be* in Black English," *Language* 45: (1969) 763–76. A technical analysis of the use of one feature, invariant *be,* in Negro dialect.

William Labov. *The Social Stratification of English in New York City* (Washington, D.C.: Center for Applied Linguistics, 1966). A broad, detailed analysis of the social and linguistic factors which affect several pronunciation features in New York City speech. Not limited to Negro dialect.

Labov. "Contraction, Deletion and Inherent Variability of the English Copula," *Language* 45 (1969) 715–62. A technical analysis of the absence of forms of *to be* in Negro dialect with implications for linguistic theory.

William Labov, Paul Cohen, Clarence Robins and John Lewis. *A Study of the Non-Standard English of Negro and Puerto Rican Speakers in New York City.* Volume I: Phonological and Grammatical Analysis. Final Report, Cooperative Research Project No. 3288, U.S. Office of Education (1968). Probably the most comprehensive linguistic and social analysis of Negro speech in existence. Based on the speech of teen-age peer groups from Harlem.

Roger W. Shuy, Walter A. Wolfram and William K. Riley. *Linguistic Correlates of Social Stratification in Detroit Speech.* Final Report, Cooperative Research Project No. 6–1347, U.S. Office of Education (1967). Preliminary social and linguistic analysis of several speech features of Detroit speakers of both races.

Walter A. Wolfram. *A Sociolinguistic Description of Detroit Negro Speech* (Washington, D.C.: Center for Applied Linguistics, 1969). A technical linguistic and social analysis of several of the most important grammatical and pronunciation features in Negro speech in a large metropolitan center.

Systematic Relations of Standard and Non-Standard Rules in the Grammar of Negro Speakers

William Labov and Paul Cohen

William Labov and Paul Cohen in their article also make use of rules as organizers for description. They describe Black English according to how its sets of rules differ from those of so-called standard English. They go beyond Fasold and Wolfram in that they postulate different levels of rules, according to transformational-generative grammatical theory. Labov and Cohen suggest that the most abstract or "deepest" rules are basically the same for Black English and other varieties of English, while the rules closer to the "surface" account for the differences between Black English forms and other English forms.

Other linguists such as J. L. Dillard and Marvin Loflin do not agree with Labov and Cohen on this point. Several feel there are basic differences between the "deep" rules for Black English and for other English varieties and would contend there is much more distance between Black English and these other varieties than Labov and Cohen acknowledge. However, the main point is that there are sets of rules which govern all varieties of English.

This article is perhaps more difficult to read than the other two in this chapter due to the theoretical framework behind the description, but it is well worth the effort because of the importance of the concepts Labov and Cohen are presenting. The authors also make educational applications throughout the article.

Since the last Project Literacy Conference, we have continued our studies into the structural and functional conflicts between standard English and the non-standard vernacular of the urban ghettos. Perhaps one of the most difficult tasks, technically, was the completion of interviews with a random sample of 100 adults in three areas of South Central Harlem. The resistance to interviewing (1) on the part of the most critical age groups (working class Negro men 20 to 30 years old) has reached a peak for many reasons, social and political, but by various devices we did succeed in completing the cells of our stratified sample: we are now able to compare subjects along the axes

From "Systematic Relations of Standard and Non-standard Rules in the Grammar of Negro Speakers" by William Labov and Paul Cohen.

Northern vs. Southern, older vs. younger, middle class vs. working class
(2) and male vs. female.

In these face-to-face interviews we utilized our knowledge of the culture
and of the factors which control language behavior to stimulate a range of
language behavior from most casual to most formal styles. (3) Many of the
questions were focused upon the intersections of two or more of the "focal
concerns" of lower class culture in general and also the particular concerns
of the Negro people. We are analyzing these materials with particular
attention to the functions for which verbal skills are positively evaluated.
More immediately, we have been able to draw from these interviews a
complex set of quantitative phonological and morphological variables
which display the general sociolinguistic structure of the speech community. Table 6 shows some preliminary figures derived from the phonological
analysis of every fourth speaker in the sample. These three variables show
similar systematic patterns in the white community, but at different levels
and without the North-South complication. (4) The (r) index is essentially the percentage of final and pre-consonantal [r]; the (dh) index

Table 6.

*Three Phonological Variables of Non-Standard Negro Adults in South Cen-
tral Harlem*

	Style	Raised in the North	Raised in the South	Middle Class	Working and Lower Class
(r)	Casual	00	07	13	03
	Careful	25	08	40	09
(dh)	Casual	151	79	45	123
	Careful	59	79	26	83
(ing)	Casual	28	04	00	14
	Careful	48	13	59	22

is constructed from the frequency of fricative, affricate and stop for
morphophonemic *th* initially in *this, then, that,* etc. The higher the index
number, the more non-standard forms are recorded. (5) The (ing) variable
is the percentage of *-in'* forms in all occurrences of unstressed *-ing.* Note
that these three variables illustrate certain general principles:

1) In careful speech, the middle class speakers are much closer to the
prestige norm than working class speakers.

2) Both working class and middle class speakers shift away from the prestige norm when they move from careful to casual speech,

3) The shift of the middle class speakers is more extreme: in casual speech

they approach or surpass the working class in distance from the standard,

4) Speakers raised in the South do not participate in this set of sociolinguistic variables (*-ing* is an exception to this; here Southerners follow the same pattern at a lower level).

It is important to obtain a clear understanding of this sociolinguistic structure in approaching the more complex variables which are located at the intersection of phonological and grammatical rules, such as the simplification of consonant clusters. These are the elements which are probably most relevant to locating structural interference in reading problems. (6) For linguists who have been raised in the tradition of categorical rules without exceptions, there is a great temptation to regularize these variables by some bold abstraction from the data. It is simple to assume that such variation as shown in Table 6 is due to mechanical dialect mixture, external to linguistic structure, and that behind all this are two pure dialects: one with stops for all *th-*'s, for example. Such an assumption is even more convenient in disposing of the frequent *-ed* forms which occur with apparent irregularity in this speech community. The process of inferring the rules for competence from the facts of performance is then simplified to the act of discarding inconvenient data. But close study of adults, adolescents and pre-adolescents shows that such systematic variation occurs at all age levels; it is an inherent part of the structure of the language, and rules must be written to reflect this fact.

When we turn to the consonant cluster variables, we find a more intricate set of relations than those of Table 6. Figure 2 shows the simplification of clusters ending in *-t* or *-d*. The perecentage of simplification is given for casual speech and careful speech, for clusters followed by words beginning with a consonant, and those followed by words beginning with a vowel. The solid lines represent the working class speakers; the dashed lines, the middle class speakers. On the left, the diagram for monomorphemic clusters show a small stylistic shift for working class speakers, with the same slope for clusters before consonants as for clusters before vowels. But the middle class line for clusters before consonants moves sharply upward, approximating the position of the working class in casual speech. Note, however, that there is no such phenomenon for the middle class use of clusters before vowels. Here the percentage of simplification is low and does not rise sharply; we can interpret this lack of parallelism by noting that a pattern of simplification before consonants but not before vowels preserves the underlying forms of the words. If we say *firs' thing* but *first of all,* there is no doubt that the underlying form is *first.* In the right half of the diagram, the same general pattern can be observed, but at a much lower level. The grammatical status of *-ed* is obviously important to both groups, since the position is lower and the slope of the lines is greater than for monomorphemic words. Further-

Figure 2.

The Effects of Style, Class, Grammatical Status and Phonetic Environment on the Simplification of Consonant Clusters Ending in t/d: *Some Preliminary Data from Adults in South Central Harlem*

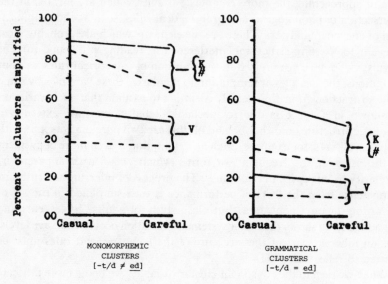

more, the middle class groups show a sharper downward shift than the working class. There is less of a tendency for the middle class to shift upward in casual speech to approximate the working class norm; that is, even before consonants we find no sharp stylistic increase in simplification. We can argue here that the middle class group has a general constraint against the dropping of the grammatical formative *-ed* as a stylistic indicator. In these respects, the middle class group approximates the behavior of white speakers as indicated in other studies. (7)

The implications of these diagrams are that we have a truly continuous variable in the case of *-ed* which is conditioned by both internal and external factors. The *-ed* has grammatical status for all of the speakers we have dealt with, at all age levels, but the effect of this conditioning factor is much smaller for the rules governing working class speakers.

This is merely one of the general questions raised by the study of the phonological-grammatical intersection. It is worth noting here that not all of the variables studied behave in this continuous fashion. On the contrary, the evidence on the clusters ending in -s/z shows that we are dealing with discrete categorical differences for both pre-adolescents and adolescents. Whereas monomorphemic forms and plurals are intact and are affected only by stylistic phonological simplification, the third-person singular -s and regular possessive -s are missing entirely from the dialect in any systematic sense.

We find many such differences in grammatical formatives among the rules which oppose this non-standard dialect to standard English. For example, the dummy *there* in *There's a difference* is regularly *it* in *It's a difference*. A question of considerable interest, which was raised at the outset of these Project Literacy conferences, (8) is whether similar or greater differences appear in the underlying phrase structure. Are the observed differences in surface structure indications of even greater differences in the deep structure, or merely the result of low-level realization rules, lexical inputs, phonological and late transformational rules? Our own investigations have regularly pointed to the latter alternative. We have frequently encountered cases where sentences differ strikingly from standard English in their surface structure, yet in the final analysis appear to be the result of minor modifications of conditions upon transformational rules, or late stylistic options.

One of the most well-known characteristics of this dialect of English is the absence of the copula in the present before predicate nouns and adjectives, locatives and comitative phrases, and the parallel absence of the forms of *to be* in the auxiliary unit *be . . . ing:*

He a friend. He with us.
He tired. He working with us.
He over there.

This pattern is paralleled and reinforced by the frequent absence of *is* and *are* in questions: *Why he here? He with you?*

Some linguists would like to produce such sentences by phrase structure rules in which no copula or auxiliary *is/are* appears. (9) The arguments for and against the presence of these elements in the underlying phrase structure might be tabulated as follows:

For	*Against*
1. *ain't* appears in the negative: *He ain't here.*	1. *ain't* is merely a negative carrier, not a copula.

2. *was* appears in the past:
   He was here.
3. *'m* remains in the 1st person:
   I'm here.
4. *'s* appears in *that's, it's, what's* [dæs, ɪs, wʌs]
5. *be* appears after modals, and in infinitival complements

6. *is* and *are* appear in tags, *He ain't here, is he?*
7. *is* and *are* are never deleted when they appear clause-finally in the surface structure, where standard English does not permit contractions: *There he is, That's what you are, I'm smarter than he is.*

2. *was* is merely a past tense marker, not a copula.
3. *I'm* is an allomorph of *I,* found in equative sentences.
4. These are single morphemes.

5. *be* represents the distinct verb found in *He be good,* as opposed to *He good.* (10)

6. ?

7. ?

Of these arguments against the presence of the copula, 1) carries weight, and 2) is persuasive. But 3) and 4) carry less conviction, and 5) is extremely difficult to purpose or follow, especially in view of the fact that there is only one form of the infinitive corresponding to the zero copula and *be*. Furthermore, we cannot conceive of any possible arguments to counter 6) or 7). 7) is particularly interesting, since it illustrates the intersection of phonological and grammatical factors which is so frequent in this area. It seems that the uncontracted forms do not disappear; it might also be noted that under emphatic stress, full forms of *is,* and *are* frequently appear where nothing is found in unemphatic sentences. (11) Similarly, we can note the extraordinary fact that the *'m* is the only form of the copula which survives, and it is the only form not affected by the phonological processes that tend to reduce final clusters and eliminate final apical consonants.

If we accept the notion that the absence of the copula is due to a transformation which deletes the *is* or *are* in certain specified environments, the question arises as to the ordering of this transformation in relation to the rest of the grammar. Argument 6) is important here. The deletion of the copula must follow the assimilation of *-t*. It seems reasonable that the deletion of the copula follows the assimilation of the *t* to the contracted form -*s,* since this extremely regular rule is a shared property of *it's, what's* and *that's.* This assimilation of *t,* one of the very general modes of consonant cluster simplification, must follow the rule which determines the phonetic form of the contracted *is:* otherwise we would have [dæz]. These and other considerations suggest that the deletion of *is* is a very late rule of the grammar, comparable to the lowest level phonological processes.

We could follow similar arguments on a more complex phenomenon, the non-standard *Ain't nobody see it; ain't nobody hear it.* This differs strikingly from standard English in that the order associated with questions (tense marker and first element of the auxiliary-noun phrase-balance of the verb phrase) is here used in a declarative statement, equivalent to standard *Nobody saw it; nobody heard it.* We cannot discuss this problem in detail here, but the general outline of the argument can be presented. We first note that this form occurs only with indefinite subjects. This suggests that it is associated with the negative concord rules which produce the well-known double negative pattern. For standard English, there is a rule which moves a negative element to combine with the first indefinite; for white non-standard English, a rule which distributes the negative to all the indefinite elements of the sentence. In the case of *Ain't nobody see it,* we have a typical pleonastic form characteristic of negative concord: one negative element in the deep structure (one meaningful negative in this case) corresponding to two negatives in the surface structure.

In this case, the negative moves to the beginning of the sentence with the tense marker, and assumes the regular form *ain't;* it also distributes to *anybody* to produce *nobody.* Such a transposition of the negative might appear strange at first, until we consider the wide range of such phenomena in standard English. Adverbs which contain negative elements move with the tense marker to the beginning of the sentence as a regular stylistic device, with roughly the same emphatic (focus) significance as the non-standard form. Thus we get *Never did he come here; Scarcely did I think so; Rarely would he do that.* Finally, we can even find a standard parallel to the movement of the negative element plus tense marker without the adverb, in the more or less archaic *Nor did anybody see him.* Thus the considerations outlined here lead us to relate the non-standard *Ain't nobody see him* to the standard rules of negative attraction: first, as the absence of the limiting condition that negatives are distributed to the *first* negative only; second, as an extension of the rule that brings negative adverbs to the beginning of the sentence with reversal of auxiliary and subject (or more simply as a continuation of the archaic standard rule with different surface formatives). (12)

Similar arguments bring us to the conclusion that sentences such as *It ain't no cat can't get in no coop* (= There isn't any cat which *can* get in any coop) are simple modifications and extensions of standard transformational rules.

We do not mean to imply that there are no differences in the underlying structure of the language of the Negro speech community. There are two elements which appear immediately as candidates for independent phrase structure rules. One is the use of *be* to indicate generality, repeated action, or existential state in sentences such as *He be with us; They be fooling around.* We do not believe that there is any simple translation of standard rules which will produce these grammatical forms. Another such element is *done* to indicate an intensive or perfective meaning as in *The bullet done penetrate my body; I done got me a bat.* Both of these are part of an aspectual system which is plainly distinct from tense; there still remains the problem of specifying their use and limitations precisely, and then relating them to the tense system. Since there is considerable disagreement on the relative roles of tense and aspect in the standard English verbal system, it is easy to understand why there is disagreement in this area.

In approaching these grammatical rules, it is not enough to determine their relative order and relation to standard English rules. We must also say something about their relative constancy within casual and spontaneous speech, the ease with which they alternate with other rules in formal speech, and their resistance to change or correction within the schoolroom situation. Of course these characteristics of the grammatical rules of non-standard English also bear upon their position in the grammar as a whole, as well as their importance in relation to reading problems.

One approach to this question is through the techniques that were used in the study of phonological variables cited above. A first step in studying syntactic patterns is to note the existence of particular forms of interest; a second step is to place them in the total population of forms which represent the same meaning and with which they alternate. The definition of this class of complementary forms or rules is not simple in many cases; but we should certainly know how frequently pre-adolescents say *He's here* as opposed to *He here* and *He be here,* together with the frequency of the relevant adverbs and other contexts which help define this alternation. In this case, and many others, there is an inherent pattern of variation in the non-standard dialect, not reducible to any constant or fixed rule.

Recently, we have begun a series of investigations which lead more directly into the problem of estimating the firmness or depth of embedding of grammatical rules in the language of children. We have utilized the device of asking for instant repetitions of standard and non-standard sentences of varying length, which has been used effectively in studying much younger children. In this case, we have been working with a group of Negro boys, ages 11 to 14, whom we know quite well. We provide strong motivation for this task by various means, and obtain all the signs of strong effort to repeat the sentences back as heard. In general, we find that standard sentences of moderate length will be repeated without delay in the non-standard form if they contravene certain deeply embedded grammatical rules:

> "I asked Alvin if he knows how to play basketball."
> —→ "I asks Alvin do he know how to play basketball."

Even if the standard sentence is said very slowly, and repeated many times, we may obtain the non-standard form repeatedly from many of the speakers. However, this is not the result with cases where the non-standard rule seems to be relatively late in the grammar. For example, we regularly obtain such repetitions as:

> "Money, who is eleven, can't spit as far as Boo can."
> —→ "Money, who is eleven, can't spit as far as Boo can."
> "Larry is a stupid fool."
> —→ "Larry is a stupid fool."

In fact, in our first series of tests, 21 out of 22 cases of *is* were repeated back without omission. In contrast, half of the sentences with negatives and indefinites were repeated back with the non-standard forms.

In a later series, we found that sentences beginning with *Nobody ever. . .* were persistently produced as *Nobody never. . .* , even after many repeated attempts. No difficulties whatever were found with the simple *is* of the copula. When we add this information, to our findings on the inherent variability of copula deletion in actual speech, and the structural arguments given above, we are forced to the conclusion that the presence or absence of *is* and *are* is governed by the operation of a low-level rule controlled by variable stylistic factors.

The behavior produced in response to the memory test leads us to a more far-reaching conclusion about the linguistic structure available to our subjects. We can ask, what linguistic competence is required to explain the rapid repetition:

> A   "I asked Alvin if he knows how to play basketball."
> B   —→ "I ask Alvin do he know how to play basketball."

In the most obvious view, we can observe that the subject failed to perform the task required. But we cannot overlook the fact that B is the correct equivalent of A; it has the same meaning and is produced by the non-standard rule which is the nearest equivalent to the standard rule. In the standard form, the order of the yes-no question is re-reversed when it is embedded with the complementizer *if* = 'whether or not.'

(A1) I asked Alvin — # — Q — he knows how to play basketball #

(A2) I asked Alvin — # — Q — does he know how to play basketball #

(A3) I asked Alvin if he knows how to play basketball.

In the non-standard form, the order of the yes-no question is preserved when it is embedded without a complementizer.

(B1) I aks Alvin — # — Q — he knows how to play basketball #

(B2) I aks Alvin — # — Q — do he know how to play basketball #

(B3) I aks Alvin do he know how to play basketball.

Thus the original Q of the deep structure is represented in the standard sentence as *if,* and in the non-standard sentence as reversal of auxiliary and subject noun phrase. The non-standard rules differ from the standard only in the absence of the *if*-complementizer placement A3.

Since the listener does perform the translation, it is clear that he does understand the standard sentence. He then rapidly produces the correct non-standard equivalent B3. Understanding here must mean perception, analysis and storage of the sentence in some relatively abstract form. If the non-standard were converted to standard, it would mean the *addition* of the *if*-complementizer rule. But as standard is converted to non-standard, we can only infer that the perceived sentence is decoded at least to the depth of A2–B2 from the point of view of production, but at least to A1–B1 from the point of view of perception and understanding.

From these considerations, it is clear that the listener is perfectly competent in (at least this) aspect of the standard grammar. The over-all linguistic structure which describes his competence is rather complex:

Perception	*Production*
→ A3 → A2 → A1⎫	
→ B3 → B2 → B1⎭	B1 → B2 → B3 →

This asymmetrical situation is apparently well-formed in the sense that the listener-speaker will use this set of rules persistently and reliably as indicated in the test situation, and we can infer that his behavior in school is not very different as he decodes the teacher's speech production or printed texts in reading. We might speak of bi-lingualism, or bi-dialectalism and underline the parallel with the extraordinary performance of some bi-lingual speakers in effecting similar transformations. However, it seems to us that such terminology pre-judges the case. If all or a great majority of the standard rules were of the type A, and operated as a unitary system for the individual, then we would use the concept of "passive bi-lingualism" without hesitation. But there is no reason to believe that this is the case. On the contrary, the results of these and other investigations indicate that there is a wide variety of conditions relating standard and non-standard rules. It is quite possible that for many speakers, the "A" rules which are incorporated into the asymmetrical situation outlined above, do not form a consistent system. They may appear as individual variables within a single non-standard system. One of the aims of our study is to investigate this set of relations among rules, and to arrive at an over-all view of the linguistic structure involved. It seems plain to us that a clear differentiation of the rule systems involved is necessary to analyze the reading performance of children whose basic speech pattern is the non-standard vernacular.

In the first part of this paper, we showed that there are general principles which govern the phonological shifting of middle class and working class speakers as they move towards and away from standard English. It may be argued that in Harlem both standard and non-standard rules are part of a larger linguistic structure which governs the shift between them. The data on syntactic behavior is not yet rich enough for us to show such systematic alternation, and we do not argue that it necessarily follows the same pattern. We do argue, however, that standard and non-standard syntactic rules can be shown to be variants of slightly more general rules. Furthermore, the competence of native speakers of the non-standard vernacular clearly includes the ability to perceive abstract and re-produce the meaning of many standard forms which they do not produce. It is reasonable to assume that a single grammar can be constructed which accounts systematically for the syntactic variation inherent in all styles of the speech of this community.

References

1. It is well known that younger lower class men form an unstable population and are poorly represented in random samples based on enumeration of residences. In the Mobilization for Youth survey of the Lower East Side of 1961 this group was most difficult, and the HARYOU survey of 1965 had even greater difficulties. Only 39% of the HARYOU sample interviews were with men; while the Census of 1960 showed 32% of Harlem families with incomes under $3,000, only 12% appeared in the HARYOU sample, and while only 15% of Harlem families had incomes over $7,000, the HARYOU sample had 28%. The fact that our interviewer, Mr. Clarence Robins, is Afro-American and native to the area did not eliminate the problem, and a number of devices were required to complete this cell in our sample.

2. The figures given in this paper are based on a rough first approximation to class status, based on residential area. We sampled three widely separated areas: one set of upper middle class, middle-income apartments, and two areas which included tenements and low-income apartments.

3. The devices used in the adult interview situation to elicit casual speech were essentially those of the Lower East Side survey (William Labov, *The Social Stratification of English in New York City.* Washington, D.C.: Center for Applied Linguistics, 1966, Chapter IV. However, it should be recognized that such techniques are only substitutes for more natural and effective means of controlling stylistic behavior. In working with adolescent and pre-adolescent boys, our samples of casual speech are drawn from the spontaneous interaction of natural peer groups in which each individual is recorded on a separate track.

4. See Labov, *Social Stratification of English,* Ch. VII.

5. The (dh) index is constructed by assigning (dh-1) to fricatives, (dh-2) to affricates, and (dh-3) to stops; the average numerical value is multiplied by 100, and 100 is subtracted from this figure, so that the invariant use of fricatives will give (dh)-00.

6. See William Labov, Paul Cohen and Clarence Robins, *A Preliminary Study of the Structure of English Used by Negro and Puerto Rican Speakers in New York City,* Final Report —Cooperative Research Project No. 3091, Office of Education, 1965; and William Labov, "Some Sources of Reading Problems for Negro Speakers of Non-Standard English," *New Directions in Elementary English,* ed. Alexander Frazier, (Champaign, Ill.: NCTE, 1967).

7. See Labov, Cohen and Robins, *Preliminary Study of Structure of English,* p. 40.

8. See P. Rosenbaum, "Prerequisites for Linguistic Studies on the Effects of Dialect Differences on Learning to Read," *Project Literacy Reports No. 2,* 1964.

9. See William Stewart, "Social Dialect," *Research Planning Conference on Language Development in Disadvantaged Children* (New York: Yeshiva University, 1966).

10. This argument is a rather unsatisfactory suggestion on our part; we know of none that has been proposed seriously so far.

11. It is obvious that only unstressed forms are contracted with the preceding item. There are many reasons to believe that contraction precedes deletion of the copula (e.g., the argument concerning *it's, that's, what's*; the fact that phonological rules operate upon the clusters and finals produced by contraction and therefore contribute to deletion). All of these arguments reinforce the view that the deletion of the copula is a very late rule.

12. "Reversal of the auxiliary and subject" is used here as shorthand for reversal of the tense marker, together with the next element of the auxiliary if there is one. For some of the standard rules on negative attraction, see Edward S. Klima, "Negation in English," in *The Structure of Language,* eds. J. A. Fodor and J. J. Katz (Englewood Cliffs, N.J.: Prentice-Hall, 1964).

Urban Negro Speech: Sociolinguistic Factors Affecting English Teaching

William A. Stewart

The reader should note that the two previous descriptions of Black English speech forms and rules organizing them did not attempt to give much explanation about the variation in the number of these forms used by different black speakers or within the same speaker, although Labov and Cohen did present variation in speech according to differences in style from casual to careful speech. William Stewart, in this article, does address himself primarily to variation in black usage. He correlates this variation in the number of Black English forms used in speech with what he calls informal social structures in the ghetto environment. To illustrate, he presents the concepts of *acrolect* and *basilect, acrolect* referring to the most prestigious form of Black English spoken in a given area, one which is not too different from the local middle-class standard. *Basilect* refers to the least prestigious form of Black English which also contains the greatest number of nonstandard forms frequently realized by blacks speaking the basilect. He then discusses how age-grading correlates with the production of Black English forms; to a certain point, the younger the child the greater the number of basilect forms are realized in speech.

. . . Most varieties of nonstandard, urban Negro speech would seem to derive from rural southern dialects which, because of migration patterns within the nation, have been brought into many metropolitan areas of the North and the West Coast. Although such dialects may have been generally accepted as natural or appropriate in their native region, they often turn out to be quite deviant in the Northern urban dialect context, while the fact that they have been brought in primarily by Negroes usually results in their being regarded as ethnic dialect, regardless of whether or not they had that status in their Southland home. This racial association of dialect traits combines with the usual linguistic problems characteristic of quasi-foreign

---

language relationships to produce what is undoubtedly one of the trickiest English teaching problems that urban public school systems may ever have to confront. Yet, in spite of the problems they pose, and in spite of the fact that in some cases they appear to have been around for quite a while, amazingly little attention has been paid to urban Negro dialects. . . .

. . . I am convinced that the effectiveness of English teaching in the context of nonstandard urban Negro dialects will ultimately depend upon the results of competent research into their linguistic characteristics and their sociological function. In the remainder of this paper, I will try to illustrate why this is so with a description of some of the characteristics of the linguistic situation in Washington, D.C., as I have observed it.

Washington, the District of Columbia and the nation's capital, is a predominantly Negro city and has been so officially since the Eighteenth Decennial Census listed, out of a total population of 763,956 persons, 411,737 Negroes, 345,263 whites, and 6,956 other non-whites. The numerical superiority of Negroes over whites in the District has come about, not only through a steady increase in the Negro population over the years, but also because of a heavy exodus of whites from Washington to the surrounding suburban areas. Thus, although the District's Negro population increased by 130,934 between 1950 and 1960, the white population actually decreased by 172,602 during the same period. (1) Most of these outgoing whites have consisted of members of families with children, so that the increase of Negro over white has been even greater for school-age children in Washington. Thus, according to a recent report on enrollment in the District's public day schools, the Negro pupils number 119,200, or over 85 percent of a 139,156 total. (2) Although most of the present growth of the Negro population of the District is due to internal expansion, in-migration from the South Atlantic states was until recently the major reason. At the same time, the outgoing white population is at least partially replenished by new office workers and professional types who come from various parts of the country, but particularly from the North, Midwest, and West Coast. This means that a large number of the city's residents are either not native Washingtonians, or are of parents who are not native Washingtonians.

The effect of all this in-migration from distant parts on the dialect profile of Washington has been profound. For one thing, it seems to have totally distorted the original dialect pattern—whatever it might have been. The influx of educated, middle class office and professional personnel, as well as nationwide radio and television programing, have brought into the District of Columbia prestige dialects of Standard English which are much more Northern than what must have been the older, Piedmont variety of standard dialect. At the same time, the in-migration of large numbers of uneducated, lower class Negroes from the South has swamped the traditional Washington Negro speech patterns (which were probably fairly similar to those of the older standard dialect) with South Atlantic Negro dialect traits, many of them much more deviant from Standard English than anything native to the Piedmont region. Subsequent reorganization of these dialect features (such as the dropping of some and the fusion of others with older Washington features), plus a certain amount of dialectal innovation, has contributed to the development of a new dialect configuration—one which sets the Washington-born Negro off linguistically from the immigrant, or "Bama." (3)

As a result of so much dialect mixing, the amount of structural difference which exists between the most "correct" and the most "incorrect" variety of Washington Negro speech is considerable. At one extreme, there is a dialect which is structurally quite close to the General American dialect of many educated whites, although it often has a slight Negro "flavor" to it. (4) It is essentially this kind of speech which is generally considered the "best" in the Washington Negro community, and it seems to be the model aimed at in formal education. In discussing some of the the sociolinguistic factors which seem to be important for English teaching in Washington, I will refer to this topmost dialect in the local sociolinguistic hierarchy as *acrolect* (from *acro-* "apex" plus *-lect* as in *dialect*). In most cases, what is meant by "Standard" English is either acrolect or something close to it. At the other extreme is a kind of speech which I refer to hereafter as *basilect* (from *basi-* "bottom"). (5) There are, of course, differences between acrolect and basilect in virtually all areas of their linguistic structures, but it is particularly because of their striking grammatical differences that the two almost cease to be mutually intelligible. For example, in contrast to acrolect (and even to some other nonstandard dialects), basilect does not normally inflect the verb in any way to show the difference between the simple present and the preterite, e.g., *I see it,* which can mean either "I see it" or "I saw it." (6) On the other hand, basilect has, in addition to a simple perfect construction, e.g., *I seen it* "I have seen it," a completive perfect which has no equivalent in acrolect, e.g., *I been seen it* (with primary stress on *been*) "I have seen it [already some time ago]."

In between basilect and acrolect, there are a number of other dialect strata, and it is in this middle range that the dialect behavior of the majority of adult Washington Negroes probably belongs. Within this range, even dialect behavior which is relatively high up in the sociolinguistic hierarchy is apt to show fairly strong Southern influence (such as in vowel usage and the absence of constricted postvocalic /r/), and forms which are at variance with standard usage are frequent, e.g., /ditn/ and /šutn/ instead of /didnt/

and /šudnt/ (*didn't* and *shouldn't*). Somewhat lower down in the dialect hierarchy, the patterns often resemble the popular stereotypes of uneducated speech, e.g., *I ain't got none*. Furthermore, the Washington dialect situation is characterized by a great deal of acropetal and basipetal switching which, if viewed apart from its particular sociolinguistic context, may give the impression of an unstructured and highly erratic kind of English usage.

One of the most interesting aspects of linguistic behavior in the Washington Negro community is the way in which dialect differences may correlate with certain kinds of informal social structures. Of course, correlations of this type are by no means unique to Negro communities, but, in the case of Washington, some of these phenomena are not only interesting from a theoretical point of view, but they also have a direct effect on the nature of Standard English teaching and learning in the schools. Of these, perhaps the most pedagogically interesting case in point is the relationship which apparently exists between dialect behavior and informal age-grading among many lower class Negro boys in Washington.

It does not take much careful observation of the dialect distribution in the city before it becomes evident that the consistent use of basilect patterns, even in predominantly lower class neighborhoods, is largely restricted to young children. This is so much the case, in fact, that adults in such neighborhoods often assume that basilect is simply the natural way for younger children to speak. At about the age of seven or eight, however, noticeable dialect shifting begins to take place. This includes, for example, the acquisition of certain new grammatical morphemes (such as /-t, -it/ to mark the preterite of many verbs, e.g., /kliynt/ "cleaned," /rentit/ "rented," /wetit/ "wet") as well as the moving around of others to new functions, e.g., the use of the participial verb form of basilect as a preterite form for some verbs—possible once a new perfect construction with *have* has been acquired: *He done it* "He did it" beside *He have done it* "He has done it." The ultimate effect of this process of linguistic change is that the speaker moves out of "pure" basilect and into a dialect level which is higher up in the hierarchy (although the result may still be quite distant from acrolect, and the speaker may continue to engage in a great deal of basipetal switching).

Now, what is especially interesting about this kind of dialect shifting from the sociological and pedagogical point of view is that it appears to take place quite automatically, and in fact seems fairly independent of formal education, although the change may be accelerated and linguistically affected by it. It is worth noting, however, that the change coincides rather neatly with a transition which is normally made at about the same age from "small boy" to "big boy" in the informal social structure of the local peer group. Since "big boys" seem to regard basilect as "small-boy talk" (just as adults do), the continued use of pure basilect probably becomes undesirable for a boy who aspires to status in the older age group. Even when "pure" basilect is abandoned, however, the resultant shift may involve more of a change in overt morphological appearance than in basic grammatical patterns. Thus, structural interference from underlying basilect patterns may continue to be a major problem in the learning of Standard English by many individuals who are no longer superficially identifiable as basilect users. . . .

References

1. See the U.S. Bureau of the Census, *U.S. Census of Population: 1960.* Vol. I, "Characteristics of the Population." Part 10, "District of Columbia" (Washington, D.C.: U.S. Government Printing Office, 1963), p. 11.
2. Public Schools of the District of Columbia, *Pupil Membership in Regular Day Schools on October 17, 1963, compared with October 18, 1962, by Schools, School Levels and Race* (Washington, D.C.: District of Columbia Board of Education, 1963), p. 2.
3. This locally popular designation for a lower class southern Negro is said to be derived from *Alabama,* although most of the persons to whom it is now applied are from Georgia, the Carolinas, or even Virginia. Many of the cues which Washingtonians use to differentiate between their own and in-migrant speech appear to be phonological. For example, the Southern [ɔŭ] (for General American [ɔ]) is found in the speech of many Negro Washingtonians, but in certain words only. Thus *dog* is usually [dɔŭg], but *walk* is [wɔk] and *cough* may be [kŏŝf]. Persons who use [ɔŭ] in words of the latter types are liable to be accused of "talking like a Bama."
4. This "flavor" appears to be due primarily to such paralinguistic features as voice quality, syllable dynamics, and special stylistic uses of pitch. For some individuals, this Negro flavor may be strengthened by the deliberate use of ethnic slang, and by occasional switching into dialect behavior of a less general type.
5. These designations allow the use of the established terms *acropetal* and *basipetal* for switching or shifting in the direction of the acrolect and basilect respectively.
6. That the simple present and the preterite both exist as grammatical categories in basilect, however, is clear from the fact that the two are negated differently: *I don't see it* "I don't see it," but *I ain't see it* "I didn't see it." Furthermore, a few basilect speakers do inflect the un-negated simple present with *-s,* e.g., *I sees it* "I see it" beside *I see it* "I saw it."

Chapter Four

Teachers' Attitudes Toward Black English

Only recently have attitudes toward Black English, including teachers' attitudes, been more than incidentally or anecdotally considered despite the fact it is probably one of the most important areas of research because of its implications for ghetto black children's education. Courtney Cazden, in a personal communication, noted:

> . . . teachers react adversely to children who speak Black English on the basis of speech cues alone. It is extremely important that this reaction be faced by teachers themselves. It may well be that Black English has more effect on the education of children indirectly through its effects on teachers' perceptions of and expectations for children, than it does directly on the children's ability to either communicate or understand.

To support this last statement there is growing evidence from around the world about the importance of attitudes toward language in influencing behavior. For example, because of religious and social attitudes, Hindi (Hindus' variety) and Urdu (Moslems' variety) are considered separate languages by many who speak them even though they are often mutually intelligible. In the Peoples' Republic of China, for at least partly political reasons, the sometimes mutually unintelligible varieties spoken on the mainland are all considered Chinese. In the former case, attitudes about the desirability of a division between Hindu and Moslem are more important than formal linguistic evidence for one language; in the latter example positive attitudes about a united China are more important than formal linguistic evidence of several languages.

What are some of the attitudes teachers hold toward Black English? As Cazden suggested and as preliminary findings seem to indicate, they are negative. According to Frederick Williams and Jack L. Whitehead, whose article appears first in this chapter, teachers tend to rate children who use Black English forms in their speech as less confident and eager in school than children who do not use those forms. In actuality, such a position is untenable; it is a stereotyped reaction to children who *are* confident and eager (at least in their first years in school). Yet the consequences of such

166

an attitude may, in the classroom, have a distinct effect on how the black ghetto child is treated and on how he responds in turn to the teacher's lowered expectations.

Linguistically false assumptions and misconceptions about Black English seem to be at least part of the basis for these negative attitudes toward Black English (see Chapter One). Both Kenneth Johnson and I point out in our articles that teachers tend to hold a prescriptive rather than descriptive set of attitudes toward language use. There is a "good" way to talk and a "bad" way; Black English is the "bad" way because it diverges from so-called standard English. Many, many linguists have commented on the detrimental effects of such a judgment of someone's speech. Yet teachers as well as the public at large still tend to be prescriptive and ethnocentric about language use. "Standards must be maintained" is apparently a common sentiment. Misconceptions such as "Black children don't use complete sentences" or "They have a very small vocabulary" are also apparently common feelings among teachers, as Roger Shuy details in his first selection.

The questions about attitudes important for education at the moment are two. Given many teachers' negative attitudes toward Black English accompanied by their prescriptive attitudes, what does this mean for the black ghetto child's language growth? If the effects on black children are detrimental, as many linguists including Roger Shuy (in this chapter) feel is the case, how can these attitudes be changed so that teachers will not continue to "victimize" and unjustly penalize black ghetto children? In my article, I indicate that I am hopeful that understanding certain sociolinguistic concepts about the nature of social variation in language use might be helpful. But at this time that is only a hope. Shuy, in his second article, also suggests knowledge, knowledge of Black English and the children who use it gained in a revised language arts curriculum, to combat the misconceptions and negative attitudes teachers demonstrated. He then points out that colleges and universities and American society in general are also to blame for the teachers' problems because they have abrogated their responsibility toward helping the teacher gain this knowledge.

Research is definitely needed into the effects of the teachers' attitudes and also into language attitude change. Undoubtedly part of the answer in attitude change lies in the complex of attitudes held toward the black ghetto culture as a whole. Linguistic ethnocentrism (or "linguocentrism") accompanies cultural ethnocentrism. Language is a clue to the status of a speaker. Black people living in the slums are considered to be inferior; Black English is also considered inferior. If black ghetto dwellers were to gain more political power, undoubtedly Black English would grow in prestige. But because this is a societal situation does not mean that teachers do not have the responsibility to behave in a linguistically unbiased manner toward Black English speaking children. They do. They must examine and face their attitudes, as Cazden suggests, in order not to "victimize" and further repress black ghetto children.

Language in the Classroom:
Studies of the Pygmalion Effect
Frederick Williams and Jack L. Whitehead

In this article, Frederick Williams and Jack Whitehead report on the research they have been conducting into teachers' attitudes toward children's speech, including black children who speak Black English. In their work they found that some teachers tended to judge children's speech along two main dimensions: confidence-eagerness and ethnicity-nonstandardness. In other words, a child was rated by teachers on whether or not he sounded confident and eager when he talked and on whether or not he sounded nonstandard and ethnic.

In subsequent research, Williams and Whitehead found that teachers typically rated middle-class children, both black and white, higher on both dimensions. Middle-class children's speech was seen as more confident than lower-class children's, and definitely more "standard" and less ethnic than the lower-class speech.

But most important was the finding that many teachers were making responses on the basis of the child's speech patterns. Black children's speech patterns were consistently rated less confident and eager and more nonstandard and ethnic than white children's speech, irrespective of social class status. Consistently, the teachers studied by the authors tended to assign the nonstandard and ethnic labels to a child's speech if, evidently, certain cues were present. This sterotyped response pattern by teachers, irrespective of the actual speech evidence, has important implications for classroom teachers who work with black children.

Although Shaw's *Pygmalion,* as well as our everyday intuitions, make us well aware of the relationship between speech characteristics and social attitudes, only in the last decade has this relation been examined as a topic of behavioral sciences research. Perhaps the best known studies along this line have come from the work of the social psychologist Wallace Lambert and his associates at McGill University. Among such studies have been experiments where, for example, listeners would assign personality charac-

From "Language in the Classroom: Studies of the Pygmalion Effect" by Frederick Williams and Jack L. Whitehead. *The English Record,* Vol. 21, No. 4, April 1971. © 1971 by New York State English Council. Reprinted by permission of publishers and Frederick Williams and Jack L. Whitehead.

teristics thought to be associated with speakers of tape-recorded examples of French and English speech. Unknown to the listeners was that the samples spoken in the two languages were earlier recorded by persons who were perfect and coordinate bilinguals. Thus it was interesting, if not amusing, to find that, for example, listeners rated English speakers as better looking or more intelligent than their French-speaking counterparts, or that the French speakers were more kind or religious.

To anyone who has worked with minority group children in the classroom, there is the question of the degree to which the speech of such children elicits social stereotyping in the mind of a teacher, and whether such stereotyping and associated attitudes might mediate the teacher's instructional behavior toward the child. This latter question, of course, relates to the theme of Rosenthal and Jacobson's now well-known *Pygmalion in the Classroom.* (1) These researchers found a reliable correlation between experimentally manipulated attitudes of teachers toward children and the subsequent progress of those children in their classes.

The research to be summarized in this paper reflects the first step in the above relation—that is, the degree to which the speech characteristics of children can be related to the attitudes of teachers.

Background

One main study, the details of which are reported elsewhere, (2) led to the present research involving teachers' attitudes. Sound tapes of speech samples of black and white, male and female, fifth and sixth grade children sampled from low and middle income families served as stimulus materials in this initial study. These tapes represented variations among degrees of Negro-nonstandard English as well as white children's speech variations relative to standard English as recorded in conversations between a linguistic fieldworker and the child. The conversations were in response to two initial questions and followup inquiries: "What kinds of games do you play around here?" and "What are your favorite television programs?"

In the first phase of this research, individual teachers from inner-city schools in Chicago were interviewed according to a procedure whereby selected samples of the above tapes were played, then the teacher was asked to describe her impressions of the child—e.g., his ethnicity, educational background, language and speech characteristics, and so on. Adjectives from these free-responses formed the basis for the development of rating scales that were eventually used to obtain quantitative data on teachers' attitudes. A sample of one such scale appears as follows:

THE CHILD SEEMS: hesitant—:—:—:—:—:—:—enthusiastic

In subsequent phases of the research, sample groups of teachers from the same population were administered selected tapes from the above materials which they then rated on scales like the one above. The result of this series of projects was that although teachers would use some 22 individual scales in rating children's speech, their ratings were generally symptomatic of only two main evaluative dimensions. One of these dimensions was labeled as *confidence-eagerness,* which was a reflection of highly similar ratings on adjectival scales such as "The child seems: unsure—confident" and ". . . reticent—eager." The second main dimension of evaluation was labeled as *ethnicity-nonstandardness,* as identified from the apparently global ratings given on such scales as "Pronunciation is: standard—nonstandard" or "Grammar is: good—bad," and so on. In sum, the evidence pointed to the generalization that teachers typically gave rather global evaluations of children's speech, but that these evaluations were along at least two relatively independent dimensions.

That the above judgmental dimensions had been validly identified was supported by two types of information. First, the children who had been selected from the low and middle income groups, and whose speech reflected this social stratification, were reliably differentiated on the average along the above two dimensions. That is, the middle status children were typically rated as less nonstandard and ethnic-sounding, and as more confident and eager than their lower status counterparts. Second, it was eventually possible to predict mathematically teachers' ratings on the two dimensions by using several characteristics of the speech samples as predictor variables. Thus, for example, deviations from standard English in pronunciation or use of /s/, /z/, / θ /, or / ð / phonemes and pronominal apposition were salient predictors of nonstandard ratings, and the lack of hesitation phenomena was an effective predictor of confidence-eagerness ratings.

One unexpected finding in this early research was that individual teacher-raters were sometimes quite consistent with themselves in terms of their ratings of all black children or all white children, apart from the actual income group of the children or even details of their speech samples. The latter point, of course, reflects a lack of predictability of ratings as based upon quantified characteristics of the samples. This phenomenon suggested that some teacher-raters (or some teachers in some ratings) may have been reporting simply stereotyped judgments of a category of child rather than their detailed perceptions and evaluations of what was presented on the stimulus tapes. Although the results are too detailed to be summarized here, further evidence of the stereotype biases of individual raters was revealed in a companion study (3) (using the same data) where it was found that various teacher-raters could be reliably grouped together on the basis of their commonality in rating certain types of children on certain scales.

The consistent and readily interpretable results of this earlier research prompted two main questions for further study: (4)

1) What is the generality of the two-dimensional judgmental model when the teacher can see as well as hear the child-speaker?

2) What is the relation between a teacher's ratings of children and her sterotypes of children of different income groups and ethnicities?

Generality of the Judgmental Model

In a new series of studies, the same technique for deriving rating scales as described above was undertaken, but this time, videotapes rather than simply audio tapes of children's speech samples were employed. These videotapes were obtained by interviewing children from specified income and ethnic neighborhoods of Austin, Texas and its environs. The tapes included samples of children from Anglo, Black, and Mexican-American families (5) and within each of these groups, children from low or middle-status families. Initially, six children were interviewed for each ethno-status category. The interviews were conducted in a living-room-like atmosphere by a 24-year-old Anglo female fieldworker. Each interview was from five to ten minutes in length and was guided by the fieldworker's questions about games and television (as in the earlier studies).

The adjectives used by small samples of teachers who viewed and described their impressions of the children in the videotapes were again used as a basis for developing rating scales. An experimental set of 59 scales was used by teacher-raters in a testing design whereby ratings were obtained of children in the six different ethno-status categories and each in a video-only, audio-only, and audio-video presentation mode. In this phase of the research, teacher-raters also had the opportunity to omit the use of any individual scales they thought irrelevant to their judgments.

Statistical analyses of all ethno-status and presentation modes combined indicated that the data fit a two-dimensional judgmental model nearly identical to the earlier model. The dimensions and their main correlated scales were as follows:

Confidence-eagerness

The child seems: active—passive (.86) (6)

The child seems to: enjoy talking—dislike talking (.85)

The child seems: hesitant—ethusiastic (.84)

The child seems: shy—talkative (.83)

The child seems: eager to speak—reticent to speak (.83)

Ethnicity-nonstandardness

The language shows: a standard American style—marked ethnic style (.90)

The language spoken in the child's home is probably: standard American style—marked ethnic style (.90)

The child seems culturally: advantaged—disadvantaged (.80)

The child's family is probably: high social status—low social status (.80)

Pronunciation is: standard—nonstandard (.70)

Separate analyses of ratings of children in each of the ethnic categories revealed nearly identical versions of the above results, thus testifying to the generality of the judgmental model across at least the three ethnic groups. Separate analyses of each of the presentation modes also yielded evidence of the two-factor model. However, the results closest to those given above were from the audiovisual mode, whereas by contrast the video-only mode showed relatively less use of the ethnicity-nonstandardness scales.

In sum, the results indicated a positive answer to the first question—the two judgmental dimensions of *ethnicity-nonstandardness* and *confidence-eagerness* were found relevant to the situation where teacher-raters saw the children as well as heard their speech.

Relations of Judgments to Stereotypes

In subsequent research, the second question was approached by having teacher-raters judge children who were not seen or heard but described for them in a stereotyped fashion. Ratings of the children as imagined from these descriptions were then compared with ratings of actual speech samples (videotapes). Six different stereotype descriptions were prepared, one for each category of children in the videotape samples. As examples, the descriptions for a low-status Anglo and a middle-status black child were as follows:

> He is Anglo and lives with his mother who is a laundress and his three brothers and one sister in a lower class neighborhood.

> He is black and the son of a professor of sociology at the University. He lives in an upper-middle-class neighborhood.

Ratings of all six stereotype descriptions were obtained from each teacher-rater approximately one week prior to, and one week after ratings of actual speech samples. Again ratings were also obtained for the video-tapes of the six categories of children, but this time results were analyzed directly in terms of the scales constituting the two factor model.

Results indicated a definite, but only moderate, statistical relation between ratings of the stereotypes and ratings of the children. That is to say, as a teacher tended, for example, to rate the Anglo samples as relatively high on the confidence-eagerness scales or low in ethnicity-nonstandard-ness, she *tended* to rate the actual (videotape) sample accordingly.

The implication of the foregoing relation and tentative answer to the second question, was that rather than reporting only a stereotype when rating a child, a teacher-rater may have been rating the videotape samples *relative* to her stereotypes. That is to say, stereotypes may mediate in the differentiation of the speech samples, but the teacher-rater nevertheless is still somewhat sensitive to individual differences *within* presumed categories of children grouped on an ethnicity-by-status basis.

Although the following is properly the subject of further research, it may be that a teacher's sensitivity to individual differences among children in the above categories is reflected in her tendency to exercise greater differentiation in rating actual speech samples relative to the ratings given for stereotypes. Conversely, the less sensitive to individual differences a teacher is to children of a particular category the more the ratings of actual children may be undifferentiated from a stereotype. Put in anecdotal terms, this latter example constitutes a case of the "they all look (or sound) alike" attitude.

Implications

Although studies in the current program of research continue, the findings to date suggest a number of implications. Some of these are, of course, theoretical, but for this report the practical will be emphasized.

One significant shift of thought challenging English language instruction in the schools today is that *differences* in language habits, particularly those of minority group children, have been too often confused as deficits. (7) The fact that, for example, teachers in this research program have consistently based about half of their judgmental perspective upon *nonstandardness* is symptomatic of a prescriptionist (for standard English) rather than, say, an aptness or a communicativeness criterion in evaluating children's speech. This hints of a major shortcoming in what teachers are taught about the language of school children, one of where the ends in teaching English overshadow the means. Perhaps too much is stressed about the objective of teaching (and expecting) standard English rather than the careful diagnosis of existing linguistic capabilities of children as a starting point. The designation of *nonstandard* (or particularly as some say, *substandard*) implies a classification of "deficiency" in a child's speech which overlooks that a child speaking a nonstandard dialect of English may be as developed, psycholinguistically at least, as his standard-English-speaking age mate. To emphasize the point, this is *not* to argue against the merits of standard English as an instuctional objective in American schools, but to stress that teachers might benefit from knowing more about language differences in children as a means for improving English instruction. If only for defining an instructional starting point, an ability to diagnose what a child can do linguistically in nonstandard English should introduce some efficiencies into English language instruction.

Just as the present studies imply a bias in teachers' attitudes toward nonstandardness, they also suggest ways to measure such bias and still more to guage the effects of teacher training.

As mentioned earlier, teachers' stereotype ratings appear quite consistent and do seem to influence judgments of actual speech. If these stereotypes somehow serve as judgmental "anchors," then effectiveness of teacher training in language differences might be gauged by shifts of the anchor point as well as by increased differentiation of actual speech ratings about that point. In all, the instructional goal in teacher training would be one of sensitivity to, and objective differentiation of, language differences. The goal is to reduce the effects of a teacher's stereotype bias in evaluating the language of her pupils.

As Eliza Doolittle counseled Professor Higgins, it is how you treat people that makes them what they are to you. The same advice seems pertinent to the reduction of teachers' negative stereotypes of children who speak nonstandard English.

References

1. Robert Rosenthal and Lenore Jacobson, *Pygmalion in the Classroom* (New York: Holt, Rinehart & Winston, 1968).
2. Frederick Williams, "Psychological Correlates of Speech Characteristics: On Sounding 'Disadvantaged,' " *Journal of Speech and Hearing Research,* XIII (September, 1970), 472–488.
3. Rita C. Naremore, "Teachers' Judgments of Children's Speech: A Factor Analtyic Study of Attitudes" unpubl. Ph.D. diss. (University of Wisconsin, 1969).
4. Technical reports of these studies are available from ERIC (numbers not yet assigned) as: Frederick Williams, Jack L. Whitehead, and Jane Traupmann, "Semantic Differential

Scaling of Audiovisual Recordings of Children's Speech Samples," technical report (Austin, 1970a) ED 042 756; Frederick Williams, Jack L. Whitehead, and Jane Traupmann, "Latency of Teachers' Semantic Differential Ratings of Children's Speech," technical report (Austin, 1970b) ED 042 757; Frederick Williams, Jack L. Whitehead, and Jane Traupmann, "Correspondence Between Semantic Differential Ratings of Children's Speech and Speech Anticipated upon the Basis of Stereotype," technical report (Austin, 1970c) ED 042 758.

5. The authors are aware of the problems involved in labeling ethnic groups. Since these labels are used in our technical reports of this research, we have chosen to use them again here.

6. The value in parenthesis is a correlation coefficient. These have a range from 0.0 or no correlation, to 1.0, or a perfect correlation. Accordingly, the values reported here are markedly high.

7. This issue is discussed further in Frederick Williams, "Language, Attitude, and Social Change," in *Language and Poverty: Perspectives on a Theme,* ed. Frederick Williams (Chicago: Markham, 1970).

Teacher's Attitude Toward the Nonstandard Negro Dialect—Let's Change It

Kenneth R. Johnson

Kenneth Johnson takes the position that educators have negative attitudes toward Black English or nonstandard Negro dialect as he calls it. Because of these negative attitudes or false assumptions as he also calls them, Johnson suggests that teaching "standard English" to black children has failed. (Teaching "standard" English as a second dialect is discussed in Chapter Five.) He then discusses the set of false assumptions he feels operate in the school setting to the detriment of black children. Basically the assumptions are false because they are not based on the linguistic premises discussed in Chapter One. The first false assumption is that because Black English is inferior to so-called Standard English, the cognitive development of Black English speaking children is impaired. Johnson points out that differences are not deficiencies. Other false assumptions include the attitude that Black English speaking children are "non-verbal," that their variety is a result of laziness and can be considered to be "sloppy" speech which is full of "errors." Also, Johnson suggests teachers feel these children have "poor auditory discrimination skills," e.g. they can't hear "standard" English sounds. He notes that these attitudes are still based on a deficiency rather than a difference notion. Finally he states that the teachers' attempts to teach a more standard variety as a replacement for Black English, because they feel the standard forms are so much superior, are failures because the Black English a child speaks is functional in his ghetto culture while standard varieties are not. Johnson brings up the extremely important point that languages function in a social setting, and that the Black English speaking child's setting is one in which the way he talks is acceptable. Only when he moves into the larger culture, Johnson contends, does he find a need for other varieties of English.

When disadvantaged black children enter school, one of the first of their sub-cultural patterns that is pedagogically attacked is their language. Teachers long have noticed that these children do not speak the same variety of English that middle-class children speak, but it was the linguists who pointed out that disadvantaged black children speak a variety of Eng-

lish that the linguists labeled "nonstandard Negro dialect." Teachers erroneously developed the attitude that the speech of disadvantaged black children was full of phonological and grammatical errors. Linguists pointed
out that these "errors" were systematic deviations from "correct" English
(the variety of English spoken by the middle-class and taught in the
schools), and that these systematic deviations comprised the phonological
and grammatical systems of a social class dialect.

From kindergarten through the elementary grades and to the end of the
secondary grades, teachers have had one primary goal: eradicate the nonstandard Negro dialect of disadvantaged black children and replace it with
"correct" English. The failure to accomplish this goal is remarkable. Black
children leave school at the end of twelve years still speaking the variety
of English (the nonstandard Negro dialect) they spoke when they entered
school. It would seem that this remarkable failure to get these children to
speak like middle-class people (that is, to speak standard English) would
have caused a reexamination of the attitudes and assumptions on which the
language program are based, and to alter teaching strategies subsequent to
this reexamination. No such reexamination, however, took place until recently, and then it was the linguists, not the educators, who took the lead
in conducting the reexamination. Not all educators are aware of what has
been discovered through the reexamination.

The purpose of this paper is to discuss some of the negative attitudes that
teachers have about nonstandard Negro dialect. These attitudes are more
than just attitudes, however; they are false assumptions about nonstandard
Negro dialect on which the language program is based. Another purpose
of this paper is to discuss some of the unsucessful attempts to teach standard
English to disadvantaged black children because of these false assumptions.

First, teachers have made a false assumption about the capability of
nonstandard Negro dialect to enable black children to achieve cognitive
development. This first false assumption indicates a need for these children
to learn standard English. Next, after the decision is made to teach black
children standard English, the language program is based on further false
assumptions that determine teaching strategies that do not succeed.

Many educators, sociologists, psychologists and others believe that the
nonstandard Negro dialect black children speak impairs their cognitive
development. Stated another way, nonstandard Negro dialect is a reflection
of inadequate cognitive development of disadvantaged black children. The
crux of this point of view is: because nonstandard Negro dialect is *different*
from standard English, it must be *inferior* to standard English . . . and
since language is essential to cognition an inferior language must impair
cognitive development of those who speak it. This is the basis for those who

adhere to the cognitive deficiency point of view. Of course, their point of view is bolstered by all kinds of research data.

The cognitive deficiency people, however, are wrong—in spite of their bolstering data. Because nonstandard Negro dialect is different from standard English, it's not automatically inferior. Further, language is a tool of culture—a perfect tool of culture. That is, the language of a people is always adequate to serve their needs—specifically, the cognitive needs—of a people. This means that nonstandard Negro dialect serves the cognitive needs of black children who must function in the black sub-culture. Now, it is likely that the cognitive needs of children in the black sub-culture are different from the cognitive needs of children in the middle-class culture. Thus, the cognitive development of disadvantaged black children and middle-class children may be different. It undoubtedly is different because of the difference between the two cultures. Black children may lack some of the cognitive skills of middle-class children (or, these cognitive skills may not be as highly developed as in middle-class children); on the other hand, middle-class children may lack some of the cognitive skills of black children. The point is: *difference* does not equal *inferiority.*

The cognitive development of black children is suited to the demands of the disadvantaged black sub-culture . . . and, the cognitive development of middle-class children is suited to the demands of the middle class culture. When testing for cognitive development, however, black children are given tasks which require cognitive skills and development derived from a middle-class experience. Thus, they fail these tasks, causing some people to erroneously assume that they are inferior or deficient in cognitive development. Black children do not conform to the cognitive expectations of the school— they are different not deficient (there is a distinction).

There is a great need to find out the exact nature of the disadvantaged black sub-culture, instead of comparing it to white middle-class culture to determine how it deviates from middle-class culture. Specifically, what needs to be found out is what kind of cognitive development is yielded by a disadvantaged black sub-culture experience. This kind of knowledge could completely change education programs for disadvantaged black children. Current types of compensatory education programs conducted for disadvantaged black children attempt to *compensate* for the lack of middle-class experiences of disadvantaged black children. In other words, what is attempted is to give black children middle-class experiences, and teach them standard English so they can develop the cognitive skills on which the curriculum is based. Stated simply, the attempt is to turn disadvantaged black children into middle-class children so they can fit the curriculum. This, of course, is why compensatory education has failed. If the kind of cognitive development yielded by a disadvantaged black sub-culture experience is known, then the curriculum could be based on these expectations. This would be a vastly different "compensatory" education program than we how have.

Because educators don't know the disadvantaged black sub-culture and they don't know the cognitive demands and the cognitive development of disadvantaged black children, the present types of compensatory education programs are ineffective (most educators have not even considered the possibility that education programs could be based on the cognitive development of disadvantaged black children, because their cognitive development is considered deficient). One of the requirements for success in these programs, however, is standard English. Thus, educators try to force disadvantaged black children to discard nonstandard Negro dialect and learn standard English to improve their cognitive development and equip them with better variety of English. This is the first, and most significant, of the false assumptions made about nonstandard Negro dialect.

This false assumption forces educators to teach disadvantaged black children standard English before they are capable of learning it, and before they really need to learn it. First, these children are taught standard English at a time when they are just learning the nonstandard Negro dialect (this is the variety of English spoken in their primary cultural environment, and so it is necessary that they learn it); second, young black children don't see a need for learning standard English (they aren't ready for work, it is nonfunctional in their primary cultural environment, they don't associate with speakers of standard English, except the teacher, in our racial and class-segregated society).

Disadvantaged children do need to learn standard English, however, but not for the reasons made by the cognitive deficient people. These children need to learn standard English because it is essential for vocational, social and academic success (as long as the curriculum is based on the ability to speak standard English it is necessary for academic success). [See Kochman, Chapter Five, for another viewpoint on this question.] Stated another way, disadvantaged black children need to learn standard English so they can be successful whenever they have to function in the dominant middle-class culture.

Attempts to teach them standard English, however, fail because of further false assumptions made about nonstandard Negro dialect and the language behavior of disadvantaged black children. These false assumptions, unfortunately, have become the dogma about the language and the language behavior of disadvantaged black children because of the frequency with which they appear in the literature about these children. Teachers have come to accept these dogma without question, and like most dogma, it's immoral (in this case, pedagogically immoral) to question them. Further, like most dogma, these false assumptions are comfortable to live with because they don't require strenuous explorations into the unknown. Finally, these false assumptions cause educators to adopt teaching strategies that inevitably result in failure to teach black children standard English.

The most frequent false assumption about the language of disadvantaged black children is that these children are "non-verbal." Taken literally, this means that disadvantaged black children are without language. Of course, those who advocate the non-verbal characteristic of black children don't mean the label to be interpreted literally. This extreme label, however, reflects how the advocates really feel about the language of black children—that is, these children do not have a complete language. In addition, the label implies that language differences have been equated with language inferiority. [See Labov, Chapter One, for further elaboration on this point.]

Disadvantaged black children are not non-verbal. Those black children who are severely disadvantaged (or, even damaged), however, may be "non-verbal." Specifically, black children who are suffering from poor health, malnutrition, emotional instability, or children who have physical disorders that result in a language handicap are restricted in their language development or their employment of language. Since there are, tragically, many severely disadvantaged black children the non-verbal label applied to all disadvantaged black children may have resulted from an invalid generalization made on the basis of severely disadvantaged black children. The vast majority of disadvantaged black children, however, are neither restricted in their language development and their language employment, nor do they have a language disorder in the physical sense. This majority of black children are normal in their facility to use nonstandard Negro dialect, the language of their primary cultural group. That they do not use standard English does not make them "non-verbal."

The question, then, is why black children have been labeled "non-verbal?" One reason has been pointed out: language difference has been equated with language inferiority, or language deficiency. Taking this as a basic premise, or the "proof" of the "non-verbal" nature of disadvantaged black children, advocates of this point of view have postulated that the main reason black children are "non-verbal" is their mothers do not talk to them, and when their mothers do talk to them it is only in incomplete sentences or in sentences which are "poorly" constructed. Again, just because black mothers speak to their children in sentences that differ in construction from standard English sentences does not mean that these are inferior to standard English sentences and stunt the language development of the children. It is probable that disadvantaged black mothers don't speak directly to their children as often as middle-class mothers do. This alone, however, is not enough to stunt the language development of black children. These children are raised in an environment that is more dense than the environment of middle-class children; thus, they hear as much, and maybe more, language than middle-class children. In addition, black children have a greater number of brothers and sisters and other children to talk with (because of the higher birth rate) than middle-class children. It is likely, then, that disadvantaged black children have as many language models to informally teach them language, and audiences on which to try out language, as middle-class children.

When disadvantaged black children come to school speaking the nonstandard Negro dialect, most seem to be as talkative as other children. By the time they get beyond the primary grades, they don't seem to be as talkative as other children—that is, when they must use language in a classroom activity. When they are out of the classroom, however, they seem to be as talkative as most children (in their homes, on the playground, during play, etc.). These children, then, are "non-verbal" only in the classroom.

There are obvious reasons for this that educators would be aware of if only their attitudes toward nonstandard Negro dialect were not so negative. First, from the time black children enter school they are corrected in their speech. Continued correction has the effect of shutting off speech. Why speak when whatever one says is incorrectly spoken? Second, much of the discussion in classrooms is about issues and topics that have no relevance to the needs, interests or backgrounds of disadvantaged black children. The higher the grade, the less relevance classroom topics have . . . and, the higher the grade, the more "non-verbal" these children seem to be when compared to middle-class children because classroom topics become more irrelevant. Thus, black children are reluctant to take part in classroom discussions and they are labeled "non-verbal."

Outside the classroom, however, black children exhibit linguistic behavior that can be labeled "highly verbal." For example, young children create many jingles and poems to verbally accompany such activities as playing games (jumping rope, hide-and-go-seek, Red Rover, kick-the-can, etc.), or bantering. Verbal bantering is a sport in the black sub-culture. Young black children learn this sport early from their elders, and they begin to participate in it at an early age. In essence, verbal bantering is the skillful and humorous use of language to "put another person down." Children who banter can hardly be labeled "non-verbal." A very special kind of bantering in the black sub-culture is "playing the dozens." Playing the dozens is to talk about another person's mother (and other female members of the family) in a derogatory manner. This can be done for humorous or insulting purposes (never for a neutral purpose). The object of playing the dozens is to use language cleverly to attain the desired affect (either humor or insult). Most black children (especially males) participate in playing the dozens, and it is highly verbal behavior. Finally, black children in the Chicago ghetto have invented a languge they call "pimp talk." Pimp talk is the affixing of a nonsense syllable to certain syllables of words. "Non-verbal" children would not be able to invent and use such a language. These verbal behaviors (word games, bantering, playing the dozens, pimp talk) are a few examples of behavior of disadvantaged black children to illustrate that they are capable of verbal behavior.

The fact is, disadvantaged black children are not "non-verbal." They are verbally different, and this does not mean that they are verbally inferior to standard English speaking middle-class children.

When educators label these children "non-verbal" it sets off a chain of events that is called "prophecy fulfillment." That is, the children are labeled non-verbal, teacher expectation is low, and the children's performance conforms to teacher expectation; in other words, children tend to achieve at the level teachers expect them to achieve. When disadvantaged black children are labeled non-verbal, and when instruction is based on other false assumptions. the children don't learn standard English.

Even though disadvantaged black children have been labeled "non-verbal," educators don't really mean it literally. Educators know these children use language, and they recognize that it is a different variety of English from standard English. The next set of false assumptions, consequently, pertains to why the nonstandard Negro dialect differs from standard English. Some educators have postulated that the reasons disadvantaged black children speak the way they do are because: they have "lazy lips and lazy tongues;" their language is "sloppy"; they attempt to "simplify" standard English; and, they have "poor auditory discrimination skills." All of these assumptions are false, and as long as educators act on the basis of these false assumptions they cannot teach standard English to disadvantaged black children who speak the nonstandard Negro dialect.

The literature on the language of disadvantaged black children is full of the assertions that these children have "lazy lips and lazy tongues" (in fairness, however, it must be pointed out that these assertions are less frequent, recently). What this means is that black children are too lazy to manipulate their lips and tongues to reproduce standard English sounds and grammatical patterns.

The nonstandard Negro dialect is spoken by a great number of disadvantaged black children. Not all of these children could be suffering with laziness of lips and tongues. Laziness is a quality, a characteristic, which is distributed among a population in a normal distribution . . . in other words, laziness should be distributed according to a bell shaped curve. There are too many black children who speak the nonstandard Negro dialect to conform to normal distribution of laziness. This assertion is another false assumption about nonstandard Negro dialect. These children speak the way they do because nonstandard Negro dialect differs systematically from standard English.

Another false assumption made about nonstandard Negro dialect is that it is "sloppy" speech (this false assumption is consistent with the "lazy lips and lazy tongues" postulation). The label "sloppy" implies that the deviations from standard English (called "errors") are made individually. That is, the deviations from standard English have no general pattern—each child is unique in his sloppiness. When one examines the deviations from standard English that are made by black children, however, one realizes that these deviations are *consistent* (which is another way of saying that these deviations are systematic). The deviations from standard English occur over and over in the same places, and they are not unique deviations . . . the children are consistent in their deviations. This is true for both phonological and grammatical deviations.

For example, black children always pronounce the final voiceless /th/ as /f/ (in words like *month, bath, both, south*), and they always omit the copula verb in present progressive tense of the verb *to be* (I talking; she listening). Now, if these deviations occur in the same linguistic environments, it means that these deviations are systematic. Stated another way, nonstandard Negro dialect has a phonological and grammatical system different from standard English. This means that nonstandard Negro dialect is not "sloppy."

This idea that nonstandard Negro dialect is sloppy (and the way to speak it is with "lazy lips and lazy tongues") has caused some people to think that in order to talk the way many black people talk, all one has to do is "mess up the English language" (leave off a few inflectional endings, don't have subject-verb agreement, etc.) and pronounce the words lazily. This is false. In order to speak nonstandard Negro dialect, one must know its phonological and grammatical systems. In other words, one must know precisely what to do with certain phonological and grammatical features of standard English. Not many people are aware of this; consequently, few people outside the black sub-culture can speak the nonstandard Negro dialect *correctly*.

As long as educators continue to view the nonstandard Negro dialect as "sloppy" they are prevented from seeing how nonstandard Negro dialect systematically interferes with the attempts of black children to learn standard English.

Interference is a phenomenon in elanguage learning that refers to one language interfering with another language. That is, when an individual attempts to learn another language, his native language imposes its phonology and grammar onto the language he is learning . . . the individual attempts to make the target language conform to the phonology and grammar of his native language. The same phenomenon occurs when a speaker of one dialect attempts to learn another dialect of the language. Black children do not learn standard English because educators do not take account of how their nonstandard Negro dialect systematically interferes with their attempts to learn standard English.

What educators must do, then, is to begin to take account of the interference when teaching standard English to black children who speak nonstandard Negro dialect. This cannot be done as long as educators view the language of these children as "sloppy."

In taking account of interference, educators must borrow techniques from teaching English as a second language to speakers of other languages. Specifically, this means that educators must first identify where nonstandard Negro dialect systematically differs from standard English (points of interference). Then, the children must be aware of these differences (without the usual accompanying stigma that is attached to the differences). Next, the children must be able to hear the difference between their nonstandard Negro dialect and standard English. Next, the children must be able to discriminate between the nonstandard Negro dialect feature and the standard English feature that are in interference. Finally, the children must reproduce the standard feature. Our current language instruction jumps from pointing out the difference between the nonstandard Negro dialect feature to reproducing the standard English feature . . . skipping over two vital steps: hearing the standard feature and discriminating between the standard and nonstandard features.

Second language teaching techniques are well developed for teaching English as a second language to speakers of other languages. Teachers of black children who speak the nonstandard Negro dialect can adapt these techniques to teach standard English to these children. This adaptation can only take place, however, if the systems—phonological and grammatical —of nonstandard Negro dialect are recognized. This can't be done if the false assumption that nonstandard Negro dialect is "sloppy" is held.

Failure to take account of the systematic nature of nonstandard Negro dialect has caused some educators to feel that black children, and others who speak the nonstandard Negro dialect, are attempting to "simplify" English. On the surface, the omission of some phonemes, and the different pronunciation given to other phonemes when they occur in particular linguistic environments seem to be efforts to simplify standard English. When one is aware of the system of nonstandard Negro dialect, however, it becomes apparent that in some instances the nonstandard Negro dialect is simpler than standard English (for example, the omission of the agreement morpheme in third person singular, present tense verbs); but in other instances, the nonstandard Negro dialect is more complicated than standard English (for example, the conjugation of the verb *to be*). Thus, nonstandard Negro dialect is neither simpler nor more complicated in the aggregate than standard English. The idea that blacks attempt to simplify English is just one more false assumption. It leads educators to add the "complexities" of standard English to the speech habits of disadvantaged black children without taking account of the systematic interference between nonstandard Negro dialect and standard English.

The last false assumption in the set of false assumptions to explain why disadvantaged black children speak the way they do and fail to learn standard English is that they have "poor auditory discrimination skills." What this means is that these children are unable to hear standard English sounds. The word "poor" implies some kind of physical impairment that prevents black children from hearing standard English sounds. It is true that these children don't hear some standard English sounds, but not for the reason implied. The reason that these children can't hear standard English sounds is due to the interference between nonstandard Negro dialect and standard English. For example, many black children are unable to hear the difference between *dough* and *door,* or *mouf* and *mouth,* or *heart* and *hard* because of phonological interference. Specifically, they can't hear the difference between *dough* and *door* because of a phenomenon in their nonstandard Negro dialect labeled "r-less-ness" (the final sounds represented by the letter *r* are eliminated); they can't hear the difference between *mouf* and *mouth* because of the systematic changing of final voiceless /th/ to /f/ in their dialect; and, they cannot hear the difference between *heart* and *hard* because of consonant elimination (speakers of nonstandard Negro dialect do not generally pronounce final /b/, /d/, /g/, /k/, /p/, /t/).

Disadvantaged black children who speak the nonstandard Negro dialect should not be treated as if their auditory discrimination skills are "poor." This implies that there is something physiologically wrong with them. Instead, they should be treated as if their auditory discrimination skills are different. This means that they are not able to hear some standard English sounds because the phonological system of their nonstandard Negro dialect interferes with their ability to hear standard English sounds.

So far, the false assumptions dealing with the nature of the linguistic behavior of disadvantaged black children and the reasons these children speak the way they do have been covered. The last false assumption that will be discussed here refers to the belief that standard English can be taught as a replacement for the nonstandard Negro dialect.

Schools have attempted to teach standard English to disadvantaged black children as a *replacement* dialect. In other words, schools have encouraged these children to discard their nonstandard Negro dialect and adopt standard English as their language. The schools have even demanded that this be done, because of the false assumption that nonstandard Negro dialect is an inferior language. The approach of teaching standard English to black children as a replacement dialect, of course, has been a complete failure. Educators should have known this, but they have been prevented from taking a rational approach to teaching black children standard English because of the false assumptions they have about nonstandard Negro dialect, and because they have not understood the relationship between language and culture.

The demand that black children replace nonstandard Negro dialect with standard English is an impossible demand, as long as black children must live and function in the disadvantaged black sub-culture.

First, language is an identity label. It forms a bond between the individual and those with whom he must live. Language tells the individual who he is and it also tells the individual the group to which he belongs. Thus, when the schools encourage black children to discard their nonstandard Negro dialect, the schools are really encouraging black children to discard part of their identity. If they adopt standard English, they cut themselves off from their primary cultural group. They cannot, of course, do this as long as they must continue to live and function in their primary cultural group.

Secondly, in encouraging black children to replace their nonstandard Negro dialect with standard English, the schools are asking black children to replace a *functional* language system with one that is *nonfunctional.* Nonstandard Negro dialect "works" in the disadvantaged black sub-culture. As it was pointed out above, nonstandard Negro dialect is generated out of the black cultural experience and it meets the demands of living in that culture. There is a dynamic relationship between nonstandard Negro dialect and the disadvantaged black sub-culture, and standard English cannot take its place in this dynamic relationship. Thus, standard English cannot replace nonstandard Negro dialect.

Thirdly, standard English—since it is not the language of the disadvantaged black sub-culture—cannot be reinforced in the disadvantaged black sub-culture. Without this reinforcement, black children can't be expected to learn it.

Educators must realize that people cannot discard the language of their culture as long as they must live in the culture. Therefore, instead of teaching standard English to black children as a *replacement* dialect, it should be taught to them as an *alternate* dialect. Standard English should be taught as an additional linguistic tool to be used in appropriate situations. The appropriate situations are whenever black children must function in the dominant culture. This raises the question: when do disadvantaged black children function in the dominant culture? Because of the racial and class-segregated nature of our society, the answer is very seldom, especially when these children are young. They must function in the dominant culture, however, when they are older—especially if they want a higher education or better vocational opportunities. This implies that standard English should be taught to black children at a much later stage in their education than it is now taught. In other words, it must be taught when black children have a recognized need to learn it. Then, it must be taught as an alternate dialect.

In conclusion, educators must completely change their attitudes and assumptions about nonstandard Negro dialect and the linguistic behavior of disadvantaged black children if these children are to learn standard English. As long as educators hold onto these negative attitudes leading to false assumptions discussed in this paper, educators can expect to continue their long and remarkable failure in teaching standard English to disadvantaged black children who speak nonstandard Negro dialect. Thus, a basic need of these children is to have teachers change their attitudes . . . and their attitudes can only be changed if teachers acquire a better understanding of nonstandard Negro dialect . . . and the nature of language itself.

Register: A Concept to Combat Negative Teacher Attitudes Toward Black English

Johanna S. DeStefano

In this article, I add another suggestion to Johnson's list as to why teachers hold relatively negative attitudes toward Black English spoken by their black ghetto students. Teachers, as well as the general public, are usually unaware of social variation in language use. They tend to view language behavior as invariable and either as "good" or "bad." So a child speaks "good English" or he speaks "bad English" under all conditions. I suggest that such a view of language is not consonant at all with what is known, that the prescriptive attitude does not fit the descriptive information linguists have gathered. Rather, language use varies with the social circumstances the speaker is in; he switches from one register (or "style" as Labov calls it) to another, depending on who he is talking to, the topic, or other social variables. This concept of register, a type of social variation, is suggested as being important for teachers to understand because of its possible effect on modifying negative attitudes.

I also bring out that teachers' negative attitudes often blind them to the fact that Black English speaking children do already use many so-called standard English forms in their school speech, probably more than Black English forms. I report on a study I conducted which suggested that black ghetto children under formal school circumstances can and do produce more "standard" forms than Black English forms. In other words, they have learned another register or registers peculiar to the school setting and do not use "ain't got" 100 per cent of the time. Further implications for modifying teachers' attitudes are also discussed.

During the past decade, linguistic theory and findings have been increasingly applied to spelling instruction, grammar, usage, composition, and other concerns of the elementary school curriculum. Yet it would be extremely unfortunate if linguists and educators were to apply to the English curriculum only their findings about the structure of language because of the obvious failure of the schools to effectively educate urban ghetto black children who speak Black English.

From a slightly revised version of "Register: Social Variation in Language Use" by Johanna S. DeStefano. *Elementary School Journal,* Vol. 72, No. 4, January 1972. Copyright © 1972 by The University of Chicago. Reprinted by permission of the publisher.

Linguistics now does include more than the study of the structure of language; it can also add to our understanding of social variations in language. It has been found that social groups differ in the language they use, and Black English is a good example of social differences in language. Also, individuals use different language in different social situations. Sociolinguistics is the study of both of these kinds of differences.

Sociolinguistics has much to offer the teacher whose pupils speak Black English. Is their speech "good" or "bad"? Can a teacher even let herself think about language variations in those evaluative terms? Should she ignore the child who says, "I ain't got none," or should she try to correct him? Do correction strategies damage a black child's self-esteem? In short, how should a teacher handle social variations in classroom language?

Sociolinguistic principles can help teachers find answers to these questions because many of these principles deal with social variation in language use, which is a linguistic fact of life. However, this fact does not seem clear to many teachers even though they face variation daily, not only in their pupils' speech but also in their own use of language.

Speakers use language differently in various situations. A teacher talks one way to her principal, another way to her fellow teachers, still another way to her pupils, and yet another way to their parents. Miss Fidditch might say to the principal, "Hubert is a constant disrupter in class"; to Hubert's parents, "Hubert has some difficulty settling down to do his work"; to her fellow teachers in the lounge, "That kid's driving me nuts with his yackity-yacking"; and to Hubert himself, "Hubert, what's wrong with you?" or "Hubert, be quiet." Notice the change in vocabulary from the educational jargon of "constant disrupter," used with the principal, to the slang terms "kid" and "nuts," used with her fellow teachers. Notice that a teacher may command a child, as Miss Fidditch did in her "Hubert, be quiet," but she probably would not give an order to the principal, to fellow teachers, or to parents.

A teacher may say "There are five *desks* in a row. Spell *desks*." As soon as the spelling lesson is over, she may say, "Now move your *dess* into a circle."

These are situational changes in teachers' speech, and changes of this kind are common. Yet many teachers seem to be unaware that they adapt their language to different social situations. There is the classic schoolboy joke about the teacher who gives a lesson on "It is I," then immediately afterward says, "It's me," in all seriousness and totally unaware of the contradiction between her lesson and linguistic reality. Such unawareness stems in part at least from perceiving speech or language use categorically. For example, listeners often feel that someone who says, "I didn't do nothing" uses the double negative consistently—100 per cent of the time. However, I have heard black ghetto children say, "I *ain't* got *none,* and he *ain't* got *any"* in the same sentence. A Black English speaker may use the double negative more frequently than a more "standard" speaker, but does not use it invariably; the teacher assumes the child's use is invariable.

What can be done about these teachers' attitudes toward Black English speakers' language use? First, the attitudes seem to be based on a lack of awareness about social variation in language. Teachers need to be informed about the dimensions of this variation. The following section has this informative purpose and presents a sociolinguistic concept dealing with social variation.

Register, a Sociolinguistic Concept

The varying of language forms to fit different situations is known as register change or switching. A register is a set of linguistic forms used in given social circumstances (1). Each register may be signaled by changes in phonology (sounds), syntax (structure), and lexicon (vocabulary).

An individual speaker usually controls a range of registers that extends from informal ones used with members of his peer group to formal ones, which include written registers if the person is literate. Miss Fidditch's comments about Hubert are samples from one speaker's range of registers.

The range of registers under control varies from individual to individual. Age influences a person's range: small children control fewer registers than adults do. Education also has an effect on range: literate adults control different registers than illiterate adults do. Socio-economic status makes a difference: an upwardly mobile adult of low status may control more registers than an adult of higher status because the low status individual controls registers he uses in his leisure culture as well as registers he uses on the job with adults of higher status.

Register in the Classroom

What does the sociolinguistic concept of register mean for teachers of Black English speaking children? It means that children who use Black English speech forms do not use them 100 per cent of the time, just as teachers do not use certain "standard" forms like "It is I" consistently. There is evidence that black ghetto children have learned to vary their speech to fit different social situations even though their age and relative lack of education limit their range of registers. (2)

Teachers often feel that there are two ways to talk, a "good" way, which includes only standard forms, and a "bad" way, which includes only Black English or nonstandard forms. Also, teachers as well as others often do not hear the standard forms the black children do use. Consequently, many black ghetto children are often told that they do not speak properly and that much of what they say is wrong. (Kenneth Johnson's article in this chapter discusses this point quite forcefully.)

It is my contention that children who speak black ghetto vernacular already control many standard English forms when they come to school and can use them in appropriate social situations. In other words, the children's range of registers already includes some standard forms. It is also my contention that these children learn to control even more standard forms from grade to grade.

Teachers need to begin to discard negative attitudes toward variation in language use. The first step toward developing a more positive approach may be to understand that so-called standard English and the language of black ghetto children consist of sets of registers in which various linguistic forms may be shared. Black English speaking children's set of registers thus already includes many "standard" forms. These children are extending their range of registers and are learning to control more so-called standard forms under circumstances which call for these forms.

A Study of the Language Instruction Register

I conducted a study (3) with 180 black children in ghetto schools in Oakland, California, to test my contention that Black English speaking children progressively gain control over registers they come in contact with after they come to school. These registers contain more "standard" and sometimes different linguistic forms than the children use in their own culture.

The children have already learned to talk one way to adults at home and another way to their playmates on the street. They have already learned to vary their language use with the social situation. When they come to school, they have control over a range of registers suitable for black children living in a ghetto culture.

In school there is a set of registers these children have not had much contact with, registers connected with middle-class culture and literacy learning. One such register, which I labeled the Language Instruction Register, concerned me because it contains forms used by the teacher when she is teaching children to read, write, and spell. I have used the word "desks" as an example—pronounced *desks* under one circumstance and pronounced *dess* under another. The pronunciation *desks* is part of the Language Instruction Register. *Masks* is also part of that register. The teacher says in a spelling lesson, "Halloween is a time for *masks*. Here is how *masks* is spelled." When the teacher is not teaching spelling or reading, she would tend to say "Put away your *mass.*" In the sentence, "I *do not* have *any* pencil," "do not" + "any" would be a Language Instruction Register syntactic form as opposed to "I *ain't* got *no* pencil," a Black English register form. Obviously "do not" + "any" is not exclusively part of the Language Instruction Register. As was mentioned above, this form and many others are shared with other registers.

The question I asked in my study was how much of the Language Instruction Register have black children who live in the ghetto and speak Black English acquired by Grade 1? By Grade 3? By Grade 5? Even though first-graders may not have been exposed to this register, it contains forms which are considered "standard" and which the children have heard over television and probably in their neighborhood. Again, it is important to remember that the use of so-called standard forms is not limited to middle-class speakers; standard forms also appear in the speech of ghetto blacks. (4)

To answer the question about how much of the Language Instruction Register was acquired by black ghetto children, equal numbers of boys and girls at each grade level were asked to repeat selected sentences. The sentences contained various Language Instruction Register forms which have semantic equivalents in the Black English registers the pupils already controlled. Each child was individually asked to repeat each sentence immediately after he heard it.

The results of this study indicated that approximately two-thirds of all the responses the black children made used forms in the Language Instruction Register. These children evidently control selected forms of the register when they are in social circumstances of relatively great formality. Formal circumstances were created to parallel those in the classroom in which the Language Instruction Register is used by the teacher and often expected of the black children. More than 50 per cent of the first-graders' responses, more than 60 per cent of the third-graders', and more than 70 per cent of the fifth-graders' responses were made in the Language Instruction Register.

An average of all the Language Instruction Register responses for all the selected forms studied masks the control the children demonstrated over various forms. In first grade, boys and girls used double negatives in their responses only 5.5 per cent of the time. Almost 95 per cent of the time the children made a response that used a form in the Language Instruction Register, such as "He *did not* have *any* breakfast." By fifth grade, the Language Instruction Register response accounted for 99 per cent of the total responses made for that form. For the Language Instruction Register form *have been* as in "I have been there," the black children in first grade did not say *have* approximately 40 per cent of the time, using instead the Black English form "I been. . . ." But by Grade 5, *have* was absent only 12.5 per cent of the time; 87.5 per cent of the responses were made in the Language Instruction Register form.

Several forms in the Language Instruction Register did not demonstrate this pattern of relatively high acquisition. One was the pronunciation of *l* in such words as *he'll* and *we'll*, in other words the contracted form of *will*. By Grade 6, only 6 per cent of the responses used the Language Instruction Register form *he'll*. The other responses used Black English forms such as *heuh* and *he*, which do not have an *l* in the final position. Similarly, in the Language Instruction Register, one says *masks* and *ghosts*. By Grade 5, only 4 per cent of the responses included the final *-sks* and *-sts*. The majority of the responses took the form of *mass* or *ghos*. Thus the children made homonyms of *masks, massed,* and *mast*. But this extremely low use of the Language Instruction Register forms by Grade 5 was not typical of the forms studied. Nine of the sixteen forms studied showed Language Instruction Register responses 80 per cent of the time or more by Grade 5.

In conclusion, the study seems to demonstrate that given the social circumstances appropriate to the Language Instruction Register, black children who speak Black English productively control a large number of forms which are part of that register. These children can respond linguistically to different social settings in their lives and are learning to respond appropriately. Consequently, the teacher cannot afford to think that these children use only Black English forms in their speech. Playground talk does seem to be different from talk in the reading circle or in the spelling lesson. These black children do seem to be increasing their range of registers. Teachers can help even more pupils do so by being aware of their efforts, acknowledging them, and helping the children gain control over forms which are a part of the registers associated with becoming literate. Teachers can also help by recognizing their own language variations; some things are said to friends but not to the principal. Teachers of Black English speaking children cannot afford categorical perception or negative attitudes toward the children's language use. They cannot afford to be unaware of social variation in language.

Speech is not "good" or "bad." Rather it contains various forms which are appropriate to different social situations. "I ain't got none" is appropriate in some circumstances and less appropriate in others. Self-esteem need not suffer if the teacher and her Black English speaking pupil understand that the pupil is expanding his speech, is learning to control more forms, and is not replacing one set of forms, which the teacher considers "bad," with another set the teacher considers "good." Sociolinguistic concepts such as register are crucial to the elementary-school classroom because of teachers' attitudes and can help make a child's school experience more educational and more humane.

References

1. M.A.K. Halliday, Angus McIntosh, and Peter B. Strevens, *The Linguistic Sciences and Language Teaching* (London: Longmans, Green and Company, Ltd., 1964).
2. Thelma Weeks, "Speech Registers in Young Children" (Unpublished paper, Stanford, Calif.; Stanford University, 1970).
3. Johanna S. DeStefano, "A Sociolinguistic Investigation of the Productive Acquisition of a School Language Instruction Register by Black Children" (Ph.D. diss., Stanford University, 1970).
4. Samuel N. Henrie, Jr., "A Study of Verb Phrases Used by Five-Year-Old Nonstandard Negro English Speaking Children" (Mimeographed, Berkeley, Calif.: University of California, June, 1969).

The Linguistic Problems of Teachers
Roger Shuy

In this selection, Roger Shuy presents information about prevalent misconceptions teachers hold toward Black English and the children who speak it. These misconceptions can contribute to creating the negative attitudes reported by Williams and Whitehead in this chapter and add to the list already compiled by Johnson and me in our articles. Shuy reports on a study done in Detroit to gather information as to what teachers of Black English speaking children know about and think of those children's speech. The findings indicated that the teachers held many misconceptions about Black English. For example, commonly held opinions were: that the children have a very meager vocabulary, that these children are not able to speak in complete sentences, and the "dialect" the children speak is wrong. The article extensively quotes specific teachers, so gives the reader a detailed account of teacher attitude and knowledge. Finally Shuy makes several recommendations as to how such ignorance of the Black English speaking child's speech can be alleviated (as it most certainly must be).

Just as the blame for a communication breakdown cannot be placed entirely on the listener (the sender might well be the source of the problem), so the language problems of the disadvantaged child cannot be viewed in isolation from the classroom. Little research has been done on the effect of teacher speech as a model for child speech or on how the teacher is capable of creating negative views toward language, standard or not, in his students. In fact relatively little research has been done on what the teacher knows, feels, or thinks about the language of disadvantaged pupils. Considerable data have been gathered on how a teacher is trained, on whether or not he feels adequately trained, and on what he actually does in the process of teaching. But assessments of what teachers really know about the language used by children and how they feel about it are infrequent. We know from *The National Interest and the Teaching of English* that the linguistic preparation of prospective English teachers is woefully inadequate. (1) It

From "Language Problems of Disadvantaged Children," Chapter 7, in *Principles of Childhood Language Disabilities,* edited by John V. Irwin and Michael Marge. New York: Appleton-Century-Crofts, forthcoming. Reprinted by courtesy of the author and Appleton-Century-Crofts, Educational Division, Meredith Corporation.

should not be surprising, then, that teachers find it difficult to describe accurately the language problems of their disadvantaged students. In the study by Anne Hughes (2) thirty Detroit teachers were randomly selected and asked to identify the language problems of their students who were designated, in one way or another, as disadvantaged.

About eighty percent of the teachers observed that their students have a limited vocabulary and many teachers offered reasons such as the following for this handicap:

> In the program, the children come with a very meager vocabulary. I think it's because of the background of the home and the lack of books at home, the lack of communication with the family, especially, if there are only one or two children in the family. Perhaps if there are more children in the family communication might be a bit better. They might have a few more words in their vocabulary.

> In the inner-city the child's vocabulary is very limited. His experiences are very limited.

These comments are typical in that the atmosphere of the home is blamed for the child's limited vocabulary. None of the teachers gave any indication that the home environment might produce a *different* vocabulary. On the contrary, it was generally felt that lack of school vocabulary was equivalent to a lack of overall vocabulary.

The widely held but erroneous concept that disadvantaged children have limited vocabularies can be traced to earlier reports on the language of the disadvantaged child. Yet, nothing in the current research of sociolinguists supports this idea. Several different reasons can be given for the rise of the notion that children in disadvantaged homes have limited vocabularies. It may be that the investigators proved to be such a cultural barrier to the children that they were too frightened and awed to talk freely, or that the investigators simply asked the wrong questions or that the student's life-style simply requires a different lexicon.

The interviewed teachers' misconceptions about the size of a disadvantaged child's vocabulary may be illustrated as follows:

> Some had a vocabulary of about a hundred and some words, I'd say; no more than that. They got along fine with what they knew. They didn't have any trouble expressing themselves. They knew the important words for them to get along okay. Some could talk your foot off. I mean, they just knew everything. The quieter ones were the ones who didn't have a large vocabulary.

The assumption that disadvantaged children use only a hundred words or so is one of the curious stereotypes of the teaching profession. What is more distressing than this exaggeration, however, is the assumption that quiet children are quiet because they have no vocabulary.

The responses of these teachers to the grammar problems of their disadvantaged students is equally naive. One third of the teachers characterized the child's greatest problem as his failure to communicate complete thoughts in complete sentences:

> I can't get them to make a sentence. Even if I have them repeat after me exactly, they don't do it. They repeat in sentences they are familiar with. They're not really sentences but fragments of sentences that are familiar to them, and they understand them. They don't realize that they aren't making a complete thought.

> Where we would use a sentence to convey a thought, they are in the habit of maybe using a phrase or just a few words to try to convey the same thought which I would presume would affect their communication to a great extent. . . .

Of the grammar of their students, the teachers offered the following comments:

> The biggest problem that I've had so far is 'I'm gonna'.

> Because there is no real honest communication between parent and child, the child isn't taught to listen. . . . He doesn't hear; he doesn't enunciate, you see.

> These children cut words off: 'could' would be 'would', such as in 'Ould you like to do this?' Too, their 'l's' were often missing.

Even when the teachers' responses reflected a clear distinction between phonology and grammar, the description was often not accurate enough to be diagnostically useful.

> Their grammar problems are many because they use substitutions, this for that.

> They use too many personal pronouns.

Although the teachers generally had more to say about pronunciation than vocabulary or grammar, there were many over-generalizations such as:

> They do have trouble with pronunciation for they fail to use their teeth and tongue and their lips. This is necessary for getting the correct sound.

> I have one child who mispronounces almost every word, but they say he does not have a speech problem.

> Many times they mispronounce because they do not know the sounds.

> Their trouble was the use of dialect for they said *hal* for *how*. It was southern dialect among some of the children which caused them to use the wrong words.

> Pronunciation is poor. Things like 'I wanna go,' or 'punkin' for 'pumpkin' and things like that. Their dialect is just hard to understand for most teachers. We were born and raised in the Midwest, for the most part.

It is indeed difficult to imagine anyone using language who fails to use his teeth and tongue and lips. The supposed substitution of *hal* for *how* indicates an awareness of the *l* problem in non-standard English but a confusion about the nature of the problem (the *l* is not inserted, it is deleted.) The parochialism of the last quotation is unsound since it is an easy matter to cite pronunciations of *wanna* for *want to* in the speech of almost any speaker of Standard English.

As for specific kinds of pronunciation problems, the teachers agreed rather clearly that disadvantaged children delete word final consonant sounds:

> They leave off last sounds, leave off beginning sounds some times. But then I have that trouble now even with the other children. I keep saying to them to put in all the letters for that's why they're there.

> Some of the children had problems with their consonants, particularly at the ends of words.

> They leave off the endings of words; instead of 'going' it's 'goin'. (Also the d's and t's give them trouble.) Even at the beginning of words you often cannot hear the beginning letter.

> I think that they're in the habit of not saying the things as clearly as we do and they say a word as 'looking' by leaving the *g* off.

The teacher's confusion of sounds and orthography is perhaps to be expected (for it seems widespread in this country) but it may be confusing to a first grade child to be told to add a *g* when the *ng* combination stands for the single sound, /ŋ/.

On the other hand, these came a bit closer to some of the significant problems of disadvantaged pronunciation than they did for vocabulary or grammer. In general, however, the analyses were too vague to be diagnostically useful. The major point that the teachers did not perceive is that there is a pattern in inner-city speech—just as there is pattern in every kind of speech. These teachers neither described the problem accurately nor understood its pattern.

One of the most important aspects involved in the language problems of disadvantaged children, therefore, focuses on the teachers' imprecise descriptions of the problem, their ignorance of how to make such descriptions and on their imperfect knowledge about a vastly neglected and underprivileged group of human beings. It is not inappropriate to observe that the linguistic sophistication of teachers is currently quite limited.

It seems very clear, then, that teachers need to learn about the current research in urban language problems, why the research is being done, how it is carried out, what is known at the moment and, every bit as important, what is not known. Further, teachers need to take cognizance of their own language in relation to that of their pupils. They need to understand language variation—the reasons underlying it and the attitudes of various subcultures toward it. Teachers should learn to listen to the language of their students. They should find out how systematic the language of disadvantaged children can be and they should develop a sensitivity to the editing processes that take place as one person listens to another.

In short, the preparation of language arts teachers must be overhauled to put language at the center of the program, accompanied wherever possible by courses in administration, techniques and evaluation. It is an indisputable fact that the most important tool for survival, for communicating and for obtaining knowledge and skills is language. This is as true for middle class children as for disadvantaged socio-economic groups. But if the circumstances under which disadvantaged children acquire this tool militate in some way against their acquiring middle class language patterns, some kind of special attention must be given them. This special attention requires the teacher to develop an ability to learn how to deal with the child's language, how to listen and respond to it, how to diagnose what is needed, how to best teach alternate linguistic systems and how to treat it as a positive and healthy entity.

References

1. *The National Interest and the Teaching of English* (Champaign, Ill.: National Council of Teachers of English, 1961).
2. Anne E. Hughes, "An Investigation of Some Sociolinguistic Phenomena in the Vocabulary, Pronunciation and Grammar of Detroit Pre-School Children, Their Parents and Teachers" (Ed.D. Diss. Michigan State University, 1967). Reprinted by permission of the author.

Language Variation in the Training of Teachers

Roger W. Shuy

In this article, Roger Shuy leads the reader from teacher attitudes directly into the following pedagogically oriented chapters (Chapters Five and Six). He suggests that although the attitudes discussed in this chapter have severe repercussions in classrooms, the teachers cannot be entirely at fault for holding them. He feels there is little in their education which helps them understand Black English speaking children. Colleges and universities have not instituted curricula which provide information about the linguistic aspects of the schools' failure to help black ghetto children. Language needs to be at the center of the language arts curriculum, he suggests, but it is not. Consequently teachers get virtually no help in understanding either Black English or the children who speak it.

Shuy then also faults the entire American "system" which does not provide for the continuing education of teachers so that those who were trained before urban language curricula were instituted can be educated in ways which will help them become better teachers of Black English speaking children. He refers to specific curricular concerns such as oral language teaching and reading instruction which are dealt with in detail in Chapters Five and Six.

Finally, he is concerned with existing language arts curricula for not having language study at their core. He briefly outlines courses which he feels should be at the center of an elementary level teacher-training curriculum in language arts and which he feels would alleviate some of the educational problems he has discussed.

With respect to social dialects, it has been clearly demonstrated that teachers find it difficult to describe accurately the language problems of their disadvantaged students. As an adjunct to the Detroit Dialect Study of 1966–67, Anne E. Hughes demonstrated vividly that randomly selected urban teachers lacked the linguistic sophistication to discuss or even to consistently identify the features of pronunciations, grammer and vocabulary with which they are presumably dealing in the classroom.(1) The general fallacies held by these teachers included the assumption that the

From "Sociolinguistic Strategies for Studying Urban Speech" by Roger W. Shuy, *Viewpoints*, Vol. 47, No. 2 (March 1971), 6-13, 21-24, Dr. Maurice L. Imhoof, editor. Reprinted by permission of the School of Education, Indiana University, and Roger W. Shuy.

lack of vocabulary used in school settings was equivalent to lack of overall vocabulary.(2) A widely held belief was that these children have a total vocabulary of only about a hundred words. The teachers also clearly indicated little or no understanding of the slum child's grammar (or, indeed, of what distinguishes grammar from pronunciation), since they suggested that the greatest problems were in saying *gonna* for *going to* and *'ould* for *could*. These teachers had considerably more to say about pronunciation problems than grammar, a fact which is . . . out of phase with current research which implies that grammatical features are considerably more stigmatized than phonological ones at least in American society.(3) The teachers predictably confused sound with orthography, often observed that the children did not use their tongues (and/or lips or teeth), and generally provided answers which, even when fairly accurate, were stated too vaguely to be diagnostically useful. Thus the case can be easily made for the lack of linguistic sophistication among teachers. . . .

Extant attempts to prepare teachers adequately for the classroom of the disadvantaged student are disappointingly weak and few undergraduate courses are offered in subjects even remotely related to the linguistic aspects of the problem. Even occasional college courses such as the Nature of Language, Introductory Linguistics, Modern Grammar, American English, etc. are seldom offered and, if offered, seldom required of teachers. If they are required of teachers, they are seldom geared to minority language problems. Thus, although one of the most urgent situations in our schools focuses on problems of language in relation to reading, composition and speech, especially among blacks and other minority groups, there is virtually no preparation for such problems in the college curricula.

Part of the reason why such courses have been slow to develop is found in the suddenness and recentness of our discovery of the problem. Although English teachers have long wrestled with the problem of making acceptable speakers and writers of English out of non-standard speakers and writers, it is only with the recent emphasis on urban problems, black awareness and a new kind of social responsibility that we have given serious consideration to the specific problems of minority groups, the black, urban poor in particular. Then, as is often the case in education, the need for teaching materials preceded any strongly felt need for theoretical bases or empirical research upon which such materials could be based. As absurd as it may seem to produce classroom materials before establishing a theoretical base for their development, that is exactly what has happened in this field today. To complicate matters even more, some sensitive teachers realizing that their training has not been adequate for their needs, are now asking for that training, preferably in condensed and intensive packages. As healthy as this situation may appear to be, it has only triggered still another problem—that of finding adequately trained professionals who can provide this training. One gets the strong feeling that the traditional language arts teacher preparation program gives far too much attention to matters of administration, teaching techniques and methods of evaluation at the expense of the study of language, the real content of their teaching. A recent national conference on educating the disadvantaged devoted less than 5 per cent of its attention during the two days of meetings on the *content* of such education. Practically all of the papers and discussion centered on funding such programs, administrating them and evaluating them. These are, of course, important matters, but one must eventually ask *what* we are funding, administrating and evaluating. If we are to merely add another course to extant teacher preparation, we may as well turn our attention to other things. For the field of the language arts needs more than another tag-on; it needs a total overhaul.

As argued by this writer in an earlier paper the preparation of language arts teachers must be overhauled to put language at the center of the program, accompanied wherever necessary by courses in administration, techniques and evaluation. (4) By far the most important tool of survival, both for communicating and for obtaining knowledge and skills, is language. For children, this is an indisputable fact. It is as true for middle class children as for disadvantaged socio-economic groups. But if the circumstances under which poor children acquire this tool militate in some way against their acquiring middle class language patterns, some kind of special attention must be given them. This special attention requires of the teacher:

1) An ability to recognize and react adequately to contrastive language patterns
2) An ability to do something about them when appropriate
3) An ability to keep from doing something about them when appropriate.

There is no evidence to date which indicates that we are training teachers adequately to handle 1). There is relatively little in the way of materials geared to accommodate 2). There is practically no understanding of 3) among teachers or, for that matter, among textbook writers.

In short, what universities need to provide for teachers in order to fulfill their educational obligations to the ghetto child (or, in fact, to any child) is information on how to deal with the child's language, how to listen and respond to it, how to diagnose what is needed, how to best teach alternate linguistic systems and how to treat it as a positive and healthy entity. Universities have come far short of assuming this responsibility.

But even if the teachers and universities were to provide optimum quality education, the larger American system is capable of negating any useful outcomes. The assumption that a student must complete his education before he begins to perform his life-function is one of the worst locksteps in American way of life. In his 1969 commencement address at Michigan State University, Yale's President Kingman Brewster, Jr. observed that colleges must make it easier to escape and re-enter. Part of the problem stems from recent reassessments of the long cherished concept of general education—the required study of the humanities, the social and the physical sciences. As Fred M. Hechinger has observed, "The most charitable objection to general education is that the world has become too complicated for the notion of a shared core of knowledge." (5) But as the components of general education have expanded with new knowledge, so have components of teacher training and other vocational preparation. The University simply has too much to do in the lockstep four-year-preparation-for-life setting. Ways must be devised for legitimizing what educators have always claimed was viable anyway, education *during* rather than just education *before*. This education must not be considered simply supplementary course work which will enable a teacher to move to a higher pay plateau or to satisfy a school-system requirement. It will, instead, require considerable cooperation between school systems, universities and unions, all of whom will be required to think of education as a continuum rather than as a four year package.

The study of language in relationship to educational and social problems stands to benefit greatly from such a system realignment. In the past five years, specialists in urban language have been called on to give lectures, workshops, courses and institutes in great quantities. Of the many types of educational settings which I have been involved with, by far the most successful has been the year-long EPDA Institute which addressed itself entirely to problems of language in education. In the period of an academic year, with a total focus on applied linguistics, fully credentialed experienced teachers had the maturation time to absorb the required new ways of thinking about language. Furthermore, they were able to wean themselves away from the syndromes which generally wreak havoc with summer institutes and workshops, including their terror at suddenly finding themselves on the other side of the desk. Such institutes, of course, are expensive as they are now constituted and their current organization is geared to compensatory education for teachers rather than to a more positive build-for-the-future model.

One of the major problems of traditional teacher training programs is that they are abstract and separated from the reality of the classroom and in no area is this more devastating than in the area of language. Unrealistic stereotypes abound. . . . We are only beginning to understand something of the tremendous importance of knowing how to observe and assess pupils' oral language, how it relates to beginning reading, how it affects spelling and composition, what should be done, if anything, about helping students learn oral standard English, and how it is affected by the language of peers, teachers and parents. Furthermore, we have done very little about teacher language, especially in terms of how teachers should assess their own speech in relation to that of the children they teach. But these things are difficult to accomplish in the traditional teacher-training program. They are not abstract and they cannot be taught effectively in the absence of real child language. Tape recordings may be helpful but real children are crucial to an accurate assessment.

It has become generally accepted in the past few years that reading is essentially a language-processing operation. The relationship of the child's only language, his oral speech, to the written symbols of oral language is the focus of much of the effective current research in reading. With the emphasis on the speech of minority groups has come the not surprising realization that the starting points in reading may differ from child to child, depending on the match of his oral language system with that of the printed word, the attempted representation of the child's oral language. This sort of understanding about reading has created a number of new approaches to reading research and materials development. Their implication for teacher training more clearly than ever argues for putting future teachers into real school settings on some sort of participatory basis at some very early stages of their preparation. If it is called practice-teaching, it should be shorn of any of the formal accounterments that have plagued such activities in the past. To school systems and unions this suggestion may seem to be a nuisance, but there is no other way to instill the importance of child language than to put future teachers in contact with it as much and as soon as possible and, of course, to give these teachers instruction on how to deal with it.

. . . At the core of every formal subject the child will ever learn and underlying much of his acceptance or rejection in society . . . is his language. This is the tool upon which all other courses build and one of the most important identifiers of his educational and economic status for the rest of his life. His language is his major device for communication which he brings with him to the first grade. It is his oral language to which any reading materials must be seen to relate and it is his oral language which may interfere with his spelling and written grammar for years to come. How little this has been understood is evident from both our teacher training programs and our research. It has taken a crisis in reading, focusing on large scale failures to teach disadvantaged black children to read, for researchers to begin to appreciate the relationship of oral language mismatch to beginning reading materials. But, as is often the case in research, the focus on the disadvantaged ghetto child will yield considerably wider benefits than we originally suspected. To the relief of those who are concerned about "spending all that money on minority groups" will come the happy ultimate realization that it takes a crisis to get research going and that some of the underlying principles discovered in the study of the language of working class black people are more widely applicable to teaching as a whole.

In another . . . paper I have outlined what I think should form the basic core of the undergraduate elementary teacher-training program in the language arts or English. (6) Briefly, these courses are

1) *The Nature of Language.* Special attention should be placed on language attitudes. Several kinds of language attitude tests are described, ranging from abstract questions about language to reactions to concrete samples of speech from a tape recording. These attitude studies would provide a starting point for the introductory course in the nature of language. Additional stress should be placed on phonetics (in order to learn how to recognize and produce differences in pronunciation) and the study of grammar (with a number of problems to be solved). Throughout, the systematic nature of language should be emphasized.

2) *Language Variation.* Beginning with regional dialects, including some data gathering and analysis experiences, the course turns its major attention to social dialects. There should be a systematic treatment of the historical origins of current non-standard, grammatical and phonological features of social dialects and some of the basic concepts of socio-linguistics, including the linguistic variable, the linguistic continuum, style shifting, and language interference.

3) *Fieldwork in the Language of Children.* Primarily an experience in gathering language data and analyzing certain features. Although special attention should be given to different techniques of language data elicitation such as sentence imitation, word games, narratives, citation forms, oral reading, etc., the primary purpose of the course is to get teachers to listen to children and be able to analyze, to a limited extent, their language.

4) *Teaching Standard English: Oral Language, Reading and Composition.* Students should be personally involved in trying to define both *standard* and *non-standard* language. They should be introduced to foreign language teaching techniques, especially as they relate to learning a second dialect. A worthwhile project in such a course would be the construction of teaching materials which focus on the grammatical features analyzed in the earlier fieldwork experiences. Students should also be encouraged to consider the effect of dialect on the beginning reading experience, especially

noting how phonology, grammar and orthography might cause serious interference to the acquisition of reading skills.

Although these four courses are suggested as a first step in the overhaul of the teacher training program, there is considerably more that must be done if we are to set our priorities in order. As was suggested earlier, something rather dramatic must be done about placing future teachers into the schools faster than we ever have before. It is difficult to justify keeping them away from real children, at least on the basis of anything we have taught them in the past. Much that we teach them about the history and structure of American education could be happily eliminated or deferred and most of the necessary content in math, social studies, and science could be condensed and focused in much the manner that I have outlined here for the language arts and reading. If the general education lockstep could be subverted, it would be possible to place future teachers in the classroom by the end of two or, at most, two and one-half years of college. As those of us who have returned to college courses after some teaching experience will attest, it takes some reality for the abstractions of college to become meaningful. The point of my suggestions here, though limited primarily to the affect which the study of social dialects can have on the training of teachers, is that special methods and techniques of instruction are fairly meaningless until the student has some notion of what in the world they might mean. The rest of the students' courses, whether they focus on methods, history, visual aids, philosophy, psychology or children's literature could be deferred until after the student has spent a school year in the classroom. But if the student gets into the classroom first for a reasonable length of time (a year at least), he will have reason to suspect that these courses may be in some way useful. If not, he may reject them with no loss of confidence caused by the insecurity of never having taught.

Quite selfishly, I see the overhaul of teacher training programs as an opportunity for linguists and educators to come to a rapprochement which is long overdue. From the view point of linguistics, this opens a door for employment which, for various reasons, has existed only marginally to date. But in a country crying for relevance and in a school setting plagued with primitive linguistic knowledge, it is hardly a time when a choice can be made. People currently trained by education departments cannot teach the courses outlined above. The field of linguistics has been relatively late in coming to grips with social and educational issues and the matter of teacher training outlined herein is as close an opportunity as the discipline may ever have.

References

1. Anne E. Hughes, "An Investigation of Some Sociolinguistic Phenomena in the Vocabulary, Pronunciation and Grammar of Detroit Pre-School Children, Their Parents and Teachers" (Ed.D. Diss. Michigan State University, 1967).
2. For classic counterevidence, see William Labov, "The Logic of Non-Standard English," in Chapter One of this book.
3. Walt Wolfram, *A Sociolinguistic Description of Detroit Negro Speech* (Washington, D.C.: Center for Applied Linguistics, 1969).
4. Roger Shuy, "Teacher Training and Urban Language Problems," in *Teaching Standard English in the Inner City,* eds. Ralph Fasold and Roger Shuy (Washington, D.C.: Center for Applied Linguistics, 1970).
5. Fred M. Hechinger, *The New York Times,* December 21, 1969.
6. "Teacher Training and Urban Language Problems."

Chapter Five
Black English and the Classroom: Oral Language Questions

In this pedagogically oriented chapter, I have tried to highlight an important controversy over the assumptions upon which "teaching Standard English as a second dialect" programs are based as well as give coverage to linguists' suggestions on how to teach a more standard variety to Black English speakers.

One of the situations facing a black ghetto child when he goes to school is that standard forms of English are stressed in the classroom. They are often used by the teacher, especially in language instruction situations (see DeStefano, Chapter Four), and are expected of the black child in many circumstances. The crucial question Kochman raises is that of the validity of the stress on more standard English varieties of English. Why can't the teacher speak so-called standard English and the child speak Black English? In fact, it has been suggested that Black English become *the* instructional variety. As would be expected, this is a controversial opinion, one not much discussed in the articles in this chapter. The prevalent feeling among many people, including linguists, seems to be that Black English fits in ghetto culture and that standard varieties fit in middle-class cultural settings such as schools. However, as the perceived role of the schools changes, this attitude may also change. Certainly there is much more questioning going on about the teaching of standard varieties to Black English speakers, especially elementary school children. It has been suggested that this "bidialectical" approach is merely another form of racism, that in effect it is telling the black child he has to learn to "talk white," that his Black English isn't good enough.

Yet the decision is often made to try to teach Black English speakers a more standard variety as a "second dialect." If this decision has been made by parents or educators in the hopes that the black ghetto child will be able to produce a greater number of more standard forms in his speech, linguists suggest that his teacher needs to be aware of three problems.

The first problem deals with *what* standard forms to teach to a Black

English speaking child. The article by William Labov and Paul Cohen deals in detail with this question.

The second problem in teaching more standard forms deals with *how* to teach those forms to ghetto black children. The article by Robert Politzer deals with this problem. Politzer considers using foreign language teaching techniques in teaching a second variety to a child who already speaks a type of English. He addresses himself to the question of how appropriate a foreign language teaching approach is to the teaching of a more standard variety, noting that an actual second language situation does not exist in the case of the Black English speaking child.

The third problem in teaching a more standard variety of English deals with how the teacher decides in what *order* to teach the forms to be taught. Walt Wolfram addresses himself to this question, suggesting that sociolinguistic criteria are more important for making the judgment as to pedagogical sequencing than purely linguistic ones.

Social Factors in the Consideration
of Teaching Standard English

Thomas Kochman

Thomas Kochman questions the assumption upon which programs teaching so called standard forms (teaching Standard English as a second dialect) to Black English speakers are based. He feels that such programs are of little educational value for several reasons. He contends that these programs do not develop language ability in the person, that they are not efficient in teaching standard forms, and that they are based on a spurious and "exaggerated importance" given to so-called standard forms by teachers. Kochman maintains that speaking "standard" English doesn't help a black get a job and that it doesn't increase his effectiveness in using language.

After he states why these programs are basically useless, he presents a discussion of the problems facing their use if educators insist on using them. First, there is the problem of motivation in language learning. Motivation is based on two factors: desire to identify culturally with those who speak the language, and the functional value of the variety. Blacks may not want to identify culturally, to be assimilated into "mainstream" culture. As Kochman puts it, the black may not want to become white, so doesn't see the value of learning "standard" English. The second argument often presented is that a more standard variety is needed if one is to get ahead in American society. This is the functional motivation. But the ghetto black knows he does not get the job because he is black, not because he speaks Black English.

The second problem teachers of "standard" English must face is that the black child is not reinforced in his use of more standard varieties. Kochman's question is: where in his life is he going to need to speak it? He concludes with the assertion that these programs to teach "standard" English accomplish nothing because Black English is stigmatized by the fact it is spoken by blacks, not because it is an "inferior" dialect. In other words, any variety of English spoken by blacks would be stigmatized merely because it is associated with ghetto blacks.

The purpose of this paper is twofold: one, to weigh the educational value of an oral language program which attempts to teach standard dialect to

From "Social Factors in the Consideration of Teaching Standard English" by Thomas Kochman. Reprinted with permission of the *Florida FL Reporter* from the special anthology issue entitled *Linguistic-Cultural Differences and American Education,* Vol. 7, No. 1, Spring/Summer 1969, pp. 87-88, 157; Alfred C. Aarons, Barbara Y. Gordon, and William A. Stewart, eds.

speakers of a nonstandard dialect, and two, to consider the probable success of such a program, given present social trends.

My first quarrel with such a program is that it does not develop the ability of a person to use language which I would further define as performance capability in a variety of social contexts on a variety of subject matter. Instead, we utilize valuable time to set up drill exercises which are designed to get the individual to replace socially stigmatized forms with socially preferred ones. I cannot endorse as valid a program that sacrifices individual language growth in exchange for some nebulous and highly problematic "social security." The child comes to us with some ability to play the horn and no ability to play the piano. This type of program presumes that a mediocre ability to play the piano is to be preferred to a better than average ability to play the horn. I cannot accept this thesis.

Underlying this approach seems to be a misapplication of Basil Bernstein's terms which falsely equates *restrictive code* and *elaborated code* with respectively, nonstandard dialect and standard dialect.

It ought to be noted, as Bernstein uses the term, *code* is not to be equated with *langue,* but *parole,* not with *competence* but *performance.* What is restrictive or elaborated is not in fact the *code* as sociolinguists use the term, but the message.

This false equation is further reinforced by the observation made by some that speakers of standard dialect possess more elaborate uses of nonstandard dialect. This coincidence is erroneously interpreted to be causal, viz., that speakers of standard dialect are more capable *because* they speak standard dialect. You hear remarks such as "there are things you can't say in nonstandard dialect." These people overlook the fact that standard dialect speakers are so designated by their educational level which often includes being better educated in the *use* of language. What limitations there are exist in the abilities of the speakers.

I might add that many elaborate users of language perform in the nonstandard dialect of the Black Urban Communities and the Kentucky mountains. People who make observations such as the one cited in the paragraph above generally know little of the high degree of prestige associated with verbal ability and consequent high degree of verbal performance in the above named sub-cultures and my guess is that they care to know even less.

The point here is that you can and do have elaborate performances in nonstandard dialect as well as standard, and restrictive performances in standard dialect as well as nonstandard.

My second quarrel with such a program deals with what can be called its efficiency quotient. How much time and drill are required to acquire the new set of language habits necessary to produce even a mediocre and restrictive performance in standard dialect. Speech teachers tell me that with maximum cooperation it takes several months of drill to get a person to say *ask* who formerly said *aks.* My own observation tells me that the input in time and effort is prodigious and the results negligible. Tying in this remark with those made earlier, how might this time be spent in a fashion more beneficial to the language growth and development of the learner?

My third quarrel deals with the exaggerated importance English and Speech teachers attach to being able to perform in a prestige dialect, far beyond its net social worth. How important is it really to getting or keeping a job, to getting the greatest amount of cooperation from your audience, or even to being necessary to the aesthetics of a speech event.

As regards getting a job, there are any number of factors that take precedence over ability to perform in standard English, such as labor supply and demand, race, membership in the dominant group, educational level, and presently, ability to threaten the establishment. Some factors influencing social and economic success are social background; race, dominant group membership; ability to manipulate people and situations; skill in exploiting others' abilities to personal advantage; acquiring political and social contacts; ability to project personality; ability to demonstrate skills of intelligence, aggressiveness, shrewdness, guile and judgment; and most important, the ability to bluff, i.e. deceive others about one's *actual* knowledge, intelligence, etc. Add to that, being a member of a group that constitutes a present threat to the establishment.

As regards the thesis that standard dialect is necessary to get the greatest cooperation from the audience, I have witnessed too many speech events where the audience accommodated the speaker on *his* terms and others where an accent actually added to the *authoritativeness* of the speaker. Also, it seems to me that speaking a *regional standard* that is different from the audience's might involve the same social handicap as speaking a nonstandard dialect. Educated South Midlanders experience much the same difficulty as uneducated ones in getting housing in Chicago. People from Chicago, New York and elsewhere seem to have different social attitudes towards regional standards and rank them differently on a social scale; yet we don't advocate that regional standard speakers accommodate the audience by modifying their speech. The point is, if we are attempting to educate people that one regional standard is as good as another why not educate them that all dialects are equally good.

The final point here is that the aesthetics of a speech event involves a great deal more than the simple use of standard dialect speech forms. I have in mind such qualities as the ability to project personality, style, self-assurance, authoritativeness, native coloring in a fluent manner, regardless of dialect.

I just read where the BBC in London is permitting the reporting of news events in dialects other than the Received Standard. They have found that news broadcasted on the scene by reporters in local dialect added a touch of "realism" to the presentation.

The second part of this paper proposes to deal with the probable success of such a program, given present social trends. The audience might well wonder why I am pursuing this aspect after I have just apparently concluded that such a program is not educationally fruitful. You ask "If it is not educationally sound, why is it necessary to consider whether it is possible." Your logic is flawless, but unhappily it is based on the illusory assumption that what is done in the classroom is done only after it is decided that it is worth doing. My observations at English, Speech and TESOL [Teaching English to Speakers of Other Languages] conventions, and in school classrooms in the past, persuade me that teachers and supervisors are concerned almost exclusively with methodology—"how to teach it" —and are gratuitously deaf to the logically antecedent question of "whether to teach it at all." This portion of the paper is especially aimed at them.

What are the teaching problems facing the teacher who attempts to teach the prestige form of a dialect to, let us suppose, black children, against whom the focus of such a program is generally directed? The two teaching problems he will have to face are social in origin. They are the problems of motivation and reinforcement. Let us consider motivation first.

There are basically two reasons for wanting to learn a second language or dialect: cultural identification and/or functional need. With respect to the first reason, we must take into account the alienation black people feel; with regard to the second reason we must consider the credibility gap that has been created because of the failure of blacks who had skills to get meaningful jobs. How has language teaching contributed to the alienation and credibility gap we now face? How have both contributed to the failure and frustration of students, producing a drop-out rate of 1000 students a month in our Chicago schools?

In the past and generally up to the present time children have encountered in the English and Speech classroom the prescriptive approach. This approach advanced the superiority of the standard dialect and through the process of exclusion, negation and derogation, the inferiority of the nonstandard dialect, and by direct implication the inferiority of the speakers who speak it and the inferiority of their culture which produces it. You who are unwilling to accept the implication, ask yourselves why English spoken with a French accent is socially acceptable, even "charming," while English spoken with a black accent is not. The inescapable social truth of the matter is that people's attitudes towards other people's speech are merely an extension of people's attitudes towards their culture and the people of that culture. This point is not missed by the culturally different when they enter the middle class establishment of the schoolroom.

What was the underlying perspective behind this approach? Assimilationist! What was the justification? At worst, it was arrogant ethnocentrism; at best, it recognized that the society is prejudiced and the way to escape discrimination was by losing your group identification. Your perspective and attitude said: obliterate what is culturally different, or if you can't, conceal it; relegate it to the inside of your homes. The penalty for nonassimilation was social ostracism, so the groups that could assimilate did, but often with much bitterness and resentment, and then only partially.

The groups that couldn't assimilate or chose not to, like American Indians, blacks and Mexican-Americans, were and are relegated respectively to the societal oblivion of the reservation and the ghetto. They have been the invisible people of our society.

The assimilationist approach made people resentful, resistant to learning. Now it has made them angry enough to demand, through petition and boycott, an end to this kind of attitude and teaching.

It is to the credit of the linguistic approach that it has at least recognized that the speaker's native dialect has cultural value for him and is not to be tampered with. It advances the teaching of standard English as a second dialect. It is a step in the right direction but it hardly goes far enough. The problem is in its supposedly "realistic" approach. It says, "People make social judgments all the time. We live in a socially stratified and deterministic society. Recognize it! Conform to the existing social order and its rules." Unfortunately, the linguistic approach accepts as social determinant the same obnoxious and racist standards as the prescriptive-assimilationist approach and in so doing merely perpetuates the alienation begun with its predecessor.

If a child does not wish to identify with the larger society, emphasize the *functional* value of performing in standard dialect; "He'll need it to get a better job," or "Teach it to him so that he will be able to decide later on whether he wants to use it or not." This "functional need" motivation falls on unbelieving ears. The black child knows that he pays the social price for being black, not because he does or does not speak standard dialect. He asks, "Why do I have to speak better than the white man to get the same job." Do you need to be able to perform in standard dialect to be a carpenter, plumber, brick layer, construction worker, or printer, or to be any trade or non-trade union employee? How many white collar jobs require the ability to perform in standard dialect? Are blacks going to believe that they are being discriminated against in all of these jobs because they don't speak standard dialect? In 1963, for those blacks who attended college, their median income was only 60% of that of whites with comparable education. In 1966, blacks with an eighth grade education earned 80% of what whites earned with comparable education. If educational level, which is a far more significant employment factor than ability to perform in standard dialect, has not been effective in reducing the disparity between black and white income why should blacks believe performing in the prestige dialect will. According to a 1967 report entitled *Chicago's Widening Color Gap,* "Negro college graduates in Chicago earn less than white high school drop-outs." It is to be noted also that the higher the educational level, the greater the disparity between black and white income.

With regard to the problem of reinforcement, where is the child going to use, outside of the classroom, the dialect the teacher is attempting to teach him inside? And if he can't find a place to use it, how is he going to acquire a "new set of language habits." The area in which he lives reinforces his native dialect, not the standard. In Chicago, it is not unusual for a black child to have attended 100 per cent black schools up to and through high school. Clearly, the linguistic approach presumes that *integration* will take place; either that black families will move into white areas or that black children will be bussed into white areas where reinforcement of standard dialect can take place. Demographic statistics show a contrary trend, viz., black communities are becoming "blacker" and white communities "whiter." Even in communities such as Maywood, Joliet and Wheaton with which I am partly familiar, with a majority white population, the blacks invariably live in segregated housing, and socialization in the high school is almost invariably *intra*-group with very little chance of reinforcing prestige dialect patterns assuming even that white high school students speak them.

Finally, the linguistic approach is based on a social fallacy, viz., that the social order is immutably stratified, that the social judgments that people are making today are the same judgments that they will be making fifteen or even five years from now. I find this assumption challenged by present social trends. The walls of racism are even today starting to crumble and those teachers using the linguistic-integrationist approach will find themselves accused of having made a pact with the same devil as those using the prescriptive-assimilationist approach.

I see our society experiencing the throes of social reform this very minute. Our cherished prejudices and practices are being assaulted at every turn, besieged with long hair and "bad manners" on the one hand and Black

Power and creative disorder on the other. What if blacks succeed in changing the social order so that they and their culture will no longer be regarded as inferior by the larger society? What if, in twenty years, you will regard a black accent comparably to the way you regard today the accent of a German professor, French singer, or British actor? Does it really matter how people of status speak? You say, what if the social order is not changed? Then I ask you, what have you accomplished in your program: the ability to avoid some stigmatized forms because the people who speak them are?

Will speaking better remove the stigma attached to that person? At the Democratic convention, Julian Bond [state legislator from Georgia] probably spoke "better" than most people there. Will speaking better make Bond president? I doubt it, but Black Power might.

It ought to be clear by this time that what is emerging in our society today is a resurgence of ethnic pride as well as attempts by ethnic communities to establish control over their own destiny. Not only are the culturally different resisting or rejecting the assimilationist pressure of the present establishment, they are also no longer relegating or subordinating their own culture to the inside of their homes. Ultimately, the choice of what is to be taught and how it is to be taught is the learner's and educators, like everyone else in our society, will have to respond to the challenge of being "relevant" in both our goals and our methods or be faced with empty classrooms and "student schools."

My conclusion is apparent. The present efforts to teach a prestige form of speech to nonstandard speakers are educationally wasteful and the effective realization is socially improbable, unless the express desire and cooperation of those learning it are forthcoming. That decision will be neither yours nor mine to make!

You who will persist in your efforts despite the resistance of your students, their parents and communities, do so at your own peril.

Reference

1. Pierre de Vise, *Chicago's Widening Color Gap* (DePaul Univ., Dept of Sociology, Inter-University Social Research Committee, Report No. 2, Dec. 1967) pp. 80–81.

Some Suggestions for Teaching Standard English to Speakers of Nonstandard Urban Dialects

William Labov and Paul Cohen

This article by William Labov and Paul Cohen deals with the question of what standard forms to teach to a Black English speaking child. The authors organize the forms into grammatical patterns (syntax), sentence patterns, and articulation and pronunciation. Within each of these sections they caution that the forms which follow the most general rules should generally be taught first so that the child becomes aware of the two systems of so-called standard English and Black English and the differences between them. The authors also include suggestions as to how to teach specific standard forms to the Black English speaker. Because of these pedagogical suggestions, the article is included even though some of the description of Black English forms overlaps with material contained in Chapter Four. And certainly the contrastive analysis presented in the article is a necessary base for the methodological suggestions in the following articles.

Some nonstandard forms are special cases that affect only one or two words of the language; but many are instances of general rules that operate in the nonstandard vernacular in a regular way and can affect the form of every sentence. It is plain that the more general rules should be introduced first in a teaching program, no matter how prominent and striking the isolated items may be. For example, the use of *less'n* in *He won't come less'n I call him* is a Southernism that is quite unacceptable in the standard English of New York City, but the problem appears only when the particular word *unless* is to be used. In a sentence like *He go downtown,* on the other hand, the particular verb *go* is irrelevant: the student must be taught the regular rule for the third-person singular *-s* for every regular verb in the language. The order of the material given below reflects this reasoning: within each section, the items are presented which involve the most general rules, and each item is presented under the form of the most general rule that applies, according to our present knowledge of the language.

The nonstandard dialect forms shown here are most characteristic of the

Negro children living in areas where large numbers of migrants have recently arrived from the Southern United States. New York City has received Southern speakers chiefly from the Atlantic Coastal states. In other Northern and Western cities, such as Chicago or Los Angeles, most migrants have come from different regions of the South, but the resulting dialect patterns in the urban centers have been surprisingly similar; the obvious differences are due to the Northern base rather than the Southern influence.

Some of the nonstandard features discussed are used by groups outside the Negro communities discussed above. These more general nonstandard forms are marked with an asterisk, *.

Grammatical Patterns

Forms of the Verb

1. *The -s of the present tense.* It has been widely noticed that many nonstandard speakers from the community discussed here make an extraordinary number of mistakes in person-number agreement—a much higher number than in the community at large. Attempts to correct these forms one at a time are almost certain to fail. Most of the children concerned have no regular rule for adding *-s* to the verb when the subject is third person singular. Their normal vernacular forms in casual, every-day speech are

> I know, you know, he know, she know, it know, we know,
> you know, they know
> I do, you do, he do, she do, it do, the man do, we do,
> you do, they do

The regular forms of the sample present should be taught from the outset, without assuming that any child necessarily possesses even a passive knowledge of the standard rules. Sometimes, the *-s* does appear with the third person singular, or with other persons, but this simply reflects the fact that children have learned that *-s* is used in school language. Their partial learning does not extend to the regular rule for placing this *-s,* and as a result it may appear in almost any position:

> *I sees it*
> *They runs down the street*
> *Somebody get hurts*
> *He can goes out*

2. *The -ed of the past tense.* In the nonstandard speech considered here, there is some basis for the *-ed* of the past and perfect tenses of the regular verb, but in the great majority of cases this inflection is not pronounced.

> *He walk' home yesterday.*
> *I have live' here.*

The *-ed* is pronounced more often after verbs ending in *-t* or *-d* (*started* or *added*) or before a vowel (*walked along*), because part of the difficulty with *-ed* has to do with rules of pronunciation in which consonant clusters are simplified (see below). But even when children pronounce this *-ed*, it may not act as a signal of the past tense for them. A good diagnostic sentence is:

> *When I passed by, I read the sign.*

Children who pronounce the *-ed* in *passed,* but say *read* to rhyme with *need,* are clearly not interpreting the written signal, and do not have the rule of the standard dialect for the past tense. Similarly, we can infer that children who read aloud *"He pickted on me",* do not know the regular rules for the forms of the *-ed* ending. (1)

All of the children concerned use the past tense for many common irregular verbs such as *give-gave* and *run-ran* and the problem is chiefly with the *forms* of the regular verb. On the other hand, nonstandard speech does allow a freer *use* of the historical present in narrative than is permitted in colloquial informal speech. Thus we find

> *I walk home last night.*
> *He stay home yesterday.*

Children therefore need training in the use of the *-ed* ending as a signal of the past tense, and in the consistent use of the past tense in formal narratives.

3. *The verb to be.*   There are many differences between standard and nonstandard rules in the use of the verb *to be.* Most commonly, the finite forms do not appear in the present, whether they are copulas or auxiliaries, and students need to be taught from the beginning that standard English does not permit this.

> *He here now.*
> *But everybody not black.*
> *You out the game.*
> *She lookin' good.*

On the other hand, we find the non-finite *be* inserted in the same slot, primarily in context of generality or repeated action and particularly in the present tense:

> *Most of the time he be in the library.*
> *He be doin' that all the time.*

> *So it all don't be on her; it be half on me and half on her.*
> *They always be messin' around.*

This use of *be* is very persistent, more than most of the other plainly marked Southernisms, and it may be difficult to show *directly* why it is incorrect. Standard English does allow *be* in many similar situations, and one would need a very good knowledge of English grammar to understand why *be* is not allowed in *They be here* but is perfectly standard in

> *Be here.*
> *They might be here.*
> *I demand that they be here.*

The best approach to the *be* situation is probably *indirect*. The students must be taught the finite forms of *to be* in the present very thoroughly, especially in context of generality and repeated action, where otherwise the bare infinitive *be* would occur.

4. *The future.* In many cases, the general use of *be* is difficult to distinguish from the standard future. Because *-l* is usually vocalized (see below), there may be little difference between

> *She be comin' home* and
> *She'll be comin' home.*

For this reason, it is best to use the *uncontracted* forms of the future in standard English, and give students practice in using these in place of the colloquial futures

> *I'm a hit you.*
> *He goin' (-gone) hit you.*
> *He hit you tomorrow.*

*5. *Irregular preterit and perfect forms.* Though children who speak this form of nonstandard English do use many irregular forms correctly, a large number of irregular Southern preterits and perfects are encountered. It is necessary to teach the standard forms of such common verbs as *begin, break, come, do, drink, drown, give, go, know, lie, ring, run, see, sing, sit, sneak, take, throw, and write.*

*6. *The passive.* The colloquial passive with *got* is normally the only one used in the nonstandard vernacular, as in *He got stung,* and children need practice in the standard form.

7. *Perfective done.* A highly marked Southernism is the use of *done* to emphasize the completed or accomplished state of an action:

> *The bullet done penetrate my body.*

This is not a common form in Northern cities, but when it does occur, it poses difficulties since there is no simple literal equivalent in standard English. It is best treated as an unacceptable Southernism similar to *less'n* or *tote,* though it is plainly more important than these in the original nonstandard grammar.

Forms of the Noun

8. *The plural -s.* The plural inflection is almost intact in nonstandard speech dealt with here. This *-s* behaves in quite the opposite manner from the third-singular *-s* or the possessive *-s:* it is used regularly by most young children, and where it differs from standard English it is even more general: it is extended to form a double plural in *mens, womens, childrens, peoples, teeths.* When the *-s* is missing, it is most frequently in fixed contexts like *eight year old, ten cent.* In short, the standard rule is known, and the teacher's task is chiefly to correct a few irregularities.

9. *The possessive -s.* The possessive *-s* which is added to nouns in standard English has no representation whatsoever in the nonstandard grammar discussed here. The normal form of the possessive is

> *John old lady house.*
> *That's Nick boy.*
> *His father sister husband.*

The standard rule must be taught without any assumption that it is necessarily part of the speech of any of the children, as is the case in the third-singular *-s* of the verb. The only place where it does occur regularly is with possessive pronouns:

> *It's mines.*
> *That's hers.*

The use of *mines* must be corrected to *mine,* an individual item. (2), (3)

10. *Pronoun forms.* There are several highly marked irregularities of pronoun forms to be considered, especially among possessive pronouns. The principal nonstandard form is *they* for *their,* as in *They brought it on they own selves. You* is sometimes not distinct from *your,* and both of these are partly the result of rules of pronunciation (the loss of final *-r*). We also find an even more deviant form with the pluralizer *them* substituting for *his* or *their*:

> *His eyes are—All of them eyes are orange, or reddish.*
> *They were in Larry and them hallway.*

Because of these several irregularities, the possessive pronouns should be taught systematically.

Other word forms

*11. *Adverbs in -ly.* The *-ly* inflection, turning adjectives into adverbs, is rarely used among nonstandard speakers, and should be taught as a regular rule from the outset. At the same time, the use of the irregular adverbs such as *well* must be taught.

*12. *Comparatives in -er.* There are many difficulties with the comparative, but the simplest is in the choice of *more* or *-er.* The use of both is common: *He is more taller than me; He is pure blacker than you;* students need practice in using one or the other. (4)

Sentence patterns

There are a very large number of syntactic problems which could be discussed here: the most important are those which concern the basic transformations of the question, the negative, and the embedded question, but there are many equally general rules which occur less frequently.

13. *Do-support in questions.* In the rules of the nonstandard vernacular, the normal form of the question transformation is usually found: the childish *How he can fix that?* is largely replaced by the standard *How can he fix that?* by the 5th or 6th grade. But with the simple verb, we get forms such as

> *How he fix that?*
> *How it taste?*
> *Why they listen to me?*

There is some reason to think that these are derived from the standard forms by deletion of *do.* In any case, the use of overt *do*-support must be taught, to relate *He fixes that* to *Does he fix that?*

14. *Negative patterns.* In the most general kind of nonstandard English, *ain't* is simply the particular equivalent of *be* plus negative. But in the nonstandard English considered here, *ain't* stands for the negative element alone. Since *do* support is largely missing, we find

> *He ain't start it.* for *He didn't start it.*
> **He ain't started to go.* for *He hasn't started to go.*
> *He ain't finish.* for *He isn't finished.*

In the past tense, we have *wasn't* or *weren't*, though without any regular person-number agreement. In negative questions, the *ain't* element is regularly brought to the front of the sentence, so that *do*-support is not needed

*Ain't that a shame?

The same pattern is extended in declarative statements with a strong affect to yield:

Ain't nobody see it: ain't nobody hear it parallel to literary forms, *Nor has anyone seen it; scarcely has anyone seen it.* As a result of these many differences in negative patterns it is necessary to introduce the standard rules in a systematic way from the very beginning.

*15. Negatives with indefinites: the "double negative."

It is difficult for many teachers to correct the nonstandard "double negative" because the rules for the standard form are not taught systematically. Briefly, in standard English there is a general rule which states that a negative element in a sentence is attracted to the first indefinite in the sentence; these negatives also include *scarcely, hardly, never, rarely,* which are brought to the very beginning of the sentence. So instead of *Anybody can't do that,* we have standard *Nobody can do that.* Instead of *Anyone hardly knows that* we have standard *Hardly does anyone know that.* A sentence like:

No one will do anything to anybody.

has a corresponding passive:

Nothing will be done to anybody by anyone.

The general nonstandard rule is much simpler: it says that a negative is attracted to *every* indefinite in the sentence. So a single negative element, instead of being represented by one negative form, is represented by many:

Nobody don't know.
Nobody won't do nothing to nobody.
I ain't never had no trouble with none of them.

The double negative will therefore occur only in sentences which originally contain indefinite pronouns or adverbs, and any practice in avoiding double negatives (perhaps better called "negative concord") must be with sentences containing such indefinites.

The particular nonstandard forms used in the Negro communities of the North differ from the general nonstandard form in one important way: the negative element can be transferred to the pre-verbal position in embedded clauses without producing a new negative meaning that contradicts the first. Thus the general nonstandard form:

> *There ain't no cat can't get in no (pigeon) coop.*

is the opposite of

> *There ain't no cat can get in no coop.*

But in the Negro community, we can have:

> *It ain't no cat can't get in no coop.*

meaning the same as

> *It ain't no cat can get in no coop.*

With these rules in mind, the teacher should be able to construct forms for teaching the standard rules for negative attraction to any of the students concerned.

16. *The dummy it.* One of the most characteristic forms of the nonstandard speech being considered is the equivalent of *There was, there is* or *there are.* Instead of these forms, we have *It is . . .*

> *It's a policeman at the door.*
> *It was one in the hall this morning.*
> *It ain't no cat can't get in no coop.*

The contraction *it's* is normally pronounced with the *t* assimilated to the *s*, to rhyme with *hiss.* Occasionally this unstressed form is voiced to rhyme with *his*, and teachers will hear the form as equivalent to dropping the subject:

> *"Is" raining.*
> *"Is" a policeman at the door.*

However, if any element is dropped, it would usually be the copula:

> *It a policeman at the door.*

Therefore, the teacher need not spend time teaching the student to replace dropped subjects, but rather to retain the copula, and replace nonstandard *it* with standard *there* in the proper contexts.

17. *Embedded questions.* We frequently encounter sentences of the following form:

> **Let me see could I think of some right away.*
> *I don't know how old are he.*
> **I don't know how did I do it.*
> *She could see is the boy nose bleed.*

In these sentences, we find that the order of the original question is preserved, with auxiliary or question word first and subject second. It would seem that standard English reverses the question in the embedded or indirect form to return to the original order of a simple declarative (or exclamation).

> *I don't know how old he is.*
> *I don't know how I did do it.*
> *Let me see if I could think of some right away.*
> *She could see if the boy's nose is bleeding.*

Notice that in many of these sentences a deleted *if* must reappear. The nonstandard retention of the inverted order preserves the question meaning which is conveyed in the standard *if.* To teach the standard rules for this construction, it may not be enough to drill the student on word order: in addition, the teacher may want to show how the meaning of wondering or questioning is preserved in the *how* or the *if* which precedes the embedded sentence.

18. *Pleonastic or "double" forms.*   The redundancy or doubling of forms seen in the negative concord is a characteristic of many deviant forms in this speech pattern considered here. The commonest such forms are demonstrative with locative adverbs:

> *This here one is a Davis.*

We also have frequent combinations such as *only but*

> *I didn't play wit' only but Wayne and Tyrone.*

The conjunction *and plus* is even more common:

> *And plus I bought me some spinach and rice.*

Parallel to this is *or either:*

> *Or either they'll say . . .*

It is characteristic of the Southern dialect pattern that quantitative adverbs are multiplied:

> *You play with them near about mostly every day*
> *So he'll bring in almost close to two hundred a week.*

Finally, we can note the redundancy of certain prepositions with relative adverbs:

> *. . . right around the corner where I used to live at.*

In all of these examples, the nonstandard forms show extra material which is not required or allowed in the standard dialect. In addition to drills on the patterns involved, the teacher should be able to show how the extra material contributes nothing to the meaning of the sentence.

19. *Adverb placement.* There are many subtle and difficult rules involved in the placement of adverbs such as *almost, even, mostly, all over;* these are principally quantifiers of the verbal action as a whole. We can see that nonstandard speakers show many deviations from standard usage in placing these adverbs, even though we may not be able to state the exact rule affected in each case, nor find a single generalization to cover all the difficulties.

> *That's what mostly we call 'em.*
> *. . . even a guy might pick a garbage can.*
> *Almost my life was lost.*
> *The longest place I stayed was -uh- in North Carolina.*
> *So, this is a crazy world we absolutely livin' in,*
> *and everything contradicts its own self.*
> *But he act all stupid.*
> *He got dirt all on his knees.*

20. *Difficulties with the comparative.* In addition to the simple problem of form of the comparative adjective, we find a great many difficulties with complex comparative, superlative and equative constructions:

> *I know he was the most award winner in track.*
> *I'm about the only one that has the less, I think.*
> *He can run the same fas' as I can.*
> *So she got the same accent of her mother.*
> *I had just as many friends up here than I had down there.*
> *Everybody got the same equal amount.*

Since this is one of the most complex areas of English grammar, it is not surprising that speakers run into difficulty. It is apparent that the high school teacher must gradually introduce students into the more complex constructions with sufficient practice to enable them to avoid such problems as those shown here.

*21. *Relative pronouns.* The general pronoun used in the nonstandard dialect is *which.* It must be replaced with *who* in some obvious cases:

> *John, which is seven, Linda which is six . . .*

But in other cases, *which* is used as a general connective which has no direct equivalent in standard English:

They were poor, which we all was poor, but I mean . . .
I had some older brothers—you know, which these boys they were older than I am.
From there I move to 115 St., which I was livin' there for about two years.

In these cases, the best equivalent is a simple *and*: the speaker must be taught to give up the sense of vague anaphoric reference which he tries to register with *which*, but which standard English cannot provide unless it is tied to a particular noun phrase.

22. *Count nouns vs. mass nouns.*   There are a great many nonstandard uses of nouns to be considered which can not be corrected efficiently unless the teacher first introduces the notion of *count nouns* and *mass nouns.* Count nouns such as chair and table have plurals and take the indefinite article *a.* Mass nouns such as *cash* or *police* have no plural forms, do not occur with the indefinite article *a,* but do occur with no article or the indefinite *some.* Thus we have

> *Give me a chair, Give me some chairs.*
> *Give me cash. Give me some cash.*

but not

> *Give me chair. Give me some chair.*
> *Give me a cash. Give me some cashes.*

With such a distinction in mind, the teacher can show that the following sentences are unacceptable because the nouns are treated as count nouns rather than mass nouns:

> *Give us a tater chips.*
> *Dat's a dope (that is, narcotics).*
> *He's training to be a police.*
> *I don't use those slangs.*

Articulation and Pronunciation

The most general principle involved in the articulation of the nonstandard speech considered here is the same as that in standard English: less information is provided or less precision required for sounds at the ends of words than for sounds at the beginnings of words. For example, initial *t* is a forcefully articulated consonant, with a burst of air that affects the quality of the next sound; but final *t* need not be released at all, and in this case is recognized through its effect on the preceding sounds. Nonstandard English carries this principle much further than standard English, in the simplification of final consonant clusters, the loss of final *r, l* and of other tongue-tip consonants: *t, d, s, z,* and to a lesser extent, *n.* In all these cases the teacher can benefit by observing one general rule: that a rule for the pronunciation of a consonant or vowel is usually sensitive to the sound immediately following the one concerned. Thus when a consonant cluster or single consonant is followed by a word beginning with a vowel, it is much more likely for the full form to be pronounced than when the next word begins with a consonant. The teacher can apply this rule in giving practice in pronunciation. (However, it does not always follow that the sound is easier for the student to *hear* in a phrase; the teacher's clearly released final *-t* in *just* may be heard more clearly than in *just a minute*).

1. *Consonant cluster simplifications.* English has a wide range of consonant clusters at the ends of words, but by far the most common are those in which the second element is *t, d* or *s, z.* These two pairs are related in the same way: *t* and *s* are voiceless consonants, and *d* and *z* are the corresponding voiced consonants—that is, the vocal cords are vibrating as these consonants are formed.

We should also observe that the consonants *t,d* and *s,z* are also the major inflections of English. The first two are the signals of the past and perfect tenses, and the second two appear in many different grammatical forms: the third-person singular present form of the verb, the plural, the possessive, the adverbial *-s* in *besides,* and the contracted forms *let's, it's,* etc. When these final elements are grammatical inflections, the appearance of *t* or *d, s* or *z,* is predicted by the first consonant of the cluster:

after voiceless consonants	t	s
after voiced consonants	d	z

(If the first consonant is a *t* or a *d,* then in the past tense there is no cluster—the inflection is an unstressed vowel and *d;* if the first consonant is a sibilant—a hissing or hushing sound, then there is no cluster in the other cases—the inflections occur as unstressed vowel plus *z.*)

Of course there are some consonant clusters which are merely parts of the basic word: as in *fist, find, hold, belt, six* (siks). In this case, the final consonant cannot be predicted after some consonants.

In the nonstandard English of the larger community there is a very high rate of simplification of such clusters such as *fist* or *find.* Even among educated speakers, words such as *just* are often simplified. But this process does not take place when the second element is a grammatical signal. Furthermore, the cluster is usually kept intact when the next word begins with a vowel. These facts show that we are dealing with a simple pronunciation factor which has no effect upon the grammar of the language.

However, in the nonstandard English of the urban centers being considered here, the line between grammatical rules and rules of pronunciation is not so easy to draw. The clusters are frequently simplified—in many cases just as often when the second consonant is a grammatical signal.

In the case of -*t* and -*d* clusters as in *act, walked,* and *grabbed,* it is the second element which disappears. There is some tendency for the cluster to be pronounced more often when the cluster contains a grammatical element, but only a small tendency; and there is some tendency for the cluster to be pronounced when the next word begins with a vowel, but also only a small tendency. On the whole, we can say that there is a basis for the teacher to use in giving the child practice in the standard forms, and it may be especially helpful if the word is given in a phrase with the next word beginning with a vowel:

> not *I walked home,* but *I walked away.*

In the case of clusters ending in -*s,* we find a wide variety of different results depending on the grammatical element involved. As noted above, the -*s,* is simply missing in the basic vernacular for the third person singular form of the present verb and the possessive. But for the plural -*s,* and the adverbial -*s,* the clusters are only occasionally simplified, and here too it will be helpful to give practice with phrases in which the next word begins with a vowel. In the case of *it's, let's, that's,* etc., there is rarely any influence of pronunciation on grammar, since it is almost always the first element which disappears, assimilated to the -*s:*

> *Le's go; i's hot; tha's right.*

There are a few clusters ending in -*k* and -*p* which behave like simple words in -*st: desk* is des', *ask* can be *as'* as well as aks, and *wasp* is was'. Here again a following vowel will help bring out the missing consonant except in the case of certain words where a basic change in the underlying "dictionary" form has taken place. In words like *tes', toas', ghos',* the apostrophe is truly a fiction for many children, for their plurals are *tesses, toases, ghoses,* and the standard forms *test, toast, ghost* must be taught as brand new items.

2. *Final and pre-consonantal -r.* In the New York City community at large, the basic vernacular (along with many educated varieties) is "r-less." The consonant -*r* that appears in spelling is never pronounced at the ends of words or before final consonants as in *car* and *card, core* and *cored.* Instead, the vowel is lengthened and may be followed by an unstressed center vowel. This feature is also characteristic of Southern speech, so that in the urban centers we find the same "r-less" pronunciation.

The pronunciation of this final and pre-consonantal *r* is rapidly being accepted as a standard of correct speech among younger educated people, and the community at large. However, r-less speech is certainly not "incorrect," and a great many teachers and educated speakers are completely r-less. At first sight, one would think that there is no reason to teach the pronunciation of *-r* to disadvantaged youth. Nevertheless, it may be good *strategy* to teach the pronunciation of the final *-r,* for many reasons. First, this variable is one of the most important marks of careful speech for younger people in New York City. Even though the older generation may still use prestige forms of r-less speech, the younger generation has turned to the general Northern pattern of r-pronunciation as the norm. This tendency is even stronger in the Negro community, which is becoming oriented more and more towards the Northern model of *careful* speech (although the Southern-based dialect forms are still the basis of affective or family speech). Second, and more importantly, the introduction of final *-r* will do a great deal of work in helping to teach standard grammar. In the use of the auxiliary and copula verb *to be,* the second person singular and plural form *are* is strongly reinforced by *r*-pronunciation. In the past tense, person-number agreement depends upon the distinction of *was* and *were,* strongly supported by *r*-pronunciation. The possessive adjectives *your* and *their* are distinguished much more easily from *you* and *they* when final *r* is pronounced. In r-less dialects, all these differences depend upon subtle differences of vowel height and obscure glides which are easily lost.

Finally, the pronunciation of final *r* may be very helpful in teaching students the full forms of words which have been altered in their underlying system. The r-less speakers of the larger community rarely drop *r* when a vowel follows, as in *four o'clock* or *Paris,* and as a result the standard spelling forms of the words are easy for them to grasp. (There is an *r* in *four* because it is produced in *four o'clock.*) But speakers of the Southern-influenced dialect are r-less in a stronger sense: for many of them, there may not be enough support for inferring the existence of an *r* in *four* (or *car, beer, Paris,* or *Carol*) because the following vowel does not bring out the *r* with the necessary regularity or reliability, and many words may then be persistently misspelled without the *r* in school.

For all these reasons, it may be advisable for teachers in New York City schools to introduce the use of final *-r* in the most formal styles, in pronouncing words aloud, and to have children practice the pronunciation of final *-r,* even though this is not a vitally important feature in itself.

3. *Final -l.* The situation with final and pre-consonantal *l* in *pal, help,* etc., is parallel in many ways to final and pre-consonantal *r.* However, there is one important difference: there is no standard dialect in which it is acceptable to omit final *-l.* Homonyms such as *too* and *tool, go* and *goal* are not recognized in standard English, though there are speakers in the larger community who show such a pattern.

The Southern-influenced nonstandard dialect shows a much greater loss of -*l* than in the community as a whole. Normally, -*l* is replaced by a back unrounded glide, which is often difficult to hear, and after back rounded vowels *u* and *o*, it tends to disappear entirely. Again, we find serious grammatical consequences of this fact, since *She be goin'* and *She'll be goin'* can be very difficult to distinguish.

Practice in the pronunciation of final -*l* will be easier for the student if the training exercises have *l* followed by a vowel, as in *a pal of mine.*

4. *The pronunciation of th.*   Initial *th* in *thing* and *then* shows roughly the same pattern in this nonstandard dialect as for most nonstandard speakers. A weakly articulated t-like sound is used in *thing* and a similar d-like sound in *then*. Occasionally a strongly articulated *t* or *d* is heard, and then the word *thin* becomes homonymous with *tin* or (more commonly), *then* with *den*. The voiceless *th* in *thin* is more frequenty an affricate—that is, an intermediate sound that begins like a *t* and ends like a *th.*

In the middle of words, and more importantly at the end of words, speakers of this nonstandard dialect frequently use -*f* and -*y* in place of the corresponding *th* sounds: *Ruth* is not distinguished from *roof,* and *bathe* rhymes with *rave.* This shift is not characteristic of any nonstandard dialect of the adult community at large, though children do show *f* and *y* for *th* sounds and Cockney English is noted for this feature. The great difficulty for the teacher and student alike is that the difference between English *f* and *th* is extremely hard to hear as a rule. Unless the consonants are carefully pronounced, and hearing conditions are ideal, even trained groups of phoneticians will not be able to transcribe these sounds reliably. Therefore the teacher will have to determine, by careful testing and visual observation of the student's lips, whether or not (a) he normally produces final *th* in careful speech and (b) whether or not he can hear the difference when the sounds are very carefully pronounced. It is interesting to note that hypercorrection is rarely found: *f* is used where standard English has *th,* but not the reverse—*roof* is not pronounced as *Ruth.* The same observation holds for initial position: we almost never find a case of *den* pronounced as *then.* The fact that the confusion is in one direction only differentiates this consonantal situation from the typical vowel situation, where fluctuation back and forth is much more common.

5. *The loss of other final consonants.*   The losses of final consonants discussed above are the most regular cases, but we also note the absence of individual final consonants such as -*t, -d, -s,* and less commonly -*n, -k, -g* and -*p.* As an example, one illiterate teenager form South Carolina can best be quoted as saying:

I ma' a ba' spee' for *I make a bad speech.*

Though final *-d* is often lost entirely, it is even more commonly pronounced as a lenis *-t*, so that *rabbit* and *rabid* can not be distinguished, and *David* rhymes with *save it.* Final *-n* is frequently heard as nasalization of the preceding vowel, and it rarely disappears in any absolute sense.

In one way, these erratic losses are more important for the teacher than the regular processes discussed before. A few children have a great deal of difficulty in understanding and being understood because they have the most extreme forms of the rules for final simplification, and most of their syllables actually end with vowels. In their speech, there is so much unexpected homonymy that intelligibility suffers badly. Teachers who notice such cases can recognize them as exceptional, and make sure that they obtain special correction.

6. *Some problems with initial clusters.*   Though the most serious difficulties are found at the ends of words, there are a number of Southern-influenced characteristics of initial consonant clusters. Initial *str-*, for example, is occasionally heard as *skr-* so that *stream* is said as *scream, street* as *skreet.* Initial *shr-* is variously *sw-, sr-, shw-: shrimp* is the word most characteristically affected. There are various combinations in which *-r-* is lost, chiefly after *th-* (and often after *b, p, k* and *g*), and where a back rounded vowel follows: the Southern forms *th'ow, th'ough* are very common.

Vowels

When dealing with vowels, it is more important to bear in mind the relations between the sounds, and the distinctions that can be made, than the actual sounds themselves. Many descriptions of non-standard dialects draw attention to the "substitution of sounds," such as the use of *i* for *e* in *pen* and *friend.* While such statements do refer to real examples, teachers who try to follow them will be puzzled to note that the same speakers will sometimes "substitute *e* for *i*" in *pin* and *wind.* In this situation we are actually dealing with a single underlying fact: that many speakers of this nonstandard dialect do not distinguish *i* and *e* before any nasal consonant, and therefore either *e* or *i* may appear without making any significant difference for them. A teacher who thinks in terms of such contrasts—trying to see what is "same" and "different" for these students—will be dealing with the entire problem directly, while a teacher who tries to correct each "mistake" as it occurs will be faced with an unending task and frustrated students. In each case, the teacher should be on the alert for the existence of sets of homonyms among the students which differ from her own and from those of standard English. The facts for any given case can be determined by giving a simple perception test. Then the teacher can give a number of ear-training exercises (using essentially the same procedure as in the perception test) to teach the students to hear the distinction. Training in the actual production of the standard distinction comes last, and will be greatly facilitated if the students have already learned to hear and recognize the differences in the speech of others. With these preliminary remarks, we can proceed to describe the various vowel problems quite briefly.

7. *The merger of fear and fair.* In the speech of many nonstandard speakers, all of the words which rhyme with *fear* also rhyme with *fair* and the class of words that rhyme with *fair* in standard English. Thus *steer* and *stair, cheer* and *chair, mere* and *mare, hear* and *hair* are homonyms, usually pronounced with a sound close to that of the second element in standard English. In the South, this merger is most characteristic of Coastal South Carolina, and speakers from this area are most apt to show it. A similar situation is not unknown in the nonstandard English of the New York City speech community in general, where many younger speakers merge *fear* and *fair* in their r-less dialect—in this case, with a sound closer to *fear* in standard English.

8. *The merger of moor and more.* Words which rhyme with *moor* in standard English are not distinguished from words which rhyme with *more:* thus *moor* and *more, lure* and *lore, tour* and *tore* are homonyns. Again, this merger is common in the community at large, with a sound closer to that of *moor*, while the Southern-influenced form is closer to that of standard *more.* This general situation should not be confused with the pronunciation of particular words such as *sure, poor,* and *your* which in many dialects are pronounced with the vowel of *more,* even when the *moor-more* distinction is made in other words.

In the South, we find another nonstandard feature of pronunciation in words of this class: *poor, sure, door,* etc. are pronounced to rhyme with *Poe, show, dough* with a long *o* instead of an ingliding open *o.* This is the usage represented as *po', do', sho'* in the dialect literature. In some manuals of pronunciation it is referred to as "drooping the *r*" but of course final *-r* is not pronounced in any word in this dialect. The nonstandard feature which is stigmatized is the use of a vowel different from standard English: an up-gliding *o* instead of an in-gliding one.

9. *The merger of pin and pen.* As noted above, one of the most general Southern features is the lack of a distinction between short *i* and *e* before

nasal consonants. Thus *pin* and *pen, tin* and *ten, since* and *sense, him* and *hem, gym* and *gem,* are the same.

10. *Monopthongization of dipthongs.* A number of homonyms result when the up-glide of the English dipthongs is lost: long *i* can merge with short *o* and broad *a,* and *oi* can merge with the long open *o* of all. Thus we can have homonyms:

time = Tom	oil = all
mile = moll	joy = jaw
pride = prod	Roy = raw
fire = far	loin = lawn

It should be noted that these mergers are not common before voiceless consonants: the diphthongs are usually intact before *p, t, k, f, s,* in *pipe, night, knife, lice, choice,* etc. Furthermore, we find that speakers with a strong Southern background will often lose the glide of the diphthongs *without* the mergers shown above. The vowel of *time, mile,* etc., shifts forward to keep the distinction between *time* and *Tom, mile* and *moll;* for the same speakers, the vowel of *hall, jaw, raw,* etc., has a back up-glide (similar to that in *hole, Joe, row*) so that these words are not pronounced the same as *oil, joy, Roy* even when these have monophthongs.

Extensive perception training is not necessary for these words, since almost all of the speakers have the ability to produce the diphthongs in their careful speech. In fact, the oscillation between diphthongal and monophthongal forms is one of the main features of style shifting in the Southern influenced community. But the ability to produce the diphthongal form consistently in the stream of speech may require considerable practice.

11. *The phonetic forms of the and a.* In standard English, there is an automatic alternation between the ordinary forms of the articles and those which precede words beginning with a vowel. The article *a* becomes *an* before a vowel and *the,* usually pronounced with a short vowel sound like that at the end of *sofa,* is said with a long *e* to rhyme with *be.* Thus *the apple* rhymes with *sea-apple.* But in the Southern-influenced nonstandard dialect, these rules are not followed. *A apple* is quite regular, and *the apple* rhymes with *a apple.* This tendency to allow one short vowel to follow another is the same as that found in the treatment of final -*r.* Where most *r*-less dialects preserve the -*r* between vowels (and even insert it where it is not found in the spelling), the nonstandard dialect considered here allows *fo' o'clock.* It would seem that all three of these features can be treated at once by the teacher, to bring home to the student the general idea of alternate forms before words beginning with a vowel.

12. *Some individual words.* There are in this nonstandard dialect many individual words which differ in pronunciation from Standard English, and these pronunciations may be surprisingly resistent to correction. Some are long-standing representatives of an oral tradition which goes back to Anglo-Saxon times: e.g., *aks* for *ask*. Some involve phonetic principles which have operated irregularly but persistently in the history of English, such as the reversal of *r* and other consonants ("metathesis") in *purpose* for *propose, pattren* for *pattern*. Some individual words show assimilation of one consonant to the following one: *bidness* for *business*. Initial unstressed vowels are frequently dropped where standard speakers never drop them: *'lectric, 'leven, 'zackly, 'zample*. These dialect features form a long but heterogeneous list, and the traditional method of correcting them as they occur may be as effective here as any other one.

13. *Combinations of nonstandard features.* It seldom happens that any one of the nonstandard features mentioned above seriously interferes with communication, although they may mark the speaker as a member of a particular class of society. Combinations of these individual rules or features may, however, add up to expressions which are quite unintelligible to speakers of standard English. For example,

She wow!

is a common expression which equals standard *She is wild*. Four different rules of the nonstandard dialect are operating here:

1. The copula is deleted.
2. The consonant cluster *-ld* is simplified with loss of final *d*.
3. The final *-l* which results is vocalized.
4. The diphthong *i* is simplified by a loss of the glide.

The resulting form differs from the standard "she wow" by a slight difference in the rounding of the high back glide, and as we frequently find in such cases, this difference is not enough to maintain the distinction between *wow* and *wild*. Therefore a standard speaker will find it very difficult to trace the original semantic intention of the nonstandard speaker as a result of this intricate combination of phonetic rules.

References

1. On the other hand, children who (in the prior example) pronounce *passed* as *pass*, but *read* to rhyme with *bed*, obviously have the ability to understand the written *-ed;* their variation from standard English is thus largely in the area of the pronunciation of consonant clusters.
2. That is to say that since *yours, his, hers, ours, theirs* all end in *-s* the generalization to *mines*

is easily understandable and should be pointed out as an irregularity in standard English that must be learned in particular.

3. There is another *-s* inflection of interest in the study of nonstandard English: the adverbial *-s* of *besides, sometimes, nowadays,* and perhaps *nights* (as in *He works nights*). There are both grammatical and pronunciative factors involved here, but they have not yet been worked out in detail.

4. The basic standard rule involves using *more* with words of more than two syllables, *-er* with monosyllables, and one or the other with particular dissyllables; but there is some variation, both optional and obligatory, even from this rule. The superlative is formed in a parallel manner.

Problems in Applying Foreign Language Teaching Methods to the Teaching of Standard English as a Second Dialect

Robert L. Politzer

Robert Politzer, in this article, is concerned with how to teach a more "standard" variety as a second dialect to Black English speaking children. The appropriateness of applying foreign language instruction techniques to this problem is questioned because of the fact that an actual second language situation does not exist in the case of Black English. Politzer suggests that there must be modifications in the foreign language approach due to the differences between the language situations.

In his discussion of these modifications he emphasizes five areas of concern. The first is the role of the native dialect, in this case Black English. He points out that Black English does not have the same social status a foreign language does, which calls for modifications in the foreign language approach to teaching a more standard form of English. Secondly, a definition of what is standard and nonstandard is necessary in this type of instruction, something which is very difficult to ascertain in American English. So Politzer suggests that a form be considered nonstandard if it interferes grammatically with a more widely used form. The third area of concern is that of special factors affecting the student who is to learn "standard" English. Politzer discusses motivation as a central issue as did Kochman in this chapter and comes to much the same conclusion as Kochman. One cannot count on the motivation of black students to learn a more standard variety, for a whole host of social reasons. His fourth concern is teaching methodology, in this case the audio-lingual approach, which he feels needs to be drastically altered before it will be helpful to Black English speakers. Finally he is concerned about teacher training, feeling that teachers who work with black children need to know the major differences between Black English and other more standard varieties.

In the literature dealing with teaching of standard English to the culturally and economically disadvantaged the suggestion is often made that they be taught standard English by teaching methodologies taken from foreign

From "Problems in Applying Foreign Language Teaching Methods to the Teaching of Standard English as a Second Dialect" by Robert L. Politzer. Research and Development Memorandum No. 40, Stanford Center for Research and Development in Teaching, December, 1968. Reprinted by permission of Robert L. Politzer.

language instruction. (1) While there is no general agreement about the preferred foreign language methodology, the suggestion itself implies that there is agreement on one important fact: the cultural and economic disadvantages are accompanied and further magnified by a linguistic disadvantage. Most of the culturally and economically disadvantaged are not native speakers of standard English, but speakers of a nonstandard dialect. Yet in many situations, both in school and out of school, they are treated as if they were speakers of standard English. As a consequence, they are given little or no opportunity to learn the standard language, because the schools—which ought to provide this opportunity—have in fact been most guilty of assuming that *all* children are native speakers of standard English. Thus, children whose native language is a nonstandard dialect are expected to learn to read as if they were already speakers of standard English, to use teaching materials prepared for speakers of standard English, and to grasp the reading rules which are formulated in standard English. . . . (2)

. . . We do not expect anyone who does not know a foreign language—let us say French—to perform tasks which assume knowledge of French as a prerequisite. We do not expect that person to learn to read French as if it were his native language; we do not teach him other subjects in French; nor do we ask him to take I.Q. tests in French, simply because it is obvious that knowledge of a language must be created before it can be used as a tool for communication. However, we do ask speakers of a nonstandard language to perform tasks requiring knowledge of the standard because —unlike the foreign language situation—the communication failure caused by the lack of knowledge of the standard language is not always obvious, and may be only partial, in which case the result is even more insidious.

In spite of the many and obvious parallels between foreign language teaching and the teaching of a second dialect, there are also many differences between the two situations. This article will therefore be a series of comments on the second dialect teaching situation with special emphasis on these differences and with specific reference to the following areas: (a) the role of the native dialect; (b) the definition of the standard; (c) special factors affecting the pupil; (d) teaching methodology; and (e) teacher training.

The Role of the Native Dialect

From the purely linguistic point of view, the native dialect of the pupil normally will belong to any one of the following three categories:

A. Dialects associated with the influence of a specific foreign language.

B. Pidgin or Creole dialects.

C. Social or regional substandard varieties of English (not classifiable under A or B above).

Within the United States the major examples of category A are, of course, supplied by the substandard dialects of the immigrant ghettoes, by the dialects of the Puerto Rican or Mexican urban populations, and by the dialects of the Mexican-Americans of the Western and Southwestern states.

Both pidgin and Creole dialects are linguistically different from both categories A and C in that they completely lack some of the major grammatical structures of English. They may have developed under the influence of some other language or languages, but unlike those dialects typical of category A these linguistic influences usually cannot be directly ascertained. The major and perhaps the only examples of pidgin dialect spoken within the United States are the pidgin English of Hawaii (3) and the Negro patois called Gullah spoken in parts of Virginia and Georgia (4).

Within the group C dialects belong all the nonstandard varieties of English which are derived from an English substrate. The differentiation between regional and social dialects is not always easy to make. Regional substandard speech can be easily transformed into nonregional (social) substandard by migrations—e.g., from Southern rural areas to the urban ghettoes of the North. An obvious example of regional substandard is the dialect of the "poor whites" of Appalachia. Another obvious example for group C is that of the various dialects within the Negro community, which may, in fact, still bear traces of a former Creole type of speech (5). However, for all practical purposes, it seems that there is enough grammatical similarity between the various Negro dialects and other English dialects to justify their classification in category C.

Whatever the exact linguistic category of the pupil's native dialect, in the second dialect teaching situation it accounts for the same linguistic interference which the pupil's native language provides in foreign language teaching. The persistent mistakes which a native speaker of English makes in French can largely be accounted for through his native English. The persistent mistakes made by, let us say, a speaker of Mexican-American English or of a Negro dialect in his attempts to speak standard English are attributable to the structure and grammar of his native dialect.

The parallel between native nonstandard dialect and native language ceases, of course, if we consider the problem of educational status. In foreign language teaching, the status to be accorded to the native language of the pupil is not a problem. Whether or not to use the pupil's native language in class is a purely pedagogical decision which does not reflect on the status of the native language. However, in the case of teaching a second dialect, the role and status to be accorded to the pupil's native dialect can become a source of considerable controversy. There are several options available: (a) we can deny the substandard dialect any status whatsoever and make its elimination the avowed goal of instruction; (b) we can conduct instruction in such a way that we simply ignore the substandard speech, without openly attempting to attack and eliminate it; (c) we can accord some status to the substandard and even attempt to raise its prestige by including it in the instructional process in various ways which imply varying degrees of status or recognition. For example, the substandard may be discussed openly in class; or, it may be compared with standard English and presented as a legitimate, alternate way of speech, not only permissible but perhaps even desirable in certain situations. It may even be accorded official recognition to the degree that instruction in some subject, or perhaps initial instruction in reading or writing, is carried out in the native (non-standard) dialect.

Of the options mentioned above it is probably the first one—elimination of the substandard—which has traditionally dominated the teaching of standard English. Of all the possible options it is also the one which at present seems to be least likely to be advocated by any of the experts. There are evidently various and complementary reasons for this point of view. To expect the actual elimination of the pupil's native dialect is probably a futile goal in any case. Few poeple ever really forget the dialect of the home environment in which they were raised. From the purely practical or realistic point of view, the teaching of standard language should aim not to eliminate the native dialect but rather to produce a bilingual pupil, or—to use a term coined by Charles Ferguson (6)—to produce a state of diglossia, i.e., a situation where even within the speech community speakers can switch from one type of speech to another according to what type seems appropriate in the specific situation.

If bilingualism or diglossia is the ultimate goal of instruction, then it becomes necessary to consider the extensive research on the effects of bilingualism. One of the most important recent findings is that bilingualism does not cause any slowdown or deficit in intellectual development. In fact, the bilingual child may have certain advantages in the ease with which he forms and expresses concepts, provided that the bilingualism is not accompanied by anomie, which is the feeling of loss of identification with a specific cultural group. (7) Thus a direct attack on the home language of the pupil is likely to produce exactly this uncertain identification, and would be an obvious departure from the now widely recognized need to provide pride in the native cultural environment of the pupil—one aim of what is now being called "self-enhancing education." As it has been so nicely stated by Frank Riessman, "One's native language is not to be denied lightly, for it is, in very basic ways one's own self". . . . (8)

. . . It is in the linguistic situation involving social or regional substandards that the exact status to be accorded to the native dialect becomes most problematical. In some situations, e.g., in the Mississippi Action Project, the decision has been made actually to use the native dialect of the pupil for instructional purposes. Consequently, teaching materials have been written in the native dialect in order to introduce elementary school children to reading and writing in the vernacular rather than in the "foreign language" of standard English. (9) Two arguments can be advanced in favor of this procedure. One is the already mentioned need to provide status and cultural identity through the overt use of the pupil's native language; the other is the general argument that initial education, especially the introduction of reading and writing, can be made almost insurmountably difficult if the pupil's already complicated learning tasks are confounded with the problem of learning a foreign or quasi-foreign language. (10) Whether these attempts to provide instruction in the dialect will accomplish any of these goals—either self-enhancement or the ultimate facilitation of learning reading and writing of standard English—remains to be established. In any case, it will be difficult to generalize the results obtained in one situation to another situation because dialects vary in their actual distance from standard English and socio-economic factors are seldom identical in different situations.

Some recent experiments (11) have shown that, in some situations at least, initial instruction in the nonstandard dialect does not contribute to greater achievement in terms of retention of subject matter or level of conceptualization. There is also some evidence that the speakers of the substandard dialect have little interest in raising the status of their speech. Professor William Labov points out that by and large the language standards of the adult Negro community are no different from those of the white community. The demand recently made by the black students of Ravenswood High School in East Palo Alto, California, that a standard African language (Swahili) be offered as part of the curriculum indicates that the linguistic aspects of self-enhancing, cultural-identity education will perhaps be met by the teaching of a standard language rather than by trying to elevate nonstandard speech to a higher status. Thus, we may tentatively conclude that the actual classroom utilization of the nonstandard should be confined demonstrations of *contrasts* between standard and nonstandard while *comparisons* between the two should be carried out in a way that makes it clear that they are simply alternate and equally legitimate modes of communication.

The Definition of the Standard

The problem of what does constitute standard English exists primarily in what some linguists might call the rather superficial or "surface" aspects of pronunciation. There may also be disagreement in the area of grammar (of the "It is I" versus the "It is me" type), but the major features of standard English grammar are, by and large, agreed upon. Even in the area of pronunciation, the definition of the standard is not likely to cause major problems in linguistic categories A and B. Dialects created by obvious foreign language intrusions and pidgin dialects both usually have phonetic features which are so different and distant from English that the variations possible within English seem somehow relatively unimportant by comparison. The situation is not unlike that arising in foreign language teaching, where the question is whether to teach Latin American Spanish or Castilian Spanish. Generally, the criterion is "whatever may make the most sense," although more often than not the choice may be made by an arbitrary decision.

In the case of linguistic situation C, the definition of the standard becomes a more delicate and somewhat touchy problem: how does one distinguish between permissible variations within the standard as opposed to substandard speech? What is "standard American" pronunciation? The speech used by radio and TV commentators? Some sort of Middlewestern American? The following is a simple example of the possible confusion: many of the features of Negro speech are also found in the speech of Southerners—even of those who are highly educated. What sense would it make to teach a speaker of a Negro dialect that certain features of pronunciation were not standard English if the very same features occurred in the speech of a President of the United States?

There are, of course, various ways in which one could establish criteria for defining what does, or at least what does not, constitute standard pronunciation. We would like to label these criteria as either sociological, phonemic, or grammatical. Sociological criteria would be based on the simple recognition that for some strange and often undefinable reasons certain pronunciations are associated with ignorance and are considered substandard while others are not. *R*-less pronunciation and the adding of postvocalic *r* (Cuba*r* and Wa*r*shington) are acceptable—after all, weren't they in the speech of a beloved President of the United States? The famous

Brooklynese mispronunciation of vowel plus *r* (b*oi*d for bird) is a sign of ignorance and is likely to keep the speaker from gaining any kind of social recognition—or a teaching position in New York. For purely practical reasons, the teacher of standard English is undoubtedly forced to take into consideration these linguistically rather arbitrary dicta of society. At the same time, however, he must realize that they are arbitrary and not make the old mistake of teaching that standard English is defined by the speaker's avoidance of certain socially unacceptable pronunciations. In this connection, it is important for the teacher to remember that certain pronunciations may in time become "unacceptable" because they are associated with a particular class or minority group. Thus, if the prejudice against a pronunciation is the result of the prejudice against a minority group, manipulating the speech of the minority is not likely to have any real influence on prejudicial attitudes themselves.

Phonemic criteria for establishing standard English would attempt to avoid pronunciations which would, by introducing additional homonyms into standard speech, create problems and misunderstandings in general communication or in reading instruction. Actually even this criterion is ultimately contaminated by pure sociological considerations. Homonyms exist in the language in any case: some are accepted parts of even the most rigorous standard, e.g., *pane, pain.* Others are so widely accepted that few if any listeners—or even classroom teachers engaged in the process of reading instruction—would question the pronunciation that accounts for the phonetic merger, (e.g., *merry, marry, Mary* merge in a large part of the Middlewest). What makes mergers like *pin* and *pen* unacceptable is ultimately a sociological criterion. Still, just because some homonyms are permissible, there is no reason why communication (and reading instruction) in standard English should be encumbered by yet an additional array of homonyms. Avoidance of homonyms could thus be used as a possible guideline.

The safest and in our opinion most defensible guideline for establishing minimum requirements for a standard pronunciation is furnished by the grammatical criterion: a pronunciation must be considered a substandard (and conversely an alternate standard pronunciation must be taught) if it interferes with the possibility of using standard grammar. As has been shown and discussed in some detail by William Labov and Paul Cohen, (12) there are various substandard pronunciations which make it impossible to use standard grammar. Principally, these substandard pronunciations consist in the dissolution or complete effacement of final consonants or consonantal clusters, on which much of English grammar depends: e.g., final -*s* as plural sign or a sign of the possessive or the third person singular;

-*ed* as a sign of the past tense or the past participle. The failure to produce the significant markers of tense or person can hardly be considered a "surface difference" between standard and dialect, and a minimal pronunciation requirement for standard English must necessarily include an adequate pronunciation of final consonants and consonant groups of grammatical significance.

Special Considerations Concerning the Pupil

In any learning situation the pupil's contribution to achievement is obviously determined by his motivation and his aptitude. In teaching the disadvantaged, both motivation and aptitude may represent special problems. In learning a foreign language the factors involved in motivation have been classified as instrumental and integrative. (13) Integrative motivation is associated with a desire to become acquainted with or to identify with the cultural and/or ethnic community which uses the foreign language. Instrumental motivation is based on the clear recognition of some sort of material advantage to be gained by the knowledge of the foreign language. The motivation associated with having to get a good grade or to fulfill a requirement must ultimately be classed as instrumental. At any rate, the extent to which either integrative or instrumental motivation are significant factors in the teaching of standard English to the disadvantaged is highly debatable.

In the already mentioned Keaukaha experiment (teaching standard English to children speaking Hawaiian pidgin), the experimenters were able to adopt "a very uncomplicated position in the matter of student motivation" based among others on the assumption that children "come to school expecting to do everything the teacher tells them to do . . ." and that "they want to please the teacher and be praised for doing what she is doing exactly as she does it." (14) Obviously none of these assumptions are likely to stand up in an urban ghetto situation. Integrative motivation for learning standard English is likely to be created by convincing the pupil of the material advantages to be gained through the use of the standard language. Even the instrumental motivation created by grades may be nonexistent in many cases, since the entire value system of the school may be completely foreign and strange to the minority-group child. As a matter of fact, the motivation problem may very well be the most crucial one in the entire complex of problems concerning the contribution of the school to the betterment of the disadvantaged in general and the solution of the language problem in particular. This fact has been rather dramatically brought home by several studies, most recently by a research study undertaken at Columbia University (15) that demonstrated (a) that the value system held by members of a Harlem street gang, which stressed such concepts as "toughness," "skill in fighting," etc., was in direct conflict with acquiring standard English because it was associated by gang members with effeminate types of behavior; (b) that achievement in language arts and especially the ability to read showed an amazingly high inverse correlation with the degree of adherence to the value system of the peer group. In other words, the teaching of standard English may in some cases take place in a situation characterized not only by a lack of motivation to achieve but, beyond that, by a motivation *not* to achieve. . . .

Teaching Methodology

Just what is meant by using foreign language teaching methodology in the teaching of a second dialect is, in itself, debatable. Here we would like to comment on the two features of modern foreign language teaching methodology which are perhaps the most characteristic of the so-called "new key" in foreign language teaching; namely, the audio-lingual approach and its chief pedagogical instruments, pattern practice, and dialogue memorization. An audio-lingual approach—in the broadest general meaning of the term—implies that, especially in the initial stage of construction, all new elements of language are learned through listening and speaking activities, before the very same elements are introduced in the reading and writing process.

The audio-lingual principle can be applied to the language teaching of the disadvantaged in two ways: (a) reading and writing can be introduced in the native dialect in which the child has already reached some audio-lingual proficiency; and (b) the standard dialect can be taught audio-lingually before reading and writing are introduced. We have stated already that it is the second application which is likely to have more permanent interest and importance. In general, this approach would lead us to emphasize audio-lingual training, perferably early in the school program. Further research will be needed to determine such details as the optimal time lag between audio-lingual learning and exposure to reading and writing, or the optimal quantity of materials to be learned audio-lingually before reading and writing are introduced. As have been pointed out by several researchers, (16) the question of the optimal time lag, if any, between audio-lingual and visual learning is far from settled even in the domain of foreign language teaching. The teaching of a second dialect can, at this point, not even rely on secure findings in the sister discipline of foreign language instruction.

Whether the standard tools of present modern foreign language teaching, namely pattern practice and dialogue memorization, can be used in the learning of a second dialect is even more debatable. Obviously, they have to undergo rather drastic modifications. In many of the "new key" approaches to foreign language teaching, children are given new foreign language names and asked to pretend to be members of the foreign culture while acting out situational dialogues. The application of this principle in a situation presumably dominated by the need for establishing identity of and pride in the self would be quite clearly nonsensical. If dialogue memorization and the acting out of dialogues are used at all, the learner of the standard dialect must always remain himself, and the dialogue must clearly and unambiguously take place in a situation in which the standard dialect, rather than the native dialect, is required. The experience of some programs in standard dialect teaching has shown already (17) that the dialogues, and the situation used in the teaching process, must be perceived as having a real and highly functional value for the learner.

The pattern practice exercise of foreign language teaching generally takes three forms: (a) repetition exercises, in which utterances are simply echoed by the pupil; (b) substitution exercises, in which the linguistic construction remains constant but different sentences are produced by the pupil by his substituting words for other grammatically equivalent words; and (c) transformation or conversion exercises, in which sentences of one construction type are converted into another by a constant linguistic manipulation, (e.g., passive sentences are made interrogative). One of the most questionable aspects of pattern practice, at least in the form in which it is most widely used in current textbooks, is its disassociation from any conceptual or tangible reality. (18) There is considerable, and mounting, evidence that the type of pattern practice that involves playing with linguistic symbols as empty shells is of debatable value in foreign language instruction. (19) In second dialect teaching, where the linguistic problem is accompanied by a very real and subtle problem of cultural difference, the manipulation of empty verbal symbols will have no beneficial effect whatsoever—if for no other reason than that the pupil's motivation is not likely to last through the attempts to manipulate verbal behavior in the abstract realm, dissociated from any real communication process.

The more promising programs of second dialect instruction indicate that the stories and topics which are used must be of real interest and importance to the pupil. (20) Overtly contrasting the native dialect and standard language may be necessitated by the similarity of the two dialects. As Labov and Cohen (21) have pointed out, the speaker of a nonstandard dialect often has only comprehension competence in the standard language, while in the nonstandard dialect he is competent at *both* comprehension and active expression. The result is that in many cases, depending perhaps on the real or linguistic depth of the difference involved, speakers of nonstandard English will give nonstandard echo-repetition responses to standard language stimuli. Under these circumstances, it is probably necessary to give very intensive training in the perception of the differences between standard and nonstandard speech, especially if we do not want to perpetuate a situation—frequently observed by the author—in which the standard speech of the teacher and the nonstandard speech of the pupil simply coexist in language drills as well as in actual communication.

Teacher Training

The desired qualifications for the foreign language teacher have been subject to considerable discussion. There is presently at least some general agreement on what these qualifications should be. As expressed in a statement issued by the Modern Language Association of America, (22) and followed as general guidelines in most teacher training or retraining programs, these qualifications are expressed as language proficiency (ability to understand, speak, read, and write the foreign language); knowledge of the civilization and culture of the foreign country; familiarity with applied linguistics (chiefly the appreciation of the interference which is exerted by the pupil's native language); and teaching methodology.

If we attempt to translate these qualifications for foreign language teachers into the second dialect teaching situation we must keep in mind that the "foreign language" becomes "standard English." Just as in foreign language teaching, proficiency in the language to be taught is an obvious requirement. An important similarity between the two situations is the fact that native speakers do not necessarily make good foreign language teachers. Not everyone who can speak standard English should be considered qualified to teach it, either as a foreign language or as a second dialect. The teacher of standard English should have a thorough and linguistically accurate knowledge of the structure of the language which he is teaching, and a clear perception of the differences between speech and writing. Perhaps the most important parallel between the qualifications for foreign language and second dialect teachers lies in the applied linguistics area. Here, the qualification of the foreign language teacher consists chiefly of his knowledge of the structural differences between the target language and the native language of the pupil.

This latter qualification, when transferred to the second dialect situation, is as desirable as it may be difficult to achieve. Our knowledge of the linguistic structure of nonstandard English dialects is relatively meager. In addition, substandard dialects are many and varied. Thus, it would be unreasonable to expect that a person trained to teach standard English as a second dialect would have a thorough knowledge of all or even many of the substandard systems. Under these circumstances, a more realistic goal of teacher training may be to make the prospective teacher of standard English as a second dialect aware of the chief examples of the main types of interference which can be expected from the nonstandard dialects, and to impart to him, not so much a detailed knowledge of the substandard, but an attitude which recognizes that substandard dialects are regular systems of communication in their own right—and are not disadvantaged, incomplete, immature, or irregular manifestations of a standard dialect.

References

1. William S. Carroll and Irvin Feigenbaum, "Teaching a Second Dialect and Some Implications for TESOL," *TESOL Quarterly,* 1 (1967), pp. 31–40.

   William A. Stewart, "Foreign Language Teaching Methods in Quasi-Foreign Language Situations," *Non-Standard Speech and the Teaching of English,* Language Information Series 2, Center for Applied Linguistics (Washington, D.C.: 1964).

2. William Labov, "The Non-Standard Vernacular of the Negro Community: Some Practical Suggestions," *Seminar in English and Language Arts* (mimeographed), Temple University (1967).

3. Stanley M. Tsuzaki, "Hawaiian English: Pidgin, Creole, or Dialect," *Pacific Speech,* 1, No. 2 (1966).

4. John Bennett, "Gullah: A Negro Patois," *South Atlantic Quarterly,* 7 (1908).

   William A. Stewart, "Continuity and Change in American Negro Dialects," *Florida FL Reporter,* 6:1 (1968).

5. William Stewart, "Creole Languages in the Caribbean," *Study of the Role of Second Languages;* F. A. Rice, editor (Washington, D.C.: 1962).

6. Charles A. Ferguson, "Diglossia," *Word,* 15 (1959), pp. 325–40.

7. Elizabeth Peal and W. Lambert, "Psychological Monographs," *The Relation of Bilingualism to Intelligence* (Washington, D.C.: 1962), p. 546.

8. Frank Riessman, "Digging the Man's Language," *Saturday Review,* 49 (September 10, 1966), pp. 81–91, 98.

9. Evan Keislar and Carolyn Stern, "Effects of Dialect and Instructional Procedures of Children's Oral Language Production and Concept Acquisition," *Urban Education,* 3 (1968), pp. 169–76.

10. W. E. Bull, "The Use of Vernacular Languages in Fundamental Education," *International Journal of American Linguistics,* 21 (1955), pp. 288–94.

11. Keislar and Stern, "Effects of Dialect and Instructional Procedures."

12. William Labov and Paul Cohen, "Systematic Relation of Standard and Non-Standard Rules in the Grammar of Negro Speakers," *Project Literacy Reports,* No. 8 (Ithaca, N.Y.: Cornell University, 1967), pp. 66–84 [in Chapter Three of this book].

13. R. C. Gardner, "Motivational Variables in Second-Language Acquisition" (Ph.D. diss., McGill University, 1960).

W. E. Lambert, "A Social Psychology of Bilingualism," *Journal of Social Issues,* 23 (1967), pp. 91–109.

14. Dale P. Crowley, "The Keaukaha Model for Mainstream Dialect Instruction," *Language Learning,* 18 (1968), pp. 125–38.

15. William Labov, and Clarence Robins, "A Note on the Relation of Reading Failure to Peer-Group Status in Urban Ghettos," *The Teachers College Record,* Volume 70, Number 5 (1969) [in Chapter Six of this book].

16. John B. Carroll, "Research on Teaching Foreign Languages," in *Handbook of Research on Teaching;* ed. N. L. Gage (Chicago: Rand McNally and Co., 1963).

Wilga M. Rivers, *The Psychologist and the Foreign Language Teacher,* (Chicago: University of Chicago Press, 1964).

17. Crowley, "The Keaukaha Model for Mainstream Dialect Instruction."

18. See Robert L. Politzer, "Some Reflections on Pattern Practice," *Modern Language Journal* 48 (1964), pp. 24–29.

19. J. W. Oller, and H. Obrecht, "Pattern Drill and Communicative Activity: A Psycholinguistic Experiment," *International Review of Applied Linguistics in Language Teaching,* 6 (1968), pp. 167–74.

20. Crowley, "The Keaukaha Model for Mainstream Dialect Instruction."

21. Labov and Cohen, "Systematic Relation of Standard and Non-Standard Rules in the Grammar of Negro Speakers."

22. PMLA (Publication of the Modern Language Association of America), "Qualifications for Secondary School Teachers of Modern Foreign Languages," *PMLA 70,* 4, Part 2 (1955), pp. 46–49.

Sociolinguistic Implications for Educational Sequencing

Walt Wolfram

Walt Wolfram, after surveying some of the materials commonly used in teaching more standard varieties of English to Black English speakers, found no consistent order in the presentation of various standard forms. He feels a more consistent priority for presentation is needed so as to increase the effectiveness of the materials, and he feels such an order is possible.

He suggests five sociolinguistic factors as helping determine the order in which the standard forms should be presented. The first is the degree of social stigmatization certain Black English forms have. If a multiple negative form, e.g. "ain't seen none," is highly stigmatized, as it is, its standard equivalents, e.g. "haven't seen any," should be promptly taught. Picking up Labov and Cohen's suggestion (this chapter), Wolfram states that another factor is the generality of the rules involved. The more general rules should be taught first because of their greater applicability. A third factor is phonological versus grammatical forms. Wolfram feels the grammatical should be taught before the phonological and states his reasons. The fourth factor is regional versus general social significance. If a form is nationally stigmatized as are multiple negatives, then the standard equivalent should be taught before one with only regional stigma. The fifth factor he suggests is the relative frequency with which the forms appear. If a form appears in speech more frequently than another, the most frequent one should be taught first as in the case of third-person singular present-tense -s.

Finally, Wolfram states that educators must consider how these five factors correlate before making the final decisions about the sequence of standard forms to be taught. For example, multiple negatives are highly socially stigmatized (factor 1) all over the country (factor 4), are used frequently in speech (factor 5), are grammatical rather than phonological (factor 3), and are part of the general system of rules covering negation in English (factor 2). Consequently, the standard form of negation should be stressed early in a program designed to teach standard forms to Black English speakers.

Within the last several years the teaching of standard English to Black English speakers (i.e. the variety of English spoken by lower socioeconomic class Negroes) has been of growing concern to urban educators. Subse-

From "Sociolinguistic Implications for Educational Sequencing" by Walt Wolfram, in *Teaching Standard English in the Inner City,* edited by Ralph W. Fasold and Roger W. Shuy. (Washington, D.C.: Center for Applied Linguistics, 1970). © 1970 by Center for Applied Linguistics. Reprinted by permission of the publisher.

quently, materials for teaching standard English in an urban setting have been produced, and a casual survey of these materials is sufficient to observe that there are differing philosophical and methodological approaches which characterize them. Furthermore, the features dealt with in these lessons and the order in which the lessons are presented vary significantly.

Although the different philosophical and methodological approaches underlying materials have now received some attention, one aspect of methodology for which there is no specific discussion is the order in which standard English features should be presented. This failure may stem from the assumption that it is common knowledge which features of standard English should be given precedence in teaching Black English speakers. However, if this were the case, one would expect that all materials would conform to a similar pattern of sequencing, a situation which does not exist.

Another possible reason for the failure to deal with pedagogical sequencing may stem from the assumption that the ordering of lessons is irrelevant, that any order convenient to the teacher is satisfactory. Several reasons can be suggested to challenge this assumption. First of all, both objective and subjective evidence (1) suggest that not all features of Black English have the same social connotations. There are some features which immediately categorize the socioeconomic class of the speaker; others, however, may correlate with ethnicity but have little or no social significance within the black community. The fact that all features of Black English do not have equal social connotations suggests that some should be given precedence over others in the acquisition of standard English. Another reason for maintaining the relevancy of lesson sequencing is motivational. Students are much more aware of the social consequences of Black English vis-à-vis standard English than they have been given credit for, (2) and the precedence of minor rather than major differences between dialects may discourage students at an early stage in their acquisition of standard English. A final reason is quite practical. The realization that any course in standard English will probably not cover as much material as would be desirable means that some features should be given priority over others in the lesson material. One way of programming this priority into the lesson material is through the sequencing of lessons.

Having suggested several reasons for the relevancy of pedagogical sequencing, what criteria may be used in determining the relative order of the lessons? Several sociolinguistic factors can be suggested as a basis for determining the most relevant order of lessons. (3)

1. Social Diagnosticity of Linguistic Variables

Since the purpose of teaching standard English is to assist students in adopting a dialect which is not socially stigmatized, a primary consideration in the sequencing of materials must be the way in which social groups are separated from one another on the basis of linguistic features (i.e. the social diagnosticity of linguistic items). As was stated above, all linguistic features do not correlate with social status in the same way. Some features set apart social groups from one another much more discretely than others. Recently, I have suggested (4) that it is useful to distinguish between *gradient* and *sharp* social stratification of linguistic features. Gradient stratification refers to a progressive increase in the frequency of occurrence of a variant between social groups without a clearly defined difference between contiguous social groups. The incidence of post-vocalic *r* in the black community is an example of gradient stratification. Figure 3 illustrates the differences in *r* absence for four social classes of Negroes in Detroit, upper-middle (UMN), lower-middle (LMN), upper-working (UWN), and lower-working (LWN) class Negroes.

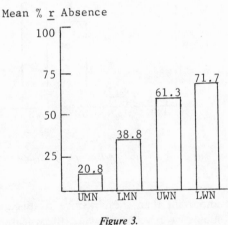

Mean % r Absence

Figure 3.

Post-Volcalic r *Absence: An Example of "Gradient" Stratification*

One observes that there is a progressive increase in the absence of post-vocalic *r* between the four social groups; none of the groups are discretely differentiated on the basis of *r*. But there are other variables which indicate a sharp demarcation between contiguous social classes (i.e. sharp stratification), such as the absence of third-person singular, present-tense-*s*. Note the incidence of -*s* third person singular absence in Figure 4.

In contrast to the absence of post-vocalic *r*, we observe that the middle class groups are sharply differentiated from the working class groups by the incidence of -*s*. Contiguous social groups (in this case, lower-middle and upper-working classes) reveal significant differences in the incidence of -*s* third-person singular. We conclude that linguistic features revealing sharp stratification are of greater social significance than those showing gradient stratification. From a social viewpoint, then, materials dealing with sharply stratified linguistic features should precede those dealing with gradiently stratified features.

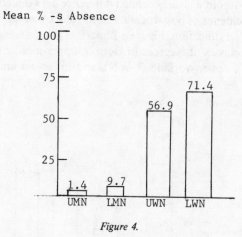

Mean % -s Absence

Figure 4.

Third Person Singular -s Absence: An Example of "Sharp" Stratification

Perhaps more important than the objective stratification of linguistic features are the subjective reactions toward these features. (5) William Labov (6) has suggested that the subjective evaluation of socially diagnostic linguistic features can be classified into three basic types:

indicators, which show social variation but usually not stylistic variation, and have little effect upon the listener's judgment of the social status of the speakers

markers, which show both social and stylistic variation and have consistent effects upon the conscious or unconscious judgment of the speaker's status by the listener *stereotypes,* which are the overt topics of social comment in the speech community, and may or may not correspond to actual linguistic behavior.

The different levels of subjective reaction to socially diagnostic linguistic features have definite implications for the ordering of materials. Materials should start with those features which are on the most conscious level of awareness, the stereotyped features. In terms of objective stratification, stereotyped features generally show sharp rather than gradient stratification. Since, as Labov points out, there are a number of stereotyped features which do not correspond to actual sociolinguistic behavior, it must be warned that we are referring to stereotyped features which relate to actual speech. One must also warn that stereotyped features often refer to single items, in which case they would not be given precedence because they do not meet the criterion of rule generality (cf. principle 2). One stereotyped feature of nonstandard speech (both Negro and white) is that of the so-called "double negative" (but more accurately called "multiple negation") such as *He didn't do nothing.*

The relative social diagnosticity of a particular feature may not only vary from linguistic variable to variable, but within a given variable, based on independent linguistic constraints such as environment and structural type. Take, for example, the absence of the final member of a consonant cluster in word-final position (e.g. Black English /dɛs/ for standard English 'desk'). This type of pattern affects items in which both members of the cluster are part of the same lexical item (i.e. monomorphemic, as in Black English /gɛs/ for standard English /gɛst/ 'guest') but also clusters which result when the addition of the grammatical suffix *-ed* results in a cluster (i.e. bimorphemic clusters such as Black English /gɛs/ for standard English /gɛs-t/ 'guessed'). The social significance of these two types are not equal, however. The former type, monomorphemic clusters, reveals a gradient stratification whereas the latter, the bimorphemic clusters, tend to reveal sharp stratification. In terms of social importance, bimorphemic clusters would therefore take precedence over monomorphemic. Likewise, in the analysis of copula absence among Negro speakers, there are certain types of constructions in which the absence of a copula is much less socially significant than others. The absence of a copula with the intentive future *gonna* (e.g. *They gonna go now*) is commonly used by middle class Negro speakers although they typically do not reveal copula absence in other types of constructions such as predicative nominals, adjectives, and locatives. It is plain that the presence of a copula with *gonna* should follow the teaching of copula with other types of constructions (e.g. predicate adjective such as *he nice*) in preparing the lesson materials on copula.

2. The Generality of Rules

Another important factor in determining the relative order of materials is the generality of the rule(s) involved in the realization of a particular Black English feature. Some nonstandard forms affect only a small subset of words or a single item whereas others involve general rules that operate on the form of every sentence of a particular structural type. Labov and Cohen (7) note that:

> it is plain that the more general rules should be introduced first in a teaching program, no matter how prominent and striking the isolated items may be.

The more general the rule, the earlier it should be introduced in the materials. For example, the nonstandard use of multiple negation affects all negative sentences with an indefinite, including indefinite pronouns (e.g. *He didn't do nothing*), determiners (e.g. *He didn't have no homework*), and adverbs (e.g. *He hardly never does his homework*). On the other hand, the Black English use of existential *it is* as a correspondence of standard English *there is* (e.g. Black English *It is a lot of trouble on that street*) only concerns one item. Standard English lesson materials will probably deal with both of these nonstandard features; however, based on the generality of rules governing the nonstandard usage, it should be obvious that multiple negation will appear in the earliest stages of lessons but "existential *it*" in the later lesson materials.

3. Phonological Versus Grammatical Variables

In many current materials designed to teach standard English, it has sometimes been assumed that it makes little difference whether one begins with phonological or grammatical variables. Therefore, some materials focus on phonological features before grammatical features while others reverse the order. There is good reason to suggest that the teaching of standard English to Black English speakers should focus on grammatical features before phonological features. In the first place, the social significance of phonological and grammatical features tend to differ. In my description of four phonological and four grammatical variables, it was pointed out that there is an important difference between the social diagnosticity of phonological and grammatical variables (8). Grammatical features tend to show sharp stratification whereas phonological variables tend to reveal gradient stratification. (9) Three of the four phonological variables investigated reveal gradient stratification, but all four variables which were treated as grammatical indicate sharp stratification. (10) As a general principle then, it is safest to begin with grammatical rather than phonological features.

Another factor favoring the introduction of grammatical features first is the type of differences observed between social groups. The social distribution of grammatical features show that there are qualitative differences between groups; that is, middle class groups often indicate complete absence of certain grammatical variants (such as multiple negation, suffixal -*s* absence, 'distributive *be*', etc.) which are present in working class speech. But phonological features most often reveal quantitative differences between social groups. Thus, *d* for potential *ð* in word-initial position (in such words as *then, that, those*), the lack of constriction for post-vocalic *r* (in words like *car, beard, mother*), the absence of the final member of a consonant cluster (in words like *desk, ground, cold*), monophthongization of potential upgliding diphthongs (in words like *time, ground, boil*), and syllable final *t* for *d* (in words like *good, bad, stupid*) all reveal quantitative differences between social groups. Qualitative differences tend to be more socially obtrusive than quantitative differences and therefore should be taught first. In some cases phonological and grammatical patterns intersect with one another to account for certain stigmatized features. We have already seen how this can happen with word-final consonant clusters. To take an example of a somewhat different type, consider the Black English use of invariant *be* in a sentence such as *he be home*. There is evidence to consider that this construction is derived from three different sources, two of which are phonological and one grammatical. (11) Invariant *be* may be derived from an underlying *will be* in a sentence such as *He be in pretty soon;* in a sentence such as *If he had a walkie talkie, he be happy* it is derived from *would be;* but in a sentence such as *He be busy all the time*, it is the realization of a grammatical category unique to the Black English speaker, "distributive *be.*" Although one may initially assume that all three uses of *be* are equally stigmatized, there is good reason to suggest that this is not the case. In the first place, the negative formations of these three constructions in Black English are *He won't be in in a few minutes, If he had a walkie talkie he wouldn't be happy*, and *He don't be busy all the time* respectively. Only the last example is socially obtrusive to the middle class speaker.

A second reason for suggesting that "distributive *be*" is more socially stigmatized than the other two uses is that standard English speakers sometimes produce a contracted form of *will be* (*'ll*) and *would be* (*'d*) which is phonetically not very different from the first two uses of *be*. But no standard English speaker would ever use *be* in its distributive sense. We thus see that where the intersection of phonological and grammatical patterns takes place, grammatical differences between standard English and Black English should be given precedence.

4. Regional Versus General Social Significance

Many large Northern urban areas have been drastically restructured within the last 50 years because of the inmigration of Southern Negroes. Due to the extent of the intersectional migration and the segregation patterns of such in-migrants in the North, the speech patterns of many Negroes living in the North have not been adapted to a Northern dialect of English. In a Northern locale, some features which are acceptable Southern speech patterns have been transformed into class and ethnic patterns. Thus, in a city such as Detroit, "r-lessness," the neutralization of the ɪ/ɛ contrast before nasals, [as in *pin* and *pen*] and monophthongization (12) of potential upgliding diphthongs have taken on a social significance even though they are acceptable patterns used by the middle class in certain parts of the South. On the other hand, there are a number of factors which have social significance regardless of the regional locale in which they are found. Thus, the absence of third person singular, present-tense -*s,* the use of invariant *be,* and multiple negation are socially diagnostic in all regions of the United States.

Several reasons can be suggested why features having general social significance should be dealt with before those whose social significance is regionally restricted (e.g. just in a Northern city). First, those features which reveal general social significance tend to be more socially diagnostic than those showing only regional significance. In terms of our distinction between sharp and gradient stratification, one observes that in Northern cities, acceptable Southern features reveal gradient rather than sharp stratification among the Negro population. But general nonstandard features often show sharp stratification. We thus see that our distinction between features showing regional and general social significance correlates in an important way with relative social diagnosticity of items.

Second, in terms of the widest possible audience of students for lesson materials, general features should be given priority over regional features. Recent investigations of Black English in a number of big cities in the United States indicate that there is a "common core" of Black English characteristic of lower socio-economic Negroes in different regions. This observation means that lesson materials may be produced which can be used in more than one region. However, to develop materials for the broadest possible use, the general socially diagnostic features should be given precedence over the regionally significant items. By placing these regionally

Black English Feature	sharp stratification [+] / gradient stratification [-]	general rule [+] / non-general rule [-]	grammatical feature [+] / phonological feature [-]	general significance [+] / regional significance [-]	frequent occurrence [+] / infrequent occurrence [-]
-s third person singular (e.g. he go)	+	+	+	+	+
multiple negation (e.g. didn't do nothing)	+	+	+	+	+
-s possessive (e.g. man hat)	+	+	+	+	-
invariant be (e.g. he be home)	+	+	±	+	+
copula absence (e.g. he nice)	+	+	-	+	+
been auxiliary in active sentence (e.g. he been ate the food)	+	-	+	+	-
existential it (e.g. It is a whole lot of people)	+	-	+	+	+
word-medial and final ð and θ (e.g. /tuf/ 'tooth')	+	+	-	+	+
word-final consonant clusters (e.g. /gɛs/ 'guest' and 'guessed')	±	+	-	+	+
word-initial ð (e.g. /dɛn/ 'then')	-	+	-	+	+
monophthongization (e.g. /tahm/ 'time')	-	+	-	-	+
post-vocalic r and l (e.g. /cah/ 'car')	-	+	-	-	+
syllable-final d (e.g. /bɛht/ 'bad')	-	+	-	-	+
ɪ/ɛ before nasals (e.g. /pɪn/ 'pin' or 'pen')	-	-	-	-	-

Figure 5.

Matrix of Cruciality

significant features in later stages of lessons (if they are to be included at all) their relative importance can be appropriately diminished (i.e. they can easily be excluded where not applicable or, in terms of time limitations, where lessons can most conveniently be eliminated or condensed). Although one might think that this principle is obvious to those responsible for developing lessons, many current materials are surprisingly negligent in this regard. Some teachers have taken far too much interest in relatively minor features such as the monophthongization of upgliding diphthongs (e.g. /tahm/ 'time', /bɔh/ 'boy') and the neutralization of the ɪ/ɛ contrast before nasals (e.g. /pɪn/ 'pin' or 'pen'), although these are quite acceptable patterns used by middle class Southerners. In justification of such interest, some teachers explain that if such differences are not taught, the students will be unable to discriminate between such words as *pin* and *pen*. While this may certainly be the case (apart from contextual disambiguation), this common type of "interdialectal homophony" (i.e. distinguishable words in one dialect are indistinguishable in another dialect) is no need for concern. It is a common phenomenon of dialects which have kept dialectologists busy and non-linguists amused for some time now. The same teachers who may attempt to spend inordinate amounts of time drilling students to contrast *pin* and *pen* may make no distinction between *cot* and *caught* in their own speech without ever having noticed it. Although it may sound unnecessarily judgmental, the preoccupation with such items as *pin* and *pen,* while well-intentioned, may ultimately be traced to dialectal ethnocentrism.

5. The Relative Frequency of Items

A final factor in the determination of lesson sequencing is the relative frequency with which an item or pattern potentially occurs. Some nonstandard patterns occur only infrequently during the course of a normal discourse. Even though some of these features may indicate sharp stratification, the infrequency of their occurrence makes them less essential than others in preparing lesson materials. For example, a comparison of the potential incidence of third-person singular present-tense -*s* with the possessive marker -*s* for 48 Detroit informants reveals that the former structural pattern is over four times as numerous as the latter. (13) It is therefore understandable why many people are more consciously aware of the absence of -*s* on third person forms than they are of the absence of -*s* on possessives.

Another example of a relatively infrequent occurring feature is the Black

English use of *been* as an auxiliary in active sentences such as *The boy been ate the pie.* Although this use of *been* clearly correlates to social class in the Negro community, the rarity of this type of construction in natural discourse suggests that the "non-use" of this type of form should only be taught after many other features which occur much more frequently.

6. The Intersection of Sociolinguistic Principles in Determining the Sequencing of Materials

When determining the order of lessons, each Black English feature must be considered in terms of the total configuration of sociolinguistic principles. The fact that a particular item reveals sharp stratification is, in itself, not adequate for including it in the preliminary stages of the lessons. Nor is the distinction of frequent versus infrequent patterns sufficient reason for determining order by itself. Only when the intersection of the various principles is considered can an adequate justification for sequencing be established. The determination of order may be viewed in terms of a sociolinguistic matrix. In Figure 5, a number of features cited as examples in the above discussion are evaluated in terms of such a matrix. For the most part, the evaluation is based on a binary opposition (e.g. either an item is considered frequent [+] or infrequent [−]). Where binary judgments cannot be made (e.g. the intersection of phonology and grammar or different levels of social significance based on subcategories of a variable) this is indicated by [±].

The way the matrix is set up, the more [+] evaluations a particular feature has, the earlier it should be introduced in the lesson material. This means that items given a [+] rating for all of the sociolinguistic principles should be introduced at the earliest stage, those with more [+] than [−] ratings at the next stage, and those with more [−] than [+] ratings at a still later stage. Such features as -*s* third person singular, multiple negation, and invariant *be* (particularly its grammatical source) should be treated in the earliest lessons. A next stage should deal with such features as word-medial and final $\underline{\theta}$ and consonant clusters, whereas features such as ɪ/ɛ contrast before nasals, syllable final *d,* and post-vocalic *r* should clearly be treated in the later lessons.

I have attempted to show how sociolinguistic considerations have important implications for teaching standard English to Black English speakers. The application of these five principles can only increase the sociolinguistic relevancy of standard English programs and improve their efficiency.

References

1. Walter A. Wolfram, *A Sociolinguistic Description of Detroit Negro Speech* (Washington, D.C.: Center For Applied Linguistics, 1969).
   Roger Shuy, Joan C. Baratz and Walter A. Wolfram, final report, Research Project No. MH 15048–01, *Sociolinguistic Factors in Speech Identification,* National Institute of Mental Health (1969).
2. *Ibid.*
3. The limitation of this discussion to sociolinguistic factors is not meant to imply that other factors may not affect the ordering of materials. For example, the pedagogical lessons on constructions introduced earlier may affect the order of items to a certain extent. Since the focus of this paper is the sociolinguistic factors, other factors will not be considered here.
4. Wolfram, *Sociolinguistic Description of Detroit Negro Speech.*
5. Shuy, Baratz, and Wolfram (1969) show that lower socioeconomic class speakers who use stigmatized variants often have the same low opinion of these forms as do middle class speakers who do not use them. Therefore the label "stigmatized" refers to a working class as well as a middle class evaluation of such forms.
6. William Labov and Paul Cohen, "Stages in the Acquisition of Standard English," *Social Dialects and Language Learning,* ed. Roger W. Shuy (Champaign: National Council of Teachers of English, 1964) p. 102.
7. William Labov and Paul Cohen, "Some Suggestions for Teaching Standard English to Speakers of Non-Standard Urban Dialects" (New York: Bureau of Curriculum Research., Board of Education of the City of New York, 1967) [in Chapter Five of this book.]
8. Wolfram, *Sociolinguistic Description of Detroit Negro Speech.*
9. McDavid (1965:15) notes that "the surest social markers in American English are grammatical forms, and any teaching program should aim, first of all, at developing a habitual command of the grammar of standard English."
10. This does not mean that ALL socially diagnostic grammatical features reveal sharp stratification or that ALL phonological features show gradient stratification since research does not show this to be the case. For example, the Black English correspondence of standard English $\underline{\theta}$ and $\underline{\delta}$ in certain positions, which is *f* and *v* respectively, shows sharp stratification. On the other hand, the Black English use of pronominal apposition (e.g. *The man, he did it*) is a grammatical feature which reveals gradient stratification.
11. Ralph W. Fasold, "Tense and the Form *be* in Black English," *Language,* 45, pp. 763–76. Wolfram, *Sociolinguistic Description of Detroit Negro Speech.*
12. Monophthongization is technically not quite correct for the pronunciation of 'time' as [taɔm] instead of [taym]. The distinction actually is found in the direction of the glide; in the former case there is a central glide and in the latter a high front glide. For convenience in this paper, the central gliding variant will be referred to as monophthongization.
13. Wolfram, *Sociolinguistic Description of Detroit Negro Speech.*

Chapter Six
Black English and Reading

One of the major concerns about ghetto black children's education is why so many of them are not learning to read or are far behind national norms in reading achievement. This situation has caused acute concern among educators, parents, society at large, and also among linguists. It has generated in linguistic literature a growing number of articles dealing with various linguistic aspects of the reading problem. Perhaps because of the overtly verbal nature of reading and perhaps because of linguists' concentration on language factors, most of the articles deal with the possible effect Black English phonological and syntactic forms might have on a black ghetto child's chance of learning to read. But I have also selected articles which question the centrality of the role of Black English in reading problems and make suggestions as to the possibility of factors other than language forms contributing to the widespread failure of ghetto black children to learn to read.

There is a growing tendency to look at reading not just as a linguistic or phycholinguistic process, but instead to put it into a social context. Children bring their culture with them when they come to school to learn to read. Sometimes that culture, especially the peer group culture, does not place a particularly high value on reading as William Labov and Clarence Robins show in their article. These differences between the values held by black peers and by teachers are being considered to be of more importance in determining reading success or failure. Calling them "sociocultural" differences in his article, Walt Wolfram feels they are possibly more important than purely linguistic factors. Obviously, research is called for in order to determine more clearly what influence cultural and social factors do have over learning to read.

As far as linguistic factors contributing to reading failure are concerned, one of the major concerns has been about the effects of the distance between Black English and the more standard forms black ghetto children have to learn to read. Many linguists agree that the differences between the varieties probably do contribute to the problems faced by Black English speakers, but they tend to disagree as to the magnitude of those differences. There are quite different pedagogical implications arising from how these differences are perceived. For example, William Stewart takes a position of maximal differences and consequently recommends that primers be rewritten in Black English so the child can learn to read easily and successfully before transfer to more standard materials. Such a position has tended to be quite controversial because of many people's, including many blacks, negative attitudes toward using Black English as a written form.

On the other hand, Kenneth Goodman feels that the varieties' differences can be handled by the black reader himself if he is allowed to make his own sound-letter and syntactic matches by reading orally in Black English from material containing more standard forms. Walt Wolfram, in his article, summarizes very clearly the major present reading proposals made by linguists.

Unfortunately, due to lack of research, these positions and recommendations must remain speculative and highly tentative. Until that research is conducted, as a stop-gap measure which Wolfram suggests, a teacher could follow Goodman's suggestion about orally reading in Black English. It does not require elaborate materials or elaborate training for the teacher and definitely has some positive benefits for ghetto black children.

Dialect Barriers to Reading Comprehension
Kenneth S. Goodman

In this very perceptive and relatively early article, Kenneth Goodman talks about the difficulties in learning to read from the viewpoint of "divergent speakers." He suggests that some standard phonological, grammatical, and semantic forms may present a reading problem for these children. Although he does not say "Black English" speakers, his article is directly applicable to black ghetto children. He feels that since these children know their own dialect so well, it forms an excellent base for instruction and warns that teachers cannot be ethnocentric and negatively judgmental about the children's language.

He then goes on to discuss points of divergence among dialects including sounds and grammar. He suggests that the sound-symbol correspondence based reading materials will not be helpful to Black English speaking children because their correspondences are different from those of the authors or teachers. He then describes various grammatical and vocabulary differences he feels are relevant to learning to read.

He ends by suggesting that the most useful approach to help these children learn to read is to let the Black English speaking child read orally in his own variety so that he will be able to make his own sound-letter correspondences and syntactic matches. Goodman makes suggestions as to the key aspects of this approach, but makes none to change the beginning reading materials. He suggests that the child be helped to make his own adjustments between his dialect and the more standard forms he is learning to read.

The task of learning to read is not an easy one. But it's a lot easier to learn to read one's mother tongue than to learn to read a foreign language, one which the learner does not speak. Actually each of us speaks a particular dialect of a language. Each dialect is distinguished from all other dialects by certain features as: some of its sounds, some of its grammar, some of its vocabulary. The dialect which the child learns in the intimacy of his own home is his mother tongue. All physically normal children learn to speak a dialect. Whatever happens to his language during his life, however fluent and multilingual he may become, this native dialect is his most deeply and permanently rooted means of communication.

From "Dialect Barriers to Reading Comprehension" by Kenneth S. Goodman. *Elementary English,* December 1965. Copyright © 1965 by the National Council of Teachers of English. Reprinted by permission of the publisher and Kenneth S. Goodman.

Since it is true that learning to read a foreign language is a more difficult task than learning to read a native language, it must follow that it is harder for a child to learn to read a dialect which is not his own than to learn to read his own dialect.

This leads to an important hypothesis: *The more divergence there is between the dialect of the learner and the dialect of learning, the more difficult will be the task of learning to read.*

This is a general hypothesis. It applies to all learners. If the language of the reading materials or the language of the teacher differs to any degree from the native speech of the learners some reading difficulty will result. To some extent also there is divergence between the immature speech of the young learner and adult language norms in the speech community. Children have mastered most but not all of the sounds and syntax of adult speech. A further divergence reflects the fact that older members of any language community are less influenced by language change than are the youth. Thus the teacher may cling to language which is obsolescent in form or meaning. Books particularly lag behind language change since they freeze language at the date of composition. Though this paper is mainly concerned with gross dialect differences it must be remembered, then, that the reading problems discussed apply to some extent to all learners because minor dialect differences are features of even homogeneous speech communities.

The Divergent Speaker

For purposes of discussion we'll call the child who speaks a dialect different from that which the school, text, or teacher treats as standard, *the divergent speaker.* Divergence, of course, is relative and there is by no means agreement on what standard American English is. Divergent is a good term however, because it is neutral as a value term and it is important, perhaps critical, in considering the problems of the divergent speaker to avoid labeling his language as bad, sloppy, or sub-standard. We need to keep clear that, though some dialects may carry more social prestige than others, they are not necessarily more effective in communication. H.A. Gleason has said, "It is a safe generalization to say that all languages are approximately equally adequate for the needs of the culture of which they are a part." (1) Dialects represent subcultures. Therefore it can similarly be said that all dialects are equally adequate for the needs of the subculture of which they are a part.

Every child brings to school, when he comes, five or six years of language and of experience. His language is closely intertwined with the culture of his community; it embodies the cultural values and structures the way in which he may perceive his world and communicate his reactions to others.

His language is so well learned and so deeply embossed on his subconscious that little conscious effort is involved for him in its use. It is as much a part of him as his skin. Ironically, well-meaning adults, including teachers who would never intentionally reject a child or any important characteristic of a child, such as the clothes he wears or the color of his skin, will immediately and emphatically reject his language. This hurts him far more than other kinds of rejection because it endangers the means which he depends on for communication and self-expression.

Things that other people say sound right or funny to a child depending on whether they fit within the language norms of his dialect. He has become exceedingly proficient in detecting slight, subtle differences in speech sounds which are significant in his dialect and he's learned to ignore other differences in speech sounds that are not significant. He uses rhythm and pitch patterns of his language with great subtlety. He enjoys puns on language which employ very slight variations in relative pitch and stress. By the time divergent speakers are in the middle grades they have learned to get pleasure from the fact that an in-group pun based on their common divergent dialect is unfunny to an outsider like their teacher who doesn't share the dialect.

All children develop vocabulary which falls generally within the vocabulary pool of their speech community. Through repeated experience common for their culture they have begun to develop complex concepts and express them in their mother tongue.

In every respect the process of language development of the divergent speaker is exactly the same as that of the standard speaker. His language when he enters school is just as systematic, just as grammatical within the norms of his dialect, just as much a part of him as any other child's is. Most important, it is a vital link with those important to him and to the world of men.

There are some differences between the problems of the divergent speaker in an isolated rural community where a single dialect is the common speech and has been for several generations and the problems of the divergent speaker in the center of one of our great cities. This latter child may live in a virtual ghetto, but his friends and neighbors represent a variety of language backgrounds. Transplanted regional dialects become social class dialects. As the city-dweller grows older he comes into increasing contact with the general culture and its language. In the home community the idiolects, the personal languages of individuals, will cluster closely around a dialect prototype. But the dialects of urban divergent speakers are much more varied and shade off from distinct divergent dialects to standard speech. Variables such as family origin, recency of migration, degree of isolation from influences outside the subculture, attitudes toward self, personal and parental goals are some of the factors which may determine idiolect.

Divergent Languages or Dialects

Language diversity among divergent speakers complicates the task of understanding the literacy problems which they have. The basic problems will be the same but the specific form and degree will vary among individuals.

Teachers need to give careful consideration to the separate characteristics of several kinds of language divergence. They need to first differentiate immature language from dialect-based divergence. Language which is immature is always in transition toward adult norms. Teachers need not worry too much about immaturity in language since desired change is virtually inevitable. On the other hand, whatever the teacher does to speed this change is in the direction the child is moving. He can confirm the teacher's advice in the speech of his parents. But if the teacher "corrects" the dialect-based divergent language, this is at cross purposes with the direction of growth of the child. All his past and present language experience contradicts what the teacher tells him. School becomes a place where people talk funny and teachers tell you things about your language that aren't true.

Another point that needs to be clarified is the difference between standard regional speech and some imaginary national standard which is correct everywhere and always. No dialect of American English ever has achieved this status; instead we have a series of standard regional dialects, the speech of the cultured people in each area.

It's obvious that a teacher in Atlanta, Georgia, is foolish to try to get her children to speak like cultured people in Detroit or Chicago, just as it's foolish for any teacher to impose universal standard pronunciations which are not even present in the teacher's own speech. I'm referring to such hypocrisies as insisting that *u* before *e* must always say its own name and therefore *Tuesday* is /tyuzdey/. Cultured speech, socially preferred, is not the same in Boston, New York, Philadelphia, Miami, Baltimore, Atlanta, or Chicago. The problem, if any, comes when the Bostonian moves to Chicago, the New Yorker to Los Angeles, the Atlantan to Detroit. Americans are ethnocentric in regard to most cultural traits but they are doubly so with regard to language. Anybody who doesn't speak the way I do is wrong. A *green onion* is not a *scallion*. I live in Detróit not Détroit.

I can carry my books to work but not my friends. *Fear* ends with an *r* and *Cuba* does not. Such ethnocentrisms are unfortunate among the general public. They may be tragic among educators. Too often we send children off to speech correction classes not because their speech needs correction but because it isn't like ours. Pity the poor child who finds himself transplanted to a new and strange environment and then must handle the additional complication of learning to talk all over again. And, of course, if the child is a migrant from the rural South to the urban North, his speech marks him not only as different but socially inferior. He is told not just that he is wrong but sloppy, careless, vulgar, crude. His best defense is to be silent.

In his classroom the divergent speaker finds several kinds of language being used. First is the language or bundle of idiolects within dialects which he and his classmates bring with them as individuals. Represented in their language or dialect is the language or dialect of their parents and their speech community. Next there is the language of the teacher which will exist in at least two forms. There will be the teacher's informal, unguarded idiolect and his version of correct standard speech; the way he says things off guard; the way he strives to speak as a cultivated person. Another version of the standard language will be the literary form or forms the child encounters in books. To this we must add the artificial language of the basal reader. Artificial language is not used by anyone in any communicative situation. Some primerese is artificial to the point of being non-language, not even a divergent one.

The Consensus of Language and the Uniformity of Print

Two things are in the divergent child's favor. First, all speakers have a range of comprehension which extends beyond the limits of their own dialect. All of us can understand speech which differs from our own, particularly if we are in frequent contact with such speech. As they grow older, urban children are in increasing contact with a number of dialects other than their own. Secondly, the English orthography has one great virtue in its uniformity across dialects. No matter how words are pronounced, printers across the country usually spell them the same. Though we get some mavericks like *guilty* and *judgment,* we spell *pumpkin* the same whether we say *pəŋkin* or *pəmpkən* and *something* the same whether we say *səmpthin* or *səmpm.* This standardization of print for a multidialectal speech suggests that part of the problem of learning to read for divergent speakers could be eliminated if teachers let children read in their own dialects and if teachers got rid of the misconception that spelling determines pronunciation. One child asked his teacher how to spell /ræt/. "R-a-t," she said. "No, ma'am," he responded, "I don't mean rat mouse, I mean right now."

Points of Divergence Among Dialects

Now if we examine the areas in which dialects differ we can perhaps shed some light on the barriers divergent readers face. Let us start with sound.

Sound Divergence

Intonation

Dialects differ in intonation. Perhaps what makes an unfamiliar dialect most difficult to understand is its unexpected pitch, stress, and rhythm. Teachers often complain when they first begin to work with divergent speakers that they can't understand a word. But after a short time they seem to tune in on the right frequency. They catch on to the melody of the dialect. Since intonation is essential in understanding oral language, it is logical to assume that it must be supplied mentally by readers as they read in order for comprehension to take place. How much comprehension is interfered with if the teacher insists on intonation patterns in oral reading which are unnatural to the divergent reader can only be conjectured at this time. But there is no doubt that this is a source of difficulty to some extent.

Phonemes

Phonemes are the significant units of speech sounds which are the symbols of oral language. All American dialects share more or less a common pool of phonemes. But not all dialects use all these phonemes in all the same ways. They pattern differently in different dialects. Since phonemes are really bundles of related sounds rather than single sounds, it is likely that the range of sounds that compose a particular phoneme will vary among dialects. Vowel phonemes are particularly likely to vary. Even within dialects there are some variations. Good examples are words ending in -og, such as /dog/, /fog/, /frog/, /log/; or are they /dɔg/, /fɔg/, /frɔg/, /lɔg/? In my own idiolect I find I say /frɔg/, /fɔg/, /dɔg/, /lɔg/, but I also say /cag/, /bag/, /smag/.

Obviously, phonics programs which attempt to teach a relationship between letters and sounds cannot be universally applicable to all dialects. The basic premise of phonics instruction is that by teaching a child to associate the sounds which he hears in oral language with the letters in written language he will be able to sound out words. But a divergent speaker can't hear the sounds of standard speech in his nonstandard dialect because he does not have them or because they occur in different places in his dialect than other dialects. The instruction may be not only inappropriate but confusing. When he reads the lesson he may then be forced to sound out words which are not words in his dialect. To illustrate: Take a child who normally says /də/ rather than /ðə/ and /nəfin/ rather than /nəθin/. Teaching him that the digraph <th> represents the first sound in *the* and the medial consonant in *nothing* makes him pronounce words not in his dialect and throws a barrier across his progress in associating sound and print.

New Reading Materials and Sound Divergence Among Dialects

Recent attempts at producing beginning reading materials which have regular one-to-one correspondence between letters and phonemes will not solve this problem and may actually compound it since there will be a tendency for teachers to assume that the matched correspondence of sound and letter is to be uniform throughout the reading materials. For example, they might assume *frog* and *log* to have the same vowel sound and so teach the sounds to be the same when a student might well use /a/ as in *father* in one and /ɔ/ as in *caught* in the other. The matched phonemic-graphemic books assume that there is a uniform spoken set of sounds that can by ingenuity and counting of data be inscribed with a uniform written alphabet. This is not true, when the spoken language is viewed as a national-international phenomenon or when it is viewed as a local phenomenon in a heterogeneous cultural country as one of our urban centers.

Transcription of the sound language in i/t/a [initial teaching alphabet] faces the same problems. It has a wider alphabet and can therefore transcribe more literary and sensible English than the limited lexicon of the American linguistic readers. The British i/t/a materials, however, cannot be read literally except with the "received pronunciation" of the BBC. When as an American I read about "levers" in an i/t/a book I must say /liyvərz/. The principle that spelling is the same across dialects is sacrificed and i/t/a spelling requires pronunciation narrowed to one special class dialect. Teachers using these materials need to make some adjustments for the dialects used by themselves and their students. There may be, no doubt is, a spoken language in common but it is not so uniform as is the common spelling system.

Another place where sound divergence among dialects affects the handling of reading materials is the traditional sets of homophones. Homophones, words that sound alike, will vary from dialect to dialect. *Been* and *bin* are homophones in my speech. In another dialect *been* would sound the same as *bean* and in still another *Ben* and *been* would be sounded alike. Bidialectal students may bring up new sets of homophones. One teacher asked her class to use *so* in a sentence. "I don't mean sew a dress," she said. "I mean the other so," "I got a *so* on my leg," responded one of her pupils.

Grammar Divergence

The Suffix

Inflectional changes in words involve using suffixes or internal changes in words to change case or tense. In certain dialects of American English speakers say *He see me* rather than *He sees me*. They are not leaving off an *s*. There isn't any in their dialect. Similarly, plurals may not use an *s* form. *I got three brother,* is common in Appalachian speech. One teacher reported to me that her pupils could differentiate between *crayon* and *crayons* as written words and respond to the difference by selecting plural and singlular illustrations, but they read the words the same, one crayon, two /kræyən/. The problem is not an inability to see or say the *s*. It doesn't seem to belong in the pronunciation of *crayons*. The inflectional ending *s* to indicate plural is not in the grammar of this dialect.

Most Americans will add /əz/ to form plurals of words ending in /s/ /z/ /š/ /ǰ/ /č/ as in *busses, mazes, washes, colleges, churches,* but in the Blue Ridge Mountains this ending also goes with words ending in /sp/, /st/, /sk/ as in /waspəz/ /pohstəz/ /tæskəz/. (2) This kind of difference will be reflected in the child's reading. The differences are systematic within the child's dialect. In terms of the school and teacher they may be divergent, or as we say, incorrect, but in terms of the reader and his speech community they are convergent, that is, correct.

Not only suffixes vary, but also verb forms and verb auxiliaries. When a child says, "I here, teacher," as the teacher calls the roll, he is not being incomplete. No linking verb is needed in this type of utterance in his dialect. There is a difference in the syntax of his dialect and other American English dialects. Fortunately such differences are minor in American English. One area of difference seems to be the use of verb forms and verb markers. *We was going, They done it, We come home,* all are examples of this phenomenon.

Vocabulary Divergence

An area of dialect divergence that people are most aware of is vocabulary. Most people are aware that *gym shoes* in Detroit are *sneakers* in New York, that in Chicago you may *throw* but in Little Rock you *chunk,* that a Minnesota *lake* would be a *pond* in New Hampshire. Perhaps there is less awareness of words which have similar but not identical meanings in different dialects. All words have a range of meaning rather than a single meaning. This range may shift from place to place. The meaning of *carry* may be basically the same in two dialects but some uses will be correct in one dialect but not in the other.

Vocabulary differences among dialects may cause reading difficulty and must be compensated for by the teacher who uses texts printed for a national market.

I've dealt primarily here with the barriers to learning how to read that result when the readers have divergent languages. There are of course other important problems which grow out of the differences in experience, values, and general subculture of the divergent learners. Readers can't comprehend materials which are based on experience and concepts outside their background and beyond their present development.

The Reading Program for Divergent Speakers

Let's address ourselves to a final question. What is currently happening as the divergent speaker learns to read? I've found that divergent speakers have a surprising tendency to read in book dialect. In their oral reading they tend to use phonemes that are not the ones they use in oral language. Their reading often sounds even more wooden and unnatural than most beginners. There is some tendency to read their own dialect as they gain proficiency, but in general it appears that teachers are more successful in teaching preferred pronunciations than reading. What is lacking is the vital link between written and oral language that will make it possible for children to bring their power over the oral language to bear on comprehending written language.

There seem to be three basic alternatives that schools may take in literacy programs for divergent speakers. First is to write materials for them that are based on their own dialect, or rewrite standard materials in their dialect. A second alternative is to teach the children to speak the standard dialect before teaching them to read in the standard dialect. The third alternative is to let the children read the standard materials in their own dialect, that is, to accept the language of the learners and make it their medium of learning. The first alternative seems to be impractical on several counts. Primarily the opposition of the parents and the leaders in the speech community must be reckoned with. They would reject the use of special materials which are based on a non-prestigious dialect. They usually share the view of the general culture that their speech is not the speech of cultivation and literature. They want their children to move into the general culture though they are not sure how this can be brought about.

The second alternative is impractical on pedagogical grounds in that the time required to teach children who are not academically oriented to another dialect of the language, which they feel no need to learn, would postpone the teaching of reading too long. Many would never be ready to learn to read if readiness depended on losing their speech divergence in the classroom. The problem is not simply one of teaching children a new dialect. Children, the divergent among them, certainly have facility in language learning. The problem involves the extinction of their existing dialect, one which receives continuous reinforcement in basic communications outside of the classroom. William Labov's research in New York indicates that divergent speakers do not seem to make a conscious effort to use language forms which they recognize as socially preferred until adolescence. Younger children may hear differences but lack the insight to realize which forms are socially preferred. Of course, teenagers may deliberately avoid preferred forms, too, as they reject adult ways and adult values.

In essence the child who is made to accept another dialect for learning must accept the view that his own language is inferior. In a very real sense, since this is the language of his parents, his family, his community, he must reject his own culture and himself, as he is, in order to become something else. This is perhaps too much to ask of any child. Even those who succeed may carry permanent scars. The school may force many to make the choice between self-respect and school acceptance. And all this must be accomplished on the faith of the learner that by changing his language he will do himself some good. As one teenager remarked to me, "Ya man, alls I gotta do is walk right and talk right and they gonna make me president of the United States."

The only practical alternative I feel is the third one. It depends on acceptance by the school and particularly by the teacher of the language which the learner brings to school. Here are some key aspects of this approach:

1) Literacy is built on the base of the child's existing language.

2) This base must be a solid one. Children must be helped to develop a pride in their language and confidence in their ability to use their language to communicate their ideas and express themselves.

3) In reading instruction, the focus must be on learning to read. No attempt to change the child's language must be permitted to enter into this process or interfere with it.

4) No special materials need to be constructed but children must be permitted, actually encouraged, to read the way they speak. Experience stories must basically be in their language.

5) Any skill instruction must be based on a careful analysis of their language.

6) Reading materials and reading instruction should draw as much as possible on experiences and settings appropriate to the children. While special dialect-based materials are impractical, we may nonetheless need to abandon our notion of universally usable reading texts and use a variety of materials selected for suitability for the particular group of learners.

7) The teacher will speak in his own natural manner and present by example the general language community, but the teacher must learn to understand and accept the children's language. He must study it carefully and become aware of the key elements of divergence that are likely to cause difficulty. Langston Hughes has suggested an apt motto for the teacher of divergent speakers: "My motto as I live and learn, is dig, and be dug in return."

My own conviction is that even after literacy has been achieved future language change cannot come about through the extinction of the native dialect and the substitution of another. I believe that language growth must be a growth outward from the native dialect, an expansion which eventually will encompass the socially preferred forms but retain its roots. The child can expand his language as he expands his outlook, not rejecting his own subculture but coming to see it in its broader setting. Eventually he can achieve the flexibility of language which makes it possible for him to communicate easily in many diverse settings and on many levels.

I'd like to close with a plea. You don't have to accept what I've said. I don't ask that you believe or that you agree with my point of view. My plea is that you listen to the language of the divergent. Listen carefully and objectively. Push your preconceptions and your own ethnocentrisms aside and listen. I think that you'll find beauty and form and a solid base for understanding and communication. And as you dig you'll find that you are indeed dug in return.

References

1. H. A. Gleason, *An Introduction to Descriptive Linguistics* (New York: Holt, Rinehart and Winston, 1961).

2. *Ibid.*, p. 62.

On the Use of Negro Dialect in the Teaching of Reading

William A. Stewart

William Stewart is concerned about the evident problems black children
have in learning to read. He feels the structural interference (language form
interference as opposed to social factors causing interference) of most consequence in producing these problems is in the grammar of Black English, not
in its phonological or lexical differences from more standard varieties. He
feels the grammatical differences are great enough to cause comprehension
problems, so recommends that Black English patterns be used in beginning
reading materials. Stewart also proposes a set of stages to move the child from
reading Black English to reading more standard varieties. He also discusses
a suitable orthography for Black English primers, as the variety is basically
a spoken one. He decides on using a "standard English" type (the conventional one) with a few special accommodations for Black English. Finally he
writes a story in Black English of the type he has in mind for reading materials
and discusses its rationale in detail.

. . . Now, it is undoubtedly true that sound-spelling-meaning correspondences between spoken Negro dialect and written standard English are
less regular (or, at least, less obviously regular) than between spoken standard English and written standard English. Still, they are by no means neat
in even the latter case. For example, speakers of standard English must
learn to deal with the correlation to different meanings of the written
distinction between homophonic *son* and *sun,* just as speakers of Negro
dialect (or, indeed, of southern varieties of standard English) must learn
to deal with what for them are homophonic *pen* and *pin.* And, of course,
spellings like *of* and *island* are not representative of the pronunciation either
of Negro dialect or standard English. Yet, most speakers of standard English do not seem to be hindered very much by such sound-spelling-meaning
irregularities when they are learning to read—a fact which would suggest
that absolute parallelism between phonology and orthography is not really

a prerequisite to literacy in English. Indeed, even relatively inexperienced readers seem to be able to cope with a fair amount of sound-spelling irregularity, provided that they are familiar with the spoken forms of the words and are able to get sufficient cues for associating the written and spoken forms from the lexical and syntactic context.

Probably more serious in its consequences for reading instruction is the way in which differences between Negro dialect pronunciations and standard English spellings can be misinterpreted by reading teachers when they attempt to evaluate reading success through *viva-voce* performance. Unfortunately, there seems to be no simple way of deciding whether, in a particular instance, /ges/ represents a Negro dialect pronunciation of *guest,* or a misreading of it as *guess.* It would be more likely to be the former, but the background and training of many reading teachers would incline them to see it as the latter. And, although linguists know that a verb need not be accompanied by an explicit marker of the past tense to have past-tense meaning in Negro dialect (or, sometimes, even in standard English—cf. *hit,* which never takes a past-tense marker), most reading teachers would probably assume that, when a Negro child reads a sentence like *They guessed who he was* to sound more like *They guess who he was,* this is evidence that he has missed the past-tense meaning of the verb *guess.* In fact, the Negro child may merely pronounce written *guessed* as /ges/ for the same reason that he pronounces *guest* as /ges/—because final /st/ clusters turn into /s/ in his dialect. The failure to articulate a final written *-ed* when reading aloud no more indicates that a Negro child has failed to perceive the past-tense meaning of a written verb having it than reading *He hit me yesterday* aloud is an indication that the speaker of standard English has failed to perceive the past-tense meaning of *hit.* Clearly, the requirements for acceptable reading aloud must be distinguished from the requirements for effective reading comprehension.

Even in those cases in which phonological differences between Negro dialect and standard English look like they ought to make phonological identification of the written word more difficult for the Negro-dialect speaker, and thus interfere with reading comprehension, this may not always turn out to be so. For, if the differences are regular enough, which they often are, then the Negro-dialect speaker may be able to set up his own sound-spelling correspondences between them—ones which will be different from those set up by a speaker of standard English, but which will allow effective word identification nevertheless. For example, most varieties of Negro dialect regularly have /f/ and /v/ where standard English has /θ/ and /ð/ respectively. And the standard-English sounds are regularly represented in the written language by *th* (usually standing for the voiceless

/θ/, but also for the voiced /ð/ in certain circumstances). But the fair amount of regularity between standard English /θ/ and /ð/ and Negro dialect /f/ and /v/ on one hand, and standard English /θ/ and /ð/ and the spelling *th* on the other allows the Negro-dialect speaker to set up his own reading rule which tells him, in effect, "Read /f/ (or, in certain circumstances, /v/) for *th*, when not at the beginning of a word." Thus, he will read /bref/ for breath and, with the additional knowledge that *th* before final *e* usually stands for the voiced counterpart, he should read /briyv/ for *breathe*. And, since /bref/ and /briyv/ are exactly his functional equivalents of standard English /breθ/ and /briyð/, the correct word identification of *breath* and *breathe*, in terms of his own spoken vocabulary, will be made. For the reading of word-initial *th*, other reading rules would be set up, since the Negro-dialect reflexes of initial /θ/ and /ð/ in standard English are more complicated.

If, as the foregoing observations seem to indicate, the adverse effects of purely phonological differences between Negro dialect and standard English on reading comprehension are but slight, then the case for structural interference in a Negro-dialect speaker's attempts to read standard English will have to be made on other linguistic grounds. A substantial number of lexical differences between the two kinds of English would serve this purpose, but one of the striking features of the relationship between urban Negro dialect and standard English is that it involves very little lexical divergence. Consequently, if there really is significant dialect interference in the reading process, it can be expected to derive from grammatical differences between Negro dialect and standard English, and particularly from ones which are more or less independent of non-significant (for reading) phonological differences.

There are actually many grammatical differences between Negro dialect and standard English which, whether caused by different transformations or by different grammatical processes of a "deeper" type, are nevertheless clearly independent of regular phonological differences between the two kinds of English. Examples of transformationally-derived grammatical differences are encountered in the use of question-type inversion in Negro-dialect verb phrases where standard English uses *if* (meaning "whether") with no inversion, e.g. *See can he go* for *See if he can go*, uninverted verb phrases after certain question words in Negro dialect where standard English requires inversion, e.g. *What it is?* for *What is it?*, and multiple negation in Negro dialect where standard English has single negation, e.g. *He ain't never bought none* for *He hasn't ever bought any* or *He has never bought any*. As with many of the regular phonological differences between Negro dialect and standard English, the Negro-dialect speaker is usually able to establish correspondences between grammatical differences of this type—provided, of course, that the context is clear and that such constructions do not pile up in rapid succession. But even so, misinterpretation is quite possible when a standard-English construction happens to resemble in form some Negro-dialect construction other than the one to which it is functionally equivalent. For example, a seemingly unambiguous standard-English sentence like *His eye's open* may be misinterpreted by a Negro-dialect speaker as meaning "His eyes are open", simply because it resembles in form the Negro dialect sentence *His eyes open* (with that meaning) more than it does *His eye open* (the Negro-dialect equivalent of the original standard-English sentence). And this, incidentally, is yet another example of a case in which *viva-voce* performance would be of no help to the reading teacher in deciding whether there was a misinterpretation or not, since the pupil's pronunciation of standard English *His eye's open* and Negro dialect *His eyes open* would be identical.

Intelligibility problems of a different order—at once more subtle and more ingrained—are posed by grammatical differences between Negro dialect and standard English which originate deeper in the respective grammars than do differences of the preceding type. Because they are not likely to involve simple one-to-one correlations, and because they may not even use the same perceptual information about the real world, these deeper grammatical differences are apt to lie beyond the scope of the intuitive methods by which speakers of one dialect normally determine structural equivalences between their own and some other dialect. It is this type of grammatical difference which underlies the dissimilar use of *be* in Negro dialect and standard English. In Negro dialect, *be* is used with adjectives and the *-in'* (= *-ing*) form of verbs to indicate an extended or repeated state or action, e.g. *He be busy, He be workin'.* On the other hand, the absence of this *be* usually indicates that the state or action is immediate or momentary, e.g. *He busy, He workin'.* The auxiliary or tag for *be* in Negro dialect is *do*, e.g. *Do he be busy?* as a question form of *He be busy*, while the explicit form use in the non-*be* construction is usually *is*, e.g. *Is he busy?* as a question form of *He busy.* This means, of course, that *be* and *is* are entirely different morphemes in Negro dialect. But in standard English, there is no such grammatical distinction, and *be* and *is* are merely inflectional variants of one and the same verb. Thus, for the two grammatical constructions of Negro dialect, standard English has but one grammatical equivalent, e.g. *He is busy, He is working,* in which the immediacy or duration of the state or action is left entirely unspecified.

Thus far, this difference between Negro dialect and standard English in the grammatical recognition or not of a contrast between extended or repeated states and actions and immediate or momentary ones may seem to have little significance for reading comprehension, since the Negro-dialect speaker is obviously not going to encounter his own *He busy* and *He be busy* constructions (which mark the distinction) in a standard-English text. In form, the closest standard-English constructions to these will be the *He is busy* type, which is functionally equivalent to both of the Negro-dialect constructions, and the *He will be busy* type, which represents a future state or action only. Now, if this were indeed the extent of the matter, it would certainly be reasonable to assume that the differences in form between the standard-English and Negro-dialect constructions would alert the average Negro-dialect speaker to a possible difference in meaning between them. But one more bit of information is necessary to a full under-standing of just how much such a seemingly minor grammatical difference can affect intelligibility. This is that exposure to the standard-English use of present-tense forms of the copula (i.e. *am, is, are*) has made many speakers of nonstandard Negro dialect—even very young ones—aware that their own *He busy* and *He be busy* types of construction are not "proper" in form. Consequently, they often attempt to "correct" these on their own by adding one or another of the standard English auxiliaries to their *He busy* type of construction, and by changing the *be* of their *He be busy* type of construction into *bees* (on analogy with correcting *he work* to *he works*) and, when they realize that even this is nonstandard, into *will be*. Now, even assuming that those who do this will always end up with forms like *He is busy* (with appropriate person accord of the auxiliary throughout) for *He busy*, and *He will be busy* for *He be busy*, it is nevertheless the case that these phonologically and morphologically "standard" forms are still nonstandard Negro dialect in their grammar and meaning. This means that Negro dialect speakers—even ones who appear to know "correct" grammar—are apt to misread standard-English *He is busy* constructions as neces-sarily implying immediacy (which they do not), and *He will be busy* con-structions as possibly indicating repetition or long duration (which they do not) as well as futurity.

Taken altogether, the grammatical differences between Negro dialect and standard English are probably extensive enough to cause reading-compre-hension problems. Even in cases where the differences do not actually obscure the meaning of a sentence or passage, they can be distracting to a young Negro-dialect speaker who is trying to learn to read, and who can find but few familiar syntactic patterns to aid him in word identification. It is true that this child must eventually be taught to read standard-English sentence patterns, but it is open to question whether he should be made to cope with the task of deciphering unfamiliar syntactic structures at the very same time that he is expected to develop effective word-reading skills. One simple way to avoid placing a double learning load on the lower-class Negro child who is learning to read would be to start with sentence patterns which are familiar to him—ones from his own dialect—and then move to unfamiliar ones from standard English once he has mastered the necessary word-reading skills. In that way, reading ability could actually become an aid to the learning of standard English.

A third objection which might well be raised to the use of Negro dialect in beginning reading materials is that it would reinforce the use by lower-class Negro children of their nonstandard dialect, and thereby serve as a barrier to their eventual acquisition of standard English. But such a claim would be predicated on two false assumptions about language learning and language use. The first false assumption is that the use of language patterns always constitutes reinforcement of those patterns in the user. Although this is a popular belief among educators, it is obviously untrue for native speakers of a language (or a particular variety of a language) who are using familiar patterns of it. If a standard-English speaker is asked to repeat (or read) a sentence like *Charles and Michael are out playing,* he will not know either the sentence pattern or the individual words any better when he is through than before he started. The reason is, of course, that he already knows these aspects of his language as well as he could possibly learn them. If this is so, then why is it assumed that, if a Negro-dialect speaker is allowed to say (or asked to read) a sentence like *Charles an' Michael, dey out playin',* he will thereby become more addicted to Negro dialect? And what sort of magic is a classroom supposed to have, anyway, that the occasional use of nonstandard pronunciations or sentence patterns within its confines is regarded as pregnant with potential effect, while the almost exclusive use of those same pronunciations and sentence patterns outside the classroom is regarded as of little consequence? The second false assumption underlying this particular argument is that the knowledge and use of one language or dialect precludes the learning and use of another language or dialect—or, put more simply, that people's capacity for learning and using different linguistic systems is severly limited. This is a particularly common belief in America, where very few educators have had any exposure to multilingualism or bidialectalism. But Europeans would be likely to be astonished or amused by such an assertion, since most of them accept it as a matter of course that one will use a nonstandard dialect in the village home and a standardized variety of the same language (or even a different language) in the city office. The fact is that, in America too, there is no linguistic reason why an individual ought not to be able to produce sentences like *Charles an' Michael, dey out playin'* in one situation, and *Charles and Michael are out playing* in another. Poor language teaching, rather than the prior knowledge of another language or dialect, is the principal cause of unsuccessful bilingualism or bidialectalism.

Instead of being ignored or made the target of an eradication program, Negro dialect should actually be used as a basis for teaching oral and written standard English. If Negro dialect is used to teach initial word-reading skills to Negro-dialect speakers, then those word-reading skills can be made the constant in terms of which standard-English grammatical patterns can be taught through reading and writing. One form which this type of language teaching could take would be to make the transition from Negro dialect to standard English in a series of stages, each of which would concentrate on a limited set of linguistic differences. An exciting aspect of this approach is that oral language teaching could be combined with the reading program to any degree felt useful. Take, for example, the Negro-dialect sentence just cited, and its standard-English counterpart. The former would become the initial stage in such a program, and the latter would be the ultimate goal. In this illustration, I will write the Negro-dialect sentence in standard-English spelling in order to simplify the transition process.

Stage 1

Charles and Michael, they out playing.
Grammatically, sentences at this stage will be pure nonstandard Negro dialect. The vocabularly, also, will be controlled so that no words which are unfamiliar to a Negro-dialect-speaking child will appear. Thus, all linguistic aspects of text will be familiar to the beginning reader, and his full attention can be focused on learning to read the vocabularly. At this stage, no attempt should be made to teach standard-English pronunciations of the words, since the sentence in which they appear is not standard English.

Stage 2

Charles and Michael, they are out playing.
At this stage, the most important grammatical features of standard English are introduced. In the example, there is one such feature—the copula. Apart from that, the vocabulary is held constant. Oral-language drills could prof-itably be used to teach person accord of the copula (*am, is, are*), and some standard-English pronunciations of the basic vocabularly might be taught.

Stage 3

Charles and Michael are out playing.
Grammatically, the sentences at this stage are brought into full conformity with standard English by making the remaining grammatical and stylistic adjustments. In the example, the "double subject" of the nonstandard form is eliminated. Oral-language drills could be used to teach this, and additional standard-English pronunciations of the basic vocabularly could be taught.

Although the complete transition from Negro-dialect grammar to standard-English grammar was effected in three stages in the foregoing example, more stages would probably be required in a real program of this type. The actual programming of these stages would have to be carried out by competent linguists, but, once done, the resulting materials ought to be usable in regular remedial-reading classes. . .

. . . Once the decision has been made to develop beginning reading materials using Negro dialect for a particular school population, then a suitable orthography must be selected for the nonstandard sentence patterns. This is an unavoidable problem, since any nonstandard dialect is, by its very nature, unwritten. But it is an important problem, since the effective use of a nonstandard dialect in a bidialectal reading program will depend to a great extent on how easy the orthographic transition between the two linguistic systems can be made. For Negro dialect, four major types of orthography are available to choose from. These are:

1) An autonomous phonemic orthography, in which words are spelled the way they are pronounced (or heard) by a speaker of the dialect. For example, if a Negro-dialect speaker normally pronounces his equivalents of standard English *bend* and *bending* /ben/ and /bendin/, then these words will be spelled so as to show these pronunciations, sound-by-sound, e.g. *ben* and *bendin.*

2) A systematic phonemic orthography, which attempts to have the spellings represent all the information necessary to determine changes which can occur in the pronunciation of words in different contexts. For example, this type of orthography would spell the Negro-dialect equivalent of standard English *bend* in a way which would show that a /d/ is pronounced in the word when a vowel follows (as it does with the suffix /-in/), while the same is not true for a word like /mown/, for standard English *moan,* i.e. /mownin/. This could be accomplished simply by spelling the Negro-dialect form /ben/ as *bend,* with a "reading rule" that *d* after *n* is pronounced only before a vowel.

3) A literary-dialect orthography, in which the purely dialectal pronunciations of Negro-dialect words are roughly indicated by minor changes in the traditional spellings of their standard-English cognates. One im-

portant device used in literary dialect is the apostrophe, which is sub-
stituted for certain letters to show that a particular sound usually pronounced in a standard-English form is not pronounced in its Negro-
dialect equivalent (e.g. *ben'* for standard English *bend*), or to indicate
sound substitutions (e.g. *bendin'* with final /n/ for standard English
bending with final /ŋ/). The examples of Negro dialect which were given
in the earlier discussion of grammatical interference were written in a
literary-dialect orthography.

4) An unmodified standard-English orthography, with no effort made to
indicate differences in pronunciation between Negro dialect and standard English. For example, the spellings *bend* and *bending* would be used
in writing both varieties of English. The negro dialect was written in
this way in the three-stage example of transitional reading materials.

   The first two types of orthography are the most scientific, since they both
attempt to indicate the pronunciation of the dialect accurately, and in its
own terms. Each of these systems has its advocates and its detractors, who
will be happy to point out its strengths and weaknesses. (1) An autonomous
phonemic orthography has the advantage of being applicable to a language
or dialect as soon as certain basic facts are known about its sound system,
and long before much is understood about contextual variations in the
structure of words. It is largely for this reason that most of the orthographies which have been devised in connection with basic literacy programs
around the world have been autonomous phonemic ones. On the other
hand, a systematic phonemic orthography has the advantage of representing the relationship between variant pronunciations of words much more
adequately than is possible in an autonomous phonemic orthography, and
hence tends to relate more closely to grammatical processes in the language
or dialect. A distinct disadvantage of systematic phonemic orthographies,
however, is that they can only be as well-formed as the state of knowledge
concerning the lexicon and morphophonemics of the particular language
or dialect will allow. And, since the lexicon of even a "primitive" language
can be quite vast, and the morphophonemics of even a "simple" dialect
quite complex, that knowledge is seldom ever as complete as it ought to
be for devising a permanent orthography. Accordingly, attempts to create
such orthographies are likely to be characterized by a certain degree of
instability, engendered by constant additions, corrections, and revisions.
   The last two types of orthography are, from a phonological point of view,
at least, much less scientific than the first two. While a literary-dialect
orthography does attempt to indicate Negro-dialect pronunciations, this is
seldom done either consistently or in the dialect's own terms. And Negro
dialect which has been spelled entirely in the standard-English fashion will

offer no clues at all as to its unique pronunciations. Rather, the effect of these two types of orthography is to show the relationship of the one form of English to the other. A literary-dialect orthography, with its altered spellings and ubiquitous apostrophe, emphasizes the dialect's phonological deviations from standard-English norms, and can create an impression of great difference—even without accommodating the actual dialect syntax. The writing of Negro dialect in an unmodified standard-English orthography, on the other hand, obscures the phonological differences between the two and, as a result, highlights whatever syntactic differences are incorporated into the writing of the sentences.

In evaluating the relative utility of these four types of orthography for writing Negro dialect in a reading program designed to phase into standard English, it is ironic that the least satisfactory one is that which has proven most effective in basic literacy programs involving only one language or dialect at a time: the autonomous phonemic orthography. What renders this type of orthography unsuitable for the task at hand is that, precisely because it would represent the sounds of Negro dialect accurately and in the dialect's own terms, it would produce Negro-dialect word spellings which would be too foreign to the spellings of standard-English cognates to permit an easy transition from reading and writing the one to reading and writing the other.

Both a systematic phonemic orthography and a literary-dialect orthography would have essentially the same drawbacks as an autonomous phonemic orthography, though conceivably to a lesser degree. But the main argument against both of these types of orthography is their complexity; the prospective reader would probably do better to spend his time and effort mastering the intricacies of the standard-English orthographic system. And, given what was said earlier about the ability of the Negro-dialect speaker to set up his own sound-spelling correspondences between Negro-dialect pronunciations and standard-English word spellings, the writing of Negro dialect in an unmodified standard-English orthography ought not to cause more problems than it avoids.

Apart from the obvious necessity of using the nonstandard *ain't* and common contractions like *it's, don't, won't, can't,* etc., in writing Negro dialect in a standard-English type of orthography, I would make one major compromise in the direction of a literary-dialect orthography. That would be to indicate, by an apostrophe, those cases in Negro dialect in which a word must take a prefix in order to become like its standard-English equivalent, e.g. Negro dialect *'bout, 'cause, 'round,* and *'posed to* for standard English *about, because, around,* and *supposed to.* In the Negro-dialect materials, word-initial apostrophes would thereby become graphic indicators of specific lexical points at which later morphological expansion of the Negro-dialect forms would have to be carried out in the transition to standard English. The usefulness of this technique lies in the fact that Negro-dialect speakers do not always know that a prefix is "missing" from their version of a particular word. Thus, the Negro-dialect form *'most* (cf. standard English *almost*), as in *'most always,* *'most everybody,* is either left that way when "proper" English is attempted, or it may be "corrected" with a suffix, *-ly,* rather than with a prefix. Although this latter step creates no conflict in meaning for the Negro-dialect speaker (since his normal equivalent of standard English *mostly* is *most of. . . ,* e.g. *Most of it ruined* and *They most of them teachers* for standard English *It has mostly spoiled* and *They are mostly teachers*), it does produce sequences like *mostly always* and *mostly everybody* which are incongruous and comical when interpreted as standard English. But even when Negro-dialect speakers do suspect that some sort of prefix is required to make a particular word into standard English, they may not be at all sure which standard-English prefix is required; or they may be sure, but be mistaken. Negro-dialect speakers may know, for example, that their forms *'cord, 'morial,* and *'vorce* all require a prefix in "proper" usage, but then they are likely to overuse *re-* (by far the most functional prefix in Negro dialect) to produce the "corrected" forms *record, remorial, and revorce,* with only one matching with standard English *record* (verb), *memorial,* and *divorce*—and that a fortuitous one. In effect, this persistent confusion which many Negro-dialect speakers experience with standard-English pretonic syllables (often in spite of "hearing" the appropriate forms from middle-class speakers from time to time) suggests that it would be of little use to write *almost, record, memorial, divorce,* etc., in beginning reading materials for Negro-dialect speakers, with the hope that they would somehow "pick up" the right usage from the spellings. It would seem more effective to write such words as *'most, 'cord, 'morial, 'vorce,* etc., in at least the initial stage of such materials, so that the learner could first become familiar with the reading of their "stems" in terms of his own pronunciation patterns, and only then to teach the appropriate standard-English prefixes by means of supplementary spoken drills, preparatory to introducing the standard-English spellings into the written text.

To close this paper, I have written a very short story, which I call "Shirley and the Valentine Card", to show what the written Negro dialect of the initial (i.e. the most nonstandard) stage of a Negro-dialect-to-standard-English reading program might look like, to serve notice on normativists that standard English has no monopoly on expressiveness, and to reassure the socio-politically timid that even radically nonstandard Negro dialect

will turn out to be comfortably unobstrusive if dialectal spellings are used ✓
sparingly enough. I have not gone so far as to structure the text of the story,
as it ought to be in a reading program, by presenting sound-spelling-meaning correspondences in a systematic way, or by organizing the distinctive
structural features of the dialect in a way which will facilitate their staging
into standard English. Rather, I present this story simply as a sample of
the language of the story. To that end, I immediately follow it with a few
specific comments on some of its features.

Shirley and the Valentine Card

It's a girl name Shirley Jones live in Washington. 'Most everybody on her
street like her, 'cause she a nice girl. And all the children Shirley be with in
school like her, too. Shirley treat all of them just like they was her sisters
and brothers, but most of all she like one boy name Charles. Shirley, she be
knowing Charles 'cause all two of them in the same grade, and he in her class.
But Shirley keep away from Charles most of the time, 'cause she start to liking
him so much she be scared of him. And that make it seem to Charles like
she don't pay him no mind. So Charles, he don't hardly say nothing to her
neither. Still, that girl got to go 'round telling everybody Charles 'posed to
be liking her. She act like she his girlfriend, too.

But when Valentine Day start to come 'round, Shirley get to worrying. She
worried 'cause she know the rest of them girls all going get Valentine cards
from their boyfriends. And she know when them girls find out she ain't get
a card from Charles, they going say she been telling a story 'bout Charles
being her boyfriend. So she keep on thinking 'bout that and worrying all day
long, even at school when she 'posed to be learning something from the
teacher and playing with the other girls. That Shirley, she so worried, she
just don't want to be with nobody. She even walk home by her own self, when
school let out.

When Shirley get home, her mother say it's a letter for her on the table.
Right away Shirley start to wondering who could it be from, 'cause she know
don't nobody 'posed to be sending her no kind of letter. It do have her name
on the front, though. It say, *Shirley Jones.* So Shirley, she open the envelope
up. And when she do, she can see it's a Valentine card inside. Now, Shirley
take out the card, and she look at it, and she see it have Charles name wrote
on the bottom.

See, Charles really been liking her all the time, even though he ain't never
tell her nothing 'bout it. So now everything going be all right for Shirley,
'cause what she been telling everybody 'bout Charles being her boyfriend ain't
story after all. It done come true!

Comments on the Language of the Story

Although Negro-dialect speakers often narrate their stories in a past-time setting, I have deliberately put "Shirley and the Valentine Card" in the somewhat less common (though still appropriate) simple present throughout. This is a useful strategy to employ in the writing of initial-stage reading materials, since it eliminates the need for introducing nonstandard past-tense verb forms, some of which would definitely require dialectal spellings, and allows for the systematic introduction of standard-English past-tense verb forms at a later time.

The language of the story is essentially a representation, in the kind of standard-English orthography I have advocated, of a variety of nonstandard dialect which is used by many lower-class Negro children in the District of Columbia—the scene of the story. (2) As it stands, this kind of Negro dialect is almost identical to that of similar children in such Eastern Seaboard cities as Baltimore, Wilmington, Philadelphia, and New York. The language of the story is fairly "pure" Negro dialect, with features from standard English kept to a somewhat artificial minimum (since, after all, the idea would be to introduce these systematically in the course of the reading program of which such a story would be part). On the other hand, because this story is arbitrarily directed to the 10-to-15-year-old range, a number of even more deviant features of the speech of younger children have been omitted, such as possessive pronouns which (except for the first person singular) are undifferentiated in form from the corresponding subject pronouns, e.g. *he girlfriend, she boyfriend* for *his girlfriend, her boyfriend.* If materials were being developed for much younger children, or for regions in which such features occur in a wider age range (in coastal South Carolina, Georgia, or Florida, for example), the dialect forms could be modified accordingly.

The other regional limitations in the linguistic structure of "Shirley and the Valentine Card" are really quite minor. A marked characteristic of the dialect used is that verbs in the simple present do not usually take a suffix -*s* for any person subject. But in some other varieties of Negro dialect, particularly those spoken in the South Central states (Mississippi, Alabama, etc.), the simple present verb is more often marked with -*s* for all persons, e.g. *I lives in Jackson.* Also, although no examples of possessive noun constructions appear in the story, South Central Negro dialect often uses a possessive suffix like standard English, e.g. *Shirley's boyfriend,* where Eastern Seaboard Negro dialect simply uses noun apposition, e.g. *Shirley boyfriend.* Finally, in the Negro dialect of the District of Columbia, as in most of the Eastern Seaboard, *got* (or *gots*) and *'posed to* take *do* (negative *don't*) as an auxiliary or tag, e.g. *Do you got a dollar?, Don't they 'posed to go with you?*, while in South Central usage the auxiliary or tag for these verbs is usually *is* (negative *ain't*), e.g. *Is you got a dollar?, Ain't they 'posed to go with you?* But the fact that, in general, the language of "Shirley and the Valentine Card" is as close as it is to the speech of Negroes of a comparable age and socio-economic level in so many parts of the United States shows reather clearly that Negro dialect from South to North, from East to West, from farm to city, and from store-front church to playground, is all part of a single sociolinguistic complex, with a single historical origin, and reveals the emptiness of the claim of some traditionalist educators that Negro speech varies too much from place to place for it to be a useful pedagogical tool.

What I have had to say about Negro dialect in the course of this paper should make it obvious that it is a highly complex yet well-formed and systematic code—just like any other language. To speak it well, or to use it effectively in pedagogical materials, requires a profound knowledge of its many phonological and grammatical rules, of subtle lexical differences (e.g. that *bright* means "light-skinned" in Negro dialect, while it means "clever" in standard English), and of countless stylistic and idiomatic details (e.g. that *sisters and brothers* is the "pure" Negro-dialect form, while *brothers and sisters* is an importation from standard English). This means that attempts to use or to write Negro dialect should not be made by unqualified persons, black or white, any more than attempt to use or write, say, French should be. For one thing, the inner-city slang or "hip talk" of teenagers and young adults should not be confused with Negro dialect in the linguistic sense, no matter how ethnically-correlated many of the slang terms may be. They are simply deliberate vocabularly substitutions, and have nothing directly to do with dialect grammar or phonology. Nor is the "stage dialect" of Negro bit-players on radio, television, or the screen necessarily close to real Negro dialect. Often, in order to insure its being understood by a wide audience, a stage Negro dialect may be created which is little more than standard English with a slightly ethnicized or southernized pronunciation, reinforced by the insertion of such general nonstandardisms as *ain't* and the double negative, and perhaps a sprinkling of southern or inner-city Negro lexical usages like *honey child* or *man*. And, although literary renditions of plantation Negro dialect (such as appears in Joel Chandler Harris' *Uncle Remus, His Songs and His Sayings*) may represent an older form of Negro dialect rather accurately, and thus share many structural characteristics with present-day Negro dialect, there are still too many intervening variables (nineteenth-century usage vs. twentieth-century usage, adult speech vs. child speech, rural forms vs. urban forms, story-telling style vs.

colloquial style, etc.) for that kind of Negro dialect to be directly useful for the purposes I have been suggesting. If used well by educators, living Negro dialect can serve as a bridge between the personal experiences of the Negro child and his acquisition of mainstream language skills. If used poorly, however, it will only add to the confusion of pupil and teacher alike. The language of the Negro child can be made an effective educational tool, but it must be treated with respect and understanding. . .

References

1. See, for example, Paul M. Postal, *Aspects of Phonological Theory* (New York: Harper & Row, 1968).
2. For a general discussion of Negro speech in the District of Columbia, including the relationship of the nonstandard dialect of Negro children to that of adults, see William A. Stewart, "Urban Negro Speech: Sociolinguistic Factors Affecting English Teaching" [in Chapter Three of this book].

Sociolinguistic Alternatives in Teaching Reading to Nonstandard Speakers

Walt Wolfram

The following summary was written by Walt Wolfram. The author critically reviews the alternative strategies in teaching reading to lower-class black children, based on current research in the field of sociolinguistics. The two main strategies discussed are the retention of extant materials with adjustments in teaching procedures and the revision of basic materials. If no change is made in materials, then the options are to teach children standard English prior to reading or allow the students to read materials with dialectally appropriate renderings. If the revision of materials is undertaken, the alternative strategies include the neutralization of grammatical differences in materials or the use of dialect primers. The review of these alternatives deals with both the linguistic and socio-cultural factors that contribute to a sociolinguistic perspective. It is concluded that the acceptance of dialectally appropriate reading of extant material should be initiated while further experimentation takes place with the revision of current materials and the use of dialect primers.

Introduction

The lagging reading level of lower-class minority groups, particularly blacks, has now become a matter of national concern. In response to this national crisis, a number of alternative approaches have been suggested in order to neutralize the discrepancy between middle-class and lower-class minority group reading achievement levels. Some of these programs have little relevance to the cultural and linguistic differences between social groups, such as programs which deal with the amount of time devoted to reading in the school curriculum or the reduction of discipline problems that interfere with productive time usage. Although these non-linguistic factors may be legitimate concerns in themselves, the sociolinguist has nothing to contribute to these areas. Other suggested programs, however, attempt to deal directly with the details of language involved in reading.

From "Sociolinguistic Alternatives in Teaching Reading to Nonstandard Speakers" by Walt Wolfram in *Reading Research Quarterly,* Fall 1970, 9–33. Reprinted with permission of Walt Wolfram and the International Reading Association.

In these matters, sociolinguistic expertise may be helpful, for it is now generally acknowledged that there are a number of linguistic differences between the language of a basal reader and the lower-class black child's indigenous dialect.

Basic to this discussion of reading materials for speakers of a nonstandard dialect is the fact that the dialect variously called "Black English," "Negro Dialect" or "Negro Nonstandard English" is a fully formed linguistic system in its own right, with its own grammar and pronunciation rules; it cannot simply be dismissed as an unworthy approximation of standard English. Although this dialect shares many features of other English dialects, it is distinct because there are a number of pronunciation and grammatical features which are not shared by other English dialects. (1)

The purpose of this paper is to describe and evaluate current approaches to the reading problem of lower-class blacks which attempt to deal with the linguistic differences between the child's indigenous system and the language of the standard English reader. It should be clear from the beginning that there is no unitary "linguistic approach"—that mythical but marketable item that has become a token of prestige in language arts curricula. Rather, there are several alternatives which attempt to eliminate the possible effect that dialect differences may have in the acquisition of reading skills. There are no panacean solutions. The advantages and disadvantages of each alternative must honestly be faced if we are to arrive at a feasible solution—one which will ultimately result in the significant reduction of reading problems in ghetto schools. The fact that we have no infallible alternative should not, however, be taken to mean that all alternatives which attempt to deal with the discrepancy between the language of the primer and the indigenous language of the child are equal. As the different approaches are evaluated, it should be apparent that some can be more highly recommended than others.

Although there are idiosyncratic aspects of practically every reading program which has been proposed, the various alternatives can be roughly divided into two main groups, those which call for different methods in teaching reading with extant materials and those which call for the development of new types of reading materials.

The Retention of Extant Materials

If the linguistic diversity between the dialect of the lower-class black and the dialect of the reading materials is going to be neutralized without altering basic materials for lower-class black children, then two options are open; either the child's language patterns must be changed to conform to standard English patterns prior to the teaching of reading, or some accomodation to the dialect in the child's reading of the traditional type of reader must be made. The feasibility of these two alternatives is discussed below.

Teaching Standard English Prior to Reading

To neutralize the difference between the "language of reading" and the language which the lower-class black child brings to school with him, it has sometimes been suggested that the teaching of standard English should precede the teaching of reading in our ghetto schools. Although this procedure may appear to be similar to the simultaneous teaching of reading and standard English that is often engaged in, it is essential not to confuse these procedures. When teachers "correct" children for dialect interference in reading as well as the authentic types of errors that occur in learning to read, the teaching of standard English is usually done in a haphazard and unsystematic way. Furthermore, legitimate dialect interference and reading problems arising from the incomplete mastery of the reading process are often not distinguished from each other. The approach suggested here, however, first concentrates on the systematic teaching of standard English before any reading is taught; when a child has acquired a productive control over standard English, the teacher may proceed to the teaching of reading. The teaching of reading begins with the assumption that the source for dialect interference has been eliminated. This is not to say that the child's indigenous dialect will be eradicated, only that he will have capacity in standard English as well as the vernacular.

Most school curricula call for the teaching of standard English eventually, but the program described here inevitably means that standard English will be taught at the initial stages of the child's experience, since the acquisition of reading is one of the earliest priorities of formal education. One might further suggest that since standard English will probably be taught anyway, it is most reasonable to teach it before the failure to learn it can inhibit reading development.

Although the above alternative is supported by a number of scholars, the assumptions about the language of the child which motivate such a position may differ dramatically. On the one hand, there are some educational psychologists such as Carl Bereiter and Siegfried Engelmann, (2) who maintain that standard English is a prerequisite for reading because the child's indigenous language system may leave him cognitively handicapped. Thus, Bereiter and Engelmann observe:

In grammar, the basic unit is the sentence, and discrete words constitute the detail from which the meaning of the sentence is derived. In reading, the basic unit is the word, and the letters constitute the detail. We have noted in Chapter 2 ["Cultural and Language Deprivation"] the inability of the essential details for understanding and constructing statements. In reading, this lack of awareness of words as discrete entities makes him oblivious of the structural wholes which spelling creates. (3)

What is seen, in this position, is the assumption that standard English must be taught prior to reading because the child comes to school with an incomplete and deficient language system. This assumption, no doubt, causes many teachers to be sympathetic to this method of attacking the reading problem of nonstandard speaking black children.

On the other hand, teaching standard English prior to reading has been endorsed by some linguistically sophisticated educators, for reasons different from Bereiter and Engelmann's. For example, R. L. Venezky asserts:

Children whose dialects deviate markedly from standard English should be taught the standard brand before they are taught reading, under the explicit assumption that it is a second dialect and not a mere correct dialect that is being taught. (4)

The position that standard English might be taught prior to reading is taken by Venezky, not because the children are assumed to have a deficient language system but because it appears to be one effective means (in Venezky's case, this alternative is combined with other alternatives) of acquiring the basic reading skills of the standard language.

If we were simply dealing with linguistic facts, teaching standard English prior to reading would certainly be an attractive alternative. Standard English will probably be taught anyhow, so why not simply learn standard English and then learn to read? We know that children are quite adept at language learning, so why not take advantage of this fact and teach them standard English at an early age? But before the potential advantages of this alternative are accepted, we must realistically consider the total sociolinguistic situation, for potential linguistic advantages cannot be treated in isolation from socio-cultural facts.

Probably the most essential sociolinguistic point that militates against this alternative is the fact that the vernacular speech of these children has persisted despite the consistent and pervasive attempts to linguistically acculturate them to standard English. Children want to speak like their peers, and the conflicts between school and indigenous value systems have repeatedly shown that school values will most often come out on the short end of a compromise. R. W. Fasold notes:

Because of the operation of social forces in the use of language—forces which are only poorly understood—it may not be possible to teach standard English to Black English speaking children unless they are interacting with Standard English speakers in a meaningful way outside the classroom. (5)

Roger Abrahams suggests that the peer group influence over speech can be expected to resist the attempts of mainstream society to adopt standard English.

Because of the functional necessity to maintain this friendship-based peer grouping, these forces are stronger than those from mainstream America which would change the most disparate black cultural patterns, and with it, certain varieties and features of Black English. . . It is asking a great deal to expect lower class blacks to give up this adaptable expressive system that has served them so well for so long. (6)

Given the pessimistic but realistic predictions about the teaching of standard English, it is therefore surprising that Venezky observes that the teaching of standard English may only involve a delay of several months in the introduction of reading. He observes:

There is no reason to believe that a delay of a few months in the introduction of reading will seriously impede any child's natural development. (7)

Thomas Kochman, who seriously questions the wisdom of teaching standard English at all, bases part of this argument for not teaching it on what he calls the "efficiency quotient." (8) By this he means the excessive time that must be spent in order to produce even a mediocre and restrictive performance in standard English. He notes that with maximum cooperation, for example, it takes several months of drilling simply to get a student to say *ask* where he formerly said *aks.* Kochman therefore concludes that "the input in time and effort is prodigious and the results negligible." (9)

Even if we take a more optimistic view on the teaching of standard English, we cannot assume that the first grade is the best time to teach it. Some sociologists and educators suggest that it is most reasonable to start teaching standard English at an age when there is an increasing awareness of the social consequences of using certain nonstandard features of speech. According to William Labov, the social perceptions of speech stratification start to match the adult norms around the ages of 14–15. (10) Because the 5–6 year old child perceives little if any social differentiation in speech, it may be argued that it is senseless to teach standard English at the first grade level, the level at which reading skills are expected to be developed. Rather, standard English should be initiated at a secondary level, when students have acquired the notion of social appropriateness for different types of behavior more fully. Irwin Feigenbaum observes:

Secondary school students are aware of social appropriateness. . . But what is to be done with students who are not mature enough to understand this concept? The author would suggest that if a student is too young to understand appropriateness, teaching Standard English and when to use it will be very difficult and perhaps fruitless. (11)

Before we can endorse teaching standard English as a prerequisite for reading, we must have evidence that it can be extensively taught given the current socio-cultural facts, and that it is most effectively taught at the initial stages of education. At this point, the socio-cultural facts which inhibit the widespread acquisition of standard English even as a second dialect do not suggest this alternative as a reasonable solution.

Dialect Reading of Extant Materials

The other alternative which retains the traditional materials does not involve the teaching of standard English in any form. Rather, it involves the acceptance of dialect renderings of standard English reading materials. Kenneth Goodman is probably the most explicit spokesman for this position when he states:

> No special materials need to be constructed but children must be permitted, actually encouraged, to read the way they speak. (12)

The child is given the standard types of reading materials and simply asked to read them aloud in a dialect-appropriate manner. If a child can read the passage in such a way that it systematically differs from standard English where his indigenous dialect differs, he has successfully read the passage. For example, if a lower-class black child reads a standard sentence such as *Jane goes to Mary's house* as *Jane go to Mary house* he is considered to have read it properly, since third person singular *-s* and possessive *-s* suffixial absence are part of the lower-class black child's vernacular. It is held that by permitting the child to read the traditional materials in his own dialect, the teacher can focus on the essentials of the reading process and the child will not be confused about reading problems which may result from dialect interference and legitimate types of reading errors arising during the course of the acquisition of reading skills.

There are some assumptions implicit in accepting what Goodman suggests as the only practical alternative for the reading problem among lower-class blacks, and our evaluation of its relative merits is based on these assumptions. First, it assumes that the standard English contained in the beginning materials is quite comprehensible to the child. Claims about the comprehension of standard English by lower-class black children vary greatly, but we still lack definitive empirical evidence on this question. At this point, the most reasonable position seems to be that for the most part, the dialect speaker has a receptive competence in standard English. The converse, standard English speakers comprehending lower-class blacks, may not necessarily be true to the same extent because of the socio-psychological factors which enter into the comprehension of the speech of a socially subordinate class by a superordinate one. (13) This position seems to be most realistic for several reasons. For one, the majority of differences between the child's vernacular and standard English appear to be on the surface rather than the underlying levels of language. (14) One might expect that differences on the surface level would usually be less imposing factors in comprehension than differences on the underlying levels of language. A more important reason for this position is found in the indirect evidence that we have from the lower-class black child's ability to perform certain types of tasks based on the perceptive competence of standard English. For example, in performing a sentence repetition test devised by Joan Baratz, lower-class black children could comprehend standard English sentences sufficiently to repeat them in the nonstandard dialect, and these were sentences which focused on the areas of difference between the child's vernacular and standard English. (15) That these children were able to give back a nonstandard equivalent given a standard English stimulus indicates that the children have understood the content of the standard English sentences.

To suggest that there is a basic comprehension of standard English sentences by nonstandard speakers does not, however, preclude the possibility that some information loss may occur when reading standard English. Thus, Walter Wolfram and Ralph Fasold have suggested:

> Certainly some lower socioeconomic class speakers read extant materials and with some apparent understanding. We would not argue that the Black English speaker is going to understand as little Standard English as a monolingual German speaker reading English, but we do suggest that there will be an inevitable information loss. (16)

If some information loss does occur because of dialect differences, what should be done about features which might be unfamiliar to the lower-class black child? Are these unfamiliar features sufficiently infrequent to warrant their retention in the materials, since any child can expect some unfamiliar constructions in reading material (for reasons we will discuss below) or will the unfamiliar constructions be sufficiently great to impede the reading process? These are empirical questions, but ones which must be faced squarely if no change in traditional reading materials is advocated.

Another factor which must be considered in using extant materials concerns the orthography, particularly if the so-called "phonics" approach to reading is employed. Although it has sometimes been argued that the traditional orthography is inappropriate for the dialect of lower-class black children, Fasold (17) has convincingly demonstrated in a formal way the adequacy of traditional English orthography for speakers of a nonstandard dialect. Hence we do not consider this factor a disadvantage as long as the teacher knows the type of sound-symbol relations which are appropriate for the dialect.

Our reference to the teacher's knowledge of the appropriate sound-symbol relations brings out another assumption of this alternative, namely, that the reading teacher is thoroughly familiar with the dialect of the children. When Goodman says that the student should be encouraged to read the way he speaks, this assumes that the teacher knows what particular dialect rendering of a given passage can be expected. Otherwise, there is no way of distinguishing legitimate reading problems arising from an incomplete mastery of the sound-symbol relations and reading differences which are the result of dialect interference. For example, if a child reads the word *thought* as *fought,* the teacher must know whether this is simply a problem of sound-symbol relations due to the incomplete mastery of these relations or a legitimate dialect rendering of *th* for the black lower-class child. In this case, the pronunciation cannot be attributed to dialect interference since there is no dialect rule which renders *th* as [f] in word-initial position. But what if the student reads *Ruth* so that it is identical with *roof?* In this case, it may be a legitimate dialect pronunciation and should not be corrected. The type of discernment which might correct the homophony of *thought* and *fought* but not the homophony of *Ruth* and *roof* assumes that the teacher knows the dialect rule which realizes *th* as [f] at the middle or end of a word, but not the beginning. Some teachers may inductively arrive at such types of discernment because of the consistency of certain types of pronunciations from dialect speakers, but if the alternative proposed by Goodman and others is to be adopted on an extensive level, it will require the training of teachers in the structural patterns of the dialect. (An acquaintance with the structural patterns does not, of course, mean that the teacher will be able to speak the dialect.)

Although the above discussion may suggest several disadvantages, it does have one very practical advantage: it can be established much more immediately than some of the other alternatives. For example, it can be adopted while further experimentation with other alternatives which require more drastic curriculum reorganization is carried out. Indeed, the teacher who thoroughly acquaints himself with the description of the dialect features and is convinced of the legitimacy of the dialect as a highly developed language system is in a position to start initiating this alternative. (18)

The Revision of Materials

A seemingly more drastic alternative to the reading problem for speakers of a nonstandard dialect involves the incorporation of new types of materials into the reading curriculum for lower-class black children. Basically, there are two approaches which have been proposed, one which involves the elimination of all features which might be unfamiliar to the nonstandard speaking child and one which involves the writing of new sets of materials which are designed specifically to represent the language and culture which the child brings with him when he enters school.

The Neutralization of Dialect Differences

One method of revising current materials for nonstandard dialect speakers would be to simply eliminate features which might predictably be problematic for the lower-class speaker because these features are not an integral part of his linguistic system. This alternative essentially follows the suggestion of Roger Shuy that grammatical choices in beginning material should not provide extraneous data. Shuy observes:

> In the case of beginning reading materials for nonstandard speakers, the text should help the child by avoiding grammatical forms which are not realized by him in this spoken language (third singular verb inflections, for example). (19)

It should be noted that this alternative would not incorporate any nonstandard features present in the dialect but absent in standard English. (20) For example, the use of *be* to indicate distributive action in a sentence such as *He be here every day* would not be used, since this feature is unique to nonstandard black speech. Accommodation would be made only by excluding features in standard English which do not have isomorphic correspondences in the dialect. It capitalizes on the presumed similarities of large portions of the grammar of these dialects so that the possibility of grammatical interference is eliminated. This alternative would only concentrate on grammatical differences since differences in pronunciation would involve most of the words in the English language. It thus appears that this alternative would involve the neutralization of grammatical differences along with the acceptance of dialect pronunciations of reading materials, as was suggested in one of the previously discussed alternatives.

There are two assumptions which are the basis for this alternative, and it cannot be evaluated apart from these. For one, it assumes that there is a sufficient "common core" between the standard and nonstandard language system which allows for the practical implementation of these suggestions into our reading materials. The validity of this assumption is an empirical question, and on the basis of Labov's research in New York (21) current research in Washington by Fasold, and this author's own research in Detroit, (22) it is certain that there are many similarities between standard English and the variety of nonstandard English spoken by lower-class blacks. The inventory of similarities is certainly greater than the inventory of differences. But the fact remains, there are differences and so we must ask if these might be of the sort which would make it difficult to effectively incorporate this type of change into materials.

To examine this problem more closely, we can take one of the sample inventories of the prominent features of lower-class black dialect, and see what changes would have to be made in order to neutralize the grammatical differences between it and standard English. For example, consider the sample inventory that Shuy delimits, which seems to be a fairly typical type of list.

Written Expression	Linguistic Feature	Oral Expression
1. John's house	possession	John house
2. John runs	3rd sing. pres.	John run
3. ten cents	plurality	ten cent
4. He jumped	past	He jump
5. She is a cook	copula	She a cook
6. He doesn't have any toys	negation	He ain't got no toys He don't have no toys He don't got no toys
7. He asked if I came	past conditional question	He asked did I come
8. Every day when I come he isn't here	negative/be	Every day when I come he don't be here (23)

What would be involved if we were to eliminate the above types of constructions from extant reading materials at the beginning level of reading? For No. 1, possession, it would mean that we could only realize possession via the preposition *of* or the verb *has.* For some items such as *John's hat* or *Bill's bike,* the use of *of* might be stylistically unacceptable even though it might be grammatical (e.g. *the hat of John, the bike of Bill*). Using the construction *John has a hat* or *the hat which John has* every time we wanted to indicate possession might lead us into even more serious stylistic difficulties. It seems that the only way in which one could eliminate such stylistic unacceptability would be to avoid some potential possessive construction. Thus, a sequence of sentences in discourse such as:

John's new bike is blue. Mary's new bike is red.
John's bike is bigger than Mary's.

might be restructured something like:

John has a new blue bike. Mary has a new bike too and it is red. The bike John has is bigger than the one Mary has.

The above type of restructuring might alleviate any potential problem area concerning differences in the use of possessive -s, but when we look at No. 2 on Shuy's list, we find that a problem with the use of third person singular present tense -*s* occurs. The use of *has* in our above sentence is therefore unjustified if we are to hold to our stated principle. In fact, this difference eliminates virtually all stories in the present tense which call for the use of third person singular forms, a rather restricting limitation to be placed on reading materials. Dealing with No. 3, plurals which might not appear in the nonstandard dialect of the child would probably take even more ingenuity if, in fact, there is any way with which this could be dealt. The elimination of structures calling for copulas, as in No. 5, would certainly add a further restriction to growing inventory of structures to be avoided, although one might maintain that copulas can be used as long as the full form (e.g. *He is big*) and not the contracted form (e.g. *He's big*) is used, based on the conclusion that the full form of the copula is an integral part of the dialect whereas the contracted form may not be. (24) Item No. 6 involves the elimination of potential multiple negatives so that sentences such as *He doesn't have any toys* would not be permitted. One might suggest that this may be remedied by using only a negative indefinite (instead of a negativized auxiliary and indefinite) such as *You have no toys* but this is not feasible since the rule which transfers the negativized auxiliary to the indefinite form (e.g. *You don't have any toys* to *You have no toys*) is not an integral part of the dialect. (25) The embedded question in No. 7 could be handled fairly simply by making a direct question out of it, such as *He asked, "can I come?"* instead of *He asked if he could come.* If one wanted to avoid constructions where black dialect might potentially use *be,* certain types of discourses involving habituality would have to be avoided, a stringent limitation if the principle is to be followed faithfully.

The above exercise demonstrates several important points with respect to the accommodation of materials for lower-class blacks. First, it shows that the feasibility of neutralization varies from feature to feature. There are some which can be handled by minor adjustments in current materials; others, however, require the elimination of significant portions of narratives or the cumbersome use of certain circumlocutions if the "avoidance strategy" which is basic to this alternative is to be carried out rigorously. It should be noted that when there are a number of different features which must be avoided in a particular type of passage, the problem of restructuring a narrative with these in mind can become quite difficult. Even if the overall differences between the standard and nonstandard dialect may be significantly less than the similarities, the clustering of differences may make this strategy virtually unusable for particular types of passages.

Material developers would not necessarily have to be as rigorous in their avoidance strategy as we have described above. One might just avoid certain types of grammatical differences while disregarding others. For example, a decision might be made to avoid grammatical differences which involve lexical changes, while disregarding those which involve affixial forms. This would mean that the use of embedded questions would be avoided since they involve a change of word order and the use of "question" *if* or *whether*. But the avoidance of constructions involving the third person singular present tense forms, certain plurals, or possessives would not be maintained since these only involve the addition of a suffixial -*s* in standard English. This procedure would reduce some of the problems caused by trying to eliminate frequently occurring inflectional forms.

There is one further aspect of the alternative discussed here which should be explicated since it may not be obvious from the presentation thus far, namely, the implicit assumption that a "dialect-free" basal reader is a legitimate end-product of this method. Venezky observes:

> Reading materials for beginning reading should, in content, vocabulary, and syntax, be as dialect free (and culture free) as possible. Given the inanity of present day materials, this should not be overly difficult to achieve. (26)

Although Venezky assumes the production of dialect-free materials is a reasonable and achievable goal, the pervasiveness of dialect patterns may be considerably more extensive than he anticipates. Venezky does not define what he means by *dialect-free*, but he presumably is referring to the fact that features which might differentiate dialects can be eliminated. That is, readers can be made "neutral" with respect to dialect. This term should not be confused with *dialect-fair*, which does not refer to neutrality, but the adaptation of materials so that they are not biased against speakers of a given dialect. As Venezky himself admits, these terms are, in reality, reflections of the more inclusive concepts, *culture-free* and *culture-fair*. The former is highly suspicious as an anthropologically valid concept because of the all-pervasive effect of cultural patterns of behavior (both linguistic and non-linguistic), whereas the latter is an essential tenet of cultural relativism. With this in mind, is the effort to accommodate different dialects and cultures in terms of one set of materials a naive attempt to achieve an unreal goal? At any rate, one must take these notions with more seriousness than Venezky suggests.

Although several apparent disadvantages of this alternative have been described, this discussion must not be concluded before pointing out some potential advantages. For one, a modification of this method may eliminate some of the most salient features of standard English which might be unfamiliar to the lower-class black child who comes to the schoolroom. Also, it would not incorporate socially stigmatized features of language, eliminating the controversy which inevitably surrounds the codification of nonstandard patterns in reading materials. The types of changes which this alternative would require in materials could, in fact, be incorporated without necessarily being noticed by teachers who are using such materials.

Dialect Readers

The final alternative dealing with linguistic aspects of the reading problem among lower-class blacks involves the use of readers which are written in the vernacular of the children. That is, every effort is made in the beginning materials to represent the cultural and linguistic content which is indigenous to the child. As a brief illustration of how such materials might differ from the conventional materials, Wolfram and Fasold have compared two versions of the same passage, one in standard English and one in the dialect of the children.

Standard English Version

"Look down here," said Suzy.
"I can see a girl in here.
That girl looks like me.
Come here and look, David.
Can you see that girl?" . . .

Black English

Susan say, "hey you-all, look down here!"
"I can see a girl in here.
The girl, she look like me.
Come here and look, David!
Could you see the girl?" . . . (27)

The second passage is a deliberate attempt to incorporate the features of the children's dialect into the basal readers. The absence of third person singular -s (e.g. *Susan say, she look*), pronominal apposition (e.g. *That girl, she. . .*), *could* for *can* and *you-all* are direct efforts to accurately represent the indigenous dialect of the lower-class black child.

It should be noted that although dialect-specific grammatical features have been incorporated, the conventional orthographical system of English has been retained. The retention of conventional English orthography has been proposed for two reasons. As we mentioned earlier, the conventional spelling does adequately represent the phonological units of the dialect at a more abstract level, so that, for example, there is formal justification for representing word-final [f] in *toof* as *tooth*. (28) From a sociological standpoint, extra-linguistic matters such as other printed material and official education also make this alternative most reasonable. For these reasons, most producers of dialect readers employ the conventional orthography. William Stewart (29) however, would make one major compromise in the direction of a literary-dialect orthography, namely, the indication, by an apostrophe, of those cases in which a word must take a prefix in order to become like its standard English equivalent. This generally involves unstressed initial syllables, such as *'cause* for *because, 'round* for *around,* and *'posed to* for *supposed to.* This adaptation is based on the fact that "Negro-dialect speakers do not always know that a prefix is 'missing' from their version of a particular word." (30)

Although it has sometimes been misunderstood by opponents of this alternative, the proposal of dialect readers does not advocate an eventual dualist reading system in American society. It is only proposed as an initial step in the adequate acquisition of reading skills. Once reading fluency has been attained in the dialect readers and the child is sufficiently confident in his ability to read, a transition from dialect to standard English readers is made. Stewart (1969) has illustrated the several stages of transition. (See pages 282-283 in this book.)

The alternative which advocates the use of dialect readers seems to be based on three assumptions: 1) that there is sufficient mismatch between the child's system and standard English textbook to warrant distinct materials, 2) the psychological benefits from reading success will be stronger in the dialect than it might be if standard English materials were used, and 3) the success of vernacular teaching in bilingual situations recommends a similar principle for bidialectal situations. Baratz maintains:

> Because of the mismatch between the child's system and that of the standard English textbook, because of the psychological consequences of denying the existence and legitimacy of the child's linguistic system, and in the light of the success of vernacular teaching around the world, it appears imperative that we teach the inner-city Negro child to read using his own language as the basis for the initial readers. (31)

In order to evaluate the potential success of such an alternative, each of these assumptions must be discussed in more detail.

From the standpoint of the reading process, one of the most crucial questions is the potential mismatch between the vernacular which the lower-class black child brings to the classroom and the standard English represented in the reading materials. To begin with, we must qualify the assertion that the lower-class black child reads a dialect which is not his own and the middle-class child simply reads a written version of the way he speaks. This argument has, in fact, often been used as an important claim for the legitimacy of dialect readers, as Wolfram and Fasold have done:

> When the child who speaks Black English is required to learn to read using Standard English materials, he is given two tasks at once: learning to read and learning a new dialect. The Standard English speaking child, by contrast, is only required to learn to read. (32)

If we look at extant materials written for middle-class children we find that this assumption must be qualified, for current materials do not always reflect the way middle-class children speak. Two reasons for this lack of isomorphism must be cited. Some of the divergence can simply be attributed to the stylistic failures of writers and editors. According to Shuy (to appear), "sometimes this dim vision is caused by the [i.e. the writers'] failure to modernize or, in this case their failure to listen to the way kids talk." Thus, for example, the use of the verb *see* in the imperative as in *See the dog* is inappropriate because in the imperative, the verb *see* is generally realized by *look at*. More consistently in error is the way pronominal reference is used in beginning readers. For example, a primer which relates a narrative without recognizing the systematic use of anaphoric reference in English violates the grammatical rules of English governing the use of pronouns on a discourse level (e.g. *Jane and Dick have a dog. Jane and Dick like the dog*). Presumably, these types of divergences can and should be remedied.

But there is also another source of mismatch between oral language and written text, and these may be due to the fact that these styles of language have different conventional forms. Rose-Marie Weber notes:

> But as we all know, the texts for beginning readers, limited as they are to a small range of vocabulary, short, short sentences, and short texts, hardly reflect the complexity of any child's spoken language. There are variations in first grade materials, of course, the *Oh, look* style differing from the *Nan can fan Dan* style in a significant aspect of their rationale. Yet, in spite of the limitations, first grade written English includes sentence types that do not ordinarily appear in speech, such as *Faster and faster went the train* and *Out ran the mouse.* (33)

Because of this observation, Weber submits:

> All in all, the detailed analysis of the differences between NNE [Negro Nonstandard English] and the standard of six-year-olds with respect to gram-

mar and what we hastily call style may fade in comparison to the differences between spoken language and the necessarily reduced language of material prepared for beginners. Every child who faces reading for the first time faces a new variety of his language. It is not at all clear that speakers of NNE are at much greater odds with their primers than are their white age mates. (34)

Although we may acknowledge that all differences between spoken and written language cannot be and should not necessarily be eliminated for the middle-class child, we must conclude that the lower-class black child can be expected to have a considerably greater divergence than the white child. And, if we follow the hypothesis of Goodman, "the more divergence there is between the dialect of the learner and the dialect of learning, the more difficult will be the task of learning to read." (35) At this point, how much more difficult the task will be because of the divergence cannot be assessed completely, but it seems reasonable to assume that it is more difficult until empirical evidence determines otherwise.

Before leaving our discussion of oral and written language mismatch, we must submit a word of caution about the style of dialect readers. To what extent should the beginning materials reflect the "pure nonstandard dialect" as opposed to the way in which children actually speak? In this regard, it is instructive to compare two passages that Wolfram and Fasold include in their illustrative reading materials, one which was simply transcribed from a dialogue as it was actually recorded and one which attempted to put a passage into "pure" dialect. (36) In the former case, there is considerable variation between forms, and as Labov (37) has observed, some of this variation cannot simply be dismissed as importation from a superimposed dialect; rather, it is an inherent part of the indigenous dialect. Some of the beginning dialect materials which start with pure dialect may, in effect, be creating a new type of mismatch between written and spoken language. That is, they have made the dialect to be more divergent from standard English in written form than it actually is in spoken form. For example, the dialect reader entitled "I Be Scared," by Olga Davis, Mildred Gladney, and Lloyd Leaverton (38) overuses the habitual use of *be* in terms of the types of constructions it occurs in and the relative frequency with which it occurs. Mismatch of this type must be minimized just as much as we minimize the difference between the mismatch of oral and written language for middle-class children learning to read.

The next assumption we must consider deals with the psychological reinforcement that such an approach might give to the child. Baratz observes that one of the prime advantages of this program is "the powerful ego-supports of giving credence to the child's language system and therefore to himself, and giving him the opportunity to experience success in school." (39)

Ideally, we must concur that a program involving language familiar to the child (and, of course, an appropriate cultural setting which must be its concomitant) will potentially hold a great opportunity for success. But if we look more closely at current attitudes toward reading materials as expressed by the community leaders and parents, we are faced with a socio-psychological fact which may force us to question whether we can predict psychological advantages for this program.

For a number of reasons, the notion of giving children nonstandard reading materials has provoked considerable controversy in communities for whom these materials have been intended. In fact, one recent attempt to experiment (one should note that this was only experimental, not curriculum revision) with dialect primers was cancelled before it ever had an opportunity to be tried. Commenting on the reasons for this cancellation, columnist William Raspberry, of the *Washington Post,* observed:

> Objections were made on a number of counts: Some found the text and illustrations 'uninspiring' or downright offensive; others concluded that white people were trying to use innocent black children for their dubious experiments . . . But most of the parents, knowing that society equates facility in standard English with intelligence, do not want to risk confirming their children in 'undesirable' speech patterns—a risk that advocates insist is virtually nonexistent. (40)

At the heart of the rejection of dialect materials by the community (i.e. educators in lower-class black schools, parents, and community leaders) seem to be several attitudes toward nonstandard dialects as a medium of education. The codification of a nonstandard language system may be viewed as a threat to the social mobility of blacks in our society. For those who are attempting to attain middle-class status (either within the black community itself or the broader society) it may be seen as a program which implicitly attempts to "keep the black man where he is." For middle-class leaders in the black community, some of the negative reactions may be fostered by embarrassment about the dialect or their own linguistic insecurity. Or, it may be viewed as a new type of paternalism toward the black community. . . .

One fact which seems basic to the negative reactions toward the use of dialect in reading is the assumption that different materials for different social or ethnic groups implies the inherent incapability of these groups to learn using the traditional methods (apparently a by-product of the American "melting pot" myth). Difference is interpreted to mean inferiority. . . .

Whether the reasons for rejecting dialect readers are real or imagined, the fact remains that the socio-political controversy over such a program and the community's negative reactions to it may seriously impede what otherwise might be an "ego-supportive" activity. The attitudes of teachers, parents, and community leaders projected to children may be sufficiently strong to affect the child's motivation.

Finally, it is assumed on the basis of vernacular learning throughout the world, that such a program can be expected to be successful. In fact, the UNESCO report on the use of vernacular languages in education specifically recommended that every pupil should begin formal education in his mother tongue. (41) For studies which compare beginning reading in the mother tongue vis-à-vis the national language, the most predominant conclusion is that "the youngsters of linguistic minorities learn to read with greater comprehension in the national language when they first learn to read in their mother tongue than when they receive all their reading instruction in the national language." (42)

Although this conclusion may be predominant, there are still scholars who have reservations about vernacular reading for one reason or another. W. E. Bull, (43) for example, cites the vast expense (both in terms of financial considerations and curricula development) that this method may involve. Venezky (44) cites many extralinguistic factors which bias experiments comparing vernacular and national language reading. He thus concludes that "the native literacy approach, although possessing obvious cultural advantages over the standard language approach, has yet to be proven scholastically superior." (45)

A more relevant consideration in terms of the vernacular reading situation for lower-class black children is the validity of using this procedure for different dialects as well as languages. One study by Tore Österberg (46) does appear to support the contention of Stewart (47) and Baratz (48) that this alternative may be just as valid for different dialects as well as different languages. Other things being equal, it would be expected that the reported success of teaching reading initially in the vernacular in other situations would recommend its usage for lower-class black children. But the fact that the socio-psychological factor we have discussed earlier may be sufficient to impede the acquisition of reading skills cannot be ignored. It should be noted in this regard, however, that in a number of bilingual situations where reading was initially taught in the vernacular, attitudes toward the indigenous language vis-à-vis the national language are quite comparable to the attitudes toward the nonstandard dialect of black children. That is, the vernacular is socially stigmatized both by the dominant class and those who actually use the stigmatized forms. Despite these attitudes, vernacular reading materials have been reported to be successful as a bridge to literacy in the national language.

Conclusion

It should be apparent from the above discussion that there is no magical potion for the reading ills of our ghetto schools. Whereas some of the alternatives seem to have more validity than others in terms of linguistic differences between standard English and lower-class black dialect, socio-cultural or psychological factors may seriously impede the implementation of these alternatives. On the other hand, alternatives which do not face these socio-cultural obstacles may not adequately deal with the linguistic differences.

But one should not mistake the attempt to honestly describe the problem areas of each alternative with the pessimistic conclusion that all is vanity. There are steps that can be taken to remedy some of the sources for reading problems immediately and there are recommendations for curriculum overhaul which definitely deserve experimentation.

A first step can be the acceptance of dialect renderings of conventional reading materials. This may, at least, eliminate some of the child's reading problems which arise from the failure to differentiate authentic reading problems and legitimate dialect differences. The advantage of such an initial step lies in the fact that it can be implemented immediately; any reading teacher familiar with the phonological and grammatical structure of the dialect can employ such a procedure. But because the differences between the dialect and reading materials are considerably greater for the lower-class black child than his middle-class counterpart, this can only be suggested as an immediate stop-gap measure.

The magnitude of the reading problem suggests that experiments must be made with alternatives which may involve the potential changing of materials and curricula. For one, an experiment should be done on the effects of neutralizing potential problem areas for the nonstandard speaking child in beginning materials. Although complete neutralization may be impossible, one could make some modifications based on a criterion such as the avoidance of grammatical differences involving changes in order or "free" morphemes but not "bound" morphemes such as certain suffixial forms.

It also seems appropriate to recommend experimentation with dialect readers. It is not necessary to institute an extended program to incorporate dialect readers into all lower-class black schools, a project which might be a 5–10 year task—only experimentation with such materials so we can find out what potential they might hold for our reading programs for lower-class blacks. Mere experimentation with such materials, however, is controversial given the current socio-political feelings of the community. But what must be done is to convince the community, including administrators, community leaders, teachers, and parents, that such an alternative may hold promise for the acquisition of reading skills and to deny its experimentation may be to deny the child what should rightfully be his—the ability to read.

References

1. R. W. Fasold and W. A. Wolfram, "Some Linguistic Features of Negro Dialect," in *Teaching Standard English in the Inner City;* eds. Ralph W. Fasold and Roger W. Shuy (Washington, D.C.: Center for Applied Linguistics, 1970), pp. 41–86. [In Chapter Three of this book].
2. Carl Bereiter, and Siegfried Engelmann, *Teaching Disadvantaged Children in Preschool* (Englewood Cliffs, N.J.: Prentice-Hall, 1966).
3. *Ibid.,* p. 274.
4. R. L. Venezky, "Nonstandard Language and Reading," *Elementary English,* 47, (1970), p. 342.
5. R. W. Fasold, "Isn't English the First Language Too?" (Milwaukee, Wis.: NCTE Annual Conference, 1968), p. 7.
6. Roger D. Abrahams, *The Advantages of Black English* (Jacksonville, Fla.: Southern Conference of Language Learning, 1970), p. 16 [in Chapter Two of this book].
7. Venezky, "Nonstandard Language and Reading."
8. Thomas Kochman, "Social Factors in the Consideration of Teaching Standard English," in *Linguistic-Cultural Differences and American Education,* eds. A. C. Aarons, Barbara Y. Gordon, and W. A. Stewart, Special Anthology Issue (The Florida FL Reporter: 1969), p. 87 [in Chapter Five of this book].
9. *Ibid.*
10. William Labov, "Stages in the Acquisition of Standard English," in *Social Dialects and Language Learning,* ed. R. W. Shuy (Champaign, Ill.: National Council of Teachers of English, 1964), p. 91.
11. Irwin Feigenbaum, "Using Foreign Language Methodology to Teach Standard English: Evaluation and Adaptation," in *Linguistic-Cultural Differences and American Education,* Special Anthology Issue, eds. A. C. Aarons, Barbara Y. Gordon, and W. A. Stewart (The Flordia FL Reporter: 1969), p. 118.
12. Kenneth S. Goodman, "Dialect Barriers to Reading Comprehension," *Elementary English,* 42, (Dec. 1965), pp. 853–60. Reprinted in *Teaching Black Children to Read,* eds. Joan C. Baratz and Roger W. Shuy (Washington: Center for Applied Linguistics, 1969), p. 27 [in Chapter Six of this book].
13. H. Wolff, "Intelligibility and Inter-Ethnic Attitudes," *Anthropological Linguistics,* 1, 3 (1959), pp. 34–41.
14. William Labov and Paul Cohen, "Systematic Relations of Standard and Non-Standard Rules in the Grammar of Negro Speakers," *Project Literacy Report No. 8* (Ithaca, N.Y.: Cornell University, 1967) [in Chapter Three of this book].
15. Joan C. Baratz, "Teaching Reading in an Urban Negro School System," in *Teaching Black Children to Read,* pp. 92–116.
16. Walter A. Wolfram and Ralph W. Fasold, "Toward Reading Materials for Speakers of Black English: Three Linguistically Appropriate Passages," in *Teaching Black Children to Read,* p. 141.
17. R. W. Fasold, "Orthography in Reading Materials for Black English Speaking Children," in *Teaching Black Children to Read,* pp. 68–91.
18. For a non-technical description of the predominant features of the dialect, see Fasold and Wolfram, "Some Linguistic Features of Negro Dialect." [In Chapter Three of this book.]

19. R. W. Shuy, "A Linguistic Background for Developing Beginning Reading Materials for Black Children," in *Teaching Black Children to Read,* p. 125.
20. In the article by Shuy in which this procedure is suggested, this is only one of several types of changes which Shuy recommends for materials which are to be used by black dialect speakers.
21. William Labov and Paul Cohen, Clarence Robins and John Lewis, "A Study of the Non-Standard English of Negro and Puerto Rican Speakers in New York City," final report, Cooperative Research Project No. 3288 (Washington, D.C.: Office of Education, 1968).
22. W. A. Wolfram, *A Sociolinguistic Description of Detroit Negro Speech* (Washington, D.C.: Center for Applied Linguistics, 1969).
23. R. W. Shuy, "A Linguistic Background for Developing Beginning Reading Materials for Black Children," in *Teaching Black Children to Read,* p. 128.
24. Fasold and Wolfram, "Some Linguistic Features of Negro Dialect," pp. 67–69 [in Chapter Three of this book].
25. *Ibid.,* p. 72.
26. Venezky, "Nonstandard Language and Reading."
27. Wolfram and Fasold, "Toward Reading Materials for Speakers of Black English," p. 147.
28. Fasold, "Orthography in Reading Materials for Black English Speaking Children," pp. 68–91.
29. W. A. Stewart, "Negro Dialect in the Teaching of Reading," in *Teaching Black Children to Read,* p. 195 [in Chapter Six of this book].
30. *Ibid.*
31. Baratz, "Teaching Reading in an Urban Negro School System," p. 113.
32. Wolfram and Fasold, "Toward Reading Materials for Speakers of Black English," p. 43.
33. Rose-Marie Weber, "Some Reservations on the Significance of Dialect in the Acquisition of Reading," *The Reading Specialist,* 7 (1969), p. 38.
34. *Ibid.*
35. Goodman, "Dialect Barriers to Reading Comprehension," p. 14 [in Chapter Six of this book].
36. Compare "Dumb Boy" and "See a Girl" in Wolfram and Fasold, "Toward Reading Materials for Speakers of Black English," p. 145 ff.
37. W. Labov, "Contraction, Deletion, and Inherent Variation of the English Copula," *Language,* 45 (1969), pp. 715–62.
38. Olga Davis, Mildred Gladney and Lloyd Leaverton, *Psycholinguistics Reading Series,* (Chicago: Board of Education, 1968).
39. Baratz, "Teaching Reading in an Urban Negro School System," p. 114.
40. *Washington Post* (March 4, 1970), p. C1.
41. UNESCO, *The Use of Vernacular Languages in Education,* Monographs on Fundamental Education, 8 (Paris: UNESCO, 1953).
42. Nancy Modiano, "National or Mother Language in Beginning Reading: A Comparative Study," mimeographed (1968), p. 9.
43. W. E. Bull, "Review of: The Use of Vernacular Languages in Education," (Paris: UNESCO, 1953), IJAL, 21 (1953), pp. 288–94.
44. Venezky, "Nonstandard Language and Reading," *Elementary English,* 47 (1970), pp. 334–45.
45. Venezky, "Nonstandard Language and Reading," p. 338.
46. Tore Österburg, *Bilingualism and the First School Language, An Educational Problem Illustrated by Results From a Swedish Dialect Area* (Umean, Sweden: Västerbottens Trycheri AB, 1961).
47. Stewart, "Negro Dialect in the Teaching of Reading," pp. 156–219 [in Chapter Six of this book].
48. Baratz, "Teaching Reading in an Urban Negro School System," pp. 92–116.

A Note on the Relation of Reading Failure to Peer-Group Status in Urban Ghettos

William Labov and Clarence Robins

In this important article, William Labov and Clarence Robins suggest that conflict between black adolescents' street culture and school culture is the major factor in the reading failure of those Black English speaking boys. The authors studied at least two major street groups (the "Cobras" and "Jets") in Harlem and found that the groups have a value system which conforms to lower class patterns but not to school values. The system is discussed in detail. The group members see school as hostile and irrelevant to their lives. Success in school, which includes reading achievement, is irrelevant to a boy's prestige and position in the gang. The authors then describe how group membership is determined. After establishing what boys are firmly in the group, they present their findings about the boys' reading ability. No one read above grade level, and only one group member read on grade level. Labov and Robins also found that no group member could read at more than fifth grade level no matter what his age. So eighth graders were consistently reading at grade five levels or below. To do something about this pattern of failure established in boys who were firmly part of the street culture, the authors proposed that a young black male be employed in the schools to act as "cultural intermediary" between those in the school culture and those in the street culture. Otherwise the reading failure pattern could well continue.

For the past several years, we have been studying certain conflicts between the vernacular of the urban ghettos and schoolroom English, especially in relation to reading failure. (1) We work primarily with peer-groups of Negro boys within the culture of the street, since we believe that the major controls upon language are exerted by these groups rather than the school or the home. Our research has recently revealed a sharp and striking relationship between participation in this street culture and reading failure. The pattern is so clear and plainly so important in understanding the

From "A Note on the Relation of Reading Failure to Peer-Group Status in Urban Ghettos" by William Labov and Clarence Robins. *Teachers College Record*, Vol. 70 (1969) No. 5, pp. 395–405. © 1969 by *Teachers College Record*. Reprinted by permission of the publisher and of William Labov and Clarence Robins.

educational problems of ghetto areas, that we are sending this brief note to all those who have shown interest in our progress reports.

The Populations Concerned

In the summer of 1965, we interviewed a sample of 75 Negro boys, age 10 to 12 years, in a geographically random sample of "Vacation Day Camps" in Harlem. Boys had to be enrolled by their parents in these recreational programs, held in schoolyards and playgrounds, so that there was a bias of selection for children from intact families with support for educational goals. Nevertheless, we found that the majority of these 10–12 year olds had serious difficulty in reading aloud such second- and third-grade sentences as

Now I read and write better than Alfred does.
When I passed by, I read the sign.

In August of 1965, we turned to the study of groups of boys in their natural associations on the streets of South Central Harlem. Our normal method of work was to interview a few individuals, locate their peer group and become acquainted with it; we then studied the language of the peer group in spontaneous interaction, and recorded the remaining individuals in face-to-face interviews. We used this approach first in studying two pre-adolescent groups in a low-income project, the "Thunderbirds" and the "Aces," against the general population of the project. We then began the study of the major adolescent groups that dominated the tenement areas from 110th Street to 118th Street between Sixth and Eighth Avenues. One of our staff members, Mr. John Lewis, acted as a participant-observer in the area. With his help, we followed two major adolescent groups, each composed of many subgroups, for two years. These groups were known as the "Cobras" and the "Jets." (2)

Our knowledge of the social structure, history, activities, and value systems of these groups is an essential aspect of the finding to be presented in this note. We traced the history of group relations and explored the value systems through individual face-to-face interviews, meetings with small groups of two or three close friends, and group sessions with six to twelve boys. In all these sessions, involving the most excited physical and verbal interaction, each person's statements and ideas were recorded on a separate track from a microphone several inches away from his mouth. We also studied group behavior in various field trips with the boys, and recorded their interaction en route. Most importantly, our participant-observer saw the boys every day on the streets, and met with them in their hang-outs and our "club-house." He was present at several moments of crisis when fighting was about to break out between the two major groups.

We also interviewed a number of isolated individuals in the same tenement areas, who were definitely not members of these groups, but who often knew about them. We are able then to assert that we reached all the major "named" groups in the area, although we did not have a representative sample of all adolescent boys. In the same areas we completed a stratified random sample of 100 adults, but only in the low-income projects did we relate our groups quantitatively to the total population. (3)

The Street Groups

The larger associations which bear the names "Jets" or "Cobras" are known to the boys as "clubs." They are not to be confused with the groups which are organized within recreation centers by adults, which are also called "clubs" and sometimes overlap in membership. The groups we studied are initiated by the boys themselves, and are disapproved of by the adults in the neighborhood. (4)

The structure and value systems of these groups are partly inherited from the period of gang violence of the 1940's and 1950's. The frequency of group fighting, however, is comparatively low. These are not "gangs" in the sense of groups which frequently fight as a unit. Nevertheless, a major source of prestige for the leaders is skill in fighting, and individual fights are very common. The inter-group conflicts which do occur are the most important sources of group cohesion; they become a fixed part of the mythology and ideology of the group, and the obligation to support one's fellow members in a group fight is strongly felt by many members.

The general value systems of these groups conform to the lower class value pattern which has been described by Walter B. Miller. (5) The focal concerns of the groups are *toughness, smartness, trouble, excitement, autonomy,* and *fate.* Intelligence or smartness is used and valued as a means of manipulating others, rather than a means of obtaining information or solving abstract problems. The specific values of the Negro nationalist movement are reflected in some groups more than others. The members of the "Cobras," within the period that we worked with them, moved from a moderately nationalist position to deep involvement with the militant Muslim religion and its complex ideology. (6) This ideology involved the members in a strong interest in learning and abstract knowledge; but the general value systems of all the groups were such that school learning was seen as hostile, distant, and essentially irrelevant.

The groups have a formal structure which may include four officers: president, vice-president, prime minister and war-lord. Junior organizations are often formed by the appointment of a younger brother of an officer to a leading position among the 10-to-13 year olds. However, this formal structure can be misleading. The day-to-day activities of the boys (7) are in smaller, informal hang-out groups, determined by geography and age; an individual's association with the larger group is often a matter of formal definition of his identity more than anything else. (8) Yet the ultimate sanction of the larger group and its fighting role is often referred to.

Sources of prestige within the group are physical size, toughness, courage and skill in fighting; skill with language in ritual insults, verbal routines with girls, singing, jokes and story-telling; knowledge of nationalist lore; skill and boldness in stealing; experience in reform schools; and connections with family members or others which provide reputation, money, hang-outs, marijuana, or other material goods. Success in school is irrelevant to prestige within the group, and reading is rarely if ever used outside of school. (9)

Group Membership

Full participation in the group consists of *endorsement* of this set of values, and *acceptance* of a set of personal obligations to others within the same environment and value system. The criterion of formal membership ("you are a Jet" or "you are not a Jet") is often disputed. A few individuals want to be members and are rejected; others could easily be members but do not care to. Full membership, as we define it, means that the individual is thoroughly involved with the values and activities of the group, and is defined as a member both by himself and by others. If some but not all of these criteria are fulfilled, we term the individual a "marginal member." The clearest evidence for full membership as against marginal status is provided by the symmetrical and asymmetrical relations in a sociometric diagram. (10) If an individual on the outskirts of the group wants to be a member, yet is prevented by the influence of other environments (family, school) and other value systems, he is classed with other non-members. In each area there are "social groups" which are strongly influenced by adult organizations: we do not include membership in such groups in the category of membership which we are studying.

It has been shown in many similar situations that group membership is a function of age. (11) Boys 8-to-9 years old are definitely outsiders for the groups we are studying, and they have only a vague knowledge of group activities. Membership is strongest in the 13-to-15 year old range, and falls off rapidly in the later teens. A few 18-or-19 year old boys act as seniors, especially if younger brothers are serving as officers, but as a rule older boys drift into different activities.

It is difficult to estimate the percentage of boys who are full participants in the street culture. However, in the one 13-story low income project which we studied intensively, (12) there were 22 boys 10-to-12 years old. Their relationships to the major peer group, the "Thunderbirds," were as follows:

members	marginal members	non-members
12	3	7

Our general experience would indicate that 50 to 60 per cent of the boys in the age range 10-to-16 are full participants in the street culture we are studying here.

Reading Records

In all of our individual interviews, we used a number of special reading tests developed to yield specific information on the vernacular phonology and grammar. (13) However, the most direct evidence for reading performance in schools is obtained from the Metropolitan Achievement Test given every year in the New York City schools. With the help of the New York City Board of Education, we were able to study recently the academic records of 75 pre-adolescent and adolescent boys with whom we had worked in the years 1965 to 1967. The substance of this report is the correlation between the Metropolitan Achievement Reading Test and group membership.

Figure 6 shows the correlation between grade level and reading achievement for 32 boys we interviewed in the 110th–120th Street area who are not members of the street culture, or whose group status is unknown (from the Vacation Day Camp series). The horizontal axis is grade level at the time of the test; the vertical axis the Metropolitan Achievement Test score. Each individual's score and grade are indicated by the location of an *x*. The diagonal lines group together those who are reading on grade level (0), one to three years above grade level (+3 — +1), or one to six years behind grade level (−1 — −6). As one would expect, there are a good many boys who are two years behind grade, which is average in New York City, but there are also quite a few on grade and some ahead of grade level. Eleven of the 32 boys are on grade or above. The general direction of the pattern is upward, indicating that learning is taking place.

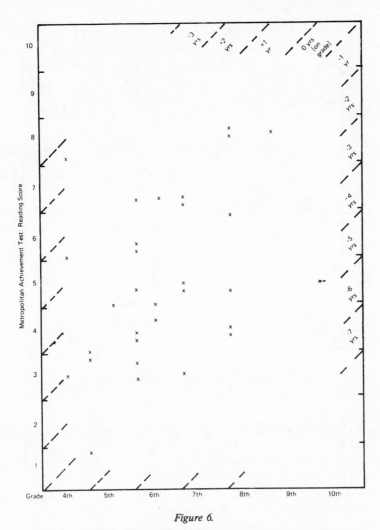

Figure 6.

Grade and Reading Achievement for 32 Non-Members of Street Groups in South Central Harlem

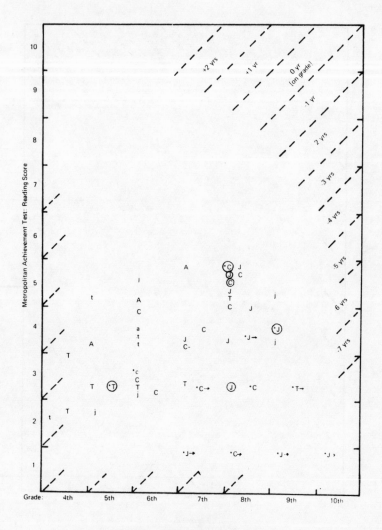

T,t = "Thunderbirds"
A,a = "Aces"
C,c = "Cobras"
J,j = "Jets"
other symbols: see text

Figure 7.

Grade and Reading Achievement for 43 Members of Street Groups in South Central Harlem

Figure 7 shows the same relationships for 43 boys who are members or marginal members of street groups in South Central Harlem. Each individual is represented by a letter symbolizing the group of which he is a member or to which he is most closely related. Upper case letters are full members, and lower case marginal members. The over-all pattern is entirely different from Figure 6: no one is reading above grade, only one boy reading on grade, and the great majority are three or more years behind. Moreover, there are *no* boys who are reading above the fifth grade level, no matter what grade they are in. At each grade, the reading achievement for these boys forms a lower, more compact group than for the same grade in Figure 6. The close concentration of boys in the eighth grade below the fifth grade level shows a limitation on achievement which is quite striking. On the whole, Figure 7 shows very little learning as compared to Figure 6. (14)

The lower achievement of group members does not indicate over-all deficiency in verbal skills. Many of these boys are proficient at a wide range of verbal skills appropriate for group activity: the verbal leaders are indicated by circles in Figure 7. While several are clustered near the highest point of achievement, there are other verbal leaders near the bottom of the diagram.

These findings are merely preliminary to our main body of correlations: we will shortly be able to provide more detailed data on a larger sample. There are a total of 170 boys whose reading abilities and language scores have been studied, and we will be able to correlate reading skill with many other factors besides membership in the street culture. However, the patterns revealed by Figures 6 and 7 are so striking that we thought all those interested in the problem should be aware of them as soon as possible.

What Is to Be Done?

The over-all view given by Figure 7 strongly reinforces our view that the major problem responsible for reading failure is a cultural conflict. The school environment and school values are plainly not influencing the boys firmly grounded in street culture. The group which does show learning contains a large percentage of boys who do not fit in with street culture— who reject it or are rejected by it. For the majority, Figure 7 confirms indirect evidence that teachers in the city schools have little ability to reward or punish members of the street culture, or to motivate learning by any means.

The usual statistics on reading achievement in urban ghettos are alarming, but they do not reveal the full extent of reading failure. Research inside the schools cannot discriminate membership in the street culture from non-membership, and educators are therefore not aware of the full extent of the cultural barrier between them and their students.

It should be understood that the educational goals of the adult Negro community are the same as that of our society as a whole. Our subjective evaluation tests, for example, show that adults in Harlem are almost unanimous in their norms of correct speech and the goals for language teaching in school. Many of the members of the street culture gradually break away and acquire these adult norms in their twenties. However, these norms are of little value for those who do not have the skills to put them into effect.

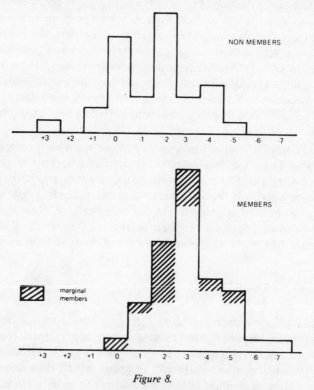

Figure 8.

Distribution of Non-Members, Marginal Members and Members of Street Culture by Years Behind Grade

The reading failure that we have documented here is typical of other performance on the academic records. The pattern of failure is so widespread in many urban areas, that one cannot hold responsible any one system, school or teacher. The majority of these boys have not learned to read well enough to use reading as a tool for further learning. For many of them, there is no realistic possibility of graduating from high school and acquiring the skills needed for the job market. In this particular note we are dealing only with the formal aspect of educational failure. In later publications, we will attempt to document the pessimism and despair with which these adolescents view their immediate future.

The absolute ceiling of Figure 7 is of course an artifact of the limited sample. We know from our own tests that there are group members who read very well, whose school records are not presently available. But even these rare individuals view the educational system with a profound cynicism. The majority of those who learn from the system are located in Figure 6.

We do not believe that the present college-educated teaching staff, Negro or white, has the specific knowledge of the street culture to solve this problem alone. Negro teachers raised in ghetto areas are not members of the *current* street culture. With a few rare exceptions, we find that success in education removes the individual from his culture so effectively that his knowledge of it becomes quite marginal. The specific knowledge of the street culture which is needed is only available to those who are in constant interaction with the peer groups on the streets. Part of the reason is that the value system, though quite general, is intensely *local* in focus. The factors that control language behavior are often local and immediate: what happened last year, last month, or yesterday to that particular sub-group is the best stimulus for evoking spontaneous speech. And the general configurations of the culture change rapidly even though the value system remains intact: a teacher raised in Harlem in the 1950's, returning to the streets today, would find it difficult to understand how and why gang fighting is no longer in style.

We hope to elaborate on these problems of communication in later publications. Here we would like to indicate briefly the form of one proposal we believe will be effective in solving the problem of Figure 7.

We propose that a cultural intermediary be introduced into the classroom in the person of a young Negro man, (15) 16-to-25 years old, with high school level reading skills, but not a college graduate. We propose the creation of a special license to allow this young man to carry out the following functions:

1) to acquaint the teacher with the specific interests of members of the class and help design reading materials centering on these interests.

2) to provide effective rewards and punishments that will motivate members of street culture for whom normal school sanctions are irrelevant.

3) to lead group discussion on topics of immediate concern to members of the class.

4) to lead boys in sports and other recreational activities in school time.

5) to maintain contact with boys outside of school, on the streets, and help organize extra-curricular activities.

We are well aware of the difficulties that any school system will have in absorbing such outside elements. The situation in most ghetto schools is plainly desperate enough so that many educators will be willing to endorse a proposal that may create such difficulties. We suggest that summer training schools be held for such special license teachers, in which regular teachers will participate, to develop jointly techniques for cross-cultural cooperation. At such training schools, it will also be possible to provide regular teachers and special license teachers with specific linguistic data of the type generated by our principal direction of research.

References

1. Data in this research note is the product of Cooperative Research Project 3288, "A Study of the Non-standard English of Negro and Puerto Rican Speakers in New York City," under OE–6–10–059. Preliminary linguistic findings of this research are published in "Some Sources of Reading Problems for Negro Speakers of Non-Standard English," in *New Directions in Elementary English*, ed. A. Frazier (Champaign, Ill.: N.C.T.E., 1967), pp. 140–167, and available in "Some Suggestions for Teaching Standard English to Speakers of Non-Standard Urban Dialects" [in Chapter Five of this book].
2. The names "Cobras" and "Jets" are here used as cover symbols for a complex of formal groups which changes over time. The "Cobras," in particular, was originally a group formed by mergers of several groups which in turn underwent mergers with other groups under successive changes in [Black] nationalist orientation.
3. See [p. 316] for relative sizes of street groups and isolated population in one project.
4. The "Thunderbirds" are a partial exception here, since the club was formed in a recreation center (and was successively re-formed with different names); however, the identity of the group was not confined to the center, and it contained members who had been banned from the center.
5. "Lower Class Culture as a Generating Milieu of Juvenile Delinquency," *Journal of Social Issues*, 14, 1958, pp. 5–19.
6. As noted above, the "Cobras" underwent a number of organizational transformations, with new officers, and merged with other groups as [Black] nationalist orientation increased.
7. Major activities are flying pigeons, playing basketball, playing cards, petty theft, playing pool, smoking marijuana, hanging out . . . although not all members participate in all of these activities. The groups as formal wholes have relatively few activities.
8. The problem of group identity, and the obligations which accompany membership, is not fully solved.
9. As one indication of the importance of reading in the group, we may consider one pair of boys who were best friends and saw each other every day. One read extremely well, the other not at all: the other's performance was a total surprise to each.
10. The most important data is derived from the question, "Who are the guys [cats] you hang

out with?," supplemented with other questions on group leaders, best friends, and all other mentions of individuals in relevant roles.

11. Cf. Peter Wilmott, *Adolescent Boys in East London* (London: 1966) p. 35. In answer to a question on main companions in spare time, 57 per cent of those 14–15 years old indicated a group of other males; 44 per cent of those 16–18 years old; and only 32 per cent of those 19–20 years old.

12. The building studied here is 1390 Fifth Avenue.

13. Gray's Oral Reading Test was also given to a section of the population for further calibration on school approaches to reading.

14. There is a close correlation between reading achievement and the Pinter-Cunningham IQ test (given in the early grades in New York City in former years) in Figure 6, and less markedly in Figure 7.

15. We specifically designate a male for this role, in contrast to a number of proposals for "para-professionals" in the schools which utilize women from the community or from college training courses. We cannot elaborate on the importance of sex differentiation here, except to indicate that we believe it is a matter of prime importance.

Index